THE FELDENKRAIS METHOD IN CREATIVE PRACTICE

THE FELDENKRAIS METHOD IN CREATIVE PRACTICE

DANCE, MUSIC AND THEATRE

Edited by Robert Sholl

methuen | drama

LONDON • NEW YORK • OXFORD • NEW DELHI • SYDNEY

METHUEN DRAMA
Bloomsbury Publishing Plc
50 Bedford Square, London, WC1B 3DP, UK
1385 Broadway, New York, NY 10018, USA
29 Earlsfort Terrace, Dublin 2, Ireland

BLOOMSBURY, METHUEN DRAMA and the Methuen Drama logo are trademarks of Bloomsbury Publishing Plc

First published in Great Britain 2021
This paperback edition published 2022

Copyright © Robert Sholl and contributors, 2021, 2022

Robert Sholl has asserted his right under the Copyright, Designs and Patents Act, 1988, to be identified as Editor of this work.

For legal purposes the Acknowledgements on p. xvi constitute an extension of this copyright page.

Cover design by Jade Barnett
Cover image © Tom and Steve/Getty Images

All rights reserved. No part of this publication may be reproduced or transmitted in any form or by any means, electronic or mechanical, including photocopying, recording, or any information storage or retrieval system, without prior permission in writing from the publishers.

Bloomsbury Publishing Plc does not have any control over, or responsibility for, any third-party websites referred to or in this book. All internet addresses given in this book were correct at the time of going to press. The author and publisher regret any inconvenience caused if addresses have changed or sites have ceased to exist, but can accept no responsibility for any such changes.

A catalogue record for this book is available from the British Library.

A catalog record for this book is available from the Library of Congress.

ISBN:	HB:	978-1-3501-5838-2
	PB:	978-1-3502-0349-5
	ePDF:	978-1-3501-5840-5
	eBook:	978-1-3501-5839-9

Typeset by Integra Software Services Pvt. Ltd.

To find out more about our authors and books visit www.bloomsbury.com and sign up for our newsletters.

CONTENTS

List of Figures   vii
Contributor Biographies   ix
Foreword *Garet Newell*   xiv
Acknowledgements   xvi

Introduction *Robert Sholl*   1

PART I Historical Perspectives on Creative Practice   15

1 Dancing the Soma-Ecstatic: Feldenkrais and the Modernist Body
   Thomas Kampe   17
2 Feldenkrais, Freud, Lacan and Gould: How to Love Thyself for Thy Neighbour
   Robert Sholl   38
3 Learning through Feeling: How the Ideas of Nikolai Bernstein and Moshe
   Feldenkrais Apply to Performer Training *Dick McCaw*   55

PART II From Science into Creative Practice   73

4 The Work of Dr Moshe Feldenkrais: A New Applied Kinesiology and a Radical
   Questioning of Training and Technique *Maxine Sheets-Johnstone*   75
5 Radical Practice: Practising Performance and Practising Oneself Is the Same
   Activity *Roger Russell*   83
6 The Feldenkrais Method for Musicians: Addressing the Need for Objective
   Measurements *Jillian Beacon, Gilles Comeau and Donald Russell*   103
7 Gaining Insight on the Impact of Feldenkrais Functional Integration in
   the Context of Piano Playing: Considerations for Measuring Posture and
   Movement Quality *Jillian Beacon, Gilles Comeau and Donald Russell* 116
   Part I The Feldenkrais Method and Pianists: A Pilot Study of Objective
       Measurement of Posture and Movement   116
   Part II Discussion and Recommendations for Future Research   124

PART III Studies in Creative Practice   135

8 Mapping Body Awareness onto Piano Performance for Artistic Rejuvenation
   Alan Fraser   137
9 Building a Model for Injury Prevention in Music Pedagogy Rooted in
   Feldenkrais's Philosophy and Methodology for Learning *Lisa M. Burrell* 158

Contents

10 A Sense of Safety: Polyvagal Theory, the Feldenkrais Method and the
    Acting Process *Victoria Worsley*   173
11 Curing the Acting Habit: The Feldenkrais Method, Actors, Compulsion
    and the Performing Arts Industry *Mark Lacey*   191
12 Tuning the Body: Acting, Dancing and Singing from Rehearsal to
    Performance *Marcia Carr*   207
13 Food for No-Thought ... Meandering between a Personal Somatic Practice
    and Feldenkrais Teaching *Sylvie Fortin*   220

Bibliography   233
Index   238

FIGURES

1	Alfred Cortot's fingering for Chopin's *Étude Op. 26 no. 6*, b. 5–6 right hand only	5
1.1	Dancer Katie Rudd in project 'Releasing the Archive' (Auckland 2016). Photograph by Thomas Kampe	20
1.2	Shoshana and Yehudit Ornstein. Photograph by Alfonso Himmelreich, copyright G. Aldor	22
1.3	Margalit Ornstein notebook from the 1930s: 'Training of the Pelvis – diagonal pelvic see-saw', copyright G. Aldor	24
1.4	Bess Mensendieck, in Elisabeth Mensendieck, *Körperkultur des Weibes: Praktisch hygienische und praktische ästhetische Winke* (Munich: F. Bruckmann [1906]1929, 10th ed.). Appendix: with permission of Stiebner Verlag	25
1.5	Noa Eshkol and peer students of Tile Rössler's school in Tel Aviv (1940s), photo by Photoservice Tel Aviv, with permission of Beit Ariella Dance Library	28
1.6	Tile Rössler teaching children in her studio in Tel Aviv in the 1950s, photography by Hela Reichmann, copyright Gideon Weinstein	28
5.1	Roger Russell and Ulla Schläfke: The Roll Map, copyright Roger Russell	88
7.1	Placement of anatomical markers for Dartfish tracking (i) canthus (outer corner) of the right eye; (ii) ear tragus; (iii) anterior acromioclavicular joint (shoulder); (iv) C7 spinous process; (v, vi, vii, viii) – T4, T8, T12 and L5 spinous processes. Copyright Jillian Beacon	118
7.2	Pre- and post-test time plots of the angle between a line connecting the C7 marker and the point of origin on the bench, and the x-axis for participant EF1. Copyright Jillian Beacon	121
7.3	Pre- and post-test time plots of the angle formed between the horizontal plane and a line connecting the C7 vertebral marker and the eye-canthus marker for participant KP2 during (A) *Für Elise* and (B) scale performances. Copyright Jillian Beacon	122
7.4	Pre- and post-test time plots of (A) eye-canthus, C7, horizontal angle, (B) C7 marker, horizontal angle, and (C) T12, L5, vertical angle for participant AL1's performance of scales. Copyright Jillian Beacon	123
7.5	Average angle of abduction between a line connecting the elbow and shoulder, and a vertical line down from the shoulder on the right and left sides in performances of contrary-motion scales before and after an FI intervention. Copyright Jillian Beacon	127

Figures

8.1	Action and reaction as the hand stands on key. Photographs copyright Igor Peyovitch, with permission of Piano Somatics Press, Novi Sad, Serbia	140
8.2	Extend the proximal phalange while flexing the medial and distal. Photographs copyright Igor Peyovitch, with permission of Piano Somatics Press, Novi Sad, Serbia	146
8.3	Wanda Landowska loads the lumbricals elastically to 'prime' the fingers for clear, varied articulation. Copyright Roger Hauert, courtesy of Editions René Kister, Genève	147
8.4	The reference movement. Photographs copyright Igor Peyovitch, with permission of Piano Somatics Press, Novi Sad, Serbia	148
8.5	Pushing through the foot, leg and pelvis into the spine and all the way to the head in FI. Photographs copyright Igor Peyovitch, with permission of Piano Somatics Press, Novi Sad, Serbia	154

Musical Examples

8.1	Claude Debussy – *Prélude* from *Pour le Piano*, b. 43–45	141
8.2	Frédéric Chopin – *Nocturne in F minor*, Op. 55 No. 1, b. 1–4 with added tenuto bars to indicate plodding, weighted melodic notes	142
8.3	Frédéric Chopin – *Nocturne in D flat major*, Op. 27 No. 2, b. 1–4	143
8.4	Alexander Scriabin – *Étude in C sharp minor*, Op. 2 No. 1, b. 1–4	149
8.5	Frédéric Chopin – *Étude in F major*, Op. 10 No. 8, b. 1–2	152
8.6	Frédéric Chopin – *Scherzo No. 1 in B minor*, Op. 20, b. 606–617	153

CONTRIBUTOR BIOGRAPHIES

Jillian Beacon is pianist, researcher and a Guild-Certified Feldenkrais practitioner. She is pursuing a PhD in Human Kinetics at the University of Ottawa as a member of the Piano Pedagogy Research Laboratory. Her research uses motion-tracking technology to study the effects of somatic training on performance attributes and postural coordination patterns of pianists. Jillian holds a Master's degree in piano pedagogy from the University of Ottawa, and a Bachelor of Music in Integrated Studies from the University of Calgary with majors in piano performance and composition. She maintains a teaching studio for piano lessons and Feldenkrais for musicians in Ottawa, Ontario. She is a practitioner, researcher and lecturer at the University of Ottawa Musicians' Wellness Centre. She enjoys adapting her knowledge of somatics and motor learning to help students of all ages and abilities more fully engage in the joy of learning music.

Lisa Burrell is on the faculty of Lone Star College and is a violinist, violist, string clinician and a Guild-Certified Feldenkrais practitioner. She is a long-time clinician in Houston public schools, colleges and universities throughout the United States. Her work integrating Feldenkrais into wellness-based curricula in music education has gained global recognition, with recent presentations and workshops in the UK, France, Azerbaijan, Portugal and Finland. For more information about applications of the Feldenkrais Method music pedagogy, visit https://lisaburrellviolin.com/.

Marcia Carr completed her training at Royal Holloway (University of London). She is a Feldenkrais practitioner. Marcia is currently Deputy Chief Examiner for the London Academy of Music and Dramatic Art (LAMDA), an Associate Artist with National Youth Theatre of Great Britain. She was Senior Lecturer at the University of West London and has taught at: East 15; RCSSD; Queen's Theatre; Belgrade Theatre; Director of Youth Theatre, Barking; Court Training Theatre; Kingston University; South Bank University; Goldsmiths University; Wolverhampton University; Winchester University and ST&M Theatre School (Amsterdam). Marcia has her own theatre companies, Impetuous Kinship and Creative Blast, working as director, choreographer and physical director.

Gilles Comeau received his PhD in the foundations of music education in 1995 and completed postdoctoral studies in piano pedagogy from 1995 to 1997 with Marc Durand and Gilles Manny. Comeau has been the beneficiary of many research grants, including a large grant from the Canadian Foundation for Innovation to set up a $1.2 million research laboratory in piano pedagogy. As head of this infrastructure, he has established partnership with many other research laboratories and research institutes and set up different multidisciplinary research groups that study various aspects of piano learning and piano teaching: music

Contributor Biographies

reading, motivation, physiological aspect of piano performance, piano-playing health injuries, video-mediated learning. He has written various scholarly research papers and his research findings have received coverage in popular media outlets (television, radio and newspapers). He has authored many books, including *Piano Pedagogy: A Research and Information Guide*; *Comparing Dalcroze, Orff and Kodály*; the five-volume series *Histoire illustrée de la musique pour les jeunes musiciens*; and over twenty education kits used by music and arts teachers.

Sylvie Fortin is full professor in the Dance Department at the University of Québec in Montreal, where she developed a graduate programme in somatic education in 2000. She is a Feldenkrais practitioner since 1994. Throughout her career, she has received funding from Canadian and Québec Research Councils for a series of interdisciplinary research projects involving dancers and non-dancers with varying bodily issues. Using both dance and the Feldenkrais Method, she has worked consistently with professional dancers, children and adults with diverse issues such as fibromyalgia, depression, eating disorders, neuromuscular and degenerative diseases, as well as stroke patients and people with addiction problems. In Montreal, she has a private practice in an interdisciplinary health clinic, where she offers Feldenkrais group classes for adults and individual Feldenkrais sessions for children with motor development challenges. She is a well-known prolific author with over 100 articles or book chapters in numerous scientific and professional journals. Sylvie's international recognition as a researcher and practitioner has led her to conduct workshops in Africa, the Americas, Asia, Australasia and Europe.

Born in Montreal in 1955, Canadian pianist **Alan Fraser** sang in le Studio de Musique Ancienne de Montreal for its first ten years, studied Tai Chi with Sam Slutsky and piano with Phil Cohen. He moved to Yugoslavia in 1990 to study with Kemal Gekić and completed a Feldenkrais professional training programme in 1992, the same year he became Gekić's assistant at the Art Academy of Novi Sad, Serbia. In 1999 he spent a year teaching at the Wuhan Conservatory in mainland China, where much of the material was transcribed for his first book, *The Craft of Piano Playing* (Scarecrow Press, 2003). Back in Serbia he continued to apply the principles of Cohen, Gekić and Feldenkrais to piano technique, producing *Honing the Pianistic Self Image* in 2010 and *All Thumbs: Well-Coordinated Piano Technique* in 2012. He has several more books nearing completion: *Play the Piano with Your Whole Self, Transforming the Pianistic Self-Image* and *Pianimals: Developing the Young Pianist's Hand*. As a concert pianist he has performed in Canada, the United States, Great Britain, France, Germany, Italy, Hungary and Yugoslavia/Serbia. He directs the *Alan Fraser Institute of Piano Somatics* held in various European and North American cities, enriching piano artistry by linking the physical dimension of piano playing to the musical.

Thomas Kampe has worked as a performing artist, researcher and somatic educator across the globe. He is Professor of Somatic performance and Education at Bath Spa University, where he co-directs the Creative Corporealities Research Group. Artistic collaborations include work with Julia Pascal, with Liz Aggiss, Hilde Holger, Tanzinitiative Hamburg, Somatische Akademie Berlin, and with Carol Brown on re-embodying the diasporic practices of Modernist choreographer Gertrud Bodenwieser. Thomas's research and writing has focused on articulating critical somatic legacies. He has collaborated with scholar Glenna Batson on writings on somatic-informed dance education, and recently edited *JDSP* Vol. 9. (2017): *Bodily Undoing: Somatics as Practices of Critique* with Kirsty Alexander. He is a practitioner of The

Feldenkrais Method and guest editor of the *IFF Research Journal* Vol. 6 (2019): *Practices of Freedom: The Feldenkrais Method and Creativity*.

Mark Lacey is an actor, director, educator and choreographer who specializes in the research and development of effective performance methods through the reinstatement of autonomy in individuals and industries. He studied physical theatre with Desmond Jones and Antonio Fava and became International Street Entertainer of the Year 1993 before going on to study acting at Central School of Speech and Drama. He qualified as a Feldenkrais teacher under Garet Newell in 2007. During his final year he became the first teacher in the UK to develop a full Feldenkrais module for a professional acting course in an accredited drama school. He went on to introduce the Method to many major acting schools, nationally and internationally. He is company director of The House of Glass Angels which supplies personal and project development for performing arts professionals who have become alienated from the industry for social-economic or health reasons. Mark's company aims to develop new models of corporate structures that reinstate trust and autonomy in the work place that maximizes productivity and quality without sacrificing employee health and wellbeing.

He has worked extensively in theatre, television and film as an actor and director, and was one of the actors working under Declan Donnellan while he developed his seminal work 'The Actor and the Target'. Mark was Associate Lecturer in drama at both Kent and Canterbury Christchurch Universities where he completed his Master's and studied the narrative potential of lip-syncing in live theatre.

Since 2004 **Dick McCaw** has been Senior Lecturer at Royal Holloway, University of London. He has edited and introduced two books: *With an Eye for Movement* (on Warren Lamb's development of Rudolph Laban's movement theories) for Brechin Books (2006) and *The Laban Sourcebook* for Routledge (2011). He has written three books: *Bakhtin and Theatre* was published by Routledge in 2016; *The Actor's Body – A Guide* was published in 2018 and his *Rethinking the Actor's Body – Dialogues with Neuroscience* in 2020, both by Methuen Drama. He is a Contributing Editor of *Theatre and Dance Performance Training* (Routledge) and *New Theatre Quarterly* (Cambridge University Press) and has written a number of articles for these and other journals. He qualified as a Feldenkrais practitioner in 2007, and he became an Instructor of Wu Family T'ai Chi Chuan in 2016.

Garet Newell was educated at Tufts University, Massachusetts, while also pursuing her interest in dance, choreography and performance. As a recipient of a graduate fellowship, she spent a year at the University of Munich, after which she moved to New York City to pursue a career in dance, completing an MA degree in Dance in Education at New York University.

She moved to San Francisco and through a chance meeting with a newly qualified Feldenkrais Method teacher became a student of Moshe Feldenkrais in his final years and graduated in 1983 from the last training programme he directed, which took place in Amherst, Massachusetts; the final year of the training was in Tel-Aviv, Israel.

She was a guest teacher at the Coloman Centre in Munich and was among the first teachers of the Feldenkrais Method in Germany, then in England where she moved in 1984. She became an Assistant Trainer and directed the first Professional Training Programme in the UK, in London, from 1987 to 1990. She became one of the first Europe-based Trainers and has since been directing four-year training programmes in the UK, through the Feldenkrais

Contributor Biographies

International Training Centre (ITC), as well as being invited to teach in training programmes around the world.

Garet played a crucial role in the formation of an international Feldenkrais community as a founding member of the International Feldenkrais Federation, as well as the European Training Accreditation Board. She lives in Sussex, just north of Brighton and Hove, and directs the Feldenkrais ITC training programmes which meet in Ditchling and Lewes, East Sussex.

Donald Russell (PhD from Massachusetts Institute of Technology) is Professor in the Department of Mechanical and Aerospace Engineering at Carleton University (Ottawa, Ontario, Canada). He also holds an associate diploma and a choir master's diploma from the Royal Canadian College of Organists and a diploma in church music studies from the Royal School of Church Music. He is Adjunct Professor of music at the University of Ottawa and an active organist, chorister and composer. His primary research interests are the biomechanics of musical performance and performance-related injuries.

Roger Russell trained with Moshe Feldenkrais (1975–82), is a Feldenkrais trainer and educational director of the Feldenkrais Zentrum Heidelberg. He is a physical therapist and has a Master's degree in movement science and movement education in Antioch University. Roger's work concerns the complex inner workings of Feldenkrais's body of work approached systematically through learning processes which span sensory-motor, cognitive and emotional processes. He helped organize the *First European Feldenkrais Conference* in Heidelberg in 1995, participated in the symposiums *Movement and the Development of Sense of Self* in 2004, *Embodying Neuroscience* in 2012, and *Movement: Brain, Body, Cognition* in Oxford in 2017 and numerous other conferences. Author of two Feldenkrais books in German, he has researched the application of the Feldenkrais Method with people with Multiple Sclerosis, as well as in infant development.

In her first life, **Maxine Sheets-Johnstone** was a dancer/choreographer, professor of dance/dance scholar. During her years of teaching dance in the studio and lecture classrooms, she choreographed twenty-five dances, performed in thirteen of these, was artistic director of five concerts, including two full-length concerts of her own works, and the organizer-director-narrator of numerous lecture-demonstrations. In her second and ongoing life, she is a philosopher, affiliated with the Department of Philosophy at the University of Oregon where she taught periodically in the 1990s and where she now holds an ongoing Courtesy Professor appointment. Her books include *The Phenomenology of Dance; Illuminating Dance: Philosophical Explorations*; the 'roots' trilogy: *The Roots of Thinking, The Roots of Power: Animate Form and Gendered Bodies, The Roots of Morality; Giving the Body Its Due; The Primacy of Movement; The Corporeal Turn: An Interdisciplinary Reader; Putting Movement Into Your Life: A Beyond Fitness Primer; Insides and Outsides: Interdisciplinary Perspectives on Animate Nature*. She was awarded a Distinguished Fellowship in 2007 for her research on xenophobia in the inaugural year of the Institute of Advanced Study at Durham University, UK, and was honoured with a Scholar's Session in 2012, Society for Phenomenology and Existential Philosophy conference, Rochester, New York.

Contributor Biographies

Robert Sholl is Professor of Music at the University of West London and teaches at the Royal Academy of Music. His research interests include twentieth- and twenty-first-century music, critical theory and philosophy, musical analysis, performance, improvisation, somatic techniques (especially the Feldenkrais Method), Music and Psychoanalysis, Music and Spirituality, listening, and film music. Robert studied the organ with Olivier Latry (Notre-Dame de Paris), and in 2016–17, he performed all of the organ works of Olivier Messiaen at Arundel Cathedral. In 2021–2 he will play all of the Vierne organ symphonies together with major works of Tournemire and chamber music and songs at Arundel. Improvisation has become a regular part of Robert's recitals, and he has released improvisations to silent films on YouTube. He has played at St Paul's Cathedral, Westminster Abbey, St John's, Smith Square, and twice both at the Madeleine and at Notre-Dame de Paris.

Victoria Worsley studied movement and performance with Monika Pagneux and Philippe Gaulier in Paris from 1984 to 1987 and worked as an actor straddling the worlds of physical theatre, new plays, classical drama, TV and film from 1985 to 2005 (somehow fitting in a degree in literae humaniores at Oxford University on the way). She co-devised and wrote a number of plays and also worked as a movement director.

Having discovered the Feldenkrais Method while training with Monika Pagnuex back in 1984, she finally trained as a professional Feldenkrais practitioner in Lewes from 2003 to 2007. Since then she has built a busy Feldenkrais practice for people from all walks of life in North London and has taught Feldenkrais and movement in a number of UK drama schools including Rose Bruford, Mountview and Oxford School of Drama. She also teaches workshops for professional actors at the Actors Centre, Sadlers Wells and with John Wright, coaches individual actors and was commissioned by Nick Hern Books to write her book *Feldenkrais For Actors – How To Do Less and Discover More*, published in 2016. She holds a second dan black belt in traditional Okinawan karate (Goju Ryu) and enjoys barefoot running.

FOREWORD

Reading through the fascinating chapters of this beautifully written and produced book, I feel that a long-held vision of mine is being fulfilled. The Feldenkrais Method has reached a level of recognition I dreamed that it one day would, and graduates of the early professional training programmes have found innovative and creative ways to apply the unique qualities of this Method in their professions. This book illustrates the accomplishment and excellence that has been reached since the Feldenkrais Method arrived in the UK, back in 1984.

As the first Feldenkrais Method teacher to move to England to teach courses, establish a practice and direct a training centre, I am very proud to see the far-reaching development of this Method through the authors of these chapters, many of whom trained with me as their Educational Director.

I discovered the Feldenkrais Method through a lifelong pursuit of a basic understanding of what it means to be human and how to practically manifest ways to improve *ourselves and our interactions in the world.*

Throughout my school years I was a 'good student' academically but was always more fascinated by activities which involved movement and expression. From my childhood, I loved my after-school classes in ballet; as a teenager I pursued jazz dance, acrobatics and performing – always considered 'hobbies'.

During my undergraduate years, I chose dance classes to satisfy the 'physical education' requirement that all students at American universities had to fulfil. I later discovered choreography and performance courses, which were offered under the umbrella of the 'Experimental College', as 'electives' to the academic requirements for my degree in Art History.

During a year abroad, thanks to a fellowship to further my studies in Art History, I made the decision to move to New York City and to choose dance as a career. I began classes with teachers from all of the major modern dance techniques at that time – Merce Cunningham, Jose Limon and with Martha Graham herself. While doing work to create a dance floor in my loft in Tribeca, a post fell on top of me and I ended up with a painful neck and upper back injury. Being already an 'alternative thinker', I searched for ways to be able to dance again through chiropractic, the Mabel Todd work with Andre Bernard, the Alexander Technique and classes in T'ai Chi Chuan.

Not being able to take part in strenuous dance technique classes, I returned to academia and enrolled in three-year MA in Dance in Education at New York University – one of the few educational institutions at that time where Dance was taken seriously as an academic subject. As part of my degree, I attended a summer course with Anna Halprin at her San Francisco Dancer's Workshop, and decided to move to San Francisco after receiving my MA in 1977.

Still looking for ways to improve from my injury, a chance meeting with a newly qualified Feldenkrais teacher was the start of a great adventure. Moshe Feldenkrais had just finished teaching a four-year training programme in San Francisco and Jerry Karzen, the teacher I had met, became the organizer of Feldenkrais's next, and last, training – in Amherst, Massachusetts, from the summer of 1980 through summer of 1983.

Foreword

Finding Moshe Feldenkrais was like finding home for me – he brought together the science and the art of movement, and in a way that it became a basis for understanding what it means to be a *potent* human *being*. The hours spent listening to and learning from him felt like the encompassing education I had been yearning for. His unique intellect was inspiring, as was his passion for awareness as the focus for learning new and more successful patterns of behaviour. Bringing together perception, sensing, thinking and moving as components of every human action was a unique understanding of his, which resolved a centuries-long division of the body and the mind.

After completing this four-year training, I was invited to join the Open Centre in London – a centre offering courses in what was then called 'human potential'. Many artists, performers, musicians and dancers found their way to my classes. I made contact with Yehudi Menuhin, who had experienced lessons with Feldenkrais while visiting him in Israel. Yehudi Menuhin recalled that in one lesson, Moshe asked him to stand on two thick cardboard rollers and, at the same time, to play his violin. It was a great example of how Feldenkrais encouraged artists to experiment with the non-habitual – therefore challenging ways of improving their already-developed skills. In 1988, the International Workshop Festival was founded by Nigel Jamieson. He invited me to do some teaching at his school and I invited him to be the patron of the Feldenkrais Guild UK, which he kindly accepted.

In 1988, Nigel Jamieson founded the International Workshop Festival (IWF). He invited me to offer Awareness through Movement lessons as 'warm-ups' for the collection of performers who flocked to London for this two-week event of creative workshops offered by leading teachers from all over the world. The appreciation of the Feldenkrais Method grew as did my association with the IWF, as Dick McCaw took over as its director and included me in each of the workshop festivals from 1995 to 2001.

Through both the Open Centre and the IWF, the appreciation of the Feldenkrais Method as a source of inspiration and practice for artists and performers grew. Many performers in 'physical theatre', such as the innovative Theatre de Complicité, teachers in university-level theatre and music departments, and dancers enrolled in the four-year training programmes to become teachers of the Feldenkrais Method. The Method came to be valued as an essential component in learning, training and education in many of the various creative arts.

As I carry on teaching the work of this multifaceted and creative genius, I am gradually seeing his vision of this Method as an integral and necessary part of education become manifest. Learning to be more aware, to sense and feel oneself and others, to know our capacities as well as limitations – all inherent in the practical and enjoyable classes and individual lessons of the Feldenkrais Method – can only bring about more fully human, human beings.

Garet Newell
Hassocks, UK, June 2020.

ACKNOWLEDGEMENTS

Firstly, I would like to acknowledge the time and patience given to this project by the contributors without whom this could not have happened. This project has come about through our collective dedication, through a shared understanding of the richness of Moshe Feldenkrais's legacy, and through a desire to share this as widely as possible. I particularly want to thank Garet Newell for her warm and wise foreword to the book.

This project has been nourished by many discussions, and by training with Garet Newell, Ned Dwelle, Roger Russell and Carl Ginsburg. I want to acknowledge the administrative help of Iuhasz Evelyn (for Chapter 4) and Janice Hortilano in the preparation of the bibliography.

I would like to thank Anna Brewer and Meredith Benson at Bloomsbury for their warm and generous help with the book. Thanks also to several unnamed reviewers whose thoughts have been incorporated into the fabric of the work. I also want to thank the University of West London (UWL) for supporting two conferences on the Feldenkrais Method, and extend thanks to colleagues and students with whom I have had discussions about the Method at UWL, and at The Royal Academy of Music.

INTRODUCTION
Robert Sholl

Towards an *Ability Studies*

In volume 1 of his biography of Moshe Feldenkrais (1904–84), the Feldenkrais practitioner Mark Reese describes Feldenkrais as grounding his Method 'in physics, biology, psychology, and neuroscience'.[1] Feldenkrais combined this background with a proficiency in biomechanics and skills in judo to develop what he called The Feldenkrais Method. This Method promotes an awareness of fine motor action for improved levels of action, skill and also healing for those who are injured. For creative artists who practise their art, the Method enables them to 'know what they are doing so they can do what they want', and 'to make the impossible possible, the possible easy and comfortable, and the comfortable aesthetically pleasurable'.[2] These ideas are at the core of creative practice.

The Feldenkrais Method bridges cognitive performance concerns with somatic educational processes, and it employs enactivist and constructivist notions of neuroplasticity and self-reflective learning. Feldenkrais's teaching focused on the development of self-directed learning, autonomy in the choice of actions and the development of curiosity through awareness. Feldenkrais understood his practices as structured, but also as improvisational processes that are concerned with challenging our habitual perception and interaction with the world. His purpose in this was to improve the creativity and the 'adaptive flexibility' of the individual, and his Method can therefore be understood as a twentieth-century emancipatory practice for the individual.[3] To improve the individual and their functioning in the world was, as he saw it in a somewhat utopian vein, to improve the world.

From its inception, the Feldenkrais Method has been used with creative artists, and indeed he regarded these types of people as paragons of human achievement.[4] Feldenkrais himself worked with such artistic luminaries as the violinist Yehudi Menuhin, the guitarist Narciso Yepes, the conductor Igor Markevitch, and the theatre director and acting coach Peter Brook.[5] The Method has grown contiguously with performance, cognitive and embodied practices in dance, music and theatre studies.

In recent years creative practitioners have started to build upon the history of somatics and to develop Feldenkrais's work.[6] Libby Worth and Dick McCaw have developed practitioner insights from the Method on Dance, Music and Theatre. These case studies also include contributions such as that by Thomas Kampe that touch upon wider historical, critical and epistemological issues raised by the Method.[7] This book expands this latter type of critical engagement, but it crucially scrutinizes the Method from outside its own confines, bringing other histories, methods, and new types of theoretical and practical reflection to the study of the Method. The book therefore does not only *apply* the Method, but takes it as a template for creative engagement and development. It reflects the ways in which the Method is not fixed, but is continually evolving as practitioners find new applications and refinements.

The chapters in this book seek to capitalize on the heritage of Feldenkrais's own thought and to enrich further the already-burgeoning literature in this area of study. Mary Spire and Jerry Karzen, as practitioners with an interest in the work of performing artists, have created programmes (sets of Awareness through Movement or ATM lessons) to address the needs of musicians.[8] Alan Fraser has published three monographs that explore how the Method can be used as a basis for improving the technique, physiology, skill and sound of the pianist, and Samuel H. Nelson's book on singing has provided a fascinating adaptation of the Method to the needs of singers.[9] Victoria Worsley's book on Feldenkrais for Actors has provided other subject-specific responses to Feldenkrais's legacy, as has the work of Dick McCaw, Other thinkers have explored the effectiveness of the Method for dealing with performance anxiety, and others are scientifically evaluating the Method.[10] The Method has also crossed over into disability studies and trauma studies with reference to both injury and rehabilitation, physiological and psycho-somatic issues.[11] These developments are all signs of the healthy expansion and critique of the Method beyond its own topics, strategies and boundaries.

The present volume absorbs many of these tributaries into what I would prefer to call *Ability Studies*. Feldenkrais has argued against the limiting ideal of 'disability'. This of course is not a denial of disability, but a rethinking of it. Some disabilities, as he has shown, are no barrier to embodied learning and improvement; according to Feldenkrais, we are all awaiting enablement at some level.[12] For instance, in the lesson with Ephram, a young Canadian boy with cerebral palsy, Feldenkrais stops at one point and tells his assembled students that 'perhaps he [Ephram] will grow up [to be] a strong, nice man like everybody else, maybe better, because he has known trouble and overcome it'.[13] The negotiation and development of a latent capacity to be enabled are essential to both artistic practice and Feldenkrais's Method. The chapters in this book explore and demonstrate an *Ability Studies* that capitalizes on the ethos of self-improvement and transformation that is at the heart of the Method.

The 'adaptive flexibility' of bodies and brains

'To make the impossible possible, the possible easy and the easy aesthetically pleasurable' in the Method was part of Feldenkrais's goal to 'restore each person to their human dignity', by using movement as a means of changing habitual patterns in the nervous system.[14] Fundamental to the Feldenkrais Method of enablement is the idea of human change associated with what he calls the self-image and in the development of choice, concepts discussed throughout this book. For Feldenkrais, the change of a person's self-image occurs through awareness. He defines the self-image, understood as part of the uniqueness of each individual, through the movement patterns of the body.[15] Feldenkrais believed that the self-image is formed by the unique identification of oneself in gravity and in proprioceptive space, but most importantly it is to be understood through the sense in which we feel that our own *particular* way of doing something – walking, speaking, thinking or playing a musical instrument for example – is sensed as uniquely our own and therefore seemingly unchangeable.[16] Feldenkrais's Method addresses the gap between our sense of ourselves in action and a somewhat utopian ideal of the self: there can therefore always be improvement in the ability to perform.

A good example of self-image and the ability to change it is found in the following anecdote. In jest, the Austrian composer Arnold Schoenberg (1874–1951) told one of his pupils that he would only have to see how the composer Gustav Mahler (1860–1911) tied his tie to know something about the purpose of his art.[17] Implicit in Schoenberg's 'jest' is that an awareness of Mahler's physical being is mimetically transferable. Everything we do – feeding, cleaning, sex, writing, walking, dancing, acting, composing music or playing a musical instrument for example – is an indivisible and unique part of our being, and for Feldenkrais these things require the participation of all aspects of our being to be successful. For Feldenkrais, an awareness of how we do something can change the quality of what we do and who we are in the world. Most of the time, however, we are unaware of this, unaware of how we tie a tie for example. Crucially, the Feldenkrais Method provides a constructive and enactivist path towards awareness. The Method affords not only the ability to learn from others, but it enables a subject to find their own original way of doing something and to be aware of how something is done.

In a lecture given in his New York Quest workshops (1981), Feldenkrais discussed the uniqueness of various creative artists: Amedeo Modigliani, David Oistrakh, Jascha Heifetz, Henry Moore, August Rodin, among others, and their ability to grow in 'their feeling of themselves, their personal image, and their relation to the outside world [i.e. through a violin, a piano, a typewriter, or a block of stone for example]'.[18] He commented on their ability to find new depths and new interest in what they are doing, and their ability to use their whole self in their activity. In using these people as exemplars of extraordinary 'ability', Feldenkrais described his Method as one that rhetorically addresses the question 'where did we stop being human beings?'

'Surely', he stated, 'Beethoven and Liszt and Gershwin and Moore, and Rodin ... [created work that bears] their own hallmark'. Feldenkrais questioned why such types of uniqueness are developed by some and not by others, and seemingly cannot be transferred. This 'hallmark' of uniqueness is present in some things we do, our handwriting for instance, but he implied that most peoples' level of awareness and their self-image are comparatively undeveloped, and that this is because, at a certain stage, development stopped for all sorts of professional, personal and societal reasons. This issue of human growth can be addressed by finding out how one learned something, how one writes or plays, paints or acts in a certain way for example, and how this uniquely expresses our 'interior self'. Feldenkrais lays the culpability for the impasse he describes at the doors of education, but more particularly at the societal compulsion for uniformity. In a workshop given to dancers at New York University in 1971, Feldenkrais stated: 'It is very difficult to become a human being. It's much easier to keep on doing what you are taught.'[19]

Mimetic learning, however, is essential to creative practice and learning. It utilizes the nervous system's inherently plastic abilities.[20] However, Feldenkrais points to a tipping point where this kind of learning is insufficient, and a time where the individual knows themselves enough to act autonomously, without compulsion and therefore in a healthy manner. In the 1981 Quest workshops, he defines his idea of health as 'being able to realize your unavowed dreams', and he discusses this in relation to the painter Salvador Dalí and his inner compulsion to find a way to be unique.[21] Health in Feldenkrais's thought is therefore intricately connected to awareness and ability. To promote this idea of health, Feldenkrais developed two ways of teaching his Method, through individual lessons called Functional Integration (FI) and through group classes known as ATM lessons.[22] Both modes of engagement between a teacher and student(s) provide forms of somatic intervention and an environment to construct and enact modes of learning designed to challenge habitual perceptions and patterns of movement and to instantiate improved function and performance. Crucially, the activity in these forms of engagement are not mimetic; students are provided with an environment in which they can find their own ways of learning through the activity. This is why Feldenkrais would often say that he was not teaching anybody, but merely providing the conditions under which learning can take place. The Method engages learning through experiment, through the development of curiosity and through the finding of new possibilities for movement, through an internal listening to small movement differentiations, and through the development of choice, flexibility and stability of action. These processes are all essential to the development of ability in performing-arts training.

Choice in action is fundamental to the Method. Awareness through Movement lessons explore a particular movement function in many different ways. If a person has twenty or more different ways to add two numbers to equal six, they have access to qualities of 'adaptive flexibility' (Thelen).[23] Likewise a person who knows many languages has a way of mitigating 'the limits of the language (*the* language which I understand) [that] mean[s] the limits of *my* world', as the philosopher Ludwig Wittgenstein stated.[24]

This development of choice and artistic fluency was one of the things that attracted me to the Method. Like many, I found the Method through injury, and it was through this that I learned of my own agency in the creation of my injury (injury is discussed in the chapters by Alan Fraser and Lisa Burrell in this book). For a performing artist, being injured and the appearance to oneself of the lack of ability or potency that this creates can become (to paraphrase the poet J.W. von Goethe) like an inner wound that needs to be nourished.[25] But Feldenkrais's Method made me realize that within this state is also, ironically, a source of potency. The longing for the 'sweet time' of the past, as Goethe puts it, should also be a desire for an even sweeter time to come. This state forces the individual to find other ways to perform. In psychoanalysis, an important background formant of Feldenkrais's thought, this problem might be addressed as 'resistance', something that Freud understood to be part of the mechanism of the cure.[26] To overcome the problem (the injury), the challenge then is to find another means of organizing one's own action, another way of using oneself. In a correspondence on the subject of colour with his brother Theo, on or around 20 October 1885, the artist Vincent van Gogh makes the following statement: 'Rembrandt and Hals, didn't they use black? And Velázquez??? Not just one, but twenty-seven blacks, I assure you.'[27] The colour black was no restriction, but a form of resistance that itself inspired greater creativity. Paradoxically also, it is being in a seemingly reduced state of potency through injury that allows one to stand back from what one does ordinarily and assess it.

In his New York Quest workshops and elsewhere in his writings, Feldenkrais clearly connects ability and learning with choice. Choice is essential to creative practice. In his *Éditions de travail* (working editions) of Chopin's music (and indeed for other composers also), the French pianist Alfred Cortot (1877–1962) included explanatory essays before each work, showing how a pianist might master technical challenges to achieve virtuosity or 'adaptive flexibility'. His discussion of Chopin's *Étude* Op. 25 no. 6, a study that deals with

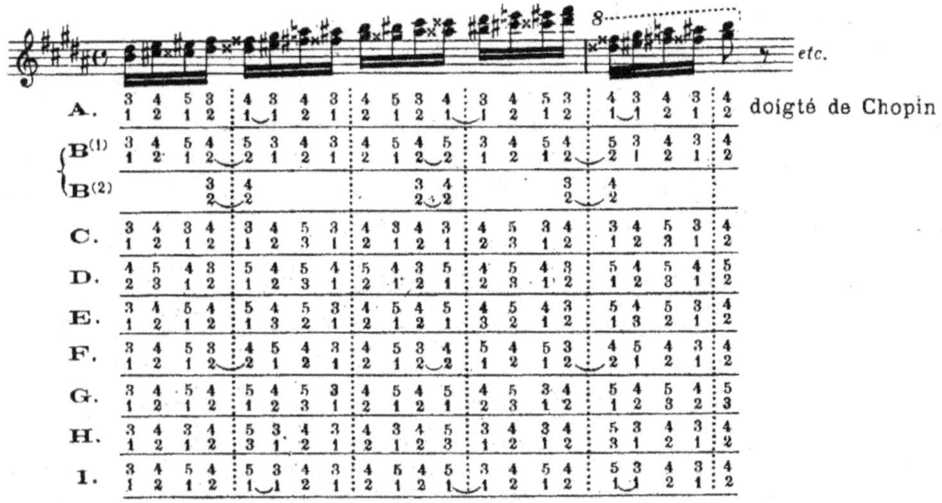

Figure 1 Alfred Cortot's fingering for Chopin's *Étude* Op. 26 no. 6, b. 5–6 right hand only.

the anatomically difficult problem of playing consecutive thirds in the right hand, is telling. Cortot gives seven possible fingerings for the opening trill figure, but then he prescribes the possibilities for the chromatic scale in Figure 1 above.[28]

This example demonstrates a method of personal awareness; in fact, it presents precepts of the Feldenkrais Method before its inception. Cortot exhorts the pianist to practise this passage in many different ways, so that they do not merely have options, different possibilities of actions, but so that they can find the *right* possibility spontaneously from this choice. Feldenkrais regarded this kind of choice as a basic human freedom. The ability to think in different ways, and the inherent ability for the brain to develop plasticity is important to action. Equally important is the overcoming of compulsion in activity. In the Quest workshops, Feldenkrais likens compulsive action with 'a memory of the troubles we had all of our life – it is an idiotic act'. He then states:

> In the things we do [that] we think that we do rightly; in those things lies our misery. It is not in the bad things we do that make us miserable; it is not in the mistakes we do; it is on the things that we think we do right for ourselves … In those things we are blind, that we are compulsive, and … this is the thing which represents our life.[29]

Awareness is the way out of this. The great Chilean pianist Claudio Arrau (1903–91) found that psychoanalysis (from 1924) was able to help him overcome the sense that he was not playing at his highest level. Arrau realized, although he does not put it this way, that the demands of concert life and the demands of his own ability had created a form of imago (an idealized image of himself created in childhood in his case) that was compulsive and vain (caused perhaps by a desire to be perfect).[30] He described the process of his work with psychoanalysis in this way: 'Over a period of thirty years, analysis helped clear my personal jungle until my full creative forces could flow freely. Layer after layer of covering and unessentials were stripped away in a process that must continue until one's death.'³¹ Arrau's description of this process of burgeoning self-awareness identifies what Feldenkrais calls the 'parasitic', a contradictory and compulsive activity that needs to be stopped in order to create clear, directed, intentional activity.³² In parasitic movement, the desire to do or stop doing is coloured by other habitual activities that, although they seem essential and pleasurable, may inhibit the clarity of a movement.³³ Parasitic movements become entangled in our self-image, and this is again where the Feldenkrais Method provides an intervention in arts training, as Roger Russell's work in this book demonstrates clearly.

Feldenkrais's Method offers a means of defeating this form of ego-compulsion (see Mark Lacey's chapter in this book for more on this). It shows up how all sorts of compulsion in public and private life are linked (they are all part of human activity), and it points up the value of intelligence in simple actions such as the ability to change one's mind. It is a reminder to slow down, to feel, sense, think; these things are preparatory to action, and not the same thing. His Method is a rejoinder to organize oneself, and that despite the expectations and invisible codes of society – what the psychoanalytical philosopher Jacques Lacan called 'the big Other'– there must be time and space to be comfortable in one's own skin.

These are seemingly hard, salient but 'obviously' intelligent lessons taught by Feldenkrais, who offers not only a blueprint, but a mechanism of how to be, feel and act as a more human person. This is why I believe this work to be among the most valuable of thought systems. It is non-religious, but can be experienced as a form of spirituality. It affords the opportunity to experience a form of comfort that can be made available to oneself instantaneously, and called into being through the quicksilver of thought. The Feldenkrais Method is therefore more than a somatic learning technique; it is an enactivist, embodied, epistemology for understanding one's being-in-the-world and the agency of others within this ecology. Many self-help philosophies (such as the work of Anthony Robbins and Steve Covey) exhort people to do more. Feldenkrais exhorted people to do less, only to find mysteriously that one can do more.

This is not a paradox, but something inscribed in our human nervous system. The Weber-Fechner law shows that there is a relationship between effort and sensation. If I were to try and lift a piano, the effort required would mean that I could not feel if a ladybird had landed on top of the piano, but if I were to lift the beautiful autumn leaf on the front cover of this volume, I might be able to tell the difference between the weight of the leaf and whether or not the ladybird was perched upon it. The ability to feel and make differentiations is vital in artistic practice, and at the foundation of the development of ability. Feldenkrais teaches that there is nothing particularly unusual about extraordinary abilities: the ability to memorize Phi (Φ) to thousands of places, the ability to be a chess master, or the ability to memorize all the piano sonatas of Beethoven; it is merely a capacity to think correctly and act, to organize oneself properly. Feldenkrais's thought therefore seeks to address these issues; it is therefore both sophisticated and extremely obvious, and this is why Feldenkrais referred to this aspect of 'how to do something' as 'the elusive obvious'.³⁴ This term embodies a search for simplicity in action that derives from a clarity of the mental intention and representation of an action.³⁵ Feldenkrais's thinking asks what it means to re-organize the whole body for action and comfort. It provides a means of reconfiguring this sense of ourselves through strategies that develop learning and 'adaptive flexibility'. This book therefore embodies a shared sense of coming to terms with Feldenkrais's quest though an interaction between historical, scientific and practical discourses.

Introduction

The Feldenkrais Method in creative practice

At his death, Feldenkrais left a rich legacy of work: books, articles, recordings of workshops, video recording of professional trainings and FIs, and many ATMs, including the 550 ATM Alexander Yanai lessons. Feldenkrais's legacy allows scholars and practitioners to intersect and engage with it in new and productive ways that develop new levels of choice, autonomy, ability, and that also explore the limitations of the Method.[36] The purpose of this book therefore is to show how the strategies of the Method can be transferred to creative practice, to contextualize, to develop and to re-think Feldenkrais's work.

This book therefore brings together scholars and artistic practitioners, not all of whom are Feldenkrais practitioners, to explore the richness of the Method and to expand what is latent within it. The book offers approaches to the Method that range across dance, music and theatre studies. The diversity of Feldenkrais's own reading is aptly reflected and extended in the range of approaches in this volume, which include philosophy, psychoanalysis, somatic theory, cognitive and movement science and theory, historical studies and praxis.

The chapters in this book come together to argue not only for the validity of the Method, but for the way in which its principles and strategies can be transferable and applicable to different theoretical and practical circumstances. It shows that the Feldenkrais Method is not just a way of thinking about somatic health, embodiment and awareness, but a vital enactivist epistemology.[37] The chapters in this book develop and demonstrate that Feldenkrais's discoveries are plastic theories and forms of embodied knowledge that provide their own multivalent forms of validation.

This book is not organized according to areas of artistic practice, but it allows the reader to make their own connections between disciplines and chapters. This construction and the resonances between the thinkers here act as a demonstration, validation and extension of Feldenkrais's strategies. Common to all of these areas are sensibilities at the heart of the Method: feeling, sensing, exploring and therefore knowing. The reader who decides to read all of the chapters or merely to dip in and out of the work will find ideas, strategies and thinking that are transferable to their own creative theoretical thinking and practice. The chapters in this book should also be understood as the foundation for a continuing dialogue between the Feldenkrais Method, theory and creative practice, and as a form of transference of experiential knowledge to expand the Method's field of immanence and reference. The contributors in the book therefore seek to extend Feldenkrais's thought, and also to explore it in ways that may not always be consonant with his thought. In this it acts as a form of Feldenkraisian re-evaluation of the Feldenkrais Method. The book therefore not only re-enforces the malleability of Feldenkrais's work, but it demonstrates ways in which theory practice can critique and extend it.

The book is divided into three sections:

I. *Historical Perspectives on Creative Practice*. This section contains three chapters that extend Feldenkrais's reading and insights from thinkers in movement, psychoanalysis, and in neuro-physiology and biology. In each case, the authors explain the origins of Feldenkrais's thinking and then apply it to creative practice in new and revealing ways that are not evident from Feldenkrais's own thought.

II. *From Science into Creative Practice.* Feldenkrais was trained as a scientist, and various disciplines (movement science, neuro-physiology, the philosophy of science and phenomenology for example) are increasingly engaging with the Method in new ways. The four chapters here present a first-hand experience of the Method, from an eminent movement scientist, from a Feldenkrais Trainer who uses cutting-edge material in the philosophy of science to understand the Method in creative practice, and finally two chapters that show how empirical study can result in practical improvement to ability.

III. *Studies in Creative Practice.* This section exposes readers to topical applications of the Method. The authors show how the theoretical contexts and strategies of the Method can be refreshed and concretized in practice. Crucially, these chapters show how practice and what I have called *Ability Studies* become part of an epistemological hinge that acts as validation, critique and refiguration of the Method. The tone of these chapters is at once personal and universal and they provide an enactivist model for the development of Feldenkrais's thought.

The chapters in this book are offered for the benefit of a wide variety of people both within and beyond the Feldenkrais community. Anyone who is a practising artist with an interest in the way theories (historical, scientific and practical) can inform and refine practice will find this book invaluable. It provides material that supports a groundswell within arts education of a more somatic-based mode of enquiry.[38] Practitioners and researchers in the disciplines of dance, theatre and music, as well as the burgeoning field of somatics will find much here to verify, extend and challenge their knowledge. Creative artists will find strategies that are transferable to their own discipline. Finally, Feldenkrais practitioners will find much that is familiar here, but they will encounter new archaeologies of the Method, and fresh thought that re-invigorates and critiques established and familiar thinking. Some repetition of the description of the Method is inevitable in such a book, and this is important for a number of reasons. One of the principles of Feldenkrais's Method, and indeed an aspect of methodological virtuosity that his work enacts, is that any problem can be addressed in multiple ways and through multiple modalities. The descriptions of the Method given by the authors therefore overlap and provide an arborescent coverage of the Method's precepts. There is no attempt to discuss or elaborate all aspects of the Method in this book.

Part I: Historical Perspectives on Creative Practice

Thomas Kampe's chapter provides one form of anthropology of the Method. He retraces the beginnings of early Modernist Dance and Body Cultures to body codes and creative emancipatory ethics found in Feldenkrais's work. He proposes that Feldenkrais's emphasis on fostering the 'mature' adult as a curious, creative and emancipated individual emerged from the early Modernist 'Körperkultur' (body culture) in 1920s Palestine which Feldenkrais encountered before he left for Paris. Drawing on his own recent field research done in Israel, he details Feldenkrais's inculcation of the work of the modern dance pioneer Margalit Ornstein (Vienna 1888–Tel Aviv 1973), Gertrud Bodenwieser (1890–1959), the European body-culture pioneer Bess Mensendieck (1864–1957), and Elsa Gindler (1885–1961) and their followers. Kampe critiques the dominant narrative of Feldenkrais's lone genius through this alternative feminist history, and it connects this anthropology to contemporary educational and somatic learning practices in dance. Robert Sholl addresses another anthropology of Feldenkrais's thought. At the beginning of his book *The Potent Self*, Feldenkrais responds to Christ's commandment 'Thou shalt love thy neighbour as thyself' (Matthew 22:39). Feldenkrais was a great reader of Freud who wrote about this injunction. Sholl shows the connections and differentiations between Feldenkrais's, and Freud's and Jacques Lacan's use of this idea. He then connects this thinking to a discussion of the Canadian pianist Glenn Gould's decision (in 1964) to stop playing the piano in public. He argues that Gould's decision to re-organize himself through recording was a way to learn to use himself more intelligently (negotiating compulsion), to refine his own self-image and to enhance his uniqueness. Finally, Sholl examines Gould as exemplar for creative artists and performance training through the development of uniqueness, 'potency' and self-awareness better 'to love thy neighbour' (conceived as the listening public).

Finally in this section, Dick McCaw focuses on another anthropology of Feldenkrais's thought. The work of the Soviet psychologist Nikolai Bernstein was an intellectual touchstone for Feldenkrais; they shared a belief that the learning movement was not purely a matter for the motor-cortex and nerves but that it involved an intricate interplay between motor output and sensory feedback. Both men were scientists with a knack for writing accessibly about complex processes. Both men were concerned with how we develop a finer sense of movement, and McCaw argues that their different (though complementary) approaches to learning and development could greatly inform our understanding of actor training. He provides a critique of muscle memorization of movement in actor training and argues that Bernstein's and Feldenkrais's thought provides tools for understanding and improving sensory intelligence for the actor.

All three chapters address the omnivorousness of Feldenkrais's interests through an international cast of interlocutors, from Israel, Austria, France and Russia. Kampe details an enabling of women through somatic cultures and he relates this to enabling in contemporary practice that utilizes this legacy. Sholl shows how the idea of self-love and care can be used intelligently to change practice and the self-image, and how Glenn Gould's legacy can be used as an unorthodox model for performance training. Finally, McCaw deals with differentiations that arise from a common heritage of thinking (Bernstein and Feldenkrais) about sensory awareness, learning, skill development and the self-image, and he turns these spotlights on the enabling process of actor training.

Part II: From Science into Creative Practice

In designing this book, I wanted to include an authentic experience of Feldenkrais's teaching. The distinguished movement scientist Maxine Sheets-Johnston here provides an objective and scientific assessment of the Method. She first encountered Feldenkrais and his Method in the late 1970s and this chapter reprints an article she wrote in the aftermath of this encounter. Sheets-Johnston describes the shock and surprise of the Method, its thinking, its processes and its effects through the body. She provides a description of what is striking, novel and valuable in Feldenkrais's approach. She differentiates it from exercise, discusses the function of memory (touched upon by McCaw) and comfort (both elaborated by Feldenkrais in his Vest workshop), of the value of indirect bodily intervention, effort, and she discusses these features of his practice with reference to a revision of dance training. She also touches upon questions of intention, attention, self-direction (rather than goal-directedness) that animate movement science and phenomenological philosophy. These are touchstones for thinking about agency and interaction, self-perception and self-negotiation through awareness that are fundamental to creative practice.

Sheets-Johnston's witness of Feldenkrais's work acts as a memory vial. Opening it triggers various epistemological tributaries that are taken up by Roger Russell's work that acts as a companion piece to this work. Drawing on literature in developmental psychology, sensory-motor development, neuroscience, biomechanics, functional anatomy, pedagogy and philosophy, Russell explores the learning and personal skills development of creative artists. He questions traditional training methods of repetition and willpower (as practice) and asks questions about the formation of artistic skill through self-discovery and the development of autonomy (see also Mark Lacey's chapter below) that extend the Feldenkrais Method into creative practice.

Russell's developmental and scientific insights are complemented by two chapters by the Canadian scientific researchers Jillian Beacon, Gilles Comeau and Donald Russell. These chapters are some of the first scientific work on the Method that assess the impact of the Method for musicians.

Their introductory chapter addresses the need for objective biomechanical measurement of musicians participating in somatic training methods such as the Feldenkrais Method, focusing on pianists. It reviews literature describing how somatic methods, including Feldenkrais's work, have been researched so far and explores how motion-tracking technologies could be used to objectively measure variables related to movement and body positioning in the context of piano playing. The chapter closes with a discussion about the challenges of choosing movement and postural variables to measure that respect the learning theories and teaching techniques unique to the Feldenkrais Method. The goal of this chapter is to help orient future researchers towards methodologies that will meaningfully contribute empirical research on the Method and musicians.

This chapter acts as a precursor to another chapter which discusses results from a recent pilot project using a 2D video-based motion-tracking method to examine aspects of pianists' body positioning and movement from before and after a single FI lesson given by pianist and Feldenkrais practitioner Alan Fraser (see Part III below). The results demonstrate qualitative changes in movement patterns for two of the twelve participants. The authors discuss the way objectivity, methodologies and possible future research paradigms can be developed to expand quantitative research on the Feldenkrais Method. They provide some objective ways in which scientific research can facilitate awareness and ability.

Part III: Studies in Creative Practice

The third part of this book addresses creative practice in a variety of ways. It provides a window onto the ways in which practitioners in dance, music and theatre have used the Method and the ways in which they see the Method as offering a laboratory space in which theory and practice are brought into a productive engagement. Alan Fraser's writings on piano technique have sought to address issues related to historical technical schools of thought, and to rethink them in the light of how the Method might be applied to piano playing. His particular concern here is with the structural-functional integrity of the pianistic mechanism (playing the piano with the whole self) moving beyond traditional concerns of arm 'weight' to imagine how the body can be used to draw greater resonance from the instrument. He shows how his adaptation develops the uniqueness of the individual's artistic relationship to the instrument, enabling them to sense, feel and express more. Fraser's work in this chapter develops Feldenkrais's thinking in unorthodox but innovative ways to help pianists avoid injury and improve the quality of their work.

The Feldenkrais Method has been employed extensively for purposes of healing and somatic education across the arts. Lisa Burrell's work (as a string player) draws on a distinction between 'orthopaedic' injuries and neurologically based dysfunction. She focuses on defining increasingly specific differentiations as a way of alleviating symptoms of hyper-development and overuse and promoting awareness through choices to enhance expressive capacity. Burrell writes about her work with musicians, how it is based on the learning-based/pedagogical concepts of ATM lessons, and how specific lessons address these issues. Her work also provides a critique of the limitations of the Method and its transfer to creative practitioners.

Victoria Worsley's chapter focuses on the significance of a fundamental perception of safety and the dysfunction of anxiety in performance. To address this, she turns to a discussion of play, social engagement and spontaneity which is at the core of the actor's experience. Using her own experience of training actors, she shows how Feldenkrais lessons can help actors learn to connect better with themselves and audiences. She considers how the Method could be a key tool in learning through modulating the Vagal Nerve complex (discussed by Stephen Porges) that is capable of regulating traditional fight/flight and stress responses to help actors engage with each other and the audience.

Mark Lacey's chapter opens up a different avenue of inquiry into this mechanism. He addresses the problem of the fundamental conflicts that exist between the well-being of the effective actor, the quality of their output, and the demands of the acting industry. The chapter examines actors' compulsive motivations that are non-integral, or in Feldenkrais's terms 'parasitic' and extraneous to performance, and he shows how the compulsion governs choice that leaves actors open to both self-manipulation and exploitation. Lacey explores how the use of Feldenkrais's thought might result in the transformation of the actor's sense of self (through training and industry practice) towards one of non-compulsive autonomy. The chapter therefore applies and develops this idea of self-reliance and ability development that is so fundamental to Feldenkrais's idea of health.

Marcia Carr's chapter complements the previous two chapters. She returns to a root cause of performance and anxiety and the search for a cure in autonomy by examining the ways in which the nervous system under performance conditions reverts to older physical habits. She draws on her experience as movement and voice specialist and as a Feldenkrais practitioner to examine how the Method can help the performer think through habitual action from a singing and movement lesson in rehearsal and the transferral of this thinking into performance. She therefore shows how the Method can be developed to provide what she calls a *tuning* of the body for new possibilities of 'adaptive flexibility' in performance.

The Canadian dance theorist Sylvie Fortin provides a further philosophical reflection on the nature of practice. Her study is based around a series of incisions into her own ritualistic morning somatic work: sensing, moving, stretching, strengthening, singing and expressing. She provides a delightful example of how the transference of practice feeds into being. She moves between work in education (like Kampe, Worsley, and Carr, Fortin works in a university dance department), and an adaptation of the Feldenkrais Method in her private practice and in her work with special-needs children in a private healthcare setting. She provides a critical expansion of the pedagogical, socio-political, spiritual and artistic dimensions of the Feldenkrais Method. Fortin clarifies how Somatics might be transformational for artists as well as laypeople as a personal, embodied and experiential practice.

This book therefore offers a rich development of the legacy and the ongoing relevance of the Feldenkrais Method. The chapters show how the Method has resonances in many areas of human life and how it provides a sustaining and powerful discourse for future work in creative practice.

The reader of this book will gain insight into strategies that can be used to refine their own practice. They will find that the thinking demonstrated in this book is transferable to other creative and theoretic circumstances, as much as to other academic and creative disciplines. They will be able to explore the contextualization of Feldenkrais's thought and they will find strategies and ideas for further thinking about and a refreshment of their work. For Feldenkrais practitioners, or those who work in other somatic disciplines, this book provides new readings, resources, strategies for practice with others and in particular, for those practitioners who do not work with creative practitioners, it will we hope provide a window onto the thinking that will facilitate engagement. For scholars in the burgeoning field of somatic studies, this book will also provide fresh insight, and it will expose how creative practice provides an arena in which such a Method provides a satisfying synergy between theory and practice.

In particular, the chapters in this book provide a rich and diverse range of views that act as a call to re-examine one's own practice from the beginning. The idea of beginning again, starting as if with no *a priori* knowledge in a field of enquiry was an idea Feldenkrais's work inherited perhaps from Zen thought (from D.T. Suzuki) and also from the work of G.I. Gurdjieff. This spirit of exploration allows the Method to be employed here as an interdisciplinary hinge to facilitate new qualities of practice and to illuminate fields of creative endeavour through creative applications of its own strategies. The book allows readers to spiral down into the richness of its contents and come back to the beginning with a new perspective on their own knowledge and with new strategies and resources for action. Some of the chapters in the book include addenda with practical thought and ATM lessons, but readers will find things to put into practice throughout the book.

Notes

1. Mark Reese, *Mosche Feldenkrais: A Life in Movement*, Vol. 1 (San Rafael, CA: Feldenkrais Resources, 2015), 231.
2. Sayings widely attributed to Feldenkrais in the Feldenkrais community.
3. See Esther Thelen, 'The Central Role of Action in Typical and Atypical Development', in *Movement and Action in Learning and Development: Clinical Implications of Pervasive Developmental*

Disorders, ed. Ida J. Stockman (San Diego, CA: Academic Press, 2004), 71. See Campbell Edinborough, 'The Resilient Body: Developing Resilience and Presence Using the Feldenkrais Method', in *Ways of Being a Body: Body and Performance*, ed. Sandra Reeve (Axminster: Triarchy Press, 2013), 111–22.

4   See Feldenkrais's lecture 'Learning, Free Choice, Individuality', *New York Quest Workshop*, 1981 (San Diego, CA: Feldenkrais Resources, n.d.).

5   See Feldenkrais, 'Eight lessons in Awareness through Movement' (1978), available at https://mindinmotion-online.com/long-lost-lessons/ (accessed 12 May 2020).

6   See Martha Eddy, 'A Brief History of Somatic Practices and Dance: Historical Development of the Field of Somatic Education and Its Relationship to Dance', *Journal of Dance and Somatic Practices*, Vol. 1 (2009), 5–27, and *Bone, Breath and Gesture: Practices of Embodiment*, ed. Don Hanlon Johnson (Berkeley, CA: North Atlantic Books: 1995).

7   Special edition of *Theatre, Dance and Performance Training*, Vol. 6, No. 2 (2015), ed. Libby Worth and Dick McCaw.

8   See Mary Spire's *How to Understand and Work Effectively with Musicians* (San Diego, CA: Feldenkrais Resources, n.d.), and Jerry Karzen's workshop: *In Tune with Yourself: Feldenkrais for Musicians* (San Diego, CA: Feldenkrais Resources, 2010). See also the lessons and discussions available at feldenkraisresourcesformusicians.co.uk (accessed 31 May 2020), and *The Feldenkrais Journal*, Vol. VI, ed. Thomas Kampe and Clifford Smyth (May 2019).

9   See Alan Fraser, *The Craft of Piano Playing: A New Approach to Piano Technique*, 2nd edn. (Lanham, MD, and Plymouth: Scarecrow Press, 2011); *Honing the Pianistic Self-Image: Skeletal-Based Piano Technique* (Novi Sad: Maple Grove Music Productions, 2010); *All Thumbs: Well-Coordinated Piano Technique* (Novi Sad: Maple Grove Music Productions, 2012); and *Piano with Your Whole Self* (2020) available at https://store.alanfraserinstitute.com/product/5, and Samuel H. Nelson, *Singing with the Whole Self: The Feldenkrais Method and Voice* (Lanham, MD, and London: Scarecrow Press, 2001).

10 Victoria Worsley, *Feldenkrais for Actors* (London: Nick Hern Books, 2016). See Dick McCaw, *Training the Actor's Body: A Guide* (London: Methuen, 2018), and *Rethinking the Actor's Body: Dialogues with Neuroscience* (London: Methuen, 2020).

11 See Blake Howe, Stefanie Jensen-Moulton, Neil Lerner and Joseph Strauss, 'Introduction: Disability Studies in Music, Music in Disability Studies', in *The Oxford Handbook of Music and Disability Studies*, ed. Howe, Jensen-Moulton, Lerner and Strauss (New York: Oxford University Press, 2016), 1–14.

12 See Feldenkrais, *Awareness through Movement: Health Exercises for Personal Growth* (London: Arkana, 1990), 67–8.

13 See Feldenkrais, 'Functional Integration with Cerebral Palsy, Session I', in *The Work of Dr Mosche Feldenkrais*, 2 DVDs (San Diego, CA: Feldenkrais Resources, 2007); also available at https://www.facebook.com/watch/?v=136092850277964 (accessed 12 May 2020), and Sholl, 'Feldenkrais's Touch, Ephram's Laughter, Gould's Sensorium: Listening and Musical Practice between Thinking and Doing', *Journal of the Royal Musical Association*, Vol. 144, No. 2 (2019), 397–428.

14 'What I'm after isn't flexible bodies but flexible brains. What I'm after is to restore each person to their human dignity.' Saying widely attributed to Feldenkrais in the Feldenkrais community.

15 Feldenkrais, *Awareness through Movement*, 10–24, 130–8, and Sean Gallagher and Andrew N. Meltzoff, 'The Earliest Sense of Self and Others: Merleau-Ponty and Recent Developmental Studies', *Philosophical Psychology*, Vol. 9, No. 2 (1996), available online at https://www.ncbi.nlm.nih.gov/pmc/articles/PMC3845406/ (accessed 12 May 2020). See also Carl Ginsburg on infant development in *The Intelligence of Moving Bodies: A Somatic View of Life and Its Consequences* (Sante Fe, NM: AWAREing, 2010), 112–43.

16 Feldenkrais, 'Bodily Expressions', trans. Thomas Hanna in *Embodied Wisdom: The Collected Papers of Mosche Feldenkrais*, ed. Elizabeth Beringer (San Diego, CA: Feldenkrais Resources, 2010), 3. See Gallagher, *How the Body Shapes the Mind* (Oxford: Oxford University Press, 2005), 45–7.

17 H.H. Stuckenschmidt, *Schoenberg: His Life, World and Works*, trans. Humphrey Searle (Richmond, Surrey: Oneworld Classics, 2011), 110.

18 Feldenkrais, 'Learning, Free Choice, Individuality', *New York Quest Workshop*, 1981.

19 Cited in Dianne Hancock, 'Teaching the FM in UK Higher Education Performer Training', *Theatre, Dance and Performance Training*, Vol. 6 No. 2 (2015), ed. Worth and McCaw, 163.

20 See Susan Hallam, *Music Psychology in Education* (London: Institute of Education, 2006), 18, and Simone Dalla Bella, 'Music and Brian Plasticity', in *The Oxford Handbook of Music Psychology*, ed. Susan Hallam, Ian Cross and Michael Thaut (New York: Oxford University Press, 2016), 325–42.

21 Feldenkrais, 'Lifting the head on the back simple flexion one side in imagination', *New York Quest Workshop*, 1981.

22 On FI see http://www.feldenkrais.com/functional-integration.

23 Feldenkrais, 'Learning, Free Choice, Individuality', *New York Quest Workshop*, 1981.

24 Ludwig Wittgenstein, *Tractatus Logico-Philosophicus*, trans. C.K.O (no name given) (London: Routledge and Kegan Paul, 1958), section 5.62, 151.

25 J.W. von Goethe, *Erster Verlust* (1815). https://www.oxfordlieder.co.uk/song/1407 (accessed 8 September 2020).

26 Jean Laplanche and Jean-Bertrand Pontalis, *The Language of Psychoanalysis*, trans. Donald Nicholson-Smith (London: Karnac, 1973), 394. See also Sigmund Freud, 'A Short Account of Psycho-analysis' (1924), in *The Standard Edition of the Complete Psychological Works of Sigmund Freud*, Vol. XIX, trans. James Strachey (London: Penguin, 1961), 196.

27 Available at http://vangoghletters.org/vg/letters/let536/letter.html (underlining in source).

28 Chopin's own fingering is marked A in this table. This is available at http://ks.imslp.net/files/imglnks/usimg/0/06/IMSLP367631-PMLP01970-Chopin_Etudes_opus_25_-_Cortot_(french).pdf

29 'Finding lightness and ease in the arms and in yourself. Rolling with interlaced hands on the back', *New York Quest Workshop*, 1981.

30 Joseph Horowitz, *Arrau on Music and Performance* (New York: Dover, 1992), 53–4, 57.

31 Claudio Arrau, 'A Performer Looks at Psychoanalysis' [February 1967 in *High Fidelity*] in Horowitz, *Arrau on Music and Performance*, 246.

32 See Horowitz, *Arrau on Music and Performance*, 203.

33 See Feldenkrais, *The Potent Self: A Study of Spontaneity and Compulsion* (Berkeley, CA: Frog, 1985), 25 and 28.

34 Feldenkrais, *The Elusive Obvious*, with a foreword by Norman Doidge (Berkeley, CA: North Atlantic Books, 2019).

35 For Gallagher, *Enactivist Interventions: Rethinking the Mind* (New York: Oxford University Press, 2017), 10 and 77, and also Gallagher, *Action and Interaction* (New York: Oxford University Press, 2020).

36 The Method is not for example a form of medical intervention, nor, despite the importance that psychoanalysis had for Feldenkrais and his own reading in this subject, is it a substitute for seeing a qualified psychiatrist/psychologist.

37 In this regard, Feldenkrais's friend David Ben-Gurion wanted to create a University that taught all of its subject through the Method. See Meyer Levin, 'The Man Who Stood the Prime Minister on His Head', available at https://feldenkraisvancouver.com/wp-content/uploads/2016/12/The-Man-Who-Stood-the-Prime-Minister-on-His-Head-Levin.pdf

38 See, for example, Louise Atkins, 'Healthy Conservatoires', available at https://www.healthyuniversities.ac.uk/wp-content/uploads/2016/05/louise_atkins___healthy_conservatoires.pdf

PART I
HISTORICAL PERSPECTIVES ON CREATIVE PRACTICE

CHAPTER 1
DANCING THE SOMA-ECSTATIC: FELDENKRAIS AND THE MODERNIST BODY
Thomas Kampe

Introduction

This chapter retraces body codes and emancipatory ethics found in the work of Moshe Feldenkrais (1904–84) to the beginnings of early Modernist European Dance and Body Cultures. The author suggests that Feldenkrais's emphasis on fostering the mature adult as a creative and emancipated individual emerged from the early Modernist 'Körperkultur' (body culture) and dance beginnings that formed important part of the cultural milieu in 1920s Palestine. Feldenkrais experienced holistic dance/gymnastic studies with Israeli expressive modern dance pioneer Margalit Ornstein (Vienna 1888–Tel Aviv 1973) before moving to Paris. Ornstein was influenced by the work of Viennese choreographer Gertrud Bodenwieser (1890–1959) and European body-culture pioneer Bess Mensendieck (1864–1957), both visionary emancipatory proto-somatic pioneers. While revealing similarities between Mensendieck's, Bodenwieser's and Feldenkrais's ethos and practices, the chapter also places Feldenkrais into the context of post-1940s Israeli body culture which drew on European Modern Dance and holistic Reform-Gymnastic practices including the work of Elsa Gindler (1885–1961). By offering an alternative and feminist history, this chapter reviews the beginnings of Feldenkrais's work not as the work of a monolithic genius but as situated within an interdisciplinary milieu that emerged from utopian and diasporic Modernist artistic and educational endeavours.

Dancing the soma-ecstatic

This chapter argues that the emancipatory dimensions within Feldenkrais's work emerge through his own first-hand encounters and experiences with proponents and practices of reform-gymnastics and education, and through his contact with European Modern dance practitioners who understood dance as an increasingly important 'factor in education'.[1] This Western Modernist Body Culture and Dance milieu 'explored new kinds of thinking about the bodily experience', where movement is understood as vessel for personal, artistic and social activation and transformation.[2]

Rothe proposes that beyond methods of training developed by men such as Rudolf Laban, Rudolf Bode or Jacques-Dalcroze, it was mainly women practitioners of the *Lebensreform* – Life reform movement – who 'intended to draw together psychological feeling, bodily experience dance and musical elements, into an all embracing, free and creative way of life. This plan revoled about the body'.[3]

Such practices of reform-gymnastics became part of an emancipatory educational Zeitgeist and milieu that privileged self-directed development against heteronomous learning. As Weaver concludes:

Reform-gymnastics proposed a different approach where the voice of the teacher and external bio-mechanical reasoning was replaced by developing an awareness of the student's inner rhythms and of the requirements of his organism.[4]

There appear to be immediate affinities between the European Modern dance heritage that asked for a 'thinking in terms of movement as contrasted with thinking in words' and the embodied 'thinking without words, with images, patterns and connections' leading 'to a new way of action' which Feldenkrais proposes.[5] Both aim to blend analysis with experience, action with reflection, exploration with discovery, and heightened self-awareness with a capacity for self-directed interaction with the environment.[6]

The synergies between the Feldenkrais Method and psycho-physical movement approaches developed within the twentieth-century theatre and dance cultures are rarely discussed in literature by Moshe Feldenkrais, nor in his recently published biographies or works that analyse his cultural milieu.[7]

It therefore seems surprising that in the edited conversation of 1965 between Moshe Feldenkrais and theatre director Richard Schechner, Feldenkrais reveals detailed insights into the training approaches developed by Russian theatre practitioner Konstantin Stanislavski (1863–1938).[8] Stanislavski's later approach to acting which highlighted embodiment and action is akin to Feldenkrais's own rationale for privileging movement as an accessible educational lever to access an awareness the unity of 'whole self'.[9] Feldenkrais sets out that his approach is 'mainly concerned with learning a better mode of action and uses of the body, from which the person can learn directly, in his own body language'.[10] This ability to learn directly from uses of the body is equally articulated in early-twentieth-century writings by Stanislavski whose work was concerned with the 'organismic functioning of man', where thinking and feeling are necessarily an embodied whole.[11]

Like Feldenkrais (in his book *Awareness through Movement*), he was concerned with accessing the person's agency, creativity and potential through movement. 'We are more at home with physical action than with the elusive nature of emotion. Here we can find our bearing better, here we are more inventive, and more certain than with subjective elements which are difficult to capture and fix.'[12] Stanislavski's system of *Spiritual Realism* was inspired by his personal encounter with Modern Dance pioneer Isadora Duncan (1877–1927) in Moscow in 1907. Modern Dance, as an emerging twentieth-century genre concerned with embodied forms of human expression through dynamic action, seemed to provide 'an imaginative richness in material and a search for truth', at the heart of Stanislavski's psycho-physical training system and rehearsal practice.[13]

Between 2014 and 2019 I collaborated on the research project *Releasing the Archive* with choreographer and dance scholar Carol Brown and dancers of The New Zealand Dance Company. The research intended to re-embody Modernist Dance practices formulated by Viennese choreographer Gertrud Bodenwieser through accessing choreographic and training practices transmitted through members of the original Viennese companies, archival notes, books, photographs and writings by Bodenwieser. Bodenwieser was the first Professor for Dance and Choreography at the Viennese Staatsakademie, and resigned shortly before the Nazis took over governance in March 1938. As a displaced Jewish dance-maker she spent twenty years in exile in Australia where she and her disciples laid foundations for Modern Dance development.

Our initial research was concerned with re-animating body codes embedded in Bodenwieser's work through Feldenkrais-informed preparatory and interventional processes. These included the use of Awareness through Movement (ATM) lessons, touch interaction, and reflective non-corrective trial and error modalities as part of the choreographic experiments with the dancers.

The dialogue between the introspective, somatic Feldenkrais processes and the ecstatic Modern dance 'body-based testimonies' explored seemed surprisingly fluid and empowering for dancers involved.[14] Dancer Katie Rudd reflects on a change in agency, body image and three-dimensional use of body shaping in her dancing:

> I am learning to be more open and lengthened spatially, and that there are more sides/fronts to my body, not just the mirror. A lot of contraction and openings. Movement at is extreme. Wide and spatial.[15]

Dancer Lucy Lynch describes a shift in capacity for core-initiation from torso and pelvis in her dancing as an organically liberating resource for greater variation in movement choices, as a result of engaging with a soma-ecstatic Feldenkrais/Bodenwieser dialogue:

> I felt an obvious change and difference in my body and also how both techniques informed my way of moving. […] I found both techniques can lead me to discover more possibilities of how I move around my pelvis and how I include my back movement into my way of moving. It gives me so much more freedom of how I could use my body and how I create movements in many different ways, instead of just focusing on the movement of my limbs.[16]

Bodenwieser was a leading proponent of *Ausdruckstanz* (dance of expression) which she described as *The New Dance* which 'does not content itself with being enchanting and entertaining only; it wishes to be stirring, exciting and thought-provoking'.[17] Such 'stirring, exciting, and thought-provoking' dance practice might be easily reframed as de-familiarizing, un-conditioning, stimulating and reflective processes that challenge the participants' habitual self-image and ways of world-making, similar to working modalities at the heart of the Feldenkrais Method.

Bodenwieser's choreographic work requires a systematically trained dancer-body that, in similar ways to the body-coding Feldenkrais prescribes is poly-centric and omni-directional in coordination. She understood Modernist dance and body cultures as being part of a 'great revolution of freeing the human mind' and placed great attention to the training of a liberated, emotionally expressive dancer.[18]

Drawing on the reform practices of François Delsarte (1811–71) and Bess Mensendieck (1864–1957), Bodenwieser sought to develop an education which activates the mover to sense, initiate and organize movements from their core. She describes this as 'the torso being given the melody of the composition, while the lower parts of the body carry the structure, the bass of the symphony'.[19]

Such body-coding lends itself easily to preparatory practices developed through the application of Feldenkrais lessons. While the Feldenkrais Method aims to foster the development of greater self-awareness in the mover, lessons are designed to improve an organic functioning

The Feldenkrais Method in Creative Practice

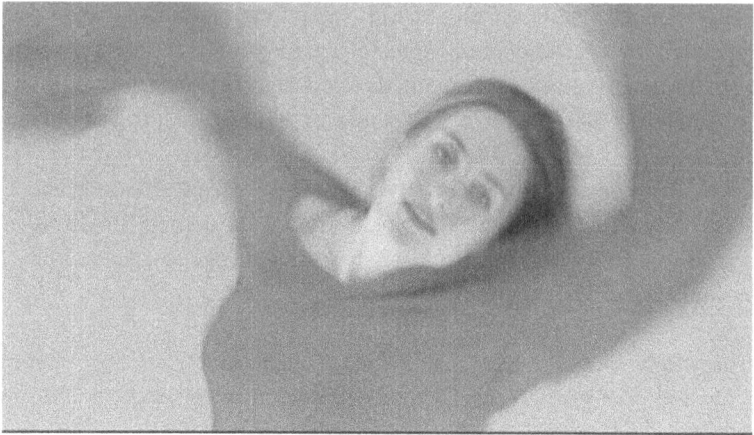

Figure 1.1 Dancer Katie Rudd in project 'Releasing the Archive' (2016).

through providing a focus on smooth control of changes in gravity response, spatial orientation and initiation in different body areas. Numerous *Awareness through Movement* ATM lessons aim to mobilize the mover's pelvis in rocking or see-saw movements, enable successive flow through the spine, or activate the dynamic and rotary relationships between the mover's torso and limbs.

The research project revealed several affinities between preferred body-codings within the work of Gertrud Bodenwieser and Feldenkrais's organic movement practices. At times, simply enlarging patterns explored in a Feldenkrais lesson led directly to a Bodenwieser movement vocabulary, such as large back arching waves through the spine, or a spiralling use of the limbs in figure of eight forms. More so, her emancipatory vision towards freedom, non-conformity and creativity of the individual and a focus on induction and discovery are akin to discovery-based pedagogies developed by Moshe Feldenkrais, not concerned with correction and conditioning, but with 'development' of the individual through embodied inquiry. Feldenkrais claims that such 'development stresses the harmonious coordination between structure, function, and achievement. And a basic condition for harmonious coordination is complete freedom from either self-compulsion or compulsion from others'.[20]

Dancer Shona Dunlop MacTavish describes a corporeal-affective-cognitive unity in the learner that this Modern Dance culture aimed to foster in the dancer: 'True dance for Bodenwieser meant discovery, discovery which combined the exploration of thoughts and feelings, simultaneously with the penetrating study of the body and its anatomical structure and the impetus of movement as a whole.'[21] It becomes clear that in both, Feldenkrais's pedagogy and the above Modernist dance practices, the curious aware agent-self is activated in dialogue with a quest for heightened physiological functioning, creative inquiry and capacity for self-care.

The Ornstein connection

> Life is Movement. Everything that lives is in continuous movement.[22]

> Man's life is a continuous process, and the improvement is needed in the quality of the process, not in his properties or disposition.[23]

In his biography of Feldenkrais, Mark Reese briefly states that Moshe Feldenkrais 'studied Ballet with one Mrs. Ornstein' during the 1920s in Palestine.[24] This is confirmed in the writings of theatre director Gaby Aldor, daughter of Modern Dancer Shoshona Ornstein (1911–98) and granddaughter of Palestine/Israel Körperkultur-pioneer Margalit Ornstein (1888–1973). Aldor clarifies that Ornstein taught not ballet, but reform-gymnastics and Bodenwieser-influenced 'Expressive Dance – artistic dance' or 'Künstlerischer Tanz'. Ornstein, who emigrated from Austria to Palestine in 1921, reveals aspects of structure and learning mood of her classes in her diaries:

> A lesson is constructed like this: floor exercises at the beginning, then swing exercises in groups of eight, for each group in different way – standing, walking or jumping. As Professor Bodenwieser used to say: if you enjoy it you will understand it faster.[25]

Aldor emphasizes that Moshe Feldenkrais was a lifelong friend of the Ornstein family, stating that Feldenkrais 'changed the way dancers treated their bodies, he opened a door for them'.[26] Yet, surprisingly she emphasizes a reciprocity of influence of Modernist body-culture knowledges on the later work of Feldenkrais.

> I think that they built some sort of groundwork that connects rationality and wisdom – like methods of von Laban, of very high physical awareness, what later went into Feldenkrais – with the capacity for inspiration. It shows up in all the exercises in Margalit's blue notebooks and I think that it's terrific – that it is really a kind of groundwork that characterizes Israeli dance too.[27]

Feldenkrais had first-hand knowledge of modern gymnastics and dance. He was in personal correspondence with the Ornstein sisters – the twin dancers Shoshona and Yehudit – while he lived in Paris in 1931, advising them not to give up their careers in dance. Surprisingly, a letter by Yehudit from 1929 states that Feldenkrais also taught at the Ornstein studio in Tel Aviv. 'We had a wonderful dance lesson. I am really so foolish that I always forget how good it is to dance. […] After class we had a Feldenkrais lesson.'[28] Both Aldor and Burckard conclude that these 'Feldenkrais lessons' were most likely self-defence lessons taught by Moshe Feldenkrais to members of the Haganah. Margalit's husband Jacques Ornstein was a leading member in the secret paramilitary organization.[29] Before emigrating to Palestine in 1921, Margalit had been a student of dance of Gertrud Bodenwieser at Vienna Staatsakademie from 1920, and visited Bodenwieser several times in Vienna during the 1920s to further study with her. She also sent her daughters to study with Bodenwieser and other European Modern dancers during 1928 and 1931.[30]

Ornstein taught basic movement principles to emerging Tel Aviv theatre companies such as the Tali, Ohel and Habima, 'to put the body of the "New Jew" on stage, full of vitality and breathing freely'.[31] She was interested in dramatic action and her work embraced the integration of movement and dance into emerging 'Tanztheater' – dance-theatre – forms, and the development of 'Theatertanz' – theatre-dance within existing plays. Ornstein wrote passionately about the training of theatre directors through movement.[32] She proposed that,

The Feldenkrais Method in Creative Practice

through the direction of movement, the educated theatre director 'will be able to give [...] a form that matches the characteristics of our Jewish life'.³³

While Modern Dance and body culture promised a freeing of the individual within its pre-First World War European Reform-Movement educational context, post-First World War practitioners re-articulated these new forms of educational expression as culturally affirmative instruments in various changing political contexts in Europe, the Soviet Union, the United States and Zionist Palestine. In her diaries, Ornstein quotes a letter by her husband Jacques from 1921, contextualizing her theatrical body politics. She refers to Theodore

Figure 1.2 Shoshana and Yehudit Ornstein. Photograph by Alfonso Himmelreich, © G. Aldor.

Herzl's Zionist novel *Altneuland* – The Old New Land: 'In straight lines and in powerful rhythm, inspired by the old-new homeland, the liberated body will emerge. The dance of the new Hebrew.'[34] The author argues that Feldenkrais's studying of dance and gymnastics with Margalit Ornstein forms a key part of his critical becoming and exemplifying the 'new Hebrew' male. The facilitators and theorists of such practices of 'the liberated body', though, were women who do not form part of the established master-narrative of Feldenkrais's biography.

Bess Mensendieck and Modernist Körperkultur

Margalit Ornstein had studied with body-culture pioneer Elisabeth 'Bess' Mensendieck in Vienna prior to arriving in Palestine. Mensendieck's system of 'free gymnastics system for women', her work with Gertrud Bodenwieser at Vienna Dance Academy and her studies in Jacques-Dalcroze's Rhythmic Gymnastics informed her teaching of 'Plastic Gymnastics and Rhythmic Exercises' in Tel Aviv from 1921.[35] Ornstein credits Mensendieck as one of her major influences, offering a functional training system useful for the Modern Dancer. Mensendieck developed a proto-feminist practice concerned with 'self-determination' of women through a 'subjective method of bodily education'.[36] Several key features in Mensendieck's work foreshadow the post-Second World War work of Moshe Feldenkrais – a social-constructivist perspective on embodiment, a focus on movement analysis and autonomy of the learner through internalization and observation, and an emphasis on the reactivation of the pelvis as a counter-cultural necessity for the Modern citizen. Mensendieck developed floor-based exercises, many of them resembling parts of Feldenkrais ATM lessons, including slow knee-drops from side to the side, or a gentle pressing through the feet to lift the pelvis and spine forward in a successive chain-like movement.[37] Her early writings *Körperkultur des Weibes* (1906) investigate the 'reciprocal relationship between body-life and cultural life', where body is understood as malleable construct within a patriarchal and urban cultural context.[38] Mensendieck advocated 'reliable, science- not fashion-based system of teachings' for a bodily culture where the woman-student develops 'a capacity for self-critique' and a curiosity for self-directed learning as a cultural practice.[39]

Her work was designed to improve the awareness and functioning of any existing part of 'the body-machine'.[40] This included exercises to strengthen the pelvic region, most notably a pelvic-rocking exercise she named 'the pelvic see-saw'.[41] Bodenwieser confirms Mensendieck's influence on paying 'greatest attention to the position of the pelvis' where 'we lift the front of the pelvis and lower the back of the pelvis'.[42] Descriptions of this preferred hip placement are repeatedly found in Ornstein's notebooks as 'vorgeschobenes Becken' – 'protruding pelvis'.[43] Mensendieck advocated for her students 'again to mentally engage with a bodily area, which predominantly has become so degenerated, because through wrong moral values one believed to have to exclude the whole region from our thinking'.[44] Her radical writings advocate a call for a revisioning of existing patriarchal morals through embodied processes: 'It is time, you women, that you construct your own bodily ethics, with moral values that are aligned to the reality of your bodily functions!'[45] Such a call for a collective somatic rejection of cultural

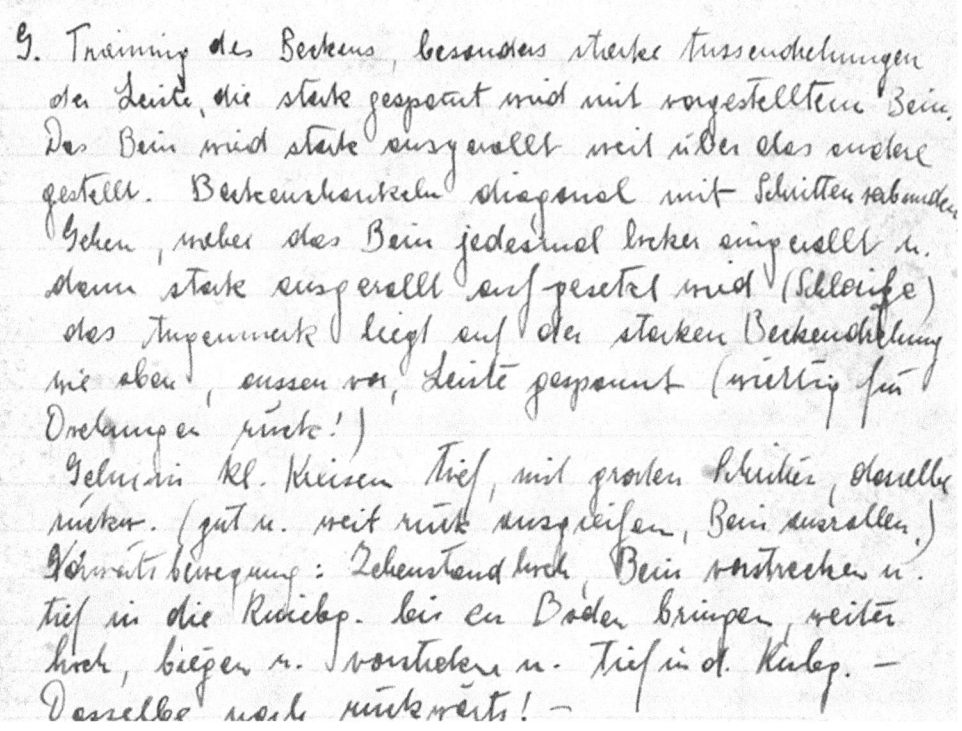

Figure 1.3 Margalit Ornstein notebook from the 1930s: 'Training of the Pelvis – diagonal pelvic see-saw'.

conditioning forms the driving force behind her profound influence within early-twentieth-century European Körperkultur.[46] The relationship between moral codes, bodily perception and function of the pelvis is discussed in similar ways in the early writings of US body-mind pioneer Mabel Todd:

> The first part of the structure to consider in the human being is the pelvis [...] we must first have an intelligent understanding of the mechanical adjustments necessary for economical functioning of the body, not allowing old postural ideas, based on moral notions, to influence our understanding.[47]

The influence of Mensendieck's writings on Todd's work as a seminal movement educator is worth further examining.

In her book *Bewegungsprobleme*, Mensendieck published a summary of her principles under *Motto* for *Mensendieck Exercises*. These consisted of a systemic perspective on movement education that embraced agency and judgement of the learner within a body-mind process that aims to construct 'an intellectualisation of the flesh' where the human willpower can direct muscular effort and functioning.[48] She lays out her motto as processes of:

Feldenkrais and the Modernist Body

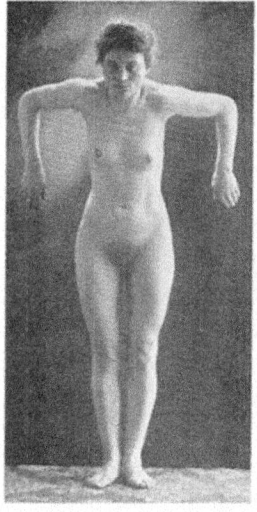

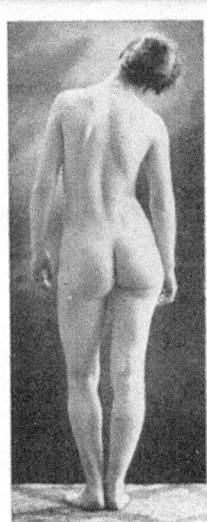

Fig. 32. Schlecht relaxiert stehender Körper

Fig. 33. Relaxiert stehender Körper mit Beherrschung der Bauchvorstülpung

Fig. 34. Korrekt relaxierte Haltung ohne Relieferschlaffung

Fig. 35. Das Stehen mit schlechter Gleichgewichtsverlagerung als Vorläufer von Skoliose

Figure 1.4 Bess Mensendieck demonstrating postural stances (1906).

> No drill-like activity
> Wiring together of muscle action and brain
> Observing
> Internalising
> Thoughtfully Comparing
> Judging
> Only self-achieved judgement is of value[49]

Her motto articulates a proto-somatic ethos akin to key principles inherent in the Feldenkrais Method concerned with sensory self-observation and notions of choice of the autonomous learner based on experience, differentiation and trial and error. However, her work appears problematic. Mensendieck sought for a wilful construction of an ideal machine-body, as a normative or 'normal body' whose perfect functioning is linked to perfect beauty. 'Unbeautiful' is understood as 'destructive' in habit or adaptation to environment.[50] Her writings reveal a eugenic position where 'illness is shameful – health is duty!' which stands in stark contrast with Feldenkrais's non-corrective and non-normative practice and ethos of 'restoring human dignity' of 'the average person'.[51]

Mensendieck's interpretation of a mind-body unity reveals itself as one-directional, where 'orders are sent out by the brain, the result being an intellectualisation of the flesh'.[52] While for Feldenkrais the sentient flesh is necessarily intellectualized, he proposes that thinking and self-image are always embodied and enacted within an environmental dialogic feedback context.

Body culture in Israel

> They all wanted you to be more connected to the true self, to nature. They were more interested in awareness. All of them. When you lift your arm very slowly you should feel your scapula. It was not very easy, when you are a 21 year old.[53]

> Because of Hitler they ran to Israel.[54]

The Jewish diaspora before, during and after the Holocaust and the Second World War brought many European, German-speaking emigrant dance- and movement-practitioners to Palestine and Israel. They embraced and developed the already-flourishing Modernist body culture in major cities such as Haifa and Tel Aviv, and in the rapidly spreading Kibbutz movement. Dancer Tile Rössler (1907–59), director of Palucca School Dresden, emigrated to Tel Aviv in 1933. There, she gained an international reputation as a dancer and ran a teacher-training programme until 1959. Writings in German from 1944 by students of Rössler reveal the holistic and emancipatory dimensions of the education she offered to a generation of movement pedagogues and dancers. Student Nava Skoroghotzi argues for dance and gymnastics systems that contribute to the 'development of the senses, imagination, self-education, and daily life experiences' of children. A highly ambitious student *Noah* writes in passionate ways:

> I want to dance, dance, dance and always dance again [...] I want my body not to be constrained by anything, so that I can execute each finest nuance of a mood, colour and idea. I want my body to be like a tender and most perfect instrument.[55]

The essay was written by choreographer and notation pioneer Noa Eshkol (1924–2007) who, on Rössler's advice, went to the UK to study with Rudolf Laban in Manchester and with Sigurd Leeder in London between 1948 and 1951. Reese and Burckard confirm that Eshkol formed a lifelong friendship and exchanged ideas with Moshe Feldenkrais already during this time in London. While Eshkol felt disappointed by the 'often arbitrary and not body-oriented' conventional dance training she experienced in England, it is questionable whether the analytical teachings and movement principles articulated by Rössler, Laban and his followers at the time and embodied by the young Eshkol had no influence on the thinking of Moshe Feldenkrais.[56] Eshkol would later invite Feldenkrais to teach at the newly established 'Body-Cultures' programme at the Tel Aviv Seminar Hakibbutzim after returning to Israel in 1951, and collaborated extensively with Feldenkrais on transcribing Feldenkrais lessons during the 1960s and 1970s into her 'EWMN' notation system.[57] Feldenkrais must have been acquainted with the bodily concerns of the Modern Dancer – a creative, reflective and clearly articulated relationship to skeletal organization, gravity and space.

Israeli Dance-Movement Therapy pioneer Yael Barkai was a student with leading figures of the Body-Culture movement between 1951 and the mid-1960s.[58] Barkai began her studies with dancer Yardena Cohen (1910–2012), and encountered Feldenkrais's classes in 1956 in Haifa.[59] Feldenkrais had been invited by German immigrant pedagogue Elly Friedman to teach gymnastic teachers as early as 1953. Barkai explains that 'the people who came were German women who wanted to develop their idea of movement, and I had heard about it – he was a famous man, and all the teachers came. I went to him for two years'.[60] While in the army during the late 1950s, Barkai encountered two women influenced by reform-gymnastic pioneer Elsa Gindler, Lotte Kristeller and Judith Bineter.[61] Barkai enrolled on the two-year diploma programme 'Body-Cultures' at Seminar Hakibbutzim run by Bineter and Kristeller since 1947, and studied with Gindler-pedagogue Miriam Goldberg and with Noa Eshkol. She continued her studies with Feldenkrais in Tel Aviv after her period in the army during the 1960s:

> At that time, he used tape recorders for his lessons, and he would stand in but he wouldn't talk. It was strange. I wish he would have talked more, but at that time it was good enough. I felt very good after the classes. I learnt to understand to look at very subtle changes, subtle ways of observing myself in the movement, and to go back to very basic movements, to feel good in my body, to slow down. It helped me to change my habits, to know how not to go beyond. It taught me to listen carefully what my body really needs. The slowness I had experienced already at college with Kristeller. She slowed me down.[62]

The work of Kristeller, Bineter and Goldberg was seminal to the development of several generations of movement pedagogues working in holistic traditions in Israel. All three leading women worked in eclectic and diverse ways. Barkai states that Bineter's pedagogy was influenced by Buddhist and Freudian concepts, 'because she wanted to break your ego where you had to clean yourself from everything'. This cathartic pedagogy was counterpointed by the teachings of Goldberg who introduced meditation into her classes, unusual in Israel at the time, and who 'taught very interesting things, such as moving with your eyes closed.'[63]

Figure 1.5 Noa Eshkol and peer students of Tile Rössler's school in Tel Aviv (1940s).

Figure 1.6 Tile Rössler teaching children in Tel Aviv in the 1950s.

Ruth Eshel describes the inductive pedagogical legacy of the 'Body-Cultures' programme run by Kristeller and Bineter as part of the 'Institute for Movement Education' (IME) at Seminar Hakibbutzim as

> a vehicle for experience and discovery of the self. The method was based on giving a verbal command with no demonstration of movement from the teacher so that the child would not imitate. The teacher would ask key questions – what? How? How many? And when? – it was the teacher's job to help the children learn to think in depth and to understand the foundations of movement – the body, energy, space and time. An advanced pupil was the one who could ask the correct question and had the technical ability to answer it him/herself.[64]

Feldenkrais pedagogue Sofia Naharin remembers her experience of working with Kristeller as assistant in dance classes for children in her private studio in the mid-1950s as seminal in her own development.[65] While Kristeller never involved herself actively as a mover, students were encouraged to 'see what you can do. She made suggestions to the students'[66]. When discussing similarities between Feldenkrais's and Kristeller's work, Naharin concludes that Kristeller's group work 'was much more creative in the movement in space' but in both approaches the 'time aspect of the work was very free, you were with yourself', Weaver states that Feldenkrais furthered his understanding of the work of Elsa Gindler through his encounters with Lotte Kristeller. Reese suggests that Feldenkrais's classes in Haifa were sponsored by ex-Gindler students. Burckard clarifies that Feldenkrais also taught regular classes before 1954 in the private Tel Aviv studio of Kristeller.[67]

Gindler never developed set exercises, but devised conditions for learning where students would be encouraged to experiment 'in pursuit of the question "Where do we end up if we simply let things happen unimpeded?"'[68] Gindler had studied *Harmonious Gymnastics* with Hedwig Kallmeyer and developed her work with Swiss pedagogue Heinrich Jacoby into a process-oriented system towards self-directed learning, improvisation, proprioception and authentic behaviour, to enable the human being to engage with complex challenges and conditions. Neudorfer refers to Jacoby's terms of 'working -through' (*sich erarbeiten*) and 'sensing' (*spüren*) as educational modalities in Gindler's work to arrive at a 'becoming quiet, awared readiness, creative indifference, sensory perception, empathy, intuition, and a feeling for self-efficacy or attunement'.[69] Gindler's student Lily Pincus suggests that such practices aimed 'to harmonize body, intellect and feeling through self-awareness'.[70] Charlotte Selver (1901–2003) describes Gindler as

> a natural scientist of extraordinary quality. She has made it her life's work to explore to what degree we human beings cooperate with the forces of nature. […] her work is bio-social in nature.[71]

What becomes evident is that Gindler had formulated a theorized practice of embodied reflective learning that placed the human exploratory organism at the heart of an emancipatory education that sought to provide means for self-direction of the dignified individual. Reese highlights the anti-totalitarian affinities between Gindler's work and the Feldenkrais Method. The author contends that these affinities emerged from Feldenkrais's dialogue with women practitioners of the reform-movement in Israel, and his ability to absorb, appropriate, re-embody and re-engineer educational concepts of the period. If Reese elaborates that Feldenkrais's key concept of 'Organic Learning' 'is related to the physical development of the body and nervous system [as] co-dependent interaction with the outer world', it is Feldenkrais's immersion in the outer world of the Israeli Gindler-informed body-culture milieu that shaped his pedagogic thinking during the 1950s.[72]

Made in Israel: Disrupting the master-narrative

Isabelle Ginot points us to the problem that within 'endogenous', self-referential, somatic discourses, notions of 'belief' tend to override critical scholarship or practice.[73] The endogenous discourse of Somatics, she argues, is under-theorized and yet exists within written and oral traditions of dissemination within individual somatic approaches. She identifies this endogenous literature and narratives as being disseminated at sites of therapeutic practices aimed at students, patients or general public. Ginot proposes that somatic discourses tend to draw on science to promote a 'form of homogeneous, non-historicized, almost eternal truth' that excludes cultural variations or the body politic. Endogenous discourses are constructed to affirm rather than critique existing practices and the undoubted achievement of their founders.[74]

Within the Feldenkrais Method a biographical master-narrative has emerged that tends to portray Moshe Feldenkrais as a male 'lone genius'. It reveals the master developing his method via his early experiments in jiu-jitsu in Palestine, overcoming his recurring knee injuries, through his knowledge in engineering, natural sciences including cybernetics, through his extensive teaching of and writings on judo, and his brief meetings with other – mostly male – scientists and somatic educators such as F.M. Alexander, Karl-Heinz von Foerster and Heinrich Jacoby. As genius creative, Feldenkrais germinates his practices in Palestine, France and the UK, and crafts a fairly coherent system in Israel where he develops and records his intensely probed experiments, and trains up his initial inheritors of the form through an organic process of osmosis. He then disseminates, markets and mass-produces his systematized product in the postmodern United States, promising a life lived to the full potential to a hungry new generation – often young Jewish men in awe of the charismatic master. Genii-women, such as anthropologist Margaret Mead or somatic pioneer Ida Rolf, and to a less extent founder of Eutonie, Gerda Alexander, also feature in this endogenous narrative, though more tangentially.

Burckard's recent biography of Moshe Feldenkrais gives an insight into the patriarchal construction of early Israeli culture. Feldenkrais's work with Prime Minister Ben-Gurion is presented as a masterstroke which promises Feldenkrais recognition and the possibility of setting up a state-funded institute.[75] When a panel with politicians and social dignitaries of Israel is formed to lobby for the setting up of such institute, the panel entirely comprises men – surprising, in a somatic milieu where most participants are women and educational ethics are shaped by women. Women, so it seems, feature predominantly as students, assistants or numerous lovers within the endogenous narrative of the becoming of the Feldenkrais Method.

There is no doubt that Feldenkrais's judo, Zen and science backgrounds informed and allowed him to develop a systemic theoretical framework for a somatic body culture that transcends prior speculations on the cognitive impact of movement on the development of the whole self. Feldenkrais also undoubtedly was able to engineer complex somatic compositions into tangible and effective toolkits for his students. All of the witnesses of the period interviewed by the author and biographers confirm his brilliance.

What seems less plausible within the Feldenkrais master-narrative is his transition from a judo practitioner to becoming a somatic theorist and practitioner of a transformative and emancipatory educational practice.[76] Burckard suggests that Kano, the founder of modern judo, already understood judo as a personality-forming practice which Feldenkrais re-articulated as 'an educational method for social adjustment'.[77] Still, it is difficult to understand the leap from the science-judo nexus informing Feldenkrais to his articulation of a coherent somatic educational practice and theory, and to emancipatory claims for the education of a more dignified individual that echo the work of the women founders of reform-body culture with remarkable detail.[78] By the 1970s Moshe Feldenkrais clearly insisted on not working just with the body, but with the whole person and their capacity to engage with their own environment. Such somatic humanism was at the heart of the well-articulated foundation of Elsa Gindler's work and her followers in Israel: 'In the centre of our work is not the human body, but the human being. The whole human being in all his capacities to relate to himself, to his body, to his life and to his environment.'[79] How can it be that ethics and practices of these women pioneers and colleagues feature hardly at all in the existing master-narrative? Was it Feldenkrais's science background or his perhaps narcissist personality that he simply did not see himself as part of a body-arts milieu, but needed to stand apart from or take a lead in from above? Were the patriarchal imaginaries and structures of Israeli society and Western-science milieu so engrained within the thinking of Feldenkrais that he simply saw little value in the contribution of his women colleagues, or that he did not make much of an effort into inquiring more deeply into the roots of their practices? Did the prodigal son, who had abandoned his secure job in Palestine before the Second World War and gave up his job with the Israeli military in 1953, feel the pressure to prove his professional success among the elite of Israel to his dominant mother Sheindel who was overtly critical of his new career ambitions? Or did he just adhere to poor academic referencing standards of the period?

From the mid-1950s, *Ausdruckstanz* in Israel came to be understood as old-fashioned and technically ineffective in comparison with the work of American Modern Dance choreographers Martha Graham, Anna Sokolow and Jerome Robbins.[80] This phenomenon matched developments in Europe and Australasia where Modern Dance was becoming an increasingly important part of soft US cultural-Imperialism. The prowess, virtuosity and systematic indoctrination-based training that US choreographic cultural exports promised, swiftly brushed away memories of the old pre-war dance and movement culture with its roots in Europe and promised a new expansive utopian American-led post-Modernity.

These developments were matched with the need to develop an Israeli national identity that differed from the pre-1948 protectorate imaginaries which had their roots in European cultural Zionism. Body-culture pioneers such as the Ornsteins, Tile Rössler, Judith Bineter abd Lotte Kristeller and many of their *Reformbewegung* followers were 'Jekkes', German-speaking immigrants, who were prescribing to their European cultural heritage. Their practices might have been persecuted, marginalized or re-appropriated in Nazi-Europe, yet they were not made or seeded in *Eretz Israel* – the land Israel – but belonged to traditions of European Enlightenment and post-Romanticism.

Feldenkrais's biography formed a completely different picture. Born into an Eastern-European Hassidic family, he brought nothing but his youth, eagerness, imagination, hunger for life, muscle power and Zionist beliefs to Palestine. His professional life started in *Eretz Israel,* and *he* personified the male *New Jew* until the end of his life – secular, yet spiritual – athletic, yet intellectual – Zionist, yet internationalist – full of impulsive vitality, yet highly educated – a fighter who had published a manual for the unarmed killing of the German enemy for the British Territorial Army, now a prophet of embodied peace and gentle self-education. After his work with Prime Minister Ben-Gurion, Feldenkrais was giving lessons to the international elite of Jewish artists visiting Israel. Feldenkrais was aware that his work had the potential to become an Israeli national icon in a culture that increasingly moved away from its Modernist European roots towards a postmodern United States. He appealed repeatedly for greater governmental support by suggesting that he had the means 'to improve the people of Israel'.[81]

Feldenkrais's contribution to the body culture of Israel as a singular male figure easily overshadows a nurturing ground provided by numerous women practitioners. In their essay 'Deconstructing the Lone Genius Myth: Towards a Contextual View of Creativity', Montuori and Purser argue that Systems Theory, feminism and constructionist twentieth-century theoretical frameworks have 'challenged the universality of the prevailing Western, male-centered conception of self, which is intimately tied to our conception of creativity'.[82] They suggest that 'in postmodern culture the author ceases to act as the sole originator of the creative product; instead, art becomes bricolage, playing around with fragments of meaning which one has not created'.[83] Highlighting 'the vital role of social forces in creativity', they stress the importance of the 'studying *both* individuals *and* the systems they create and inhabit' in order to glean an understanding of the development of creative processes or forms.[84] They further argue that:

> creative individuals seek to understand their environment and are willing to put down their own beliefs and assumptions into question in order to do so to a far greater degree than are persons who were not judged as being particularly creative. Creative persons are therefore constantly engaged in a process of self-renewal that draws on environmental factors of the destabilisation of existing concepts, values, self-images, and so forth.[85]

In this chapter the author has put forward a contextual study of the *Reform* body-culture and educational milieu that surrounded Moshe Feldenkrais in Palestine of the 1920s and the Israel of the 1950s. It reveals Feldenkrais's flexibility to absorb new cultural information and to revise and refine his own practice in highly creative ways. The author aimed to emphasize the direct contact Feldenkrais had over a prolonged period with women body-culture pioneers of Palestine and Israel. While recent literature guides us to the lived connections between Feldenkrais and the Ornstein and Gindler legacies, much research still deserves to be done to allow us to understand this complex collective narrative of situated knowledge in greater detail.

Notes

1. Gertrud Bodenwieser, 'Dancing as a factor in education', *Dancing Times* (1926), 194.
2. Katja Rothe, 'The Gymnastics of Thought: Elsa Gindler's Networks of Knowledge', in *Encounters in Performance Philosophy*, ed. Laura Cull and Alice Lagaay (London: Palgrave Macmillan, 2014), 197.
3. Rothe, 'The Gymnastics of Thought', 197. Rudolf Bode (1881–1970) was initially influenced by the rhythmical gymnastics of Jacques-Dalcroze, but developed his own school of Ausdrucksgymnastic – 'Expressive Gymnastics' – as early as 1920. Bode became a member of the NSDAP as early as 1932, and was a leading figure in propagating the racialized Nazi body culture until the end of the Second World War.
4. Judyth Weaver, *The Influence of Elsa Gindler-Ancestor of Sensory Awareness* (2006), http://judythweaver.com/writings/the-influence-of-elsa-gindler-ancestor-of-sensory-awareness/
5. Rudolf Laban, *The Mastery of Movement on the Stage* (London: Macdonald and Evans, 1950), 15. Moshe Feldenkrais, *Embodied Wisdom: The Collected Papers of Moshe Feldenkrais* (Berkeley, CA: North Atlantic Books, 2010), 88.
6. The emphasis on intra-organismic awareness within the somatic processes offered through the Feldenkrais Method, a focus on improved function as 'effective action' with a preference on embodying of a dynamism that is 'light and easy', can leave a limited dynamic and spatial range in the movement repertory of a learner or performer (see Feldenkrais, *Awareness through Movement*, 85–6). Here, Feldenkrais's modalities differ from the often 'ecstatic' and 'expressive' highly dynamic and spatially expansive and eccentric Modernist dance and movement practices.
7. Gaby Aldor, *Wie tanzt nun ein Kamel? Die Geschichte der Ornstein-Familie und die Erfindung des modernen israelischen Tanztheaters* (Wien: Mandelbaum, 2012); Mark Reese, *Moshe Feldenkrais: A Life in Movement* (San Rafael, CA: ReeseKress Somatics Press, 2015); Christian Burckard, *Moshe Feldenkrais – Der Mensch hinter der Methode* (Berlin: Piper, 2015).
8. Feldenkrais had been introduced to the work of Stanislavski and his disciple Vakhtaganov by actor and family friend Aharon Meskin in Tel Aviv already in the 1920s. Feldenkrais suggests that his approach to learning fosters in the actor 'an awareness of action', 'greater clarity and ease', a capacity for 'rediscovery', and 'a heightened ability to listening to the other person'. Feldenkrais, 'Image, Movement, and Actor: Restoration of Potentiality', *Tulane Drama Review*, Vol. 10 (1972), 125–6.
9. Feldenkrais, *Awareness through Movement: Health Exercises for Personal Growth* (New York: HarperCollins, 1990).
10. Feldenkrais, *The Potent Self: A Study of Spontaneity and Compulsion* (San Francisco, CA: Harper, 1985), 153.
11. Prokofiev, in Valerie Litvinoff, *The Use of Stanislavsky within Modern Dance* (New York: American Dance Guild, 1972), 19.
12. Valerie Litvinoff, *The Use of Stanislavsky within Modern Dance* (New York, NY: American Dance Guild 1972), 21.
13. Coralie Hinckley, in Bettina Vernon-Warren and Charles Warren (eds), *Gertrud Bodenwieser and Vienna's Contribution to Ausdruckstanz* (London: Routledge, 1999), 167. Hinckley was a member of the 1940s and 1950s Australian Bodenwieser Modern Ballets.
14. Duncan cited in Konstantin Stanislavski, *My Life in Art* (London: Routledge, 1974), 507.
15. Katie Rudd, *NZDC Questionnaire – Releasing the Archive* (Auckland: Unpublished, 2015).
16. Lucy Lynch, *NZDC Questionnaire – Releasing the Archive* (Auckland: Unpublished, 2015).
17. Gertrud Bodenwieser and Marie Cuckson (eds), *The New Dance* (Vaucluse: Rondo Studios, 1960).

18   See Bodenwieser and Cuckson, *The New Dance*, 89.
19   See Bodenwieser and Cuckson, *The New Dance*, 82.
20   Feldenkrais, *Awareness through Movement*, 51.
21   Shona Dunlop MacTavish, *Lecture on Modern Dance* (Dunedin: Dunlop MacTavish archives, 1984).
22   Margalit Ornstein, *Movement Culture as Preparation for Direction* (Tel Aviv Dance Library, 1939/1940).
23   Feldenkrais, *Awareness through Movement*, 33.
24   Reese, *Moshe Feldenkrais: A Life in Movement*, 68.
25   Margalit Ornstein (1922) in Gaby Aldor, *Wie tanzt nun ein Kamel?*, 27.
26   Gaby Aldor, email 15 March 2017.
27   Gaby Aldor, in Elad Samorzik *Pas de Troi* (2011), http://www.haaretz.com/weekend/week-s-end/pas-de-trois-1.392435 (accessed 17 December 2017).
28   Letter Yehudit Ornstein: 2 November 1929 in Gaby Aldor *Wie tanzt nun ein Kamel?* P. 94.
29   There is currently no exact information on how long and how often Moshe Feldenkrais studied with Margalit Ornstein.
30   The Ornsteins were also strongly influenced by the teaching of Rosalia Chladek (1905–95), who was developing an analytical and function-oriented training system for dancers. Through the teaching of Jarmila Kröschlova (1893–1983), Chladek was introduced to the functional gymnastics of Bess Mensendieck who's influence on the work of Margalit Ornstein and Gertrud Bodenwieser is discussed later in this chapter.
31   Margalit Ornstein, cited in Gaby Aldor, *Wie tanzt nun ein Kamel?*, 48.
32   Her two-part essay, 'Bewegungskultur als Vorbereitung für Regieführung', written in German during 1939/1940 on movement education for the training of directors, provides an analytical framework based on Rudolf Laban's movement elements of force, time and space, forming a vessel for a Zionist vision of the embodied 'New Jew'. See Yitzhak Conforti, 'The New Jew in the Zionist Movement: Ideology and Historiography', *Australian Journal of Jewish Studies* (2011).
33   Margalit Ornstein, *Movement Culture as Preparation for Direction* (Tel Aviv Dance Library 1939/19).
34   'In geraden Linien und kraftvollem, aus der altneuen Heimat schöpfenden Rhythmus wird der befreite Körper entstehen. Der Tanz des neuen Hebräers'. Margalit Ornstein in Gaby Aldor, *Wie tanzt nun ein Kamel?*, p. 42. http://www.tanz.at/index.php/verlegt/buecher/1659-wie-tanzt-nun-ein-kamel.
35   The influence of Mensendieck's work on Ornstein is evident in her notebooks of the 1920s and 1930s. Her 'Blue Notebooks' give insights into the functional foundations of the dance learning inquiries at the heart of her teachings. Here, a mobilization, strengthening and connecting the pelvis into the functioning of the legs are highlighted, perhaps akin to what Feldenkrais called a 'culture of pelvis and hip joints'. With thanks to Gaby Aldor and Kirsten Seeligmüller of Dock11 Berlin for access to notebooks.
36   Elisabeth Mensendieck, *Bewegungsprobleme – Die Gestaltung schöner Arme* (Munich: F. Bruckmann, 1927), 9.
37   Fischer describes teaching principles of Mensendieck – the breaking down of whole body movements into isolated parts, the lowering of tension of the habitually contracted body, a focus on weight-shifts and balancing exercises, and a mainly light use of force and slow tempo within the exercises. See Hans Werner Fischer, *Körperschönheit und Körperkultur* (Berlin: Deutsche Buchgemeinschaft, 1928), 214.

38 Elisabeth Mensendieck, *Körperkultur des Weibes: Praktisch hygienische und praktische ästhetische Winke*, 10th edn. (Munich: F. Bruckmann, [1906] 1929), 1. Published later as *Körperkultur der Frau* in 1908.
39 Mensendieck, *Bewegungsprobleme*, 13–14.
40 Mensendieck, *Bewegungsprobleme*, 11.
41 Mensendieck, *Bewegungsprobleme*, appendix.
42 Bodenwieser and Cuckson (eds), *The New Dance*, 48.
43 A Dutch film from 1920 shows Mensendieck and two assistants working hands-on with a client who has paralysis in his legs. While placed on his back and side, the client is gently assisted to mobilize his pelvis in relation to the leverage of his legs. The quality of touch is gentle and attentive with minimal force input, always in dialogue with the client's sensation of ease and potential. The slow explorative mobilization and connecting of the pelvis into the functioning of the legs resemble Feldenkrais's *Functional Integration* practice. Dir.: Willem de Haan (NL), https://www.eyefilm.nl/collectie/filmgeschiedenis/film/mensendieck
44 Mensendieck, *Körperkultur des Weibes*, 198.
45 See endnote 66.
46 Barbara Cuckson describes the integration of Mensendieck floor-gymnastics into her dance training as a child with Bodenwieser-company member Emmy Steininger-Taussig in 1950s Sydney: 'One of the many exercises was called "hole and bottom". We lay on our tummies and arched our backs against gravity, lifting our bottoms as high as we could without lifting our ribs or knees. From that position we then gradually "sucked our tummies in", pulling the pubic bone to earth. It took us as long as we needed and had to be a slow smooth motion. When we were flat to the floor, we repeated the exercise. You can imagine how revolutionary that movement was!!' (email Cuckson, 2019).
47 Mabel Elsworth Todd, *Early Writings* (New York: Dance Horizons 1977 [1929]), 56 and 58.
48 Mensendieck, *Bewegungsprobleme*, 17.
49 Mensendieck, *Bewegungsprobleme*, appendix.
50 Mensendieck, *Bewegungsprobleme*, 10 and 13.
51 Mensendieck, *Körperkultur des Weibes*, 107; Feldenkrais, *Embodied Wisdom*, 68 and 116.
52 Mensendieck, *Bewegungsprobleme*, 12.
53 Yael Barkai, interview 12 January 2017.
54 Sofia Naharin, interview 26 December 2017.
55 Essays from Rössler's school (1944), Tel Aviv Dance Library.
56 Noa Eshkol, in Christian Burckard *Moshe Feldenkrais – Der Mensch hinter der Methode*, 89.
57 Eshkol Wachman Movement Notation system (EWMN) was launched in 1958 by Noa Eshkol with architect Avraham Wachman, as a tool for notating and composing movement and dance.
58 Barkai's mother had encountered modernist movement culture in Berlin, before the Second World War. Her father was an instructor at a home for special education for children – A'hava (The Institute of Love) – in her German-speaking home town near Haifa.
59 Cohen was a student with Bodenwieser in Vienna during the 1930s and included improvisation – often to biblical themes – and 'a little technique with movements of the pelvis' (Barkai 2017) in her teaching.
60 Yael Barkai, interview 2017. Feldenkrais had already published books on self-defence and his major publication *Body and Mature Behaviour* (1949) when he ran his immediately popular classes in Haifa.
61 See endnote 60.

62 See endnote 60.

63 See endnote 60. Three of Feldenkrais's close collaborators and students – dancer and notator Amos Hetz, Chava Shelav and Ruthy Alon were graduates from the 'Body-Cultures' programme in Tel Aviv, and developed their own Feldenkrais-informed practice in eclectic ways.

64 Ruth Eshel, *Dance Spreads Its Wings – Israeli Concert Dance since the 1920s* (Tel Aviv: Israel Dance Diaries, 2016), 292.

65 Sofia Naharin, mother of choreographer Ohad Naharin, studied with most of the Israeli Modern Dance pioneers including Gertrud Kraus, Yardena Cohen and Miriam Goldberg. She trained as a Feldenkrais teacher in Tel Aviv, where she lives.

66 'She was a very good teacher, she was really something. There was no music in the classes. She was always present in her spirit and very, very creative. We never saw her move.' Sofia Naharin, interview (2017).

67 Barkai (interview, 2017) reveals that the exchange was 'not so flourishing' for Kristeller. Schwalbe-Kleinhuis (email 2017) suggests that Feldenkrais might have already encountered Gindler's work through the teacher Lili Ehrenfried (1896–1994) in Paris during the 1930s.

68 Elsa Gindler, *course notes* (1954), cited in Katja Rothe, 'The Gymnastics of Thought: Elsa Gindler's Networks of Knowledge', in *Encounters in Performance Philosophy*, ed. Laura Cull and Alice Lagaay (London: Palgrave Macmillan, 2014), 211. Gindler's work, at times referred to as *work on the human being – Arbeit am Menschen,* or as *After-Unfolding – Nachentfaltung*, was never given an official title. She founded her *Institute for Harmonious Gymnastics* in Berlin in 1913.

69 Heinrich Jacoby, cited in Anita Neudorfer, *Rhythmus als unsichtbare Religion. Die Rhythmusbewegung der Weimarer Republik aus religionswissenschaftlicher Sicht* (Vienna: Vienna University, 2012), 203.

70 Lily Pincus, 1981, in Judyth Weaver, *The Influence of Elsa Gindler-Ancestor of Sensory Awareness*.

71 Charlotte Selver, *Sensory Awareness and Total Functioning* (ETC: General Semantics,1957), 444–5.

72 Reese, 'Moshe Feldenkrais's Work with Movement – A Parallel Approach to Milton Erickson's Hypnotherapy', *Feldenkrais Journal*, Vol. 1 (1984), 420.

73 Isabelle Ginot, 'From Shusterman's Somaesthetics to a Radical Epistemology of Somatics', *Dance Research Journal*, Vol. 42, No. 1 (Summer 2010), 29.

74 Ginot, 'From Shusterman's Somaesthetics to a Radical Epistemology of Somatics', 29.

75 David Ben-Gurion (1886–1971) was the first prime minister of Israel, and a private student of Feldenkrais for several years from 1956 after suffering from lumbago. Feldenkrais successfully restored Ben-Gurion's well-being and famously taught him to stand on his head. The setting up of the institute never materialized. Feldenkrais hesitated to take up offers made to him in locations on the outskirts of Tel Aviv, or to become part of an existing University department.

76 Feldenkrais encountered the pedagogies of F.M. Alexander in London after the Second World War, and was introduced to the theories of developmental psychologist Jean Piaget during that period.

77 Feldenkrais, *Higher Judo: Groundworks* (London: Frederick Warne & Co, 1952), xii.

78 Feldenkrais, *San Francisco Training Transcript* (Paris: International Feldenkrais Federation, 1975), 155.

79 'Im Mittelpunkt unserer Arbeit steht nicht der menschliche Körper, sondern der Mensch. Der Mensch als Ganzes in all seinen Beziehungsmöglichkeiten zu sich, zu seinem Körper, zu seinem Leben und zu seiner Umwelt'. Elsa Gindler (1931) cited in Heinrich Dauber. *Grundlagen Humanistischer Pädagogik. Leben lernen für eine humane Zukunft* (Bad Heilbrunn: Klinkhardt, 2009); translation from German, with the male gender inflection as in original, by the author.

80 Robbins, born Jerome Wilson Rabinowitz, went to Israel in 1951 and opened avenues for US Modern Dance choreographer Anna Sokolow who started to work with the Inbal Yemenite Dance Group in 1953; Martha Graham's dance technique was first taught in Israel in the early

1950s through American immigrants Rina Shaham and Rena Gluck. Martha Graham's visit in 1956, funded by the Baroness Bethsabee de Rothschild, inspired the founding of Batsheva Dance Company as a world-leading Modern Dance laboratory.

81 Feldenkrais in Christian Burckard, *Moshe Feldenkrais – Der Mensch hinter der Methode*, 252.
82 Alfonso Montuori and Ronald Purser, 'Deconstructing the Lone Genius Myth: Towards a Contextual View of Creativity', *Journal of Humanistic Psychology*, Vol. 35, No. 3 (1995), 95.
83 See endnotes 105, 72.
84 See endnotes 105, 79 and 82.
85 See endnotes 105, 83.

CHAPTER 2
FELDENKRAIS, FREUD, LACAN AND GOULD: HOW TO LOVE THYSELF FOR THY NEIGHBOUR
Robert Sholl

Introduction

> 'I myself, I owe to Freud three tenths of my knowledge or more, three quarters of what I know, and what I am talking [about] now.'[1]

The importance of psychoanalysis in the formation of Moshe Feldenkrais's thinking is rarely discussed in the literature on this somatic thinker. One of Freud's interests was in slips of the tongue and jokes.[2] For Freud, such off-the-cuff statements reveal an unbidden truth, and an intention or desire to say something that should perhaps have remained unspoken, but that needed to be revealed. In a more Feldenkraisian sense, they reveal something of ourselves of which we are unaware.

Feldenkrais's admission above occurs in the context of a discussion of fears and habit. He advises his student audience that if they want to change there is no point in going to a desert island to escape the world; the important thing is the way in which the quality of the nervous system can be improved through engagement with the world and, crucially, with the self through movement. It is essential that 'intention can be organized properly' through a form of somatic kindness to the self in action which facilitates comfort as a primary condition for learning. For Feldenkrais, we need to find out *how* we do something, which parts of ourselves participate in our actions, and at the foundation of this, as the singer Leontyne Price (1927–) explains beautifully, is a form of self-love in action.[3] These are vital lessons for daily artistic practice.

In the introduction to *The Potent Self*, Feldenkrais discusses Christ's commandment: 'Love thy Neighbour as thyself' (Matthew 22:39, Luke 10:27). He provides a unique qualification of this injunction: 'Love Thyself as Thy Neighbour.'[4] This chapter differentiates Feldenkrais's thought on Christ's injunction from Freud's thinking this presented in *Civilization and Its Discontents* (1930), and further connects this to Jacques Lacan's (1901–81) thought.[5] I am not attempting to imply Lacan's influence on Feldenkrais, but to point towards some of the remarkable synergies that exist between their thought.

While Freud is openly hostile on a number of counts to Christ's injunction, Feldenkrais's response is more constructive. The individual must learn to love themselves first – in a Freudian reading, to overcome the innate aggression within the individual – so that they can then be a useful member of civilization, and be fully enabled to help others.

Lacan takes Freud's ideas further. In the neighbour resides what he calls *das Ding* (the 'Thing'), the quality not merely of otherness, but of something alien that reminds one reflexively of this 'Thing' in oneself. Feldenkrais's Method, I argue, provides a safe and sanitized access to this 'Thing', which is associated with personal and artistic uniqueness essential to creativity in this chapter.⁶ Awareness of the how one writes, or plays an instrument and what participates in this action, provides a means to artistic improvement.

I discuss this uniqueness with reference to the Canadian pianist Glenn Gould (1932–82). It is plausible that Gould withdrew from performance in 1964 to avoid the collective 'Things', of the public. Many performers, it could be argued, require the trauma of the 'Thing', and the gratification that comes from flaunting it through applause and critical plaudits. But at the same time, performance, on stage and at a safe distance from the unique qualities of people, also arguably protects the performer from others.

For Gould, performance and communication with his neighbour (understood as the listening public) were to be refreighted in a different form.⁷ Paul Meyers, one of Gould's record producers at Columbia, said that 'one of his reasons for his decision to quit the concert stage was that he was tired of being regarded as a "freak show"', and in an interview with Alex Trebek in 1966, Gould stated how much he 'detests audiences'.⁸ In a psychoanalytical reading of this interview, the audience here becomes a form of fetishistic absent 'object', what Lacan would refer to as *objet petit a* which acts as a detached source of *jouissance* (surplus enjoyment) that escapes symbolization, or a phantasmatic framework that allows a pay-off for Gould that results from a 'failure to integrate it into [his] universe'.⁹

Gould's turn to recording was arguably a way to counter the impermanence of performance and to ground his enjoyment of his uniqueness in a seemingly inviolable product. But it also functions psychoanalytically as a means to satisfy his own needs in default of, but ultimately for, the benefit of his neighbour.¹⁰ By withdrawing from the public to focus on recording, Gould made an intelligent decision to make them into a better prosthesis of himself.¹¹ Through this action, he comes to use more of himself and to use himself more effectively. In Feldenkraisian terms, recording was a pursuit of a form of health: 'of realizing his unavowed dreams.'¹²

The second part of this chapter brings the work of Feldenkrais, Freud, Lacan and Gould into conversation. Despite the presence in this study of psychiatric literature, there is no attempt to diagnose or pathologize Gould, nor is there much here on Gould's 'performance mechanism', as the musicologist Arved Ashby calls it, but to think through what might lie behind his 'decision'.¹³ In the Feldenkrais Method, part of the process of awareness is becoming cognizant of one's own parasitic movement – Feldenkrais's term for cross-motivational activity. In this sense the parasitic functions as part of what Freud calls 'resistance'.¹⁴ This process of self-negotiation is connected to Gould's choice, and this provides a means of understanding compulsiveness and spontaneity in action. The third part of the chapter further examines Gould's ideas of recording with reference to psychoanalysis and Feldenkrais's thought, and seeks to understand how he figured his uniqueness, a discussion developed through ethnographical evidence. The final part of this chapter turns to the value of uniqueness for current artistic education and performance training. An addendum provides some practical suggestions for developing this quality in the context of the Feldenkrais Method.

Negotiating the neighbour – finding self-love

A reader familiar with Feldenkrais's thought will find many synergies with Freud's *Civilization and Its Discontents*. Early in the book, Freud writes: 'Normally, there is nothing of which we are more certain than the feeling of ourself, of our own ego'.¹⁵ Essential to Freud's project, as it is to Feldenkrais's own work, is to show that this sense of ourselves is misleading. One of the fundamental purposes of psychoanalysis is to figure and ameliorate the gap between the sense of ourselves and our sense or imagination of the way others or society ('civilization') perceive us. In a similar vein, Feldenkrais's lessons are designed to remedy a disparity between what we think we are doing and what we are actually doing which Feldenkrais defines as our 'self-image'. In music or dance lessons, the student comes to the session with a certain self-image and discovers new perspectives on their self-image, they find new possibilities of using themselves through another's purview. Learning how to understand this gap is fundamental to creative practice and development.[16] It is also essential to the art of recording, and I would contend that Gould's turn to recording and his search for an ideal form of interpretation are also attempts to close this gap. To do this is, for Feldenkrais, a perfecting of the self-image, a process of improvement that he understands as unending.[17]

Freud speaks of learning and development based on 'the pleasure principle'. His thought resonates with Feldenkrais's ideal that the integration of learning only happens when learning is pleasurable.[18] This again is another reason that Gould I believe turns to recording; the space between the learning process and the execution of this learning becomes closer in his use of this environment, which evidently provided more satisfaction for Gould than the repetition of concert life.[19] Freud then turns to religion as a critical hinge to understand the origins of happiness and suffering. He cautions: 'An unrestricted satisfaction of every need presents itself as the most enticing method of conducting one's life, but it means putting enjoyment before caution, and soon brings in its own punishment.'[20] Instead, he advises the path of 'becoming a member of the human community', and in words that pre-empt Feldenkrais's project, he states: 'But the most interesting methods of averting suffering are those which seek to influence our own organism.'[21]

Feldenkrais takes this issue up in many ways in his teaching, not least commenting in his New York Quest workshops on how people do not know how to be comfortable in themselves. This again is another reason, I would contend, that Gould turns aside from concert life: his 'negative attitude towards audiences' cultivating, as Gould puts it himself 'an attitude of healthy indifference', was surely not comfortable and sustainable.[22]

Feldenkrais's thought here resonates as a salient alternative to Freud's. Freud suggests that people search for happiness sometimes through intoxication, the sublimation of suffering through work, through a 'delusional remoulding of reality', and what he calls 'the economics of the individual's libido'.[23] Freud then unveils a revelation that the threat to civilization comes not so much from the feebleness of the human body, nor the inadequate regulations of family life, but from within civilization itself, and in particular from within the individuals within it.[24]

Civilization for Freud imposes restrictions on the ability of individuals to be unique in order to preserve itself; this is a concept that I will discuss later in terms of Gould's recordings through which, I argue, he finds a way of turning against his 'community' (both the concert public and certain pianistic axioms) to reinvent it.[25] 'The urge for freedom, therefore', writes Freud, 'is directed against particular forms and demands of civilization or against civilization altogether.'[26] 'Civilization', continues Freud, 'is built upon a renunciation of instinct' that presupposes a 'non-satisfaction (by suppression, repression or some other means) of powerful instincts'.[27] Feldenkrais extends this when he notes that 'the best intentions when acted [on] compulsively [especially a compulsion founded on instinct] yield opposite results', and he carries the ideal of passive aggression forward by showing that loving one's neighbour to the exclusion of the self quashes spontaneity. 'Compulsive kindness or goodness of this sort', he states, 'is the symptom and the result of inhibited aggression.'[28] Gould's decision not to obey the superego demands of performance culture – to prove oneself continually through concertizing – needs to be understood in this light: he found other ways, through recording, to create 'goodness'.

Freud affirms the role of love in the relation of civilization before turning to Christ's injunction, which he finds both surprising and bewildering. He cannot accept this unconditional position for a number of reasons. Firstly, if he truly values his own love, care should be taken in bestowing it. Secondly, there is the value and worthiness of the individual who is potentially to be loved. Thirdly, there seems little point in loving someone when that love is either ignored or not reciprocated in at least equal measure and, finally, he sees it as useless to love a neighbour who may be my enemy. Instead Freud offers this alternative injunction; 'Love thy neighbour as thy neighbour loves thee.'[29] In short, he states, Christ's injunction 'runs so strongly counter to the original [instinctual] nature of man',[30] which, after the death drive, are the 'instinct(s) of aggressiveness and destruction'.[31]

Feldenkrais understands this relation to aggressiveness in a different light. Aggressiveness is not mitigated through 'libidinal sublimation', but is a *behaviour* that relates to 'the amount of confidence the person has gained through exercising the function in which she is impotent'.[32] In his San Francisco Workshops, Feldenkrais stated:

What is important is that you get the person to love himself, not just like himself. If you achieve that, you are worth your weight in diamonds. If you take a person who hates himself, has no confidence, and make him feel that he can love himself. He feels he can begin to rely on his own self and begins to have self-confidence enough to stand on his feet. Well, who can do that? No politician, no millionaire can. You can't buy that for money. Yet, you may be able to do it and that means that you are richer than any of those.[33]

It is clear from this that Feldenkrais regarded the individual's dissatisfaction with themselves, as he also makes clear in *The Potent Self*, and the individual's tendency to overcome inability through willpower to gain a 'disproportionate pleasure when he lives up to his expectations', to be fundamental impasses that can be ameliorated through his Method.[34] Gould's decision to leave the concert platform is often explained by him as a profound sense of dissatisfaction with the contingency of live performance, but it should be understood more properly as a dissatisfaction with himself and his own agency in this ecology. Recording was a way of creating self-reliance, and of standing 'on his [own] feet', as Feldenkrais puts it.[35]

For Freud, dissatisfaction was conceived of as 'the sense of guilt' which is 'the most important problem in the development of civilization'. He states that 'the price we pay for our advance in civilization is a loss of happiness through the heightening of the sense of guilt'.[36] Feldenkrais puts this in more devastating ways in *The Potent Self*; the price of effort is a loss of human dignity and choice, and the effort to overcome it is something that our civilization is there to sustain. This is very difficult to avoid or unlearn.[37]

Gould's decision therefore to step outside his community can be understood as a brave move that obviated the continual pleasing of his community. For a performer, trained to perform to and for the public, this would be no easy decision. For Feldenkrais the desire and effort to achieve (despite any satisfaction) come from a feeling, institutionalized by education, that we are not good enough. Effort is required to achieve what is demanded perhaps by the (absent) parent, the teacher or the superego demands of society or the self. Feldenkrais observes the result of this lack of love for the self in the following devastating way: 'Reluctantly, most people work themselves into snug little corners, to fit their clipped wings.'[38] Those who reject 'stereotyped behaviour' then become the yardstick 'who are used to muzzle the next generation'.[39] Gould, for many of his pianistic colleagues, as we shall see, becomes, in different senses, a yardstick. His particular form of uniqueness (originality and eccentricity) becomes an exemplar of what *not* to imitate, and this image of Gould has arguably muzzled similar maverick-style forms of experimentation. For Freud, however, the problem of uniqueness is defined in measuring ourselves against figures such as Christ. This manifests itself in what he calls the 'cultural super ego' and its demand to 'love thy neighbour'.[40] Although he does not put it this directly, Freud sees civilization as a means of economizing this concept: partially fulfilling it, or fulfilling it enough to substantiate its survival.[41] He describes aggressiveness as a 'potent obstacle' to it, but he also inadvertently creates an argument where civilization in fact needs to economize this aggressiveness or protect itself against aggressiveness by exclusion of groups of people from civilization, in order to promote and maintain its ideal of happiness.[42]

I now want to develop this understanding of aggressiveness through Lacan's development of Freud's work, and to understand this in relation to Feldenkrais's thought. In his *Seminar VII* (1958–60), in a development of Freud's thought, Lacan imagines what he calls 'the Thing' (*das Ding*), a completely alien and intrusive foreignness that is present in ourselves.[43] The Lacanian theorist Kenneth Reinhard identifies the 'Thing' as the kernel of traumatic enjoyment or *jouissance* that is articulated through the neighbour, and that then conditions our awareness of the uncanniness of social relations.[44] In *Seminar VII*, Lacan developed the antagonism between pleasure and *jouissance*. *Jouissance* is understood as an excessive, surplus meaning or excitation, which the pleasure principle (linked to the death drive) attempts to disrupt or traumatize.[45] *Jouissance* is associated with pleasure that occurs through pain.

This uncanniness and enjoyment are signalled, for example, by Elizabeth Bennett's father (Mr Bennett) in Jane Austen's *Pride and Prejudice* (1813) when he states: 'For what do we live, but to make sport for our neighbours, and laugh at them in our turn?'[46] Mr Bennett's wry and genteel observation is a screen for the aggressiveness that is held at bay and that prevents his full *jouissance* (in a Freudian sense, through a repressed desire to kill his neighbour). Lacan argues that our 'happiness' is a screen against *jouissance*, and that the more we give up *jouissance*, the more we punish ourselves (this is what Mr Bennett does to himself).[47] This is very similar to Feldenkrais's argument that in becoming compulsively good or loving our neighbour we sacrifice our personal enjoyment (or *jouissance*). Mr Bennett's comment also reveals that the antagonism of the neighbour is needed for civilization, and that some satisfaction is derived from this antagonism (pleasure and pain). To turn against this 'Thing' that is within his neighbours is to turn against himself.[48]

What Lacan is in fact describing is what Feldenkrais describes as a parasitic relationship. The parasitic for Feldenkrais describes the compulsion to perform actions, which seem necessary, but in fact impede essential human functioning or well-being.[49] In Lacan, the parasitic is conceived as a negotiation of the neighbour. For Lacan, the love of the neighbour is 'beyond the pleasure principle', that is (*pace* Freud) a 'least-suffering principle … [that]

keeps us a long way from our *jouissance*', and this guarantees ethical happiness.[50] In other words, following Freud, Lacan and indeed the example of Mr Bennett, happiness cannot be achieved through this parasitic relationship. In the negotiation of the self to achieve this form of satisfaction, there is an undoing that is necessary, a letting-go, or a renegotiation with the neighbour. This has profound consequences as we shall see for Gould's turn away from the public to recording, where this negotiation is more intelligently resolved.

Another concrete way to imagine what Lacan and Feldenkrais are describing can be imagined through the nuances that derive from a scenario on the London Underground. Firstly, I sit in a carriage and pretend to hibernate in my personal space (perhaps listening to music through headphones), and I refrain from looking at my neighbours (even if they smile at me or I think that they have smiled at me), so I temporarily close my eyes as a screen. I shelter in the anonymity of the crowd, so that I do not have to return their gaze or engage with the possibility of communication. In performing this anonymity, I also give up my own *jouissance*; because I do not engage with the others' 'Thing', and in doing this, I don't have to engage with my own.

Then, in my position of hibernation, I open my eyes and see someone who needs to sit down (perhaps an elderly person). I make an assessment of their needs, and although I am tired, I give up my seat (my comfort for their comfort). Although, this may or may not have been a spontaneous or altruistic decision (the proper Christian position), I am left with the sensation of regret, despite knowing that I have done a 'good deed' and given something that did not cost me very much (it did not cost my life or any money). My *jouissance* is spoiled, following Lacan's thinking, not only because of a lack of comfort, but because I now feel guilty for feeling like the 'good samaritan' (Luke 10: 25–37). I am left questioning whether I should feel joy in my act, whether this joy means that I have merely succeeded in negotiating past my own selfishness, and whether the service I have rendered has been good enough.

Finally, other people sitting in the carriage who also observed the elderly person and who assessed that person's needs now feel bad too. They saw me give up my seat, but they did not do it themselves. I feel uneasy with my motivations in the decisions, and perhaps most ironically, the elderly person also feels uncomfortable because they have made me vacate my seat. Through being a 'good neighbour', in this scenario everyone was a loser in some way. A further fog remains over this scene that results from the big Other (the Lacanian name for the unmentioned codes and injunctions that dominate human action): all of what transpired was done with as few words as possible (minimal communication is a necessity), and therefore what is really difficult in this scene is the unknowable 'impenetrable' desires of our neighbours.[51]

One might have a wry laugh at this scenario, but it is illustrative of the difficulties we make for ourselves, troubles that are totally unnecessary, but that we learn to live with, and that in a Feldenkraisian vein stop us reaching our potential. Worse, we enjoy these symptoms of our own collective failure – the big Other is not just 'somewhere else'; it is a creation of each and every one of us. These symptoms therefore powerfully point back to ourselves, through what Lacan calls the *sinthome*, an idea that is present in a different sense in Feldenkrais's thought. A symptom, as the musicologist Michael L. Klein explains, is 'a sign from the unconscious that demands interpretation(.) … a symptom is a message from the Real addressed through the unconscious to the Symbolic'.[52] My simple action in giving up my seat is symbolic of many things, but it points to an underlying trauma caused by obeying the compulsion of the injunction to be a 'good neighbour'. The traumatic underlying problem is registered in language and behaviour, goodness, guilt or regret for example; it can be interpreted but in fact leads back to an unassimilable and unreachable source in the self. The *sinthome* turns the telescope around on the symptom. It occurs when hermeneutics run dry and when we come to the realization that the explanations we give for the symbolic ['I did this because … '] are not the answers. The problem lies reflexively in something of which we are unaware within ourselves. 'The *sinthome*', Klein writes, 'is a form of enjoyment (*jouissance*) that comes from the constant deferral of a final interpretation demanded by the symbolic.'[53] A final interpretation of the situation on the London Underground above is simply catastrophic: it is that through our intention to do good we come to an abyss of failure. The problem lies not in my actions or my interpretation of my actions, but in the screen that I create that prevents me realizing the full toll of this situation.

What is missing here in Feldenkrais's terms is awareness of my actions. To apply the *sinthome* to Feldenkrais's thought, education and our attitudes to the body can be understood to be symptoms of civilization, but the *sinthome* that acts to bind or suture these items together is the traumatic 'Thing', an element of the Real that is within the individual, but that we defer from to preserve our *jouissance*. *Jouissance* acts as a screen to prevent our own sense of comfort in action. This is something experienced at many levels. When I roll over in bed at night, for example, I might deem the results of this action 'good enough', but the movement, upon closer examination, is perhaps not very fluent or comfortable. There is a level of self-aggression involved here that is not clear to me. Next time you are brushing your teeth, ask yourself: 'If I was brushing someone else's teeth, would I do it this way?' The question then remains of how to escape from this economy of aggression. In an earlier study, Feldenkrais identifies the masochistic heart of this problem identified by Freud:

> In a perfectly matured body, which has grown without great emotional disturbances, movements tend gradually to conform to the mechanical requirements of the surrounding world. The nervous system has evolved under the influence of these laws and is fitted to them. However, in our society we do, by the promise of great reward or intense punishment, so distort the even development of the system, that many acts become excluded or restricted. The result is that we have to provide special conditions for further adult maturation of many arrested functions.[54]

For Feldenkrais then, learning should be a form of maturation, not of accustomizing ourselves to the injunctions of the Lacanian big Other (parents, schools, society's unwritten rules [thou shalt give up thy seat to those who need it!]), or the beliefs imputed to a 'jealous God' (Ex. 20:5, 34:14).

Maturation is founded in the development of an awareness of *how* we do something and the development of 'spontaneity'.[55] Feldenkrais describes 'compulsion' in terms redolent of Freud's essay, as 'the symptom and the result of inhibited aggression', and he says that it 'is sensed when motivation for action is conflicting', or 'parasitic'.[56] He further states that:

> all creative people do things in their own way … everybody else who has ever done anything worthwhile, always had to learn to paint, think, compose – but not in the way they were taught. They had to learn and work until they knew themselves sufficiently to bring themselves to the state of spontaneity in which their deepest inner self could

be brought up and out. Such people are not free of compulsion – much to the contrary. The difference is that what they produce out of the state of compulsion has some value because of the true spontaneous nature of the production.[57]

Compulsion and spontaneity intersect through the agency of awareness and choice (discussed extensively in the Introduction to this volume). The Feldenkrais Method and so much of Feldenkrais's writing are grounded in the idea that in order to be a better human being, and to be a catalyst for society, one must be able to organize oneself. At the heart of this organization is not just an ability to choose (i.e. based on experience and judgement), but a form of self-education conceived of as building a viable and increasing set of options to effect 'adaptive flexibility' as Esther Thelen puts it.[58] Unless there is choice in any human activity – in sex, feeding, cleaning, education or in artistic creation – there can be no spontaneous action. Feldenkrais's idea of spontaneity is also achieved through self-negotiation, through 'maturation', through the ability to use the imagination, through the ability to choose, but it operates in a way that is ideally free from the parasitic.[59]

'Love thyself as thy Neighbour' is essential to these processes. It could naively be understood as a form of selfishness, but in Feldenkrais's hands – 'Love Thyself as Thy Neighbour' – becomes about self-awareness, and *giving of permission* for self-love that values the uniqueness of the individual rather than subsuming the person within civilization. Feldenkrais's alteration of Christ's injunction is much closer to the attitude taken by the Austrian neurologist, psychiatrist and Holocaust survivor Victor E. Frankl (1905–97), which might be put in a different way: 'Look to your spontaneity, your own true human freedom, which only you have the power to control, and only through this can you (choose to) help your neighbour, and choose which neighbour can, and in fact, desires to be helped.'[60]

Feldenkrais's proactive version of Christ's injunction is a recognition that to be of use to civilization, a person must improve the ability *to be* and thence *to do*. It is, to borrow another biblical passage, an exhortation to take the log out of one's own eye before dealing with someone else's splinter (Matthew 7:3). The meaning of Feldenkrais's thought is further clarified by transferring this thought to another injunction in the New Covenant. This might be understood not as 'Do unto others, as you would have done to yourself' (Matthew 7: 12), but: 'Do for yourself first, so that you may be able truly *to do* much better for others.'

This provides a new perspective on Feldenkrais's proposition that he was not teaching his students but providing conditions for them to learn: this position allowed and gave them permission to explore their own uniqueness. Feldenkrais's teaching is not prescriptive by nature, especially in the sense of 'Do *this* (as I say), and you will get *that*', nor more narcissistically 'Do as I do, and you will be as good as me!' His Method was designed to guide students to find their own spontaneity.

For Feldenkrais, pleasure was an intimate aspect of spontaneity. Pleasure then arrives *through* or *in* spontaneity and not merely through the desire to reproduce right action that may arise from the big Other (such as the implied demands of civilization or a teacher). Pleasure in spontaneity for itself would be free from the types of conditions signalled by Freud and from the parasitic in Lacanian *jouissance*. In the following section of this study, I want to examine how these concepts can be understood in Gould's decision to leave the concert platform, and how Gould came to use recording technology to create his own unique forms of *jouissance* and spontaneity for the neighbours' benefit.

The Feldenkrais Method in Creative Practice

Gould's neighbour

Glenn Gould withdrew from performing in public in 1964 and much is written about this, but not with any reference to psychoanalysis or the work of Feldenkrais. Reinhard, Eric L. Santner and Slavoj Žižek provide insight into two positions that illuminate different facets of Gould's action:

> Neurosis and psychosis represent two asymmetrical modes of the failure to love the neighbour: whereas the neurotic becomes an autonomous subject of desire in turning away from the impossibility of the command to love the neighbour, the psychotic fails to achieve subjectivity [i.e. they lose the sense of themselves in their action] while succeeding in experiencing the other as radically other, loving the neighbour not wisely, but too well.[61]

While these two positions outline stereotypes, Gould's position is more complex. His is perhaps a little closer to that of the paranoic who sees or imagines the gaze of the Other (where there is none in the recording studio), experiencing by proxy the *jouissance* of the unknown gaze or listener.[62] Gould arguably used recording as a screen to protect himself from the Other, but also to enable himself to assume a fantasy place in the listener's imagination, avoiding the traumatic presence of proximity in the concert hall.[63] His self-negotiation and decision not to play in public and escape parasitic and repetitive action can, in Feldenkraisian terms, be better understood as an attempt to create a new form of spontaneity. Gould understood continual concertizing as 'an endless series of imperfect, transient experiences of a work, which became stale and distorted through over-exposure';[64] the life of a concert pianist was an aggressive economy of duty and expectation. For him what was missing was the opportunity to sculpt an ideal interpretation rather than merely present a re-presentation.

My presentation of Gould here contrasts for instance with that of the musicologist Colin Symes who promotes the obvious libidinal and utopian interpretations of Gould's turn away from the concert platform. He avers that Gould's turn to the recording studio 'had nothing to do with the absence of an audience and everything to do with the electronic technology that had become commonplace in the recording studios of the 1960s, which has revolutionized the way records were made, and had the potential to change the way music was "represented" on disc'.[65]

Yes, Gould adored technology and had a 'love affair with the microphone'.[66] Through technology, Gould created syncretic representations of musical works, splicing many different 'takes' into one ideal or preferred recorded artistic choice. Paul Myers shows, Gould made 'as many as ten or fifteen interpretations of the same piece – each of them quite different, many of them valid – as though examining the music from every angle before deciding upon a final performance'.[67] In the recording studio, Gould seemingly becomes the archetypal 'neurotic', who also, like Reinhard's, Santner's and Žižek's 'psychotic', searches for his own true subjectivity, and seemingly fails to achieve this. Recording becomes a fantasy pursuit of an ideal interpretation and a way of realizing this 'unavowed dream'. The virtual, prosthetic and syncretic nature of recording – recording, re-recording and splicing term tape in search of an archetype, which seems like the least spontaneous means possible – can be understood in this sense as Gould's way out of parasitic action towards Feldenkraisian spontaneity and a form of health. This description of recording indicates that there is a different form of creative aggression present in recording; arguably Gould throws one economy of aggression over for another. However, Gould emphasizes often the emancipatory element of working in this way.[68]

The process of recording provided a means for perpetual improvement rather than merely production. Gould's 'decision' needs to understood not as merely motivated by technology, or just a desire to be recluse, or to produce a perfect product, but as an effective and radical act of self-love. His choice not to play, and his freedom to choose, shows an abnegation of the masochism and the masochistic culture of public performance, and of the superego cultural ideal of the contract with the listener (the neighbour) that must be fulfilled. Not performing was for Gould not some heroic hair-shirt; neither was Gould only merely hibernating from the trauma of the neighbour: the germ-ridden, coughing, fidgeting, farting, applauding, judging being that pays to make him their servant, even as he is idolized.[69]

Gould's spontaneity needs to be understood in Feldenkrais's terms. His pianism is a striking example of what Feldenkrais calls a 'maturity', embodied in 'the freedom from internal compulsion that accompanies the process'.[70] This is evidenced in his direction of his own imagination, and his work away from what he saw as the limiting mechanical and physical qualities of the piano. However, anyone who watches Gould's final films, for instance the Bruno Monsaingeon film of him playing some of Bach's *Art of Fugue* (1980), or of Bach's *Goldberg Variations* (1981), might also agree with Feldenkrais that the compulsive behaviour on display 'has some value because of the true spontaneous nature of the production'.[71] Compulsion therefore is mostly integrated into action, or action can be thought of as so 'high-functioning', in Maloney's sense, that the compulsion appears to be part of it.[72] Compulsion is essential to Gould's unique presence, to his 'Thing' which is indivisible from his physical organization (internal and external) and the particular sound he made when he touched the piano.

This 'Thing' is often passed off as 'eccentricity', but is in fact essential to Gould's persona.[73] In his uniqueness is the revelation of a kernel of otherness and foreignness that arguably brings the listener closer to their own 'Thing'. Uniqueness has a mimetic function and reminds the listener, in Feldenkrais's terms of 'where' they stopped 'being human beings': where their own unique qualities became disavowed through their own inactions as much as the pressure of the big Other.[74] The proximity of recording, especially the sort of 'tight shot' closeness with which Gould came to record (an inheritance from jazz recordings by Miles Davis and Oscar Peterson for example), brings the listener closer to his or her 'Thing'.[75] Gould imagined a certain listener autonomy whereby his 'Thing' could be manipulated by changing the different microphone levels (positioned in different parts of the hall) for example. Gould's 'acoustic orchestrations' of Sciabin and Sibelius enable the listener to become a better prosthetic articulation of his 'Thing', making them a 'conscientious consumer of recorded music', and giving them 'unprecedented spontaneity of judgment'.[76]

One way of conceiving this 'potentiality' is expressed in Gould's invisible reforming of narrative time in his recording. Gould at once undermines the unified experience of time given in a performance by making recordings that are syncretic (made of many takes spliced together). These *choices* point to perhaps the greatest irony about Gould. Despite his syncretic, choreographic recording techniques, his 'Thing' *remains*.[77]

In this sense, what the literary critic Edward Said has described as Gould's ability through virtuosity 'to draw the audience in by provocation, [and] the dislocation of expectation', is merely a symptom that points to the *sinthome* of Gould himself.[78] Recording attempts to overcome but in fact exacerbates the problem of 'symbolic castration', defined as the 'gap between [his] direct psychological identity and [his] symbolic identity' (the difference between a person's image in the world and their private self). It makes an idealized self-image. This should be understood more positively as an attempt to reintegrate the presence of the performer as recreator into the work. Recording for Gould is therefore not wholly dominated by compositional or historical interpretational imprimatur [thou shalt play this way or … !], but it offers a laboratory space for interpretation. In a Feldenkraisian sense, like in an ATM lesson, recording provided an opportunity to find different choices about how to perform a function. But recording also provided a prosthetic means for Gould to interpret himself. A musical work especially through recording therefore was, in a Lacanian sense, a medium for exploring the *sinthome* of Gould. I am not pretending in any way that Gould's recordings allow the listener to *know* Gould, but his 'Thing', his uniqueness, acts as a fascinator. Through his 'Thing', Gould's interpretations also allow something of the uniqueness of each composer being interpreted to be heard. The eccentricity and originality of Beethoven's music (Beethoven's 'Thing') are heard uniquely, and it is both irreducible and unrepeatable in this sense because of its presence in Gould's own *sinthome*.

By providing access to his 'Thing', through recording, he arguably undermines the normalization of Beethoven performance (through culture, and time and financial constraints on recording for example), and in so doing it he reframes the universalism of this music, understood as ideological homogeneity and cultural hegemony.[79] Gould steps outside the cultural expectation of the neighbour – the listener to Beethoven – who expects Beethoven to sound a particular way. He holds a mirror to the listener's 'attitude', and the degree to which the exceptional or 'eccentric' aspects of Gould come to dislocate their own 'Thing'. With these thoughts in mind, it is fascinating to sample a small ethnographic snapshot of Gould. On one website, commentators have allowed themselves the sort of free reign that anonymity provides. Gould is described as a 'psycho', as a 'one-trick pony' (i.e. he could only play Bach), as a pianist who 'butchered Beethoven', leaving an 'overall feeling of blasphemy and violation', despite his commitment to the music, playing as if 'possessed and mesmerised' by the music.[80]

In an article in the *Guardian* newspaper, revealingly entitled 'Glenn Gould: a wilfully idiotic genius?', four concert pianists more cautiously comment on Gould.[81] These comments in themselves are interesting partly as a sampling of the critical temperature and passive/aggressive ire that Gould arouses, but mostly because of the unwritten libidinal economy (the unconscious desires) of the writers. The subtexts of their commentaries could be summarized on a spectrum from 'He was cleverer than us', or 'Well, if he was so clever, why is he not like us?', to 'Ok, we know Gould was eccentric and we will tolerate this up to a point … ', to: 'Gould has betrayed our idea of Beethoven [by Artur Schnabel, Claudio Arrau, Sviatoslav Richter, Daniel Barenboim, Alfred Brendel etc.], and he should not be taken seriously as an artist. Therefore, people who are really interested in (this) music should not listen to him'. The implication here is that he transgressed 'our community', and therefore he should be understood at best as a maverick, and at worst, as a pariah.[82] But, we should reverse this, and say that it is because of such comments that Gould becomes a 'yardstick' of what is possible, a mirror to the libidinal economy of recordings (of perfection and ideals of 'correctness') and the way these have become, through late capitalism, merely another facet of the prosthetic hardwiring of civilization into the parasitic *jouissance* of technology. Gould's 'urge for freedom', as Freud puts it, enables him to transgress his community and thence to become a better prosthesis of its 'cultural ideal' and of commodity fetishism.[83] His is not a 'renunciation of instinct', that presupposes a 'non-satisfaction (by suppression, repression or some other means) of powerful instincts', but a harnessing of it. He therefore provides an ideal exemplar of Feldenkrais's qualification of Christ's injunction.[84]

Conclusion: Shake your 'Thing'!

In this chapter I have used the ideal of the neighbour as a lens to examine aspects of musical performance. The question of what the neighbour wants and what they are doing is to a large extent set aside by Gould. To ask why Gould plays Beethoven's 'Appassionata' piano sonata Op. 57 (the first movement is almost a half of the 'normal' *Allegro assai* speed used by performers) is in fact to ask questions of our indoctrination to cultural norms and presuppositions. Gould in this work becomes a provocative reaction against cultural rules and listeners' implicit desires. That he does not 'obey' the big Other (the tendency to normalization) but follows his own path is deeply disturbing for some, and yet also perversely entrancing.

Gould's prediction that 'the habit of concert going and concert giving' would disappear has not only proven unfounded, but has been substantially shown to be incorrect. This 'chief symbol of musical mercantilism' has in fact retained and enhanced its status.[85] Through social media, for example, performance has attained its own forms of celebrity culture. The 'Thing' has therefore gone virtual and acquired commercial interests: it is 'out there'.

The aspects of individuality and spontaneity demonstrated by Gould can provide a useful critique of arts-based education.[86] The search for uniqueness would facilitate immersion and mastery, rather than merely servicing a curriculum (a function of the big Other); it could bring about 'flexible bodies and brains', as Feldenkrais states.[87] The support for uniqueness would be a search for an order that does not obey the big Other's demands for the normative, for agreement, for certainty and for the ordinary, but would act as a form intra-sensory critique, listening to the potential to realize our 'unavowed dreams' within ourselves.[88] Institutions and educators bear a responsibility to think about the ways in which they can facilitate this, to learn to think beyond their own limitations and what might have worked last year, and to examine how they can balance the (big Other) demands of the profession with the development of artistic uniqueness, and the demands of art itself.

Feldenkrais always said that he wasn't teaching but merely providing ideal conditions for people to learn. This was, as I have shown in this study, to shift the emphasis back onto the development of the uniqueness of the person through a form of learning where there is exploration rather than judgement. This would be a way of learning where mastery is attained through time spent finding multiple different ways to do something rather than working with the fear of meeting the unknown and often unrealistic expectations of society, teachers, other performers and the listening public.

This requires a form of slow learning, moving and listening softly, listening the way in which our limitations are self-generated (by culture and our own habits especially) and the ways in which we challenge these limitations. The Feldenkrais Method promotes a dialogue between outside and inside; to change one way of acting, the way we hold our head, the tonus of the hand, the spine, chest and ribs, the skin between the eyes, is to change everything. To develop a soft, comfortable way of doing, employing skill not will, requires a way of listening and learning that facilitates more joy, flexibility, autonomy and a sense of the uniqueness of what we do as creative artists.

Gould provides an exemplar of this kind of self-investment, and of the ways in which different ways of learning and different kinds of creativity can coalesce. To follow the examples of Feldenkrais and Gould would be not only to value and reward uniqueness, but to understand how multiple 'uniquenesses' can be facilitated. This would be a conduit 'to know what you are doing, so you can do what you want'. At the heart of this ideal is a cherishing of the 'Thing', loving oneself first better to 'love thy neighbour'.

Addendum

Listening to children practise an instrument is often very instructive. They often vocalize what adults might sublimate. 'I don't like practise' … 'this is too hard' … 'Why do you (the composer, the teacher, the big Other) want me to do this?' or there is sometimes just a deep sigh (as if from the soul), which combines these thoughts and others as if the weight of humanity's burden of difficulty since the beginning of time has found its harvest home. 'To improve' therefore means to improve not just a localized problem, but something much more profound. It is important to develop a sense of our own creaturely feeling, using our own intelligence to move in the most elegant and aesthetically pleasurable way. Feldenkrais at one point in his Quest workshops states that this acquisition 'is priceless'.[89] If we do not do this we might feel 'Oh, what I am doing is not good enough' and even 'I am no good'. But this sense and intelligence need space in order to be enactivated. Here is a suggestion to alleviate this impasse. We need to move slowly to find out *how* we do something, and to learn the patience to do this. But how does one do this? Take any technical problem in your work, and do it very slowly, but before you do it, have the intention to do it in the softest, most pleasurable, most luxuriant and comfortable way possible. Pay attention to the smallest parts of the movement – the beginning and end of a single note for example, or how you move from one note to the next. How could you enjoy every part of what you are doing (and of yourself) to the utmost?[90]

Part of this question is concerned with listening to habitual action and how one can include more of oneself in an action. Which parts of yourself participate in the action of laughing at a joke? For some people it seems that their whole body is involved – they seem to be enjoying the joke more than others, even if they are may be unaware of what is happening. This type of awareness is crucial and needs focus. For example, how can a violinist use their pelvis, and weight transference through the feet in their action, or how can a pianist use their sternum in their action, or how can an organist employ subtle movements in their ribs when they play the organ pedals with their feet? Can a singer choose to sing with vibrato or not, and can they control this vibrato as a means of expression rather than as habit or as a demand of the big Other? Thinking in these imaginative and non-habitual ways is a ramification of Feldenkrais's teaching; it leads to an understanding that difficulty (in doing something) is not really present in the object (the score for example), but is present in an incomplete self-image, in both thought and movement patterns. Finding out what this is requires a form of listening to what is missing – to what is missing in our self-listening and what our habits of listening are – and *doing* in this way I suggest helps find this missing key.

This is not done to please someone else or to say to someone else – 'look how good I am; look how nicely I do it!' Rather, this kind of learning develops a sense of pleasure, as the quality of the activity and the engagement of your whole self in the activity improves so that you come to be as you would like to be; we can perhaps learn to love ourselves sufficiently so that we can love our neighbour better. In this way of working you can find something of your uniqueness as a creative artist, and also discover something of the contribution that you can make to your art.

Notes

1. Moshe Feldenkrais, 'Discussion of Habits and Fear', in *New York Quest Workshop*, 1981 (San Diego, CA: Feldenkrais Resources, n.d.).
2. Sigmund Freud, 'Jokes and Their Relation to the Unconscious' (1905), in *The Standard Edition of the Complete Psychological Works of Sigmund Freud*, Vol. VIII, trans. and ed. James Strachey (London: Vintage books, 2001).
3. Leontyne Price at https://www.youtube.com/watch?v=EqVu_wlxTzM (accessed 10 June 2020).
4. Feldenkrais, 'Introduction: Love Thyself as Thy Neighbour', in *The Potent Self: A Study of Spontaneity and Compulsion* (Berkeley, CA: Frog Publications, 1985), xxxvii–xliv.
5. Freud, 'Civilization and Its Discontents' (1930), in *The Standard Edition of the Complete Psychological Works of Sigmund Freud*, Vol. XXI (1927–31) trans. and ed. James Strachey (London: Vintage books, 2001). See Jacques Lacan, *Seminar VII, The Ethics of Psychoanalysis*, ed. Jacques-Alain Miller, trans. Dennis Potter (Routledge: London and New York, 1992), 220–34.
6. Feldenkrais, 'Learning, Free Choice, Individuality', *New York Quest Workshop*, 1981.
7. See Geoffrey Payzant on Gould's attitude to audiences and other pianists' attitudes in *Glenn Gould: Music and Mind*, 23.
8. Rhona Bergman, *The Idea of Gould* (Philadelphia, PA: Lev publishing, 1999), 48. Interview with Alex Trebek in 1966 at https://www.youtube.com/watch?v=1nZTgAGSajA (accessed 29 April 2020).
9. See Slavoj Žižek, 'Love Thy Neighbour? No Thanks!', in *The Plague of Fantasies* (London: Verso, 1997), 58–9, 61.
10. Žižek, 'Love Thy Neighbour? No Thanks!', 65.
11. Freud, *Civilization and Its Discontents*, 91–2.
12. Feldenkrais, 'Discussion: Relationships, Change and the Self', *New York Quest Workshops*, 1981. On Feldenkrais and Gould see also: Sholl, 'Feldenkrais's Touch, Ephram's Laughter, Gould's Sensorium: Listening and Musical Practice between Thinking and Doing', *Journal of the Royal Musical Association*, Vol. 144, No. 2 (2019), 397–428.
13. Arved Ashby, *Absolute Music, Mechanical Reproduction* (Berkeley: University of California Press, 2010), 92. On Gould and psychoanalysis, see Geoffrey Payzant, *Gould: Music and Mind* (Toronto: Van Nostrand Reinhold, 1978), 73–4, and Peter Ostwald, *Glenn Gould: The Ecstasy and Tragedy of Genius* (New York: Norton, 1997), 102–3. See also S. Timothy Malony, 'Glenn Gould, Autistic Savant', in *Sounding Off: Theorizing Disability in Music*, ed. Neil Lerner and Joseph N. Straus (New York: Routledge, 2006), 121–35.
14. Feldenkrais, *The Potent Self*, 23–9 and 111–26, and Jean Laplanche and Jean-Bertrand Pontalis, *The Language of Psychoanalysis* (London: The Hogarth Press, 1973), 394.
15. Freud, *Civilization and Its Discontents*, 65.
16. See Feldenkrais, *Thinking and Doing* (Longmont, CO: Genesis II, 2013).
17. Feldenkrais, *Awareness through Movement* (London: Penguin, 1972), 87–9, 136–7.

18 Freud, *Civilization and Its Discontents*, 67.
19 See Betty Lee, cited in Payzant, 34.
20 Freud, *Civilization and Its Discontents*, 77.
21 Freud, *Civilization and Its Discontents*, 77 and 78.
22 Payzant, *Glenn Gould: Music and Mind*, 22–3.
23 Freud, *Civilization and Its Discontents*, 76–81, 83 and Feldenkrais, *The Potent Self*, xli.
24 Freud, *Civilization and Its Discontents*, 86.
25 Freud, *Civilization and Its Discontents*, 95.
26 Freud, *Civilization and Its Discontents*, 96.
27 Freud, *Civilization and Its Discontents*, 97.
28 Feldenkrais, *The Potent Self*, xxxvii, and 34–5 on symptoms.
29 Freud, *Civilization and Its Discontents*, 109–10.
30 Freud, *Civilization and Its Discontents*, 112.
31 Freud, *Civilization and Its Discontents*, 119, 122.
32 Feldenkrais, *The Potent Self*, xliii, xlii.
33 Feldenkrais, *San Francisco Feldenkrais Method Training* (San Diego, CA: Feldenkrais Resources, 1977).
34 Feldenkrais, *The Potent Self*, xxxviii.
35 Payzant, *Glenn Gould: Music and Mind*, 21.
36 Freud, *Civilization and Its Discontents*, 134.
37 Feldenkrais, *The Potent Self*, xl.
38 Feldenkrais, *The Potent Self*, 92.
39 Feldenkrais, *The Potent Self*, 92.
40 Freud, *Civilization and Its Discontents*, 142.
41 Freud, *Civilization and Its Discontents*, 142–3, 145.
42 Freud, *Civilization and Its Discontents*, 149.
43 Lacan, *Seminar VII*, 62.
44 Kenneth Reinhard, 'Towards a Political Theology of the Neighbor', in *The Neighbour: Three Inquiries in Political Theology* (Chicago: The University of Chicago Press, 2013), 32.
45 Dylan Evans, *An Introductory Dictionary of Lacanian Psychoanalysis* (London: Routledge, 1996), 150.
46 Jane Austen, *Pride and Prejudice*, Chapter 57 at https://www.gutenberg.org/files/1342/1342-h/1342-h.htm#link2HCH0015
47 Reinhard, 'Towards a Political Theology of the Neighbor', 45.
48 Lacan, *Seminar VII*, 229, 65.
49 See Feldenkrais, *The Potent Self*, 108.
50 Lacan, *Seminar VII*, 227–8, 82.
51 Žižek, *Against the Double Blackmail: Refugees, Terror and Other Troubles with the Neighbours* (London: Penguin, 2016), 73.
52 Michael L Klein, *Music and the Crises of the Modern Subject* (Bloomington and Indianapolis: Indiana University Press, 2015), 102–3.
53 Klein, *Music and the Crises of the Modern Subject*, 118.
54 Feldenkrais, *Higher Judo* (London: Frederick Warne, 1962), 47.

55 Feldenkrais, *The Potent Self*, xl.

56 Feldenkrais, *The Potent Self*, xxxvii, and 11.

57 Feldenkrais, *The Potent Self*, xl.

58 Esther Thelen, 'The Central Role of Action in Typical and Atypical Development', in *Movement and Action in Learning and Development: Clinical Implications of Pervasive Developmental Disorders*, ed. Ida J. Stockman (San Diego, CA: Academic Press, 2004), 71.

59 On the imagination, see Feldenkrais, *Thinking and Doing*, 8–9. He writes: 'Any thought developed in accordance with this plan will be manifest in the unconscious and become realized in actual life.'

60 Victor E. Frankl, *Man's Search for Meaning* (London: Rider, 2004), and Feldenkrais, *The Potent Self*, xliv.

61 Reinhard, Santner, and Žižek, 'Introduction' to *The Neighbour: Three Inquiries in Political Theology*, 7. On Gould's pre-performance activities, see Payzant, 76, and Malony, 'Glenn Gould, Autistic Savant', 121–2.

62 Žižek, 'Love Thy Neighbour? No Thanks!', 73.

63 Žižek, 'Love Thy Neighbour? No Thanks!', 85.

64 Bazzana, *Wondrous Strange: The Life and Art of Glenn Gould* (New York: Oxford University Press, 2005), 260.

65 Colin Symes, 'Variations on a Theme of Nelson Goodman as Arranged by Glenn Gould for the Piano Phonograph', in *Recorded Music: Philosophical and Critical reflections*, ed. Mine Doğantan-Dack (Hendon: Middlesex University Press, 2008), 49.

66 See Gould in Payzant, 37.

67 See Myers in Payzant, 50, and Gould, 'The Prospects of Recording', in *The Glenn Gould Reader*, ed. Tim Page (London: Faber, 1984), 338–9.

68 Gould, 'The Prospects of Recording', 339, and 'We Who Are About to Be Disqualified Salute You!', *The Glenn Gould Reader*, ed. Tim Page (London: Faber, 1984), 250–5.

69 See T.W. Adorno, *Introduction to the Sociology of Music*, trans. E.B. Ashton (New York: The Seabury Press, 1976), 106.

70 Feldenkrais, *The Potent Self*, 101

71 Feldenkrais, *The Potent Self*, xi.

72 Malony, 'Glenn Gould, Autistic Savant', 121–36.

73 See Bazzana, *Wondrous Strange: The Life and Art of Glenn Gould*, 316–29, and Laplanche and Pontalis on the ideal-ego, 201.

74 Feldenkrais, 'Learning, Free Choice, Individuality', *New York Quest Workshop*, 1981.

75 Gould in https://www.youtube.com/watch?v=JllD47HIees (accessed 4 May 2020).

76 Gould, 'Strauss and the Electronic Future' (1964), in *The Glenn Gould Reader*, 93, 99.

77 Gould, 'The Prospects of Recording', 338.

78 Edward Said, *On Late Style: Music and Literature against the Grain* (London: Bloomsbury, 2007), 117.

79 See Žižek in *Against the Double Blackmail*, 75–6.

80 http://www.talkclassical.com/1186-goulds-beethoven.html (accessed 4 May 2020).

81 https://www.theguardian.com/music/2012/sep/20/glenn-gould-wilfully-idiotic-genius (accessed 4 May 2020).

82 An important aspect of this transgression is that Gould appears to usurp the image of the artist as servant of music to place himself seemingly outside the audience's gaze, but, as I argue, he

    merely finds a better way of using himself through technology. See Tim Hecker, 'Glenn Gould, the Vanishing Performer and the Ambivalence of the Studio', *Leonardo Music Journal*, Vol. 18, *Why Live? Performance in the Age of Digital Reproduction* (2008), 79. Hecker's argument that Gould's work in the studio was a form of 'self-erasure' (p. 77) and 'retreat' (p. 83), although supported by biographical evidence, is diametrically opposed to the thinking in the chapter.

83   Freud, *Civilization and Its Discontents*, 96.

84   Freud, *Civilization and Its Discontents*, 97.

85   Gould, 'The Prospects of Recording', 331–2.

86   See Thomas Kampe, 'The Art of Making Choices: The Feldenkrais Method as Soma-critique', in *Attending to Movement: Somatic Perspectives on Living in This World*, ed. Sarah Whatley, Natalie Garrett-Brown and Kirsty Alexander (Axminster: Triarchy Press, 2015), 86–7.

87   Saying attributed to Feldenkrais and widely understood in the Feldenkrais community.

88   See Sylvie Fortin, 'Looking for Blind Spots in Somatics' Evolving Pathways', *Journal of Dance and Somatic Practices*, Vol. 9, No. 2 (2017), 146.

89   'a) Pressing and lifting on the side, opening and closing hand to stand b) Variations in standing c) Pressing again on side, making a wave'. *New York Quest Workshop*, 1981.

90   Such a comment might seem simple or simplistic, but it is part of what Feldenkrais calls 'the elusive obvious'.

CHAPTER 3
LEARNING THROUGH FEELING: HOW THE IDEAS OF NIKOLAI BERNSTEIN AND MOSHE FELDENKRAIS APPLY TO PERFORMER TRAINING
Dick McCaw

Introduction

I have been involved in actor training since I became associate director of the International Workshop Festival in 1989, and then artistic director in 1993. As its title suggests, the festival focused on providing continuing training and development for professionals working in the performing arts. There were Feldenkrais sessions at the end of every working day and a weekend or week-long workshop in every programme. In other words, in my conception of performer training, the Feldenkrais Method was central. This chapter will examine how the ideas of Feldenkrais and Russian neuroscientist Nikolai Bernstein can broaden our understanding of the dynamic principles underlying performer training. (I thank the late Carl Ginsburg, an inspiring Feldenkrais trainer, for introducing me to Bernstein's work.) The central idea shared by both men lies in the title of this chapter: we learn through feeling. This may seem self-evident, but many performers and sports people still use expressions like 'muscle memory' which assume, firstly, that movements are remembered in the muscles and not the brain, and that what we are learning are the motor elements involved in a movement. The process is analogous to uploading a movement program into the circuitry of a robot, an analogy which reveals the shortcomings of such a theory of learning and movement. Have you seen how robots move? With what comical awkwardness they negotiate bumps and slopes in the floor, or objects in the room? If you think of learning to move in the real world, then very quickly it becomes clear that one cannot write programs for every eventuality the robot will encounter. So now, they are 'teaching' robots how to learn from their movements. By means of heuristic algorithms the robots establish a learned connection between a given motor output and the sensory feedback resulting from that output. Its memory is no longer a fixed program which has been installed, but an ever-developing database which guides future movements. Robotics has moved from a static to a dynamic conception of motor control. In other words, heuristic programs are being devised whereby robots can learn through feeling.

This chapter explores how concepts deployed by Bernstein and Feldenkrais lie at the heart of the work of Clive Barker (an actor and trainer) and Peter Brook (a director who devised trainings for his actors). Both men created situations in which their actors or students of acting could learn through their experience of doing. Just as with the example of the robot, this process of learning involved finding out how to do something, rather than having to commit a specific movement program to memory. When asked to define training, Brook replied, 'to make the actor simply more sensitive'. There are several other aims in Barker's and Brook's actor trainings: they are to develop:

- a creative intelligence whereby an actor has a wider range of movement responses;
- an intelligence that enables an actor to make sense of a given situation;
- a capacity to learn how to learn, or put another way, to learn how to learn from practice.

I want to explore how two scientists, both of whom were inventive in their practical experiments and committed to the public dissemination of scientific knowledge, can help us understand some broader principles that underlie the aims and modalities of these two actor trainings.

Part I: The ideas of Nikolai Bernstein

In an article about Bernstein and Feldenkrais, Carl Ginsburg describes the shock of realizing that Bernstein's *The Development of Dexterity* 'contains ideas about movement, learning, and the nervous system familiar to us from the work of Feldenkrais'.[1] He goes on to ask 'How is it possible that Bernstein could have so clearly understood through experimentation the same ideas when no one else in the field came close?'[2] In his 2015 biography Mark Reese similarly notes how the thinking of Moshe Feldenkrais recalls the work of this 'Russian physician and researcher who, contemporaneous with Moshe, theorized about the learning of skills. Both were years ahead of their time and shared much in their approach'.[3]

According to Mark Latash *The Development of Dexterity* was written 'in the second half of the 1940s in an attempt to make Bernstein's theory on multi-level movement organization accessible for readers with minimal background in physiology and mechanics'.[4] Ginsburg adds that Bernstein 'specifically tackles the question of learning, and in a way that separates him from his contemporaries and aligns him with Feldenkrais'.[5] He also wrote a book on Biomechanics that had a major influence on Meyerhold's theatrical training of the same name.

In order to establish the connection with Feldenkrais, Reece offers a long quotation from Bernstein:

> A motor skill is not a movement formula and certainly not a formula of permanent muscle forces imprinted in some motor center. *Motor skill is an ability to solve one or another type of motor problem.* It becomes clear now, how tremendous the work for the nervous system is during the development of such a skill, how many deviations, variations, and special cases it must actually meet or consider ... The learned movement must *be actually performed many times* in order to *actually experience all the sensations* which form the basis for its sensory corrections. [...] Certainly, the most sensible and correct training would be organized in a way that combined a minimization of effort with a large variety of well-designed sensations and that created optimal conditions for meaningfully absorbing and memorizing all these sensations.[6]

Many of the questions that will be explored in this chapter can be found in the above passage: what is a movement skill, or, put another way, what is that we know that enables us to perform a movement skilfully? What kind of training is required to achieve that skill? Bernstein's conception of dexterity is far from being a set of skills, but rather a movement intelligence, or indeed a sensitivity to movement.

The notion of 'skill' is central to the thinking of both men, and it is important to grasp Bernstein's argument that a motor skill is neither 'a movement skill' nor some kind of program printed in a muscle ('a formula of permanent muscle forces imprinted in some motor center'). It is not, in other words, a fixed routine that is learned and then subsequently repeated. Did Reece pick out this quotation (as did Ginsburg in his 1998 article[7]) because the focus on sensory rather than motor activity resonated with Feldenkrais's Method of Awareness through Movement? While it is undoubtedly true that training should consist of subtle variations of a movement, we should also realize that unlike machines which are designed to repeat movements, it is actually quite difficult for humans to reproduce the same movement in all its detail. The very means by which we move obliges us to focus on sensory control rather than motor output. The last sentence of the passage explores how the amount of 'effort' in motor output affects the clarity of our sensory experience of that movement. On the one hand, Bernstein writes about a 'minimization of effort' in terms of ergonomic efficiency; on the other, he argues that such minimization would create 'optimal conditions for meaningfully absorbing and memorizing all these sensations'. It is precisely this equation between effort and sensation that concerned Feldenkrais who, as we shall see later, drew on the Weber-Fechner ratio to explain their functional interrelation.

One could say the learning in the Feldenkrais Method takes place when one can become aware of the effect that a movement has upon one's entire body. We therefore need to know how two types of nerve – the sensory and the motor – communicate with each other. This happens through 'synaptic communication'. To explain how two neurons communicate with each other, Kandel uses the image of one person whispering into another's ear:

> Thus, like lips whispering very close to an ear, synaptic communication between neurons has three basic components: the presynaptic terminal of the axon, which sends signals (corresponding to the lips in our analogy); the synaptic cleft (the space between lips and ear); and the postsynaptic site on the dendrite that receives signals (the ear).[8]

This 'synaptic communication' (synapse comes from the Greek for 'junction' or 'connection') is the basis of learning and memory. Kandel discovered that in order to guarantee the strength and durability of this connection between an axon (which carry messages *from* the cell body) and a dendrite (which carry messages *to* the cell body), the cell body of the axon produces an extra synaptic terminal. In other words, a memory, a thing learned, constitutes a physical alteration of the cell – hence the earlier reference to plasticity – which means that the brain changes itself through its functional activity. Memory is more often described with metaphors (many of which are misleading): Kandel offers us a non-metaphorical account of the organic process of memory, that is, of the connection between learning and feeling.

The difference between the movement capacity of machines, animals and humans

In my introduction, I compared the capacity of robots and humans to move, and Bernstein makes very instructive use of this comparison. He notes that machines and tools '*deteriorate with use;* they wear out, loosen up, and generally become *worse*. The best machines are those that do not require repair for long periods of time'. He then continues:

> The situation with the 'human machine' is the opposite. *The longer* a human participates in a certain activity, the *better* he or she performs it. A living organism not only does not deteriorate during work but, quite the opposite, becomes stronger, quicker, more enduring, more adroit and dexterous, particularly with respect to the type of activity that has been performed.[9]

He calls this adaptability of the 'human machine' to improve its performance of tasks 'exercisability'. Through the 'exercise' of a movement we progressively learn how better to perform it. What a wonderful concept for any person engaged in expressive movement! This concept explains how practice helps us learn through doing.

His analysis further points out that a machine moves thanks to pistons which push rods, whereas animals move thanks to muscles which contract, or pull at, bones[10]. A machine has totally prescribed angles of movement whereas the joints of animals have almost unlimited freedom of movement. Sensory control (and learning) is thus necessary in an animal whereas (like the movement program) it is part of the design of a machine. In Chapter 6 of *Training the Actor's Body – A Guide* (2018), I suggested that we perform rotations to explore the full movement capacity of our joints, and the chapter ends with an analysis of two Feldenkrais lessons where he uses the image of clock-face to sharpen our feeling of such rotations.

Joints and muscles: Degrees of freedom in movement

Above I noted how the moving parts of a machine are constructed according to a very precise design. A piston is designed to push in one direction: if its support becomes loose then it will lose this precise directionality and its action will destroy the machine. Bernstein calls this directional possibility in a joint a 'degree of freedom'. Latash and Turvey (joint editors of *Dexterity*) explain that Bernstein's 'most beloved notion in the area of control of voluntary movements was probably that of degrees of freedom'. They continue:

> He showed how rich the motor system is in degrees of freedom as compared to the most sophisticated devices and machines. He also showed how a single, additional (redundant) degree of freedom can introduce an infinite flexibility, or, in other words, an infinite number of choices.[11]

With a machine, an additional, redundant degree of freedom means that it is broken; in the more adaptable human it means the need for more careful control of the movement. Consider how the joints of the shoulder or pelvic girdle allow movement in all three planes.

And then consider what moves the bones of the legs and arms – our muscles. Bernstein explains how the reactive speed of our muscles enables us to make quick and effective corrections while engaged in a movement. But, precisely because muscles are elastic, they don't transduce 'force as carefully and precisely as rigid rods'; moreover, 'the numerous external forces that confront us from all sides lead to a situation where, in addressing a certain muscle, the brain cannot know in advance what the effects will be on the limb movements'. This motor unpredictability leads him to conclude that from 'the very onset, the brain must continuously and watchfully check *the movement based on reports of the sensory organs* and harness the movement with corresponding *corrections*'.[12] By invoking the brain, we shouldn't think he is proposing a conscious process. Most of these supremely complex and subtle processes which control our movement are completely unconscious.

Sensory nerves: Sensation as a guide to movement

Bernstein stated that learning a motor skill is not about the execution, not about some motor engram printed in the muscles, but rather the constant monitoring of its performance through the sensory system. He makes this point repeatedly through *Dexterity* insisting that an exercise trains '*not the effector itself,* not its joints, bones and muscles, but *a certain area of activity* of this organ controlled by the brain at one or another level'.[13] In a few words, Bernstein describes motor skill as a process of correction that relies upon an effective translation of sensory feedback into motor corrections, a process he calls 'reciphering':

> The brain's sensory systems gradually learn to be more and more skillful in making an instantaneous translation from the language of incoming sensations and perceptions reflecting the movement process into the language of corrective motor impulses that need to be sent to one or another muscle. We shall call this translation from the language of sensations to the language of corrections *reciphering of neural impulses*.[14]

This passage takes us back to my Introduction where Bernstein had noted the decisive advantage an organism has when the motor and sensory cells are connected, since this allows it to '*react* to external stimuli (for example, they could move directly to a potential prey or move away from a potential danger)'.[15] To repeat a phrase Reece quoted above, we are acquiring 'an ability to solve one or another type of motor problem', or, put another way, 'not a permanent cliché, but a peculiar, specific *maneuverability*'.[16] Feldenkrais will make the matter even simpler by arguing that we need to focus not on the 'what' (the content of the physical movement) but the 'how' (the way that movement is executed).

When Brook argues that actor training is about developing sensitivity, we need to understand that there are two senses of which we might be unaware: firstly, the kinaesthetic sense (of movement) and secondly the proprioceptive sense (of position).

> Proprioceptive sense means 'sensing itself' (that is, having a sense of one's own body). Sensory endings of proprioceptive organs are scattered all around the muscular fibers, tendons, and articular capsules. These endings (called *receptors*) send signals to the brain on the position of body links, joint angles, muscle forces, and so on.[17]

Bernstein goes on to explain how 'it is quite obvious that proprioception plays the first violin in sensory corrections'.[18] Thanks to our proprioceptive sense we can develop an image of ourselves in movement, another key theme in Feldenkrais's teaching, and central to many kinds of actor training, particularly that of Michael Chekhov.

Dexterity is resourcefulness, manoeuvrability and exercisability

The final pages of *Dexterity* are a sustained reflection on learning. He begins by examining learning from a phylogenetic perspective (i.e. the evolution of humans). He argues that new brain structures naturally developed in response to 'the increasing demands of life', structures that were 'more and more *trainable*. The younger a new level of movement construction is, the more capable it is with respect to meaning and complexity of solvable problems, the more flexible, adaptive, "plastic" it is, and thus, *the more exercisable it is*'.[19] Later he defines exercisability in terms of an animal's 'motor wits in unexpected situations'.[20] With these 'motor wits' we solve problems, we negotiate the unexpected and the unfamiliar. When Bernstein writes about exercise, he is describing a way of training, an attitude towards that exercise. The following quotation very elegantly sums up his pedagogy:

> The essence and objective of exercise is to improve the movements, that is, to change them. Therefore, correct exercise is in fact a *repetition without repetition*. […] The point is that during a correctly organized exercise, a student is repeating many times, *not the means for solving* a given motor problem, but *the process of its solution,* the changing and improving of the means.[21]

'Repetition without repetition' is a phrase that could have been written by Feldenkrais, who, Reece notes, 'mounted a life-long critique of repetitive exercise'.[22] Although this is relevant to any training practice, is it not also at the heart of the work of any interpretative artist, be they musician or actor? An actor has to be acutely sensitive to the rhythms and dynamics of every performance, so they are attuned to the contours of that particular space, that particular audience. Although working from a pre-rehearsed score, the interpretative artist stands or falls on their ability to achieve repetition without repetition. That is what makes a performance live. If learning happens through feeling, then the only physical structure we can feel with is our own bodies. We are both the moving structure and the instrument that can monitor, make sense and learn from our every movement. Is this not at the heart of any performer training worth its salt?

Part II: Moshe Feldenkrais

Feldenkrais turns the question of learning upon itself: he asks not only *what* it is that one learns (Bernstein's question) but also *how* one learns, what is the manner of learning? The manner is to become aware (to reflect) upon one's own unique way of doing, and thereby to see other possibilities of taking action. This extends into a reflection upon the nature of learning, and by extension, on the constitution of one's self. Thus understood, 'learning is the gift of life. A special kind of learning: that of knowing oneself'.[23] Gilbert Ryle (in his book *The Concept of Mind*) makes much of this distinction between learning 'what' and learning 'how'. He explains that 'an action exhibits intelligence, if, and only if, the agent is thinking what he is doing while he is doing it, and thinking what he is doing in such a manner that he would not do the action so well if he were not thinking what he is doing'.[24] The entire argument of this chapter turns around this central point that the execution of an action can only be improved through developing an attention to (an awareness of) *how* it is performed. Feldenkrais takes up Ryle's critique of education by arguing that most 'formal' teaching 'seems to overlook the fact that there are ways of learning that lead to growth and maturity with practically no failures. Formal teaching is more concerned with "what" is taught than with "how"; its failures are frequent'.[25] Feldenkrais considers the reflexive process of learning how to learn 'the higher function of learning'.[26]

But how does this learning take place? Feldenkrais answered above, when we learn how to move 'without any sudden change in the rhythm of breathing (usually holding the breath), or clenching the lower jaw, or tensing the neck muscles'. The gradient of Feldenkrais learning consists of becoming ever more sensitive to these unnecessary changes and involuntary tensions. Hence, he describes lifelong learning being about the process of getting to know rather than the accumulation of known facts. Feldenkrais puts the difference memorably: 'what I've learned is not another item added to a register of dead knowledge, but a dynamic correction in the process of thinking. It is knowledge that directly and immediately transforms the manner of what I am doing.'[27] 'What' one learns in a lesson with Feldenkrais is the possible change one can make in the manner of performing an action; the informational content is contained in this often minute correction.

Awareness and sensitivity – the tools of learning and development

Bernstein has already argued that dexterity is acquired through the development of one's sensitivity, a principle that is evident in the very title of Feldenkrais's group lessons, Awareness through Movement (ATM). Again, like Bernstein, he argues that we are more likely to learn about 'what is happening in our central nervous system' if we focus on changes in 'stance, stability, and attitude' rather than 'in the muscles themselves'.[28] (This is what distinguishes their approach from kinesiology.) We understand our bodies at the level of actions (such as rolling from the back to the stomach, coming to sitting from lying etc.) rather than their physiological effectors (i.e. nerves, muscle groups, joints). But whereas Bernstein confined his practice to recording functional actions, Feldenkrais created some three thousand carefully constructed ATM lessons in which the student is invited to perform small movements with sufficient force to generate an awareness of how this movement affects their physical structure. This last point cannot be sufficiently stressed: the movement has no value at the motor level, only at the sensory level. The information, the learning, is generated through the student's ability to feel, not their capacity for movement. In these lessons the greater the movement, the lesser the sensory signal (once again an evocation of the Weber-Fechner ratio). It takes practice to learn how to do less, displacing the effort from making the movement, to listening to its effects.

We have come a long way in this argument without reflecting on how Feldenkrais uses the word 'awareness'. Throughout his writings we find a remarkable consistency of definition: in *Awareness through Movement* he states that 'Awareness is consciousness together with a realization of what is happening within it or of what is going on within ourselves while we are conscious.'[29] In *The Elusive Obvious* his definition is crisp: awareness is 'conscious-of plus knowledge'.[30] Elsewhere he states that 'Awareness is a question of knowing what you're doing, knowing what you are conscious of'.[31] Consistent in all these definitions is the insistence that awareness is a state of active investigation, and as such an essential aspect of his heuristic approach to learning and teaching. A student's improvement 'comes through their awareness of themselves in action', and leading on from this, 'their freedom to choose their modes of action', which in turn are only 'available to those who have discovered themselves'.[32]

Although Feldenkrais's philosophical claims may seem idealistic, his practice was based on scientific research and methodology. Rather like Apple computer technology, the simplicity of the user interface in his lessons of ATM belies the considerable unseen technical complexity that underpins them. Thus when in the passage below he writes about feedback, it is with the knowledge of a research scientist who specialized in electrical engineering:

> Only through feedback can an action become a new habit in life, or on the contrary be rejected. But this is possible only through the light of awareness. Because awareness is a part of the correction, it is turned into the action itself; it listens to the action. Such listening, I think, is the first feedback. In other words without feedback it is impossible to condition or de-condition a grown-up person.[33]

Through the exercise of awareness we generate 'feedback', which is precisely the information that enables us to correct a movement. Carl Ginsburg created a verb 'awareing'[34] to demonstrate the activity of being aware. After a day of training to become Feldenkrais practitioners we were all exhausted, but this was mental rather than physical exhaustion, because the action, the work, involved being aware, and making constant self-correction.

In *Awareness through Movement* Feldenkrais warns that 'the exercises here are intended to reduce effort in movement, for in order to recognize small changes in effort, the effort itself must first be reduced. More delicate and improved control of movement is possible only through the increase of sensitivity, through a greater ability to sense differences'.[35] His lessons thus have a double purpose: apart from enhancing one's efficiency in action it is also about the more subtle development of a sensitivity to this ratio between effort and sensitivity. He makes this clear in a later article: 'in order to be able to tell differences in exertion one must first reduce the exertion. Finer and finer performance is possible only if the *sensitivity* – that is, the ability to *feel* the difference – is improved.'[36] There can be no learning from our doing if we cannot feel the difference between an efficient and a less efficient movement. Even awareness is learned.

Teaching and learning how to learn: Child's play

When Feldenkrais was beginning to develop his ATM teaching he reflected upon what it was that he could pass on to a colleague. He started with the realization that 'no baby is born with the ability to perform adult movements; they have to be learned while growing'.[37] Unlike other animals we have to learn basic motor skills like standing and walking and occasionally we are forced to relearn these skills. Because Feldenkrais had seriously injured his knee playing football he therefore had 'to relearn as an adult that which I had failed to learn better in my past'. This led him to realize that 'learning to learn was the thing I had to share with my colleague'.[38] Feldenkrais argued that there is 'no inherited learning in the human species whatsoever. The "lower" animals have phylogenetic learning, or inherited evolved learning of their species. The "higher" animal learns through his own individual ontogenetic experience.'[39] If the baby has 'few helpful presents from the past which work from the start', they do have 'the most useful trick of all, the ability to form his own tricks'.[40] (Recall his earlier statement about our ability to 'break up total situations of previous experience'[41] and use them to solve novel problems.) This explains why 'individual experience is more important in man than it is in any other animal'.[42] In a word, we learn through experience, constantly 'acquiring new responses to stimuli'.[43] We are not even born with the physical means by which we experience: 'Our nervous system is not born as it is when we are adults. In order to get a system to work as it does in us, the nervous system needs the outside world.'[44] Unlike machines, in the living organism there is no distinction between hardware and software: the nervous system is developed through use.

So, how should we approach our learning in and about the world? Feldenkrais replies that we should develop 'that ability to play while learning the ability to pay attention, without intending to learn; the ability to feel differences; that is, the ability to distinguish between one sensation and another very similar one'.[45] Far from being wilful paradox, this idea is at the heart of the child's heuristic form of learning through discovery. If the child didn't employ such an open and non-directed approach to their early movement experiments, it might possibly not happen upon some of the happy accidents whereby it discovers the progressive mastery of gravity in sitting, crawling, standing and finally walking. I would argue that the ability to play while paying attention is a viable definition of creativity. Feldenkrais declared that because 'learning is the most important thing for a human being', therefore it should be 'a pleasant, marvelous experience'.[46] Trying to learn fast – to get on, to make quick progress – is yet another form of misplaced effort. Feldenkrais explains that slowness 'is necessary for the discovery of parasitic superfluous exertion and its partial elimination. [...] Fast action when learning is strenuous, leads to confusion, and makes the learning unpleasant and tiring'. He continues this reflection by returning to the theme of pleasure and to learning not being about the acquisition of skills, but about the dynamic process of learning:

> In Awareness Through Movement lessons you make the impossible possible, then easy, comfortable, and finally pleasing. I believe it is more important to learn the way to learn new skills than the feat of the skills themselves; the new skill is only a reward for your attention.[47]

Feldenkrais has developed Bernstein's definition of motor skills, but crucial to both men was the insistence that we do not consider training or learning as the acquisition of a series of tricks but rather as the ability to make sense of our sensory experience.

Teaching and learning how to learn: Habit

Bernstein offers a useful definition of habits: 'We control the skill while habits control us.'[48] Feldenkrais's whole philosophy of education was based on helping his students free themselves from their often unrecognized habits. To understand why habits are limiting, let us consider more broadly the purpose of learning. Feldenkrais argues that 'learning that allows further growth of the structures and their functioning is the one that leads to new and different ways of doing things I already know how to do'. Once again we are dealing with variations of how to perform a familiar task. But why bother? Because 'this kind of learning increases my ability to choose more freely. Having only a single mode of action means my choice is limited to simply acting or not acting'.[49] What Feldenkrais describes is a person who has one way of doing; they act automatically, that is, without thinking. To act habitually is to have no choice of how one acts. Where Bernstein simply points to the essential role the sensory nervous system plays in learning a movement skill, Feldenkrais actually explains how this works in practice. In *Awareness through Movement* he states that 'the delay between thought and action is the basis for awareness'.[50] Both he and F.M. Alexander agree that in the moment's delay between intention and action one can focus on how one is going to act. The focus, once again, is not on the 'what' but on the 'how'.

The problem about learning (memorizing) movement is that it only becomes effective when performed without thinking (we don't have to think when we drive, swim or walk). In this sense all learned movement becomes a habit. But Feldenkrais notes that 'the advantage of a habit acquired by awareness is that when it shows unfitness or maladjustment when confronted with reality, it easily provokes new awareness and so helps one to make a fresh and more efficient change'.[51] Is this not precisely the 'adaptability' that Bernstein was writing about? We are dealing with an attitude of mind, a shift from a static to a more dynamic attitude towards act-performing: 'the difficulties involved lie less in the nature of the new habit than in the changing of habits of body, feeling, and mind from their established patterns.' It involves 'a change in the way an act is performed, a change in the whole dynamics, so that the new method will be in every respect as good as the old'.[52]

An example of how we can help another learn comes from psychologist Norman Doidge. He admired how Anat Baniel practised the Feldenkrais Method because she helped children learn from doing rather than setting them tests and exercises. Baniel calls it 'practicing failure', because 'children learn from their experience; they don't necessarily learn what we intend them to'. Instead, using play, she turned on [her student's] 'learning switch'.[53] This is such a useful critique of teaching methods that can often do little more than confirm a learner's sense of their inadequacy (and the teacher's superiority). The student only 'practices failure' because the educational method has failed them. Baniel recognizes that all children, all adults, are programmed to learn, and a good teacher creates the ideal situation for this innate ability to learn.

Knowing oneself as a moving whole – self-image

Finally we turn to what Feldenkrais calls 'self-image', which, like 'mature behavior', is achieved through the exercise of full awareness of ourselves as active social beings. In *Awareness through Movement* he offers a definition of self-image that is close to Bernstein's definition of proprioception. A 'complete self-image', he argues, 'would involve full awareness of all the joints in the skeletal structure as well as of the entire surface of the body'.[54] Indeed, a self-image that is 'complete and uniform with respect to all parts of the body – all sensations, feelings, and thoughts – is an ideal which has been difficult to achieve up to now in man's state of ignorance'.[55] The shape of this definition should by now be familiar. He begins with a purely physical account (keeping close to Bernstein) which then opens out to a more far-reaching concept of education.

Mature Behaviour, like awareness, is something to be learned, and moreover it is an ongoing project that is coterminous with living. Self-image is not purely physical but embraces one's 'appearance, voice, way of thinking, environment, relationship to space and time'. These may well be 'taken for granted as realities born with [oneself], whereas every important element in the individual's relationship to other people and to society in general is the result of extensive training'.[56] As with the nervous system, he stresses that our self-image only develops thanks to our interaction with our external environment. A thing that is 'taken for granted' as a reality is rejected in the same way that he rejects habits or any fixed way of doing, in favour of a dynamic approach to action and living. Thus if we want to 'change our mode of action we must change the image of ourselves that we carry within us. What is involved here, of course, is a change in the dynamics of our reactions, and not the mere replacing of one action by another'.[57] He explains that for an exercise to 'produce the development and clarification of the self-image', one must concentrate on

(1) each part of the action itself,
(2) what is felt during the action,
(3) the total body image, and the effect of the action on the body image.

Only with this constant surveillance and reassessment can one progress to new actions, orientations and adjustments.[58]

This is such a marvellous X-ray of how any training exercise should be conducted. The focus shifts from analysis of the movement itself, to feedback from the movement, to how it affects us personally.

Alan Questel, both an actor trainer and a Feldenkrais practitioner, connects this work on sensitivity with the actor's presence. He observes that 'the ability to fill a space so that an actor is seen and heard by the audience and other actors comes naturally to some, but can be developed by all of us. Through the Feldenkrais Method, we can learn to more fully inhabit ourselves in a sensory way'. Questel's notion that actors can learn to 'fully inhabit' themselves 'in a sensory way' brings together the notions of sensing and inhabiting. To explain such 'sensory inhabiting' he claims that 'in doing the Feldenkrais Method, we are practicing our sensations' which involves taking time to 'quietly listen to what we feel and to let the sensation of some of the more unknown parts of ourselves slowly emerge. This results in the ability to feel ourselves more, while expanding our self-image'.[59] The phrase 'we are practicing our sensations' articulates perfectly what I mean by sensitivity being an active state that can be developed through training.

Feldenkrais and actor training: Case studies

Clive Barker's *Theatre Games* (2010) contains a wealth of references to Feldenkrais, including his definition of intelligent movement:

(i) that the proper posture of the body is such that it can initiate movement in any direction with the same ease;

(ii) that it can start any movement without a preliminary adjustment;

(iii) that the movement is performed with the minimum of work, i.e. with the maximum of efficiency.[60]

Apart from being central to Barker's concept of actor movement, this could also serve as a gloss on Brook's experiment with the National Theatre audience in 1993. Barker's notion of stance and gravity owed an immense amount to Feldenkrais.

The greater connection between Feldenkrais and Barker is their pedagogy. He prefers to do first and talk after:

> I would never, for instance, expose the basic principles on which the work is based before I started on it. In practice, these principles are revealed only as the actor works through various stages. [...] If an actor is told in advance what the purpose of an exercise is, this knowledge might push him towards doing the exercise, 'properly' or 'well' or 'efficiently' as an end in itself, and this would interfere with the experience and sensations that are encountered in simply 'trying' it. His concentration would be on the end result, instead of on the process or means, which could defeat everything I am trying to do.[61]

This could easily have been written by Feldenkrais. Throughout our training we were told not to try and guess the (end-) point of the lesson but to focus on our present sensations. In this way Barker's theatre games are 'situations' in which an actor can learn.

> In this sense the games in this book are used as parables. They are images of action, through which general principles and laws are transformed into living sensations of cause and effect, which make the processes involved easier to understand.[62]

If there is no reference in *Theatre Games* to Feldenkrais's pedagogy, it is because only *Body and Mature Behaviour* (first published in 1949) was available when he was writing. At that stage in Feldenkrais's career he had not yet developed his ATM lessons. Even more extraordinary then that Barker's approach to experiential learning is so close to that of Feldenkrais. Both theatre games and ATM lessons are structured movement experiences by which the student can engage in active and autonomous learning through doing (with awareness). As Barker notes, 'One cannot teach "acting". One can only create situations in which the actor can learn and develop.'[63]

> The object of the games and exercises is to reveal to the actor what happens when he works, and to help him be aware of the mind/body processes involved in his work. What use he then makes of this understanding is up to him. One can never predict what value any individual will get or take from any exercise. One should never try to make an exercise or game 'work'; one should set it up and let it take place.[64]

Earlier he had warned students against trying to second guess the point of an exercise; this time his advice is addressed to teachers. A theatre game has a structure but not a fixed content – that is the responsibility of the individual players. It is thanks to Barker (with whom I worked for some twenty years) that I arrived at the realization that a game or exercise is (or should be) an empty structure, a point made throughout my *Training the Actor's Body* (2018).[65]

Many of Feldenkrais's lessons take place on the floor where one rediscovers an infant's acts of autonomous learning-through-finding-out. Similarly, Barker's games are an example of a child's 'process of learning through experimentation'.[66] He goes on, 'One goes back to the root processes of learning, by which he acquired movement skills in the first place, and this helps him rediscover lost skills, or those which have atrophied. … It substitutes for the pain of learning the joy of re-discovery.'[67] What characterizes both men's account of child learning was that it was self-directed and rooted in the child's own experience. Their approach was *heuristic* – i.e. about the student finding out for themselves, rather than being told.

> The keynote to all the work is that it is *a process of exploration and discovery*, not the direct acquisition of practical skills which the actor does not possess. The acquisition of skills is the by-product of the work.[68]

Barker's actor training is about building confidence and engendering a spirit of enquiry through taking away hang-ups and resistances, a training where the actor is given autonomy. This feeds into his vision of a theatre where 'the actor is the theatre, and the sooner we give it back to him the better.'[69] In a sense, the actor is the model of mature behaviour.

Peter Brook organized an eight-week workshop by Feldenkrais in February 1978. He explains why:

> The very basis of every actor's work is their own body – nothing is more concrete. During the experiments we have made at the International Centre for Theatrical Research we have had occasion to study various techniques which focus on the development of the actor's body, sometimes through dance, sometimes gymnastics, sometimes again through the practice of the martial arts; and it is thus that I have come to know Moshe Feldenkrais.[70]

Brook has elegantly described a whole culture of practical theatre research that was common in the 1970s through until the late 1990s when public funding began to diminish.

In a Platform Talk in November 1993 at the National Theatre he returned to the question of actor training, but declined to define what he meant by the word 'training' until the audience had taken part in a practical experiment. Already this constitutes an important pedagogical point: he chose to begin with experiential learning and then move on to discursive learning, or as he put it: 'I favour doing first and talking second.' He then gave this instruction:

> When I give you a signal, I would ask everyone to stand up, wait for a moment, then sit down together. [The audience does so]
>
> Right, everyone has now performed a simple action. There is one question. Can what you just did be improved upon or not? Have we already reached the ultimate level of perfection together?[71]

He assures them that since 'it isn't the case, let's begin to work'. He offers two ways in which the audience could stand and sit at the same time: the first 'would be the sergeant major technique, which is to say to you "Now, all together, rise to your feet, count together – one, two, three – then sit down'". Of course the audience/student learns nothing other than how to act on command. So, he offers 'another way which can lead to something quite different'. First he advises them to 'adjust' themselves 'so that you're ready without any waste of energy to be able to get up'. Without labouring the point, he returns us to readiness and Feldenkrais's principle of good organization. Next he turns to peripheral vision: 'However you're sitting, bring into your field of vision as many people as possible on either side. Know that you can feel the people around you.' His third instruction is to 'listen'. He asks the audience to listen to each other once they have all stood up together and then sit down after a pause. 'We won't say how long the pause has to be, but there is just one natural pause. Let's see if we can find a natural timing instinctively, all together, without a leader.'[72] This sense of ensemble is felt through an appreciation of rhythm.

The action is repeated and he exclaims:

Watching you, I assure you that was better than the first time. If we did this for even twenty minutes, it would be astonishing to see how it's possible for a large number of people to become more sensitive, more alert, more perceptive to one another than when they started, just by each person making a very special effort himself.

In a few sentences, in an exercise lasting probably about five minutes, Brook has summed up his approach to actor training, and one which I would argue reveals a considerable debt to Feldenkrais in its attention to awareness and feeling, rather than simply doing. After the audience had felt what it is to perform a simple action with awareness, they were 'more sensitive, more alert, more perceptive to one another than when they started'. This led to his definition of actor training.

Brook argues that training is not to make a 'cleverer or a better actor, or a better athlete or dancer. It's to make a group more sensitive to itself. Something quite different. When one does exercises, it isn't to make people more powerfully skillful, it's to make everybody from the start quite simply more sensitive. Once a group becomes more sensitive, each person feels the reward'.[73] Brook's point is that training is not only a question of tuning yourself (as an instrument), but developing a facility for tuning into what others are doing, and how they are doing it.

The final example of Feldenkrais influencing a leading practitioner is Kristin Linklater's account of a workshop he led in October 1971.[74] Linklater offers the perspective of one master-teacher on the pedagogical strategy of another. I shall focus more on her experience than on the detail of the lesson itself. Suffice it to say the lesson is performed standing, and involved shifting the weight onto the left leg while caressing the outside of the thigh of the right leg. As the hand reaches down you rest the right leg on the ball of the right foot while bending the right knee lifting the right heel. As the hand comes up, you lower the heel and straighten the knee. This is the basic structure of the exercise, the gauge being the ever-lower reach of the hand down the right leg. But this increase of reach was not the stated aim, nor were the students ever encouraged to try to reach 'lower than was comfortable'; indeed she noted how 'there was to be no stretching, reaching or trying'. Moreover no 'guidelines were given on what we should feel – nothing was labelled "right" or "wrong"'. It is precisely instructions like this that helped her to combat the 'urge to push and strain for what I thought was the aim of the exercise. So automatic is goal-oriented work that one doesn't recognize effort, as such, until led to a heightened state of awareness where subtle energy differences can be perceived'.

Rather than focusing on effort, on trying to succeed, the emphasis was on ease. When Feldenkrais asked whether she and the other students were holding back any part of the body that might participate in the action, she realized she 'was stiff in her waist', and after letting go of those muscles she was holding, 'the top of my body began to go with the rocking [...] so that I was caressing an area down to my knee – comfortably and pleasantly'.

Another aspect of the lesson's structure were the frequent periods of walking around the room to feel how the sensations developing in the right side of the body differed from the left. Once again, there was no indication of what they should feel, just an invitation to feel. By the end she could touch the floor with the palms of her hands and her legs straight 'without strain' – something she had never been able to do. After the lesson she experienced an extraordinary sense of lightness in the torso, ease in the legs and a balanced alignment through the ribcage and shoulders. 'Because there were contrasting sensations in each side, my physical awareness increased. What had happened in the course of 30 to 40 minutes was that our back muscles had slowly released while our attention was elsewhere.'

She then realized Feldenkrais's genius as a teacher, for 'while the focus was on the hand and leg, the back was decontracting and limbering'. And all this was achieved through a focus on learning through feeling, through letting go rather than trying to do.

Notes

1 Carl Ginsburg, 'Bernstein and Feldenkrais: The Fathers of Movement Science', *The Feldenkrais Journal*, No. 12 (1998), 49.
2 Ginsburg, 'Bernstein and Feldenkrais', 49.
3 Mark Reece, *Moshe Feldenkrais: A Life in Movement* (San Rafael, CA: ReeseKress Somatics Press, 2015), 183.
4 Mark Latash, 'A New Book by Nikolai Bernstein', *Motor Control*, Vol. 10, No. 1 (January 2006), 1. (Downloaded from http://journals.humankinetics.com on 19 December 2017).
5 Ginsburg, 'Bernstein and Feldenkrais', 49.
6 Nikolai Bernstein, *Dexterity and Its Development*, ed. Mark Latash, Michael Turvey (New York: Psychology Press, 1996), 181.
7 Ginsburg, 'Bernstein and Feldenkrais', 49.
8 Eric Kandel, *In Search of Memory* (New York and London: Norton, 2007), 65.
9 Bernstein, *Dexterity and Its Development*, 171.
10 Bernstein, *Dexterity and Its Development*, 38–9.
11 Latash, 'The Bernstein Problem: How Does the Central Nervous System Make Its Choice?' in N. Bernstein, *Dexterity and Its Development*, ed. Mark Latash and Michael Turvey (New York: Psychology Press, 1996), 280–1.
12 Bernstein, *Dexterity and Its Development*, 180.
13 Bernstein, *Dexterity and Its Development*, 184.
14 Bernstein, *Dexterity and Its Development*, 181.
15 Bernstein, *Dexterity and Its Development*, 53.

16 Bernstein, *Dexterity and Its Development*, 181.
17 Bernstein, *Dexterity and Its Development*, 43.
18 Bernstein, *Dexterity and Its Development*, 43.
19 Bernstein, *Dexterity and Its Development*, 176.
20 Bernstein, *Dexterity and Its Development*, 177.
21 Bernstein, *Dexterity and Its Development*, 204–5.
22 Reece, *Moshe Feldenkrais*, 74.
23 Feldenkrais, *Embodied Wisdom*, 58.
24 Gilbert Ryle, *The Concept of Mind* (Harmondsworth: Penguin, 1963), 29.
25 Moshe Feldenkrais, *The Case of Nora* (Berkeley, CA: Somatic Resources and Frog, 1977), xiii–xiv.
26 Feldenkrais, *Embodied Wisdom*, 67.
27 Feldenkrais, *The Case of Nora*, 22.
28 Feldenkrais, *Awareness through Movement*, 36–7.
29 Feldenkrais, *Awareness through Movement*, 50.
30 Feldenkrais, *The Elusive Obvious*, 95.
31 Feldenkrais, *Embodied Wisdom*, 80.
32 Feldenkrais, *The Elusive Obvious*, 96.
33 Feldenkrais, *Embodied Wisdom*, 174.
34 Carl Ginsburg, *The Intelligence of Moving Bodies* (Santa Fe, NM: AWAREing Press, 2010), 15.
35 Feldenkrais, *Awareness through Movement*, 59.
36 Feldenkrais, *Embodied Wisdom*, 37.
37 Feldenkrais, *The Elusive Obvious*, 91.
38 Feldenkrais, *The Elusive Obvious*, 91.
39 Feldenkrais, *The Elusive Obvious*, 24.
40 Feldenkrais, *The Elusive Obvious*, 81.
41 Moshe Feldenkrais, *Body and Mature Behaviour* (Berkeley CA: Frog Books, 2005), 146–7.
42 Feldenkrais, *Body and Mature Behaviour*, 39.
43 Feldenkrais, *Body and Mature Behaviour*, 38.
44 Feldenkrais, *Embodied Wisdom*, 55.
45 Feldenkrais, *The Case of Nora*, 27.
46 Feldenkrais, *Embodied Wisdom*, 185–6.
47 Feldenkrais, *The Elusive Obvious*, 92.
48 Bernstein, *Dexterity and Its Development*, 188.
49 Feldenkrais, *The Elusive Obvious*, 35.
50 Feldenkrais, *Awareness through Movement*, 45.
51 Feldenkrais, *Embodied Wisdom*, 34.
52 Feldenkrais, *Awareness through Movement*, 20.
53 Norman Doidge, *The Brain's Way of Healing* (London: Allen Lane, 2015), 193–4.
54 Feldenkrais, *Awareness through Movement*, 21.
55 Feldenkrais, *Awareness through Movement*, 155.
56 Feldenkrais, *Awareness through Movement*, 20.

57 Feldenkrais, *Awareness through Movement*, 10.
58 Feldenkrais, *Embodied Wisdom*, 102–3.
59 In Nicole Potter (ed.), *Movement for Actors* (New York: Allworth Press, 2012), 59.
60 Clive Barker, *Theatre Games*, 2nd edn. (London: Methuen, 2010), 32.
61 Barker, *Theatre Games*, 8–9.
62 Barker, *Theatre Games*, 9.
63 Barker, *Theatre Games*, 6.
64 Barker, *Theatre Games*, 51.
65 McCaw, *Training the Actor's Body* (London: Methuen, 2018), xvi, 61, 238.
66 Barker, *Theatre Games*, 63.
67 Barker, *Theatre Games*, 64.
68 Barker, *Theatre Games*, 51.
69 Barker, *Theatre Games*, 211.
70 Letter in the archives of The Bouffes du Nord, Paris.
71 Peter Brook, 'On Actor Training', in *Platform Papers 6* (London: National Theatre, 1994), 6.
72 Brook, 'On Actor Training', 7.
73 Brook, 'On Actor Training', 7.
74 Kristin Linklater, 'The Body Training of Moshe Feldenkrais', *The Drama Review: TDR*, Vol.16, No.1 (March 1972), 23–7.

PART II
FROM SCIENCE INTO CREATIVE PRACTICE

CHAPTER 4
THE WORK OF DR MOSHE FELDENKRAIS: A NEW APPLIED KINESIOLOGY AND A RADICAL QUESTIONING OF TRAINING AND TECHNIQUE
Maxine Sheets-Johnstone

At the first evening session of a weekend workshop given by Dr Moshe Feldenkrais, mention was made of the tonic neck and righting reflexes.[1] Before the first evening session ended, Dr Feldenkrais asked us to remember what he had said of those reflexes. Surprisingly enough, the following morning, he asked us to forget them, to concentrate in all seriousness upon obliterating the memory of them.

How does one go about 'voluntary forgetting'? More importantly, what happens when one tries to forget? What happens is that the thing to be forgotten clings ever more tenaciously to one's thoughts. In the process of trying to forget, remembrance becomes all the stronger and more vivid.

One of the most striking aspects of Dr Feldenkrais's work is the arrival at individual capacities in movement by means precisely contrary to common sense or to habitual modes of doing. Common sense would impel us to pinpoint attention on the thing in order to remember it; likewise certain personal habits of doing would regulate our attempts to remember. The one thousand plus movement techniques which Dr Feldenkrais has devised to increase bodily freedom all run counter to common practice, common sense and/or habitual modes of doing. In the traditional technique class, one stretches, pulling and reaching arms, legs, torso, head, now in this direction, now in that, all to effect an increased flexibility. Only by going beyond the natural or comfortable does an increase in range develop – or so we read, think and do.[2] Any one of the Feldenkrais techniques results in a dramatic increase in range of movement all the while staying within the bounds of what is easy and what is comfortable. It is for this reason that the techniques at times appear magical: one has barely done anything at all, and yet, here one is rotating in the torso 270 degrees or touching one's knees to one's forehead or achieving a greater outward rotation in the legs, and so on. The effects appear magical because the means are virtually effortless.

There is another striking aspect of Dr Feldenkrais's work which should be singled out insofar as it too runs contrary to traditional practice and oftentimes yields the same magical effect. We commonly think of the range of movement in any part of the body as being controlled wholly by the particular muscles which move that part of the body.[3] Hence the localization of movement and the development and practice of movement patterns which isolate certain body parts. If greater range is desired in the hip joint, flexion and extension of the hip joint is practised; if greater flexibility in the shoulder girdle is desired, movement patterns are practised which utilize muscles of the shoulder girdle. In other words, in traditional technique classes one always works directly with the body part in which greater freedom of movement is desired. In any one of Dr Feldenkrais's techniques, on the contrary, one works from time to time with parts of the body which are seemingly unrelated to the part focused on or at most indirectly related. For example, in a technique centring upon the mobility of the spine and hip joint, movement patterns involving the head and eyes are performed. When one returns to the rotatory movement and the extension of the hip joint, one finds an increased range which indeed seems miraculous. Why should movement patterns of the head and eyes increase the degree of freedom of movement in the spine and hip joint? Magic aside, Feldenkrais's work is a living testimonial that the body always moves as a whole and that all body parts are involved in any localization. If no one part moves in true isolation from any other part, then each part must either hinder or enhance the freedom of movement in all other parts.

Prior to considering in more detail the procedural and theoretical substance of Dr Feldenkrais's work, two final features should be noted which again are in remarkable contrast to traditional technique classes. To begin with, Feldenkrais classes include a good number of rest periods. After doing a specific movement pattern several times, one is told to lie down and rest for a few minutes. Combined with the effortless doing mentioned previously, these rest periods might seem puzzling indeed: not only does one expend minimal effort, moving easily and comfortably, one is also given time to recover from one's virtual non-expenditure of energy. In relation to the pace and intensity of a traditional technique class or training programme, such goings-on might seem worthless and perhaps self-indulgent, at least at first glance or to those who have not experienced a Feldenkrais class. Yet something is going on during those rest periods in the way of learning and more will be said of this when we consider the theoretical substance of Feldenkrais's work. For the moment it is enough to note the rest period as a most uncommon departure from ordinary classes in physical activity.

A more radical departure is evident in the use of motor imagery and the startling results achieved through it. After working on one side of the body, work on the other side may consist of nothing more than imagining oneself going through the same motor patterns done on the original side. Expressions of wonder can be heard through a class when people discover that their range of movement is increased merely by imagining themselves going through certain movement sequences. While the use of motor imagery may not be uncommon in technique or training programmes, it has certainly not been utilized in this way.[4] Common sense would lead us to believe that it is only by actually stretching that one can develop a greater range of movement.

Taken singly or as a whole, the four features described above attest to the utter novelty of Feldenkrais's work. I have contrasted his work with traditional technique classes because I want to suggest that a revision, indeed a revolution, is needed in the teaching of dance technique, particularly insofar as bodily freedom is concerned and particularly insofar as traditional classes in technique are neither individualized nor efficient. Within the traditional technique class, all people, regardless of their peculiar limitations, are made to do the same patterns and sequences of movement. Rather than being given specific techniques dealing with those limitations they are literally put in the position of magnifying them. A case in point is the classical second position sitting posture from which base certain stretching patterns are performed. I am sure that you as well as I have seen innumerable people who cannot at the same time maintain an erect spine and extended knees in that position. The bounces or stretch patterns which they perform from this already impossible position do no more than exacerbate their condition. Moreover the daily stretching required to maintain a greater range of movement is not efficient, the greater range of movement being assured only by daily practice.[5] There are, in other words, no long-range effects. One may reasonably question whether this is so because what is done bypasses neuro-physical learning, that is, it effects no change in the neuro-muscular organization of the body. As a means of gaining greater range of movement, traditional stretching techniques must be recognized as highly inefficient. To be sure, the Feldenkrais techniques do not produce instant change, but there is no doubt that long-term effects are attained, judging both from my own experience and the experiences of others whom I have interviewed. Certainly one of the reasons for these long-range effects is related not only to a different kind of doing but to a heightened and totally different kind of awareness, a central aspect of Dr Feldenkrais's work which we will discuss presently.

As prelude to that discussion, let us consider the principal procedural facets of Dr Feldenkrais's work. First and foremost, attention is directed to what one is doing and not upon what is to be done. There is no end result to be accomplished which is described or demonstrated in advance. This is in part because there is no model whom one is trying to emulate. If there is no model, there is no end product in the form of a desired and demonstrated 'doingness' or a desired and demonstrated standard of execution. On the contrary, each person is his or her own model; each person progressively discovers new points of arrival for himself or herself, new individual norms of bodily freedom. But it is also in part because there is no end to begin with in the sense of a goal to be achieved, a feat to be accomplished. There is only the here and now of what one is doing and that particular doing carries with it no unusual effort; what is already easily and comfortably accomplished cannot be a goal, for it is already actualized, not something to be attained in the future. Because there is no model and because no verbal description is given of a position to be arrived at, there is nothing that the individual is trying to attain or focused upon achieving. In essence this means that the individual is not judging himself or herself in relation to a norm or standard of execution and neither is the individual striving to accomplish something, exerting himself or herself towards some accomplishment.

So far as everyday action is concerned, human intentionality is commonly directed towards the future: crossing the street, opening the mailbox, hammering the nail, and by extension, kicking the ball over the goal post, touching the floor with one's fingertips, arriving at certain positions at certain times within a stretch sequence, and so on. Movement is commonly directed to a 'where-I-am-not-yet'. Awareness as such is not on movement per se nor yet on the body since both body and movement aim towards a future and are thus only horizontally present in awareness.[6] It is the intention to achieve something which projects the person into the future and consumes his or her attention. In contrast, when awareness is upon what one is doing and not upon something to be done, one may be directly aware of body movement, directly aware of a here-now-happening.

A further essential feature of the procedure is that one always begins with a small range of movement, a range which is easy and comfortable, which demands no unusual or extraordinary effort. As the lesson proceeds, that initial range is expanded, not through striving or effort, but as the result of repeating, several times over, a variety of movement patterns involving various parts of the body. These movement patterns are also performed within the limits of what is comfortable and easy to the individual. Coupled with the fact that there is no goal, no end product which one is trying to achieve, the small range of movement creates a doubly significant situation: one becomes acutely aware of what one is doing and at the same time makes no preparation in order to do it. Normally if we see an end product or if an end product is described to us, when we set about to do it ourselves, we gird ourselves in whatever way is habitual to us in order to accomplish it. To take a simple example, if told to stand up, people will not uncommonly prepare for that motion by contracting the muscles of the thigh and digging their feet into the floor, an exertion which, though habitual, is a totally unnecessary preparation.[7] By focusing attention on what we are doing rather than on what is to be done, we learn to discriminate between what is efficient and easy and what is wasteful and strained. A small range of movement allows us an opportunity to notice what is going on to the end that voluntary movement is indeed voluntary: we discriminate and we choose.[8] By the same token, in bypassing the habitual, one reaches one's maximum range in any technique in an entirely new way. That maximal range often comes as an astonishing surprise to the person. If someone had asked the person to stretch that far, the response would have been 'Impossible!' Yet here he or she is touching knees to forehead easily and comfortably. The person has truly discovered something and entirely on his or her own. To the extent that one discovers what has always been potentially present but unrealized, Feldenkrais's Method might be described as maieutic or socratic, Feldenkrais playing the part of a corporeal rather than conceptual midwife.

Crucial to this process of developing awareness, of bringing to light the ways of the body, are the rest periods mentioned earlier. These brief periods are not for idle reverie any more than they are for recuperation. They are periods for discriminating change. For example, prior to doing any movement patterns, and while lying in a supine position, one is asked to direct attention to various appearances of that position, perhaps the pressure of the heels on the floor, and so on. After doing several movement patterns, one is asked to return to that initial supine position and to rest. One might discover, for example, that the lumbar spine is now flatter against the floor, that the right leg is turned out further than the left, or that one side of the body is heavier than the other. During these rest periods it is not uncommon to experience the body as being of a peculiarly unusual, even distorted shape. What is interesting about these experiences is that they are not descriptive of the way I imagine my body to be, but of the way I am and feel as a body: I do not feel as if my right leg were longer than my left or as if my neck were three times longer than usual; my right leg is longer and my neck is three times longer than usual. One might speculate whether such spontaneous distortions of the felt body are modifications at the experiential level of a beginning process of neuro-muscular re-organization and of a beginning process of re-organization of the bodily schema consequent to the previously experienced and wholly novel movement patterns one has just completed. Such a speculation might not be unrelated to the theory that dreams are the body's way of organizing experiences of the previous day. Speculation aside, the point of noticing and discriminating change is, of course, learning.

What I would like to do is consider Feldenkrais's work within the larger framework of motor learning, yet not in terms of tests and measurements of performance, conditioning, modifications of behaviour and the like, but, rather, by describing the possible ways in which we can be aware of our bodies or of our bodies in movement. Possibilities of awareness disclose themselves in answer to the question 'where is attention directed in moving?', and by extension, 'where might it be directed in the act of moving?' It should be noted that examples given in illustration are not intended as absolute characterizations but as possibilities of awareness within the given context. A brief descriptive analysis of these possibilities should allow us insight into what must be considered the very foundation of motor learning, namely the immediate and direct experience we have of our bodies in any movement situation. To affirm that what we learn is bound to the 'what' of our awareness is to affirm something both trite and profound, something assumed and taken for granted and at the same time something far from articulated within the body of knowledge called motor learning.

Mention was made earlier of goal-directed movement, of situations in which a person aims at a future, a 'where-I-am-not-yet'. Someone running in a race or jogging on a cold winter day might experience his body in precisely this way. Perhaps also, the pole-vaulter experiences his or her accelerating run and air-borne flight as such a projection into a future, to a moment of clearance or to a peak and momentary suspension. Whenever a goal is charted, whenever a particular performance is to be accomplished, awareness may be wholly directed towards the feat to be achieved or to the task to be done. Both body and movement, as noted earlier, are only horizontally present within the situation, horizontal to the task to be performed. What is central to awareness is the accomplishments, a closing of the distance that separates me from my goal.

A related but totally different kind of awareness is best exemplified in learning situations wherein an accomplishment of some order is progressively pursued, where concentration is on parts which will ultimately build to a whole, and where the body is consequently experienced as a series of 'nows'. Awareness is not towards a 'where-I-am-not-yet', but of a 'here I am', 'here I am', 'here I am' and so on; in other words, of a series of precise positions, each meted out sequentially but separately in its own time. Thus, for example, the sequence 'step, together, step, hop'. My awareness focuses upon establishing myself positionally, now 'here', now 'here', such that the movement by which the points are connected is something of which I am only horizontally aware. Because I have not yet grasped the movement pattern, that is, a whole in which all of the parts are felt coherently, one position can make no claim on the next. I must continually affirm my presence anew. Corrections in such situations are in fact oftentimes a verbal or manual 'not here but here'. It is only after I have learned the parts and only as those parts begin to exist as a singular sequence for me that I have the possibility of experiencing my body as a dynamic rather than a static presence.

To be aware of the body as a dynamic presence is to be aware of the feel of movement, its peculiar qualitative flow. Such awareness is geared neither to a future nor to a series of 'nows', but exists in a different spatio-temporal order, an order in which neither time nor space has objective determination; past, present and future dissolve in the flow, in the ongoing and continuous pulsation of energy. To be conscious solely of the feel of movement is to be one with the movement: body and movement are non-differentiated. The intention is not to be nor to affirm oneself somewhere but to give oneself over to the qualitative feel of movement, to be caught up in the flow, to feel its surges, its diffusions, its wanings, its accelerations and so on. Such an awareness may be the domain not only of the dancer but of the gymnast, the diver and even the Sunday golfer as well.

In many training and technique programmes, awareness of the body in the act of moving is frequently geared towards control and/or evaluation of the body's performance. In the execution of a certain movement or skill, a tennis serve, for example, or a series of leaps, attention is focused on steering the body in motion, on directing it through the specific sequence. In such an awareness the body figures both as something to be moved and as something moving, but in such a way that we experience it from the viewpoint of an observer. In order to control or assay our performance in the very act of performance we must take a third person stance in relation to our own body. By adopting such a stance we are able to steer it along the appointed paths with the requisite force and timing. Judgements, our own or of others, teach us to correct this or that action and in effect, we not only learn how to do certain movements, but we also learn about the body. The objective stance which allows us to direct and to judge our performance in the very act of performing teaches us how the body as a system of externally related parts may be moved and how in controlling its movement we can accomplish certain skills. Since the experience is always that of an outside observer, one controls or judges the experience of body movement at the price of having it. The having of the experience is put off until the skill is learned and the performance judged adequate.

What distinguishes Dr Feldenkrais's classes is an insistence upon and a commitment to a totally different kind of awareness, an awareness of the body which is not goal directed, which is anchored in neither a static nor a dynamic presence of the body, and which is not either directed towards controlling the body moving it along appointed paths. To be aware is simply to listen, to notice, to pay attention. In listening, in noticing, in paying attention, we reach not only the lived but the 'unlived lines of our bodies'. We embark on a journey in which we progressively map the whole of our bodies, our moving selves, and in this sense ultimately reforge our body image:[9] we expand our send of 'I can do'. We refine the 'I can', and we vitalize the 'I'. What is learned as a result of this awareness is obviously not a repertoire of movement skills. In this respect, Straus's distinction between learning movement and learning to move ourselves is extremely significant.[10] In the same way that a child does not learn a movement, 'standing up', but rather learns to move himself or herself, so with the Feldenkrais technique, one does not learn movements but learns how to move himself or herself. Straus's distinction, however, may be amplified insofar as bodily awareness is concerned: in any Feldenkrais class, one is not learning about the body, one is learning the body directly; one is in touch with the source itself, learning the ways of the body from the master teacher. What needs to be emphasized is that this learning is not done from the standpoint of a third person observer; one is not watching oneself, attending to the proceedings at a distance; what one is experiencing immediately and directly is oneself. One has the experience and it is only on the basis of having that experience that one is able to discriminate and notice change.

If that we learn is indeed bound to the 'what' of our awareness, it is evident that each of the possible modes of awareness is effective of a different kind of learning and of a different thing learned.[11] When it was suggested earlier that a revolution in dance technique and training programmes was vital, it was not meant to disparage the whole affair. Each mode of awareness is what it is. On the other hand, in conception and in practice, movement programmes are by and large a layering of one skill upon the next, the emphasis being upon greater and greater heights of accomplishment. Seldom if ever are the foundations of the ever-ascending structure examined. To examine these foundations is to gain insight into the very grounds of all our accomplishments: it is to learn the ways of our bodies, a pristine learning to be sure, but one no less rich in wisdom. It is indeed radical to suggest that we reverse the order of our usual preoccupations with the body and with body movement, that instead of inspecting the body and holding it up to the light, instead of controlling it or keeping it on the horizons of our awareness, that within technique and training programmes we listen to that pristine source and hear first-hand and fully all the body has to tell us.

Notes

1. Novato Institute for Somatic Research and Training, Novato, California, 6–7 August 1976. This paper was first presented for The Association for Research, Administration, Professional Councils and Societies' Symposium. American Alliance for Health, Physical Education and Recreation Convention, Seattle, Washington, in March 1977.

2. See for example Philip J. Rasch and R.K. Burke, *Kinesiology and Applied Anatomy* (Philadelphia, PA: Lea & Febiger, 1974), 439: 'Flexibility may be gained by any exercise that forces the point beyond the range of motion in which it has been adapted, whether this exercise be passive, assistive, or resistive', or Charles B. Corbin, *Becoming Physically Educated in the Elementary School* (Philadelphia, PA: Lea & Febiger, 1969), 21: 'If flexibility is the objective, the muscles must be stretched more than normal', or Gertrude Shurr and Rachael Dunaven Yocum, *Modern Dance Technique and Teaching* (New York: Ronald Press Co., 1949), where illustrations of flexibility exercises show standards of flexibility 'for all dance conditioning'; or James Penrod, *Movement for the Performing Artist* (Palo Alto, CA: National Press Books, 1974), 84: 'Only straighten the legs to the point where there is minimum discomfort.'

3. Evidence for this conception and practice is given in the very idea of applying kinesiologic forces to increase flexibility. See for example Katherine Wells, *Kinesiology* (Philadelphia, PA: W.G. Saunders, 1971), 387. These forces are applied or utilized in respect to a specific joint, that is, the one for which an increase in range of movement is desired.

4. Motor imagery is used in various ways to improve performance, not to increase range of movement. Studies concerned with the use of motor imagery or with mental practice are concerned with whether, when and to what degree the imagery or practice influences the learning and/or the execution of certain skills. See John Drowatsky, *Motor Learning* (Minneapolis, MN: Burgess Publishing, 1975), 219–23.

5. After noting that flexibility exercises done three times a week for 10 minutes for six months only slightly increased the range of movement in the hip joint and that after one month's rest the increased range was lost, J.W. Postman writes, 'Apparently, therefore, no anatomical changes took place in the joints, nor was there any lengthening of the muscles. Presumable a real increase in suppleness can take place if the exercises are done daily and continue over a long period, as for example, ballet dancers do when they want to learn the split.' *Introduction to the Theory of Physical Education* (Cape Town: A.A. Balkerman, 1968), 224.

6. The concept of horizons of awareness is a phenomenological one originating with Husserl. See in particular his books *Cartesian Meditations* and *Ideas Pertaining to a Pure Phenomenology and to a Phenomenological Philosophy, Second Book (Ideas II)* on the subject of 'horizons'. See his Cartesian Meditation or Ideas. See also Ernest Jolk in Drowtasky's *Motor Learning*, 261: 'At any given time there is but one focal doing which presented the keypiece of the performance to which all other motor events are subordinate.'

7. Feldenkrais, *Awareness through Movement* (New York: Harper & Row, 1972), 78–80.

8. Feldenkrais, *Awareness through Movement*, 59: ' … to reduce effort in movement … the effort itself must first be reduced. More delicate and improved control of movement is possible only through the increase of sensitivity, through a greater ability to sense differences.'

9   The concept of body image used here is the phenomenological one developed by Maurice Merleau-Ponty. See his *Phenomenology of Perception* (New York: The Humanities Press, 1974), particularly the chapter on the spatiality of the body. See also Jolk in Drowtasky's *Motor Learning*, 266: 'If I have failed to acquire skills I am restricted in respect to the actions I can take in my environment.'

10 E.W. Straus, *Phenomenological Psychology* (New York: Basic Books, 1966), 53.

11 There are, as Merleau-Ponty has written, 'several ways for the body to be a body'. *Phenomenology of Perception*, 124.

CHAPTER 5
RADICAL PRACTICE: PRACTISING PERFORMANCE AND PRACTISING ONESELF IS THE SAME ACTIVITY
Roger Russell

Our embodiment is the ultimate source … of how we know [that] … in the development of thought, doing is prior to understanding.[1]

Introduction

The development of coordination is the foundation of artistic skill. Considered from a lifespan perspective, artistic training has two phases. First, there is the young artist's own self-discovery in infancy and early childhood. The second phase emerges when a young person has shown some 'talent' and makes a commitment to a training regimen, often focused on specific modes of expression in music, dance, theatre or the fine arts. Complete absorption and effortful repetition are often regarded as professional virtues in this second phase of the artist's developmental process. My professional experience has shown that the first phase contains a hidden resource that can make the second phase more rewarding.

Every artist was an infant, exploring their own body. This was literally *self-discovery*. Movement experience is at the core of this sense of self. This early self-discovery is a deep resource. It can be drawn on to enhance artistic performance throughout life. By exploring the discovery and learning process of infancy and early childhood, a learning process categorically different from the idea of 'no pain, no gain' becomes available. This kind of learning challenges almost every belief concerning what practice is and how it should be done. I will address how the Feldenkrais Method provides a learning process for performing artists to refine their professional skills by understanding, embracing and enhancing this kinaesthetic core of their lives.[2] This task will be approached through three central ideas:

- The importance of the kinaesthetic foundations of the sense of self, leading to
- A radical rethinking of how we practice, and
- How attentive practice to improve skill can reorder the kinaesthetic sense of self.

Framing the issues

In his recent book *Embodied Mind, Meaning and Reason – How Our Bodies Give Rise to Understanding*, the philosopher Mark Johnson writes:

This book develops an argument for the central importance of our bodies in everything we experience, mean, think, say, value and do …. it argues that we will not understand any of the issues that are so dear to philosophy until we have a deep and detailed understanding of how our embodiment gives rise to experience, meaning and thought.[3]

Why only an argument? Why not also a practice which offers concrete, embodied experience. Shouldn't one argue for a form of mutual engagement between thinking and acting? Following Husserl's suggestion that 'the only way to check your definition is to experience an act – you have to jump in there feet first and experience it yourself';[4] such a practice needs a conceptual framework. For this chapter, this structure is formed from philosophy, cognitive science, neuroscience and developmental psychology. The embodied vision of self has framed attempts in the past decades to free Western philosophical anthropology from the dualistic Cartesian embrace.[5] Embodied cognitive science supports this shift to a modern answer to Kant's question 'Who is a person?' by observing how the subjective sense of self includes brain, body and social world.[6] Neuroscience offers another perspective of a person as both a subject and an object of research, understood from biological, social and cultural frames of reference.[7] The practice of psychotherapy and the study of developmental psychology demonstrate that the development of the sense of self is actively embodied.[8] In his unique way, the writer and physician Oliver Sacks eloquently captured the beginnings of this lifespan developmental process:

> Implied in all this is the necessity for an adequate concept of the individual and of mind, a concept of how individual persons grow and become, and how their growing and becoming are correlated with their physical bodies.
>
> The infant immediately starts exploring the world, looking, feeling, touching, smelling, as all higher animals do, from the moment of birth. Sensation alone is not enough; it must be combined with movement, with emotion, with *action*. Movement and sensation together become the antecedent of meaning. This evolution of self, this active growth and learning and becoming of the individual, is made possible by … the individual's experiences (and needs and beliefs and desires). This process … cannot arise, cannot even start, unless there is movement-it is movement that makes possible all perceptual categorization.[9]

Understanding how movement and *this evolution of self* are intertwined offers unexpected possibilities. While many readers may believe that they are reading this book to help them improve performance, there is more at stake. Refined performance enhances one's sense of who one is; to be proud of oneself as a person and to participate in the rewards that come with mastery are crucial payoffs.

From philosophy into practice

Feldenkrais lessons can be seen as an archetype for pragmatic, phenomenological learning. The meaning of a Feldenkrais lesson is, as in the sense of C.S. Peirce and W. James, a difference in each person's sense of themselves and their skills in living. In order to find that difference, Feldenkrais lessons enable each person to step around preconceived concepts and engage in a lived phenomenology; providing an immediate experiential path for improving health, enhancing artistic and athletic performance, and redirecting the person's lifespan developmental narrative. Feldenkrais lessons unfold by attending to our sensing while exploring new choices for moving gracefully. The results can be astonishing. As a trainer in the Method, I frequently hear people ask after a lesson, 'Why does a different "me" emerge through such simple movements?'

Maxine Sheets-Johnstone provides a succinct answer to this question, 'Caught up in the adult world, we easily lose sight of … our fundamental capacity to thinking in movement. Any time we care to turn our attention to it, however, there it is.'[10] Indeed, there it is. The questions remain potent: How might we be moving and how can we be attending to this? This is a conundrum faced by everyone wishing to practise movement to improve performance. Feldenkrais lessons offer concrete answers to these questions.

From a practical perspective, we need a methodology to improve skilled performance. However, there are two epistemological handicaps to overcome. The first is easy to solve. Researchers, searching for effective methods of skill enhancement, are constrained by the rules of scientific engagement; they are limited by the requirements for objective criteria for scientific methods and academic literature sources.[11] While ignoring first person experience may be objective science, it also eliminates an important resource for discovery. The first person learning experiences which order the infant's body image are not constrained by the rules of logic.[12] These experiences emerge through the living, individual experience across developmental stages. Such real skills for living unfold outside of the laboratory, away from statistical analysis.

The solution is obvious. We agree to participate; to discover how exploratory learning works for ourselves. We admit that learning is a subjective activity. A new behaviour will be preferred by an individual, because, in some way or other, it feels good for an individual. Learning is always a subjective experience, a sense of meaningful discovery: one person at a time.[13] Feldenkrais lessons offer just such a first person methodology to explore, at any time across the lifespan, the entire range of human movement experience. This is not to downplay scientific discovery. Indeed, Feldenkrais was a man of high erudition, a scientist and engineer. Instead of ignoring science he coupled it with the subjective foundation of learning; this was the wellspring of Feldenkrais's thought.

The second handicap – based on the Cartesian assumption of personhood – is a habit of thinking. It is implicit in our language, hidden by widely held assumptions that escape detection. It prescribes a belief that humans have a mechanical body controlled by an immaterial mind. From this it follows that, like any mechanical object, the body can be changed by the application of external force to the machine itself: stretching muscles and tendons, lifting weight, stressing fascia etc. This leads us to a mindset where serious practice requires the effortful application of force to those body parts which are not following the intent of the mind.[14] However, this Cartesian assumption is mistaken. Feldenkrais's perspective of personhood is a different one. A person is a human, biological animal endowed with the capacity to choose how they act and how they learn across the lifespan. In 1964 Feldenkrais wrote:

> My contention is that the unity of mind and body is an objective reality, that they are not entities related to each other … but an inseparable whole while functioning.[15]

For Feldenkrais the body is not a machine, and the mind is not immaterial. The mind emerges as the person engages with their personal world through active, self-organizing processes of movement that can be understood as enactivist.[16] Through individual experience a human animal becomes a person. As a singular, unified person, practising movement coordination is also about refining *the sense of self*. The human learning process functions through the activity of the infant, child and adult, exploring its own body and the world into which it grows and develops.[17] Exploratory learning involves making choices about how and what to attend to, where to move and how, who to relate to, and how actively to construct a sense of self.[18]

Improving movement skill is about refining coordination, which requires enhanced information rather than imposing force.[19] Information, as the anthropologist and social scientist Gregory Bateson famously stated, is a perceived 'difference that makes a difference'.[20] Coordination can be improved quickly by maximizing feedback about differences in our sensation of ourselves (not 'the body'). Our nervous system automatically improves the effects of feedback when we minimize force and pay attention to our experience.[21] This carries a momentous consequence for how we practise improving our skills. Coordination in self-organizing, biological systems is improved through information feedback processes internal to the animal.[22] Improving movement coordination demands sensory feedback information. It requires clarity in the subjective experience of the perception of differences of movement variations. This distinction between outside force, applied to a mechanical body, or internal information as feedback for regulation of movement means that we have a choice of how we practise for improvement: effort or attention. It also frames an ethical question. When we work with other people as a teacher, coach or therapist, do we apply force to their bodies, confident that this force will correct their shortcomings as a mechanical object? Or, do we approach our task as an intersubjective relationship, helping them explore their potential as a human being with choices of how they participate with our guidance?[23]

Self-discovery

In an article from 1997, as the brain science revolution was transforming the science of human development and cognition, the neuroscientist Antonio Damasio asked, 'How does the brain build a sense of self?'[24] Many years before that, Feldenkrais touched on the same issue. Feldenkrais began his book *Awareness through Movement* with the words: 'We act in accordance with our self-image. This self-image – which, in turn, governs our every act – is conditioned … by three factors: heritage, education, and self-education.'[25] Feldenkrais answered Damasio's future question by creating a system for exploring and re-organizing the sensory-motor foundations of the sense of self. Feldenkrais invented hundreds of innovative Awareness through Movement (ATM) group lessons and individual lessons of Functional Integration (FI).[26] Those lessons have applications in any field in which people want to improve performance of any task that includes moving. These group and individual techniques are not a fixed system of instructions to correct faulty movement. Instead, a person becomes a curious explorer of their experience of moving, of who they are in motion. Furthermore, they gain an insight into who they can become by recruiting discovery learning processes every person knows from infancy.

To understand more we need to ask some other questions:

- What do we mean when we speak of self-image or sense of self?
- How do the body image and the self-image first develop in infancy?
- What exactly is the child doing as it learns to move in its social and physical world during this unfolding of self-image?
- Can we harness these developmental skills, honed in infancy, for improving performance and health at any time in the lifespan?
- Specifically, how can performing artists focus this self-education process for refining their artistic expression?

The foundations of the body image emerge in infancy as the infant learns movement skills by piecing together patterns of moving, such as those seen in the Map of Rolling (Figure 5.1) by discovering and exploring its own possibilities. Being able to understand how discovery learning in infancy and childhood functions gives each person a new choice in how they approach enhancing their performance.

Movement and the development of the sense of self

In this section I will focus on how movement is the foundation of the sense of self as seen from one perspective of developmental psychology. I will draw on the developmental psychologist and psychiatrist Daniel Stern's ideas about how the sense of self unfolds across the lifespan, beginning in infancy.[27] His model includes several domains of self-image that are active throughout our lifespan; implicit in each moment of our lives, ordering our actions, our relationships and our sense of our possibilities.[28]

According to Stern, the sense of self is initially a kinaesthetic experience which unfolds within a relationship with the caregiver.[29] Stern's name for this experience of self is telling: 'the sense of core-self'. It serves as the foundation of how the sense of self develops over the lifespan.[30] Importantly, Stern writes that we can learn to attend to any of the experiences of the sense of self with appropriate guidance, including this non-verbal experiences of core-self.

In Stern's model, the core sense of self unfolds in the first nine months of postnatal life. By then the children act[31] 'as if there is now an integrated sense of themselves as distinct and coherent bodies'.[32] Stern continues: 'Infants are gradually and systematically ordering these elements of experience to identify self-invariants.' One of those self-invariant experiences is what Stern calls *Self-coherence* – that is, the 'sense of being a non-fragmented, physical whole, with boundaries and a locus of integrated action'.[33] Self-coherence is the infant's experience of movements unifying all parts of the body in direction, timing and the muscle forces that enable successful action.[34] By the ninth month of life the process of discovery and learning enables the child to coordinate these elements of self-action as it learns to roll on the ground. This can be seen in the 'Roll Map' (Figure 5.1). The child will build on this kinaesthetic core sense of self-coherence across its entire lifespan.[35] This ability for discovery and learning of movement coherence is the learning resource each person can refine in every Feldenkrais lesson. After all, we have all mastered this skill once in our lives. But what kind of guideposts do we need to re-enter this realm of experience and explore?

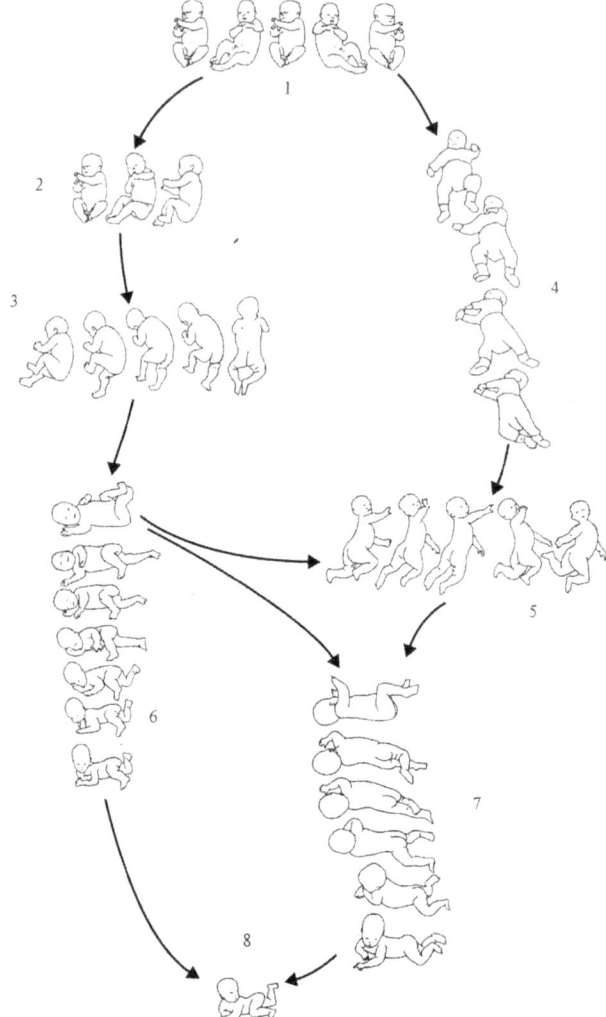

Figure 5.1 Roger Russell and Ulla Schläfke: The Roll Map.[36]

What is the child doing?

As the infant is assembling its sense of core-self, it is constructing movements that enable it to move around its world, while also mastering a discovery-learning process. As this self-discovery process unfolds, the infant achieves increasing behavioural competence and flexibility coupled with increasing motor efficiency. It is valuable to look at which new patterns of moving we see in this developmental period and, critically, how the young autodidact discovers novelty in moving without instruction.

This map presents a summary of early developmental moving; from top to bottom is a timeline over several months of how these activities emerge in the core-self period. Beginning

(1) with initial explorations of balance while on the back, the child discovers how to flex its body to maintain balance and roll to the side (2), and then onto its belly (3). It soon finds it can create a new pattern to first flex and then extend its body to roll to the belly (6 + 7). In another variation, shifting its balance the child discovers it can roll by extending its body (4) in various configurations (4 + 5) until it finds its way to the belly (7 + 8). This map can begin with the infant on its belly rather than its back. This summary, of course, does not map hundreds of variations in movement patterns depicted.

How does the infant master discovery learning?

How does this kind of discovery learning unfold without a teacher? How does the child navigate as it explores numerous movement variations and arrive at effective and efficient patterns of moving? This is the secret of self-education that artists can learn to harness for the perfection of their performance. This process of untaught learning can be mobilized in every Feldenkrais lesson. Writing about this kind of learning the development psychologists Esther Thelen and Linda B. Smith described it in terms of dynamic systems theory. They point out that

> during development, behavior is *selected* from a wider universe of possibilities … exploration is a key process for acquiring new forms; and … creation and exploitation of variability are key elements in the process.[37]

Based on literature in developmental psychology, video studies of infants, my own first person experience, as well as teaching hundreds of Feldenkrais lessons, I have coined the expression **E.V.E.S.O.** to summarize the dynamic systems learning process which Thelen and Smith have described. The person will be:

- Exploring their own system: The child explores its possibilities for perceiving and moving its own body, making
- Variations in movement patterns as they are assembled and re-assembled,
- Experimenting with the usefulness of each new movement pattern as it is assembled,
- Selecting those movement patterns which are useful and efficient, and finally
- Optimizing their behaviour by refining smooth, graceful movements which fit the self-image and the social necessities of the developing person.[38]

This E.V.E.S.O. process unfolds as the child explores new positions and patterns on a continually evolving foundation of skills. The result is a series of developmental 'milestones' which are patterns of adaptive postures and movements.[39]

Attention is a critical dimension of exploratory learning

E.V.E.S.O. learning is initiated by curiosity and by paying attention, which accelerates and focuses learning.[40] Attention plays a central role in how the brain utilizes kinaesthetic sensory feedback to coordinate patterns of moving as the infant weaves together the foundations of core-self.[41] Thus, one of the developmental tasks of the infant (and its caretakers) is to find a way to learn to coordinate three dimensions of its attentional process: arousal, focus and orientation.[42] For optimal learning, an individual needs to be quietly alert. The person needs to regulate their focus of attention and be capable of reorienting attention between internal kinaesthetic experience or the external world, and from one event to another. Finally, the child is born with an intrinsic ability to recognize the best new patterns that emerge during the assembly and tuning process.[43] Evolution has fashioned brains, bodies and movement as an integrated survival system for making choices based on a criterion that ensures effective behaviour. Feldenkrais lessons provide a way of recognizing and harnessing each of these potential resources for learning, ready to be honed into a radically different way of practising for improving skill.[44]

Feldenkrais lessons – a phenomenological guidebook to moving

> The intentional seeking out of new, alternative and novel behavioral solutions must be understood if we are to approach an understanding of the broader phenomena of development and adaptation.[45]

In this section I will show how the activities of the infant developmental process inform the body of work created by Feldenkrais. Before I do so, a short detour is important. In their book, *On Becoming Aware*, Depraz, Varela and Vermersch describe a method of attending to one's own experience which is called phenomenology.[46] The idea seems simple enough:

1. *Suspending* your 'realist' prejudice … enabling you to change how you pay attention to your experience …
2. *Redirecting your attention* from the 'exterior' to the 'interior' …
3. *Letting-go or accepting* your experience.[47]

Every Feldenkrais lesson follows these steps, as will be outlined below. Hundreds of Feldenkrais ATM lessons provide maps of most possible movement patterns. Many of these lessons follow the movement patterns of the Roll Map (Figure 5.1). The lessons usually include the surprise of recognizing that you have significantly underestimated yourself as a person. The lessons take the participant outside of their habitual horizon of movement experience, expanding their imagination of how they can perform effectively, and revealing an unexpected confidence in their own potential.

Discovery learning across the lifespan

The dynamic systems theory outlined by Thelen and Smith provides a framework for the discovery learning process in a Feldenkrais ATM lesson.[48] In every lesson the person engages with the non-verbal, kinaesthetic experience in these steps of discovery:

- **Explore** the system: The Feldenkrais student explores their possibilities for attending, perceiving and moving.

- **Variations** in movement patterns are assembled and re-assembled, providing a wide repertoire of lessons.
- **Experimenting** with what can be done with the new movement patterns that emerge.
- **Select** those movement patterns which satisfy two primary criteria. Is the new pattern useful? And, is the movement easy?[49]
- **Optimize** the easy movements for improved skill, confidence and self-efficacy; making them part of everyday living.

Feldenkrais lessons are constructed for reordering movement patterns of the entire body while helping the person to recognize their intrinsic learning capacity. A new ordering of the entire repertoire of moving emerges.[50] Instead of honing a familiar skill the goal is fundamentally to change how performance is coordinated. The activity is more effective by an order of magnitude, instead of small increments. This is how it is done.

Feldenkrais lessons guide the E.V.E.S.O. discovery learning process built with the following seven components. These can be understood as a hierarchical systems approach to learning.[51] Feldenkrais lessons usually begin with a person lying on the back, side or belly on the floor.[52]

1. The student is asked to agree to explore how they perform a simple action. Similar to play, this is an open, unprejudiced exploration.[53] The person is also exploring the embodiment of their own psychological dynamics, their curiosity and patience, their sense of agency and emotional openness.

2. Playful curiosity helps the participant regulate arousal, and redirect their attention, a key learning resource for bringing non-verbal experience into the foreground of perception.[54] One way to do this is to ask them to attend to variations of ineffective and inefficient movements: setting aside habitual goals of forcing improvement and practising curiosity for the sake of the experience itself.

3. An invitation to attend to the quality of reference movements is made. The person finds a criterion for noticing differences at the end of the lesson. This may include questions about contact with the floor, the movements of breathing, the sense of muscle tension or the sensation of the relative sizes and spatial relations of parts of the body. These 'sensory measuring sticks' reorient the neurological processes of attention to the non-verbal kinaesthetic sense of core-self.[55]

4. The student is asked to explore a series of variations of a movement pattern. In many of those variations the freedom of movement is constrained by positions or configurations of parts of the body making the *habitual solution* to the movement task being explored impossible. The person needs to find another, easier way to move. If the person can re-assemble the variations, a new movement pattern emerges almost immediately.[56] The student is asked to make small, comfortable movements. By going easy, the Weber-Fechner-Henneman movement optimization cycle immediately improves kinaesthetic information feedback.[57]

5. With the new movement pattern a shift in self-perception emerges, often surprising for the participant.[58] This brings to light a characteristic of exploratory learning that is important to understand. The E.V.E.S.O. process utilizes the non-linear emergence of new patterns, meaning the results are *in principle* unpredictable.[59] Each person

discovers a unique solution for the same movement problem posed in the lesson sequence. Observers see individuals in the group moving differently in response to the suggestions while the teacher is satisfied that they are following instructions. The discovery process brings forth a new coordination pattern of moving that is creative and relevant for each individual at that particular time.[60]

6. The student compares reference movements from step 3. The differences are often unexpected and pleasant. The new movement pattern is brought into the daily life of the person, ensuring transfer of learning.

7. Over a developmental time frame of many lessons, spanning weeks to months, the person discovers new skills of emotional regulation, attending, improved movement and self-confidence. The person experiences themselves as a skilled, successful and confident learner.

Functionally integrated movement patterns

Embedded within this structure of a Feldenkrais lesson are two insights about how we move that are elusively obvious.[61] Critical for improving performance, these facts are so much a part of our behaviour that they escape detection in our everyday approach to practising. The first is that all movement coordination is always in the form of movement patterns. Fundamentally, biology is about patterns.[62] Whether we are considering physiology, anatomy or neurology, the animal is a whole, an integrated being. Movement skill development always involves learning to coordinate movement patterns of the entire body. The second insight relates to what habits are and how they change.[63] Let us take a look at these ideas. Once recognized, they become powerful allies for improving performance.

In keeping with the phenomenological stance of the Feldenkrais Method I will begin with an experiential exploration. After that I will look at some of the theoretical foundations of the experience. The reader can test an experience about patterns and habits for themselves, right now. You can discover unexpected changes in your breathing and balance that requires no repetitive practice at all. It can be done quickly by making one simple change of the movement pattern. If you put this book aside for a moment and quickly interlace your fingers, you can find out how that works. Look at how they are interlaced. One thumb is over the other, and as you look at the other fingers you will find that each finger on one hand is on top of that same finger of the other hand, led by the thumb. If you do this many times quickly, they will always be interlaced in the same habitual pattern. Now, slow down and interlace the hands non-habitually, by moving each finger from the thumb to little finger, one finger farther. It is an odd sensation of something being not quite familiar, not quite right.

Notice that the wrists and lower arms also feel a bit odd with the fingers non-habitually interlaced. If you go back to your habit, it usually feels back to normal. In the non-habitual interlacing of the hands, notice if you sense anything unfamiliar in your upper arms or even your shoulders. You are becoming aware that small changes in the interlacing of the fingers are actually a completely different movement pattern of coordinating all of your muscles, not only the hands and fingers.

Sit quietly for a moment, hands not interlaced, with your eyes closed. As you slowly interlace the hands habitually, notice how you sense your eyes, and the muscle tension in and around the eyes, and in your face. Sense your neck too. Then, take the hands apart and interlace them, with the eyes closed, non-habitually. Does something now change in your sensation of your eyes? Not only the hands, arms and even shoulders, but your hands and eyes are continually coordinated through the brain, even when we are not attending. Sensing that the eyes change by changing the interlacing of the fingers is a surprise for most people.

You can explore this further. Find a chair with a fairly hard seat. Slide forward a bit, sensing how you are sitting on the seat bones. Careful attention will show you, as you shift your weight – very slowly – a bit right or left, that the way you shift the weight from one side to the other feels slightly different. This means that the way your brain mobilizes the entire musculature to maintain your balance is slightly different on the right and left. This is normal, but for most people unnoticed. These are examples of habitual actions: fast, unattended, useful patterns of moving for our lives. Attend also to the movements of breathing in the right and left side of your chest. You will find that the differences in balancing also makes the breathing slightly asymmetric too. This is also normal, nothing to be worried about.

If you interlace the fingers habitually, you will probably not notice any differences in breathing movements or how you shift your weight slightly on your seat bones. However, if you interlace your fingers non-habitually, you might be surprised to discover that there is a difference when you are shifting your weight from side to side. Go slowly, otherwise you will miss the subtle differences in how your balance changes or how your breathing changes when you change the interlacing of your fingers. Change them back to habitual and notice both balance and breathing are back to habitual too. Is this interesting for you? There is one last surprise. Try the same experiment in standing and shifting your weight from the left to the right foot. Slowly, attentively and without trying to do it well. Attend to how your balance on each foot is slightly different when you move to the right or left. This is normal. The surprise comes when you interlace the fingers slowly in the non-habitual way. If you then test your balance from one foot to the other, you will likely sense subtle differences in your balance than with the habitual interlacing. Notice your feet on the floor, your muscles in your legs and hips and perhaps along your back and neck, possibly in how the eyes feel if you close them and shift your balance, slowly and quietly, back and forth. By slowing changing between the habitual and non-habitual interlacing of the fingers you will have the opportunity to notice how this seemingly simple change evokes a reordering of the entire pattern of balancing in standing. This nifty little experiment surprises people. The differences, felt throughout the body, are a demonstration that our brains coordinate any movement we do as a pattern of the entire body. In theoretical biology this is called functional integration.[64] These functionally integrated sensory-motor patterns of coordination constitute the core of any skill whatsoever, and the kinaesthetic core of ourselves as a person.

We usually ignore these small differences in balance, breathing and looking for most activities. If we think of the body as a mechanical object, this phenomenon cannot be readily explained. It seems to be an irrelevant detail. If, however, we consider ourselves to be functionally integrated creatures of biology, then we can consider how small changes can make a meaningful difference to performance, skill or even safety.

These small changes of a pattern are also different for each person. For every individual, their coordination is unique, and has a unique history of how they learned. Therefore, any fundamental improvements in skill need an individual discovery pathway.[65] This leads us then to ask, how did that history of coordination of movement skills unfold for the person and how each individual's uniqueness will be impacted by Feldenkrais lessons? We now need to consider three questions. First, what is a movement pattern? Second, how are habitual movement patterns coordinated by the brain, and, third, how can that coordination be re-organized through practice?

The neurology of non-habitual patternmaking

'Habits are when we make a decision before we are aware of having a choice.'[66]

Movement skills are habits, which are familiar patterns of coordinating movement for successful action. Examples of habitual movement patterns include signing your name, organizing your breathing, face, jaw and tongue to speak your native language with a familiar accent, your way of walking that friends will immediately recognize, your personal way of expressing your feelings and your individual way of performing your art.

Our brain has a neurological plan for these learned actions, movement memories which are available when needed. We call these movement memories 'habits'.[67] Most habits are useful: speaking, our handwriting, our way of walking. Habits automatically assure performance of day-to-day living and artistic performance. One of the keys to improving skill is understanding how habits are coordinated by the brain.[68]

The neuroscience of performance shows that when a person imagines an activity, their brain plans how that intention can be carried out.[69] This unfolds in a fraction of a second. To accomplish this planning feat the brain utilizes a set of networks that function as a movement pattern generator.[70] The plan is sent from the brain's pattern generator to the spinal cord and the muscles execute the plan. There are two ways for the brain to prepare and send a movement plan to the spinal cord and the muscles. The first is by relying on habits, or second, by inventing novel patterns of moving.

When we are acting habitually, our neurological pattern generator is using familiar movement memories to guide the muscles. This enables us to do what we need to do successfully and easily. An entire pattern of movement is quickly available. We call this skill. If all goes well, we can ignore how it works. Artistic performance works like this too.

Habits are well-learned patterns of moving. They can be initiated without a conscious decision. They are inflexible and therefore reliable for well-known tasks. Habitual movement patterns are all or nothing activities. Once initiated by the brain's pattern generator, the habitual movement unfolds exactly as planned; it cannot be revised halfway.[71] However, for all of these reasons, if our unconscious, automatic and inflexible habits are insufficient for our goals, they are difficult to change. We don't know how the habit pattern generator in the brain functions.[72]

For improving skill, we need a way to re-order how the brain guides the muscles in a movement pattern. In other words, we need to invent a new plan, different from the habitual plan. Only then can we quickly learn a refined level of skill. The neurology of how this works offers a hint.

We can begin by considering that if an activity is completely new, the person has no clear plan. Learning proceeds by trial and error. The learner's brain will begin to assemble a plan for later use. This is what practising is all about: discovering a clear and precise plan for the imagined performance. This is what Feldenkrais points to in the essays in his book *Thinking and Doing*: the action is complete already in the mind.[73] However, practising is not about repeating the desired action. Because, let's face it, in most practice sessions we are not repeating the desired action. We are making innumerable mistakes. We are usually frustrated by this fact, but it is necessary to make the mistakes and then inhibit them in order to sharpen our skills. Attending to how we make each mistake will enable us to quickly inhibit the plan for that particular mistake in the next round. At some point, all possible mistakes have been discovered and inhibited, and there is nothing left to do except to be successful. In other words, learning requires that we make all possible mistakes, and compare each mistake to others that are more effective.[74] If you take the time to reflect on your own experience you can see the wisdom in this observation. Once you can clearly imagine the action, you can stop making mistakes. Your brain has discovered a clear plan and can mobilize that movement memory whenever it is imagined.

If you would take the opportunity to watch an infant doing the movements mapped out in Figure 5.1, you will see that the infant tries every possible variation of those movements. Most of those variations are not effective. However, the infant persists until it stops doing the variations which interfere with gracefully rolling over on the floor.[75] If the movement that the infant discovers is successful and easy, the infant will keep that plan in its habitual repertoire of actions and goes on with new discoveries.

Understanding the neurology of habits indicates how practising without stress can be done. The secret lies in the fact that when we imagine doing something we make a decision without our noticing. We often decide to mobilize the habit. This is not clear to us, since mobilizing a habit can be done without us being aware that we have done so. Once the decision has been made and the plan is on the way to the spinal cord for execution it is too late to change that pattern of moving. We can, however, interrupt the habitual activity and consciously create a new plan. This is what E.V.E.S.O. learning is all about.

There are two decision-making doors into the movement pattern generator network, with three keys. One door is that of emotion. The key is the desire for success. Managed by the emotional centres of the brain, the habit door is opened by most kinds of emotional drive. It has the advantage of being very fast. It can mobilize habitual movement plans and send them on to the muscles in a split second. We cannot survive if we don't have these habits available. However, it has a disadvantage if we want to learn a new way to perform. Emotionally driven practising sets the movement pattern generator at the habit setting. We don't notice that the choice has been narrowed down to one option: what we already know how to do. If we are practising under emotional pressure our brain has no choice but to mobilize habitual movement plans.[76] Ambitious or fearful practising reinstates the habitual movement pattern that limits our choices and interferes with the precision of our performance. We are trapped.[77] We want to change the pattern of action and we keep hitting the habit button. No wonder practice can feel so stressful.

The keys to the second door to the movement plan generator are different. The first key is curiosity; also, an emotional experience, but it takes you to a second door with still another key: patience. This kind of experience is managed by another – unemotional – part of your brain, the prefrontal cortex. This is our brain's network for making strategic decisions about alternative ways of acting.[78] The keys of curiosity and patience help us regulate the emotions and open the movement pattern generator for new choices. This gives us the opportunity to try out all possible patterns, all possible mistakes. The kinaesthetic feedback from these variations will help us inhibit unsuccessful or inefficient patterns of moving. Once we have inhibited all possible mistakes we will select and refine successful plans for truly excellent performance.[79] Feldenkrais lessons are constructed to utilize these neurological keys for learning in the E.V.E.S.O. learning process. The E. stands for exploring our system, in this case the system is ourselves moving. Feldenkrais lessons are the guideposts to help us navigate this biological learning process including the neurology of functionally integrated movement patterns. Finally, every person can master this learning process since they have the necessary know-how since infancy.

Changing our stories in the future

Feldenkrais lessons enable us become explorers of our own developmental histories. We re-learn how new patterns of moving can be discovered, rather than imposed. We experience that we can open our developmental future. It is not as narrow as we might assume. This kind of learning involves self-acceptance, curiosity, patience and the willingness to make mistakes, giving us the skills we need for fine-tuning our perception and movement. Another perspective on practising comes into view. We can ask, what can we attend to? How can we experiment with a variety of ways of moving, some of which will not be selected? Normally called mistakes, those variations are not bothersome side effects of E.V.E.S.O. learning. They are intended; guided by curiosity and patience, we decide to practice our mistakes. By doing so we have interfered with the unconscious programming of the habitual movement that is limiting a more skilful performance. How else could we find a more effective pattern of moving without interrupting our automatic and unconscious habit of making mistakes?

The pathway is open for change. It works, but most people are concerned that they are making their performance worse by practising their mistakes. They are missing the opportunity of a lifetime to change a mindset towards effort. Of course, during an actual performance making mistakes is not a good idea. However, in an E.V.E.S.O. practice situation interrupting the habit is a necessary condition for the reassembly of a new, more effective pattern of moving. So-called mistakes are welcome, if attended to, since the performer discovers how those particular variations are interfering with attaining a higher level of performance.

This kind of developmental learning extends our opportunities of acting in our world. We learn to say: 'I can do that.' We find ourselves acting with confidence and skill. This alone would make it worth trying the Feldenkrais approach to practice. Feldenkrais lessons enhance performance, as many stories in this book will attest. However, there is another opportunity available. We can reach deeper into our personal history. The lessons open a door to the kinaesthetic foundation of our core sense of self. We have available, to our surprise, something beyond movement exercises.

Drawing on the field of developmental psychology seems, at first glance, far from artistic performance questions. However, is the story of your development as a person and as an artist so far away from each other? We can recognize that the Feldenkrais Method is the practice that was missing in Mark Johnson's argument.[80] I suggest that you return to the first pages of this chapter. I warned that you may be in for something more than you bargained for. We have available an unexpected tool in our repertoire for learning that enables us to rewrite our story of ourselves. Daniel Stern names this story the *Narrative-Self*.[81] Other authors describe this as autobiographical memory, our retrospective description of our biography.[82] Prospective memory is a description of how our memory of our experience of ourselves orders our expectations and perception of ourselves and our world into the future.[83] This is a prospective narrative of who we can become. By re-organizing our core sense of self, we begin to discover how our memory of 'I don't know how' becomes 'I can'. Our imaginations of who we can become and what we can do show new promise. In other words, you may be approaching an opportunity to discover a new experience of health. Feldenkrais liked to say that 'Health is when a person is able to realize their unavowed dreams'.[84] What are your dreams as an artist?

Conclusion

In this chapter I have reviewed some ideas about how the experience of the sense of self can be understood. How it first develops in infancy, and what the is child doing as it is unfolding its self-image. This has led to an understanding of how we can harness these developmental skills, honed in infancy, for improving performance and health at any time in the lifespan. This is a general discovery learning process which I have named E.V.E.S.O. I have shown how the foundations of body image emerge in infancy as the infant learns movement skills by piecing together patterns of moving, such as those seen in the Map of Rolling (Figure 5.1), by discovering and exploring its own possibilities.

Being able to understand how discovery learning in infancy and childhood functions gives each person a new choice in how they approach practice for enhancing their performance. Specifically, how performing artists can focus this self-education process for refining their artistic expression. If we are willing to follow the consequences of Moshe Feldenkrais's description of the person, we can recognize that exploratory learning will lead us on pathways of practising that are radically different than what we have been taught. We learn to be patient, attentive, curios; interested in making useful mistakes, which lead us to the movement pattern variations that are both successful and graceful.

We can leave the emotional captivity of habits behind us, and discover not only improved performance but a changed person within ourselves: One who is able to explore all possibilities of making mistakes. Refined performance is the result. The grand prize? We gain an adventurous trust in our own learning ability, confident and untethered by dogma of authority or traditions. We become explorers of unexpected possibilities that were waiting for us just beyond our blind spot. We become artists for making creative decisions about how we perform and how we live.

Notes

1. Gerald M. Edelman and Giulio Tononi, *A Universe of Consciousness* (New York: Basis Books, 2000), 207.
2. This text is an updated version of an article written for a symposium *Movement and the Development of Sense of Self* in Seattle, United States, in August 2004.
3. Mark Johnson, *Embodied Mind, Meaning and Reason – How Our Bodies Give Rise to Understanding* (Chicago: The University of Chicago Press, 2017), 1.
4. Edmund Husserl, cited in Natalie Depraz, Francisco Varela and Pierre Vermersch, *On Becoming Aware* (Amsterdam: John Benjamins Publishing, 2003), 22.
5. See Shaun Gallagher, *Enactivist Interventions* (Oxford: Oxford University Press, 2017), and Ezequiel Di Paolo, Thomas Buhrmann and Xabier E. Barandiaran, *Sensorimotor Life*: *An Enactive Proposal* (Oxford: Oxford University Press, 2017).
6. Lawrence Shapiro, *The Routledge Handbook of Embodied Cognition* (New York: Routledge, 2017).
7. Larry R. Squire, Darwin Berg, Floyd E Bloom, Sascha Du Lac, Anirvan Ghosh and Nicholas C. Spitzer (eds), *Fundamental Neuroscience*, 4th edn. (Amsterdam; Boston: Elsevier/Academic Press, 2013). Georg F. Striedter, *Principles of Brain Evolution* (Sunderland, MA: Sinauer, 2005).
8. Karen E. Adolph and Justin E. Hoch, 'Motor Development: Embodied, Embedded, Encultured and Enabling', *The Annual Review of Psychology*, Vol. 70, No. 26 (2019), 1–26, 24.
9. Oliver Sacks, 'Neurology and the Soul', *New York Review* (22 November 1990), 44–50 (my italics).
10. Maxine Sheets-Johnstone, *The Primacy of Movement*, 2nd edn. (Amsterdam: John Benjamins, 2011), xii.
11. For example, 'There appear to have been no systematic attempts to determine the degree to which infants can produce new patterns of coordination or…more broadly in the lifespan of the human species, no matter the developmental age or stage.' in Karl M. Newell, Yeou-The Liu and Gottfried Mayer-Kress, 'A Dynamical Systems Interpretation of Epigenetic Landscapes for Infant Motor Development', *Infant Behavior & Development*, Vol. 26 (2003), 452.
12. Eugene T. Gendlin, 'The Responsive Order: A New Empiricism', *Man and World*, Vol. 30 (1997), 383–411.
13. These activities have been summarized by many researchers such as Adolph and Hoch, 'Motor Development', and Philippe Rochat and Tricia Striano, 'Perceived Self in Infancy', *Infant Behavior and Development*, Vol. 23, No. 3–4 (2000), 513–30, and Daniel Stern, *The Interpersonal World of the Infant: A View from Psychoanalysis and Developmental Psychology* (New York: Basic Books, 2000) [Orig. 1985].
14. Heinz von Foerster called this a trivial machine perspective. See his 'Lethology – A Theory of Learning and Knowing vis à vis Undeterminables, Undecidables, Unknowables', *Revista Universidad Eafit* (July–September 1997), 13–30. See also Gilbert Ryle, *The Concept of Mind* (Milton Park: Routledge, 2009).
15. Feldenkrais, 'Mind and Body', *Systematics*, Vol. 2, No. 1 (June 1964), 47.
16. Evan Thompson, *Mind in Life* (Cambridge, MA: Harvard University Press, 2007).
17. Melvin Konner, *The Evolution of Childhood: Relationships, Emotion, Mind* (Cambridge, MA: Belknap Press, 2010).
18. Philippe Rochat, 'What Is It Like to Be a Newborn', in *The Oxford Handbook of The Self*, ed. Shaun Gallagher (Oxford: Oxford University Press, 2013), 57–79. Esther Thelen and Linda B. Smith, *A Dynamic Systems Approach to the Development of Cognition and Action* (Cambridge, MA: MIT Press, 1994).

19 'The quantities that characterize coordination…are best thought of as informational in nature.' J.A. Scott Kelso, 'From Bernstein's Physiology of Activity to Coordination Dynamics', in *Progress in Motor Control*, Volume One, *Bernstein's Traditions in Movement Studies*, ed. Mark L. Latash (Champaign, IL: Human Kinetics, 1998), 212.

20 Aaron Sloman, 'What Did Bateson Mean When He Wrote "Information" Is "a Difference That Makes a Difference"?' at https://www.cs.bham.ac.uk/research/projects/cogaff/misc/information-difference.html (accessed 25 March 2020).

21 Roger Russell, 'The Weber-Fechner-Henneman Movement Optimization Cycle', *The Feldenkrais Journal*, No. 30 (2017). https://issuu.com/thefeldenkraisjournal/docs/2017_feldenkrais_final

22 Thompson, *Mind in Life*, 57.

23 Martin Buber, *I and Thou*, 2nd edn. (New York: Macmillan Pub, 1958/1987).

24 Antonio R. Damasio, 'A Clear Consciousness', *TIME Special Issue: The New Age of Discovery* (Winter 1997/1998), 90.

25 Feldenkrais, *Awareness through Movement* (New York: Harper and Row, 1972), 1.

26 See: http://www.feldenkrais.co.uk/index.php or https://feldenkrais.com/

27 See Stern, *The Interpersonal World of the Infant*.

28 Stern, *The Interpersonal World of the* Infant, 2000, xxv.

29 Philippe Rochat writes: 'The early inclination of infants to explore their bodies forms the cradle of self- perception and the developmental origin of self-knowledge.' Rochat, *The Infant's World* (Cambridge, MA: Harvard University Press, 2004), 28–9.

30 Stern, *The Interpersonal World of the Infant*, xxv. In Stern's model the developmental process continues with the Intersubjective Sense of Self, the Verbal Sense of Self and the Narrative Sense of Self.

31 Stern, *The Interpersonal World of the Infant*, 37–99.

32 Stern, *The Interpersonal World of the Infant*, 69.

33 Stern, *The Interpersonal World of the Infant*, 71.

34 See research in movement science and neuroscience relating to these questions: D. Gordon E. Robertson, Graham E. Cadwell, Joseph Hamill, Garry Kamen and Saunders A. Whittlesey, *Research Methods in Biomechanics*, 2nd edn. (Champaign, IL: Human Kinetics, 2014), and Thelen and Smith, *A Dynamic Systems Approach to the Development of Cognition and Action*, and Barry E. Stein, ed., *The New Handbook of Multisensory Processes* (Cambridge, MA: MIT Press, 2012).

35 Stern writes: 'All mental acts…accompanied by input from the body…to permit, support, amplify…the ongoing mental activity.' Stern, *The Interpersonal World of the Infant*, 2000, xvii. Antonio Damasio writes in *Self Comes to Mind* (New York: Panteon Books, 2010), 20, that 'the model for this scaling up of mind…can be found in the physiology of movement.… a foundation of the conscious mind'.

36 Roger Russell and Ulla Schläfke, 'The Growing World of the Child', *The Feldenkrais Journal*, Vol. 12 (1997–8), 25. This illustration summarizes observations made of four infants.

37 Thelen and Smith, *A Dynamic Systems Approach to the Development of Cognition and Action*, 130–1. Also, in the same volume in 'Goals for a Developmental Theory', xviii. These scientists have outlined in detail how exploring, selecting and optimizing movement variations lead to effective action.

38 Thelen and Smith, *A Dynamic Systems Approach to the Development of Cognition and Action*, Chapter 7: The Dynamics of Selection in Human Infants (pp. 187–211), and Chapter 9: Knowledge from Action: Exploration and Selection in Learning to Reach (pp. 247–77).

39 That all children go through similar stages implies that these patterns satisfy biological values which ensure survival. Konner, *The Evolution of Childhood: Relationships, Emotion, Mind*, and

Barry Bogin and Carlos Verea, 'Evolution of Human Life History', in *Evolution of Nervous Systems, Volume 4, The Evolution of the Human Brain: Apes and Other Ancestors*, ed. Jon H. Haas (Amsterdam: Elsevier, 2017), 37–50.

40   Michael I. Posner, *Cognitive Neuroscience of Attention*, 2nd edn. (New York: The Guilford Press, 2012). Philippe Rochat and Rachel Morgan comment, 'Self-exploration is an important process… in which infants are perceptually attentive to their own body.' Rochat & Morgan, 'The function and determinants of early self-exploration', in *The Self in Infancy: Theory and Research*, ed. Rochat (Amsterdam: Elsevier, 1995), 410.

41   Andrea Nani, Jordi Manuello, Lorenzo Mancuso, Donato Liloia, Tommaso Costa and Franco Cauda, 'The Neural Correlates of Consciousness and Attention: Two Sister Processes of the Brain', *Frontiers in Neuroscience*, Vol. 13 (2019), 1169.

42   Miller writes: 'During development attention becomes more systematic and selective. They learn how to pay attention in different situations, fitting the attention to the setting.' Patricia Miller, *Theories of Developmental Psychology* (New York: W.H. Freeman, 1993), 358.

43   Edelman and Tononi, *A Universe of Consciousness*, 79–138. The authors demonstrate that a value system is essential for learning. For movement coordination, see Klaus Schneider and Ronald F. Zernicke, 'Jerk-Cost Modulations during the Practice of Rapid Arm Movements', *Biological Cybernetics*, Vol. 60 (1989), 221–30. Karl Friston, 'The Free-Energy Principle: A Unified Brain Theory?' *Nature Reviews Neuroscience*, Vol. 11 (2010), 127–38.

44   Russell, 'The Weber-Fechner-Henneman Movement Optimization Cycle'.

45   Karl M. Newell and P. Vernon McDonald, 'The Evolving Perceptual-Motor Workspace in Infancy', in *Advances in Psychology*, Vol. 97. *The Development of Coordination in Infancy*, ed. Geert J.P. Savelsbergh (North-Holland: Elsevier Science Publishers, 1993), 194.

46   Natalie Depraz, Francisco Varela and Pierre Vermersch, *On Becoming Aware*, 25.

47   This is Husserl's concept of epoché. Natalie Depraz, Francisco Varela and Pierre Vermersch, *On Becoming Aware*, 25 (italics in the source).

48   Thelen and Smith, *A Dynamic Systems Approach to the Development of Cognition and Action*, and Beatrix Vereijken, *The Dynamics of Skill Acquisition*, Academisch Proefschrift, Vrije Universiteit (Meppel: Krips Repro, 1991).

49   Easy, smooth movements save energy. See Tamar Flash and Neville Hogan, 'The Coordination of Arm Movements: An Experimentally Confirmed Mathematical Model', *The Journal of Neuroscience*, Vol. 5, No. 7 (July 1985), 1688–703.

50   Including the biomechanical system of bones and muscles guided by the emergence of new information in the nervous operations.

51   Howard H. Pattee, *Hierarchy Theory: The Challenge of Complex Systems* (New York: George Braziller, 1973), and Michael L. Commons and Sara Nora Ross, 'The Hierarchical Complexity View of Evolution and History', *World Futures*, Vol. 64 (2008), 399–405.

52   There are many more options than this. In his training group in San Francisco (1975–8) Feldenkrais claimed that he had developed lessons in seventeen different positions. Personal Notes, 1976.

53   Edward S. Reed, *Encountering the World* (Oxford: Oxford University Press, 1996), and Francesco Mannella, Vieri G. Santucci, Eszter Somogyi, Lisa Jacquey, Kevin J. O'Regan and Gianluca Baldassarre, 'Know Your Body Through Intrinsic Goals', *Frontiers in Neurorobotics*, Vol. 12, No. 30 (2018), 1.

54   Dav Clark, Frank Schumann and Stewart H. Mostofsky, 'Mindful Movement and Skilled Attention', *Frontiers in Human Neuroscience*, Vol. 9, No. 297 (2015), 1–23, and Catherine E. Kerr, Matthew D. Sacchet, Sara W. Lazar, Christopher I. Moore and Stephanie R. Jones, 'Mindfulness Starts with the Body: Somatosensory Attention and Top-Down Modulation of Cortical Alpha Rhythms

55 in Mindfulness Meditation', *Frontiers in Human Neuroscience*, Vol. 7, No. 12. doi: 10.3389/fnhum.2013.00012 (13 February 2013), 1–15.

55 Barry Stein, ed. *The New Handbook of Multisensory Processes* (Cambridge, MA: MIT Press, 2012). See also Michael I. Posner, *Cognitive Neuroscience of Attention*, 2nd ed., 2012.

56 Newell, 'Change in Movement and Skill: Learning, Retention and Transfer', in *Dexterity and Its Development*, ed. Mark L. Latash and Michael T. Turvey (Mahwah, NJ: Lawrence Erlbaum, 1996), 393–429 and J. A. Scott Kelso, *Dynamic Patterns* (Cambridge, MA: MIT Press, 1995),

57 See Russell, 'The Weber-Fechner-Henneman Movement Optimization Cycle'.

58 Russell, *Dem Schmerz den Rücken kehren* (Paderborn: Junfermann Verlag, 2002).

59 Kelso, *Dynamic Patterns*, 1–95.

60 Considering a person as an open, non-linear, far from equilibrium, complex adaptive system means that the initial conditions based on each person's history at the beginning of the lesson are unique. See Kelso, *Dynamic Patterns*, and Thelen and Smith, *A Dynamic Systems Approach to the Development of Cognition and Action*.

61 See Feldenkrais, *The Elusive Obvious* (Capitola, CA: Meta Publications, 1981).

62 In the case of the example of interlacing the fingers the surprising discovery is that the entire body is included in the changes of the pattern rather than only the hands and fingers. Further reading: Neil A. Campbell, Lisa A. Urry, Michael L. Cain, Steven A. Wasserman, Peter V. Minorsky and Jane B. Reece, eds, *Biology: A Global Approach*, Global Edition: 11th edn. (New York: Pearson, 2018).

63 Ann M. Graybiel and Kyle S. Smith, 'Good Habits, Bad Habits', *Scientific American*, Vol. 310, No. 6 (June 2014), 38–43.

64 Gilbert A. Chauvet, *Theoretical Systems in Biology: Hierarchical and Functional Integration*, Vol. 1 (Oxford: Pergamon, 1995), and Volume 3: *Organisation and Regulation* (1996).

65 This is what the Feldenkrais Method offers (see note 5, above).

66 Feldenkrais, Amherst Training, 1980, personal notes.

67 Ann M. Graybiel and Kyle S. Smith, 'Good Habits, Bad Habits', and Henry H. Yin and Barbara Knowlton, 'The Role of the Basal Ganglia in Habit Formation', *Nature Reviews Neuroscience*, Vol. 7, No. 6 (June 2006), 464–76.

68 Yin and Knowlton, 'The Role of the Basal Ganglia in Habit Formation', 464–76.

69 Joaquin M. Fuster, *The Prefrontal Cortex*, 5th edn. (Amsterdam: Elsevier, 2015), 1–6 and 333–85.

70 The cerebral cortex, cerebellum and basal ganglia are central hubs in this pattern generator: Carol A. Seger and Brian J. Spiering, 'A Critical Review of Habit Learning and the Basal Ganglia', *Frontiers in Systems Neuroscience*, Vol. 5, No. 66 (30 August 2011), 1–99. https://www.frontiersin.org/articles/10.3389/fnsys.2011.00066/full

71 Yin and Knowlton, 'The Role of the Basal Ganglia in Habit Formation', 464–76.

72 Yin and Knowlton, 'The Role of the Basal Ganglia in Habit Formation', 464–76.

73 Feldenkrais, *Thinking and Doing* (Longmont, CO: Genesis II Publishing, 2013).

74 Feldenkrais, San Francisco Feldenkrais Training, June 1975–August 1977. San Francisco, Humanistic Psychology Institute, 1976, Personal notes. See also Knight Dunlap, *Habits: Their Making and Unmaking* (Oxford: Liveright, 1932).

75 Llinás writes, 'The reduction of all possible choices to a useful set of the most probable solutions... is a necessary prerequisite of effective behaviour.' Rodolfo R. Llinás, *I of the Vortex: From Neurons to Self* (Cambridge, MA: MIT Press, 2002), 168. See also Beatrix Vereijken, *The Dynamics of Skill Acquisition*.

76 For more information about the neuroscience of habits, see Ann M. Graybiel and Kyle S. Smith, 'Good Habits, Bad Habits', *Scientific American*, Vol. 310, No. 6 (June 2014), 38–43, and Richard

E. Passingham and Steven P. Wise, *The Neurobiology of the Prefrontal Cortex* (Oxford: Oxford University Press, 2012).

77 Yin and Knowlton, 'The Role of the Basal Ganglia in Habit Formation', 2006, 464–76, and Ann M. Graybiel and Kyle S. Smith, 'Good Habits, Bad Habits', 39–43.

78 Richard E. Passingham and Steven P. Wise, *The Neurobiology of the Prefrontal Cortex* (Oxford: Oxford University Press, 2012), and Joaquin M. Fuster, *The Prefrontal Cortex*, 5th edn. (Amsterdam: Elsevier, 2015).

79 'The results of the experiment were startling. They found that every subject corrected his errors with the use of negative practice, but positive practice did not produce these results. With positive practice, the errors were partially eliminated, but with negative practice, errors were completely eliminated' (p. 100). Gordon B. Johnson, 'Negative Practice on Band Instruments: An Exploratory Study', *Journal of Research in Music Education*, Vol. 10, No. 2 (1962), 100–4.

80 Johnson, *Embodied Mind, Meaning and Reason – How Our Bodies Give Rise to Understanding*, 1.

81 Stern, *The Interpersonal World of the Infant*, xxiii–xxxiii.

82 H.L. Williams, M.A. Conway, M.A. and G. Cohen, 'Autobiographical Memory', In *Memory in the Real World*, 3rd ed., ed. G. Cohen and M.A. Conway (Hove, UK: Psychology Press, 2008), 21–90.

83 M.A. McDaniel and G.O. Einstein, *Prospective Memory: An Overview and Synthesis of an Emerging Field* (New York: Sage, 2007).

84 Feldenkrais, Amherst Feldenkrais Training, 1980, personal notes, and Feldenkrais, 'On Health', in *Embodied Wisdom: The Collected Papers of Moshe Feldenkrais*, ed. Elizabeth Beringer (Berkeley, CA: North Atlantic Books, 2010), 53–8.

CHAPTER 6
THE FELDENKRAIS METHOD FOR MUSICIANS: ADDRESSING THE NEED FOR OBJECTIVE MEASUREMENTS
Jillian Beacon, Gilles Comeau and Donald Russell

Carl Czerny wrote that 'the movements of the body have so great an influence on piano-forte playing, that a good and graceful position must be the first thing to which the pupil's attention should be drawn'.[1] The notion that poised and erect posture is essential to piano playing persists in pedagogical traditions today. Somatic training approaches such as the Feldenkrais Method (FM) offer strategies that can help musicians move beyond static ideas about posture to develop a more nuanced and dynamic understanding of how habits of body use influence the ability to play freely and expressively. Many musicians claim that FM has helped them recover from playing-related pain (PRP) and go on to play better than ever before.[2] These claims have increased awareness of FM in music education, leading to its incorporation in prestigious music training programmes around the world. However, at present, access to FM in music education is not widespread, with access largely limited to elite training schools or special programmes in workshop settings. With the high prevalence of PRP among both professional[3] and pre-professional musicians[4] well documented in research, music educators require access to more effective strategies for helping their students remain healthy throughout their study.[5] It is urgent that experts in somatic modalities like FM find ways to include their perspectives in the academic and administrative conversations taking place about how to better address musicians' health and well-being.

An important and currently lacking part of this conversation is scientific research that not only offers objective evidence of FM outcomes for musicians, but also investigates the neurological and physiological mechanisms underlying the Method's perceived benefits. Although a plethora of anecdotal evidence is available in the form of testimonials and practitioner-reported case studies, the body of research on somatic training is small, with very few studies on musicians. If FM is capable of helping musicians play and feel better, high-quality research studies can highlight its strengths and reveal its limitations. A body of scientific literature on FM outcomes for musicians could increase music educator's knowledge about the Method and facilitate greater trust in its techniques. This knowledge would help educators make informed decisions about incorporating FM into evolving pedagogies concerning musicians' health that increasingly emphasize body awareness. Musician-centred research would also help FM practitioners learn how their techniques could best be adapted to help musicians in the contexts of practice and performance.

The goal of this chapter is to help orient future researchers towards methodologies that will contribute empirical research on FM and musicians. It addresses the need for objective measurement of musicians' motor behaviour in response to somatic training methods such as FM, focusing on pianists. Our discussion pertains to research on physiological measurements of body-positioning and movement without extending to psychological outcomes or assessments of performance quality. The first section reviews literature on how somatic methods, including FM, have been researched so far with both musicians and non-musicians. The second section discusses the strengths and limitations of various biomechanical approaches for measuring body-positioning for FM research, with the goal of helping researchers choose the best methods for their own research questions. The chapter closes with a discussion about the unique challenges of choosing variables representing movement behaviour that respect the learning theories and teaching techniques that make FM unique.

Evidence of somatic training outcomes for musicians

Musicians were one of the earliest groups to recognize how Feldenkrais's Awareness through Movement (ATM) or Functional Integration (FI) lessons could benefit them as artists. In ATM, students actively explore movements based on verbal directions given by the practitioner, and the classes are often done in groups. These lessons seek to create a comfortable and safe context for individuals to become aware of subtleties in sensations and movement quality as they explore variations in patterned movements. Students are encouraged to approach the movements non-performatively, focusing on the quality and ease of the experience, rather than the 'correctness' of execution. The goal of ATM is to help students' nervous systems learn to seek out movements which are more comfortable, efficient or adaptable, rather than persisting in familiar patterns which may limit motor dexterity or contribute to discomfort. During an FI lesson, students experience a one-to-one interaction during which the practitioner gently moves the student's body while they are recumbent. Practitioners seek to move the student in ways that seem comfortable and familiar to them rather than forcibly manipulating the body through stretching, pressing or pulling. It is theorized that as the practitioner joins the student's existing movement tendencies, habitual patterns of muscular tension release as the work of the muscles is overtaken by the support of the practitioner. The Method seeks to work with, and not against, the nervous system's preferred patterns of motor behaviour so that new movements introduced by the practitioner are experienced as simple, pleasurable and congruous with the person's sense of themselves. The benefits of FM in music performance have been documented anecdotally, with many musicians testifying to improvements to musculoskeletal pain[6] or performance anxiety[7] through exploration of Feldenkrais FI and ATM lessons. Intriguingly, many musicians also attest to more elusive improvements in musical expressivity and technical control. It is common for students to report an increased sense of well-being or that their playing seems to improve even after only short-term exposure in workshop scenarios. For example, Scotty Barnhart, trumpet player and director of the Count Basie Orchestra, had the following to say in a YouTube interview after receiving two Feldenkrais lessons for the first time from practitioner Alice Boyd for a PBS documentary: 'I feel a whole lot better. I am energized and I feel alive. Things I didn't know I was doing wrong she fixed! So, now I am standing up more on the balls of my feet. My body is aligned a whole lot better. I am breathing easier, and it is just easier to play.'[8] Qualitative descriptions of improvements to musicians' musculoskeletal pain symptoms are also common. For instance, Nelson[9] presents a descriptive case study of a female violinist suffering from debilitating neck pain at the Eastman School of Music. Nelson documents her progress, describing how after seven FI lessons her neck pain no longer bothered her in regular playing situations and she felt that her playing had improved overall.

Testimonials and practitioner-reported results such as these are invaluable because they convey pertinent details about individual experiences and document the process and outcomes of FM from the perspectives of practitioners and their students. However, they do not constitute research-based evidence from a scientific perspective. Student accolades and practitioner reports of best-case scenarios could be susceptible to bias, and often contain vague descriptions of qualitative experiences that are difficult to measure quantitatively. Although descriptive case-study reporting should continue, researchers can now begin using information from testimonials and descriptive case studies to formulate and scientifically investigate hypotheses about specific mechanisms underlying the more general positive effects reported by students and practitioners using objective measurement.

Scientific research on the Feldenkrais Method

Most research on FM has investigated its suitability as an intervention for musculoskeletal pain. Comprehensive reviews of research studies on FM, including those investigating musculoskeletal pain, can be found in a review published by Jain and colleagues,[10] and systematic reviews by Ernst and Canter,[11] and Hillier and Worley.[12] These reviews suggest that although almost all studies on FM report positive outcomes from participation in the Method, methodological limitations, including high potential for bias, small sample sizes, lack of baseline testing and use of unverified measures, prevent definitive conclusions being made about FM as a treatment for various musculoskeletal disorders based on the data available at this time. Although research results about the impact of FM on pain symptoms are ambiguous,[13] some studies suggest that FM may help improve patients' self-efficacy for pain management when compared to traditional physiotherapy treatments.[14] The reviews indicate that researchers studying FM have struggled to meet the demands of randomized controlled trials (RCTs), citing difficulty in recruiting a sample of participants of ample size and homogeneity to permit statistical analysis of the results. In addition, RCTs are unable to capture the diversity of individuals' responses to FM lessons, since RCT methodology necessitates the selection of discrete dependent variables which can easily be compared between large experimental and control groups. Many practitioners worry that this approach risks misrepresenting the Method by reducing it to discrete, generalizable outcomes and overlooking the potential for individual variation which is central to the Method.

Objective measurements of musicians' body-positioning and movement

An alternative to studying the impact of FM on subjective experiences such as participant reported pain or functionality could be to measure motor behaviour using motion-tracking technology. This approach has not yet been pursued in music research, but it may offer practical solutions to the problems posed by large-scale studies on subjective measures. The primary objective of most somatic methods is to influence biomechanical functioning by disrupting habitual patterns of motor behaviour, or 'self-use'. This is especially true of FM, which purports to help students learn about themselves using practitioner-directed and student-directed movement as a platform for exploratory, sensorimotor learning.[15] By bringing awareness to movement, the Method seeks not only to change a person's habits of movement, but in doing so also change how they experience their entire self.[16] Therefore, it could be posited that any positive benefits musicians may incur from the Method regarding pain or performance quality could be linked to observable changes in motor behaviour, which could be objectively measured by researchers given the appropriate tools. Assessing the impact of somatic training on variables relating to body-positioning and movement of musicians seems like a logical next step in research, especially considering that somatic practitioners routinely use visual assessments of body-positioning and movement as an aspect of their teaching.

A few pioneering studies can be found that quantitatively measure the impact of somatic methods on movement and postural biomechanics, primarily in non-musicians. For instance, Kutschke measured the neck and shoulder postural alignment, range of motion and muscle activity in healthy people after participating in twenty Alexander Technique sessions over eight weeks. Surface electromyogram (sEMG) measurements from this study indicate that muscle activity in the neck and shoulder altered after the Alexander training, and that measurements of forward head posture improved significantly for the intervention participants, especially during sitting and typing.[17] Other studies have found evidence that patterns in postural muscle recruitment are altered in individuals trained to teach Alexander Technique.[18] These studies provide evidence that long-term exposure to somatic training could impact motor control strategies for posture, and suggest further study on patterns of muscle activation is warranted with FM.

There are also some first examples of studies on the impact of somatic training on musicians that include assessments of posture and movement. These include the studies on music performance quality and body use of instrumentalists by Valentine and Williamon,[19] and Wong,[20] which both incorporate posture quality rating scales to examine practitioner-reported differences in musician posture characteristics from before and after somatic training interventions. The study by Valentine and Williamon randomly assigned eighteen musician participants (consisting of wind players, string players, keyboardists and singers) to receive thirty-minute Alexander lessons once a week for 12 weeks ($n=10$), or to undergo ten sessions of neurofeedback training over 6 to 8 weeks ($n=8$). Researchers video-recorded musical performances from before and after the training, and the videos were randomly ordered and assessed by experts external to the college. The experts rated the posture of the musicians before and after the interventions using a rating scale developed by the practitioner conducting the lessons in the study. The scale examined ten categories of Alexander Technique movement and posture goals, including 'head-neck-back' relationship and 'upper-limb/back'. It was found that the Alexander Technique participants demonstrated improvements in seven out of ten categories of the Alexander Technique movement and posture goals when compared with the neurofeedback participants. The clearest improvements in posture were noted in the singers in this study.

In the study by Wong, ten pianists were assigned to undergo a fifty-minute Feldenkrais, Body Mapping or Alexander Technique lesson. A panel of eight somatic training practitioners rated the 'body usage' of participants in the video recordings of participant performances of scales, Beethoven's *Für Elise*, and Schumann's *Wilder Reiter* from before and after the somatic training interventions. The researcher developed a seven-point Likert scale that required raters to assess the quality of body usage in the head/neck, shoulders, arms, torso, legs and feet from 'very good usage and coordination' to 'severe misusage'. Statistically significant post-somatic improvements were only noted for head and neck usage, although raters tended to rate body usage as slightly better in the post-somatic lesson videos for the other areas of the body as well.

These two studies are important because they are the first examples of scientific evidence that somatic training can impact playing posture in musicians. However, research has called into question the validity of visual assessment scales as tools for reliably measuring posture in scientific research.[21] Visual assessments of posture tend to have a poor inter- and intra-rater reliability; measurements are often not highly repeatable between different measurers using the same scale, and measurements can fluctuate within the same measurer from day to day.[22] Assessment instruments like postural rating scales must be assessed for reliability and validity to be considered scientifically valid.[23] Evidence of this validation process is lacking from existing studies on somatic education with musicians. This illustrates a need for more objective measurement tools when assessing aspects of body-positioning or movement quality.[24]

As of yet, no studies with musicians have used objective measurement tools to quantitatively measure posture and movement from before and after somatic training. Lee and colleagues have demonstrated the feasibility of this approach in their kinematic analysis of a cellist and flautist before and after an eight-week training programme involving yogic breathing and physical therapy exercises.[25] Feldenkrais researchers could use a similar approach and employ motion-tracking tools, such as optical-based motion-capture systems or video-based motion-tracking software, to collect quantitative data on how musicians' movement strategies evolve with FM experience. The next section presents possible methods of objectively measuring body-positioning and movement for this purpose, assessing the benefits and drawbacks of each approach in the context of research pertaining to FM and musicians. The discussion considers different analytical approaches for defining posture and movement variables from data acquired using motion-tracking technology.

Quantitative measurement of instantaneous body-positions

One biomechanical approach for objectively examining the physiological impact of FM is to take instantaneous measurements of body-positioning to quantify joint angles and alignment of anatomical locations at specific points in time. This approach involves taking photos with a camera or tracking motion with an advanced optical system and either choosing specific points in time to take measurements or taking an average of multiple measurements. Researchers using this method must choose which parts of the body will be measured, which strategies will be used to assess the quality of the positions and how data will be selected for analysis. Markers must be placed on relevant anatomical landmarks so that their positions can be tracked and distance and angle measurements can be taken.

Plumb-line approach

Since many somatic practitioners are concerned with alignment of points of balance in the head, shoulders, and spine, hips, knees, and ankles,[26] and since poor postural alignment in these parts of the body is frequently cited as a factor in the development of playing-related musculoskeletal disorders (PRMDs),[27] researchers may wish to examine vertical alignment of these points to investigate somatic training outcomes with pianists. Traditionally, vertical alignment in these parts of the body has been assessed against plumb lines to check if important structural joints are vertically arranged in such a way that the body can balance freely. This principle is frequently used in chiropractic, physical therapy and somatic training assessments, and has been used as a criterion for assessing posture quality in resting positions in research.[28]

Plumb-line approaches to posture measurement rest on the assumptions that vertical alignment and postural symmetry represent postural ideals that are associated with musculoskeletal health. However, the usefulness of straight plumb lines as diagnostic criteria for posture has been questioned, and evidence shows that the points of balance at the ear, shoulder, hip, knee and ankle are not generally arranged in a straight vertical line in standing positions in healthy subjects.[29] Postural symmetry in the right and left sides of the body in the anterior and posterior views is also occasionally used as a standard representing postural health for diagnostic purposes. However, research demonstrates that asymmetry in the resting positions of the pelvis, shoulder and trunk is normally observed in healthy, pain-free individuals, raising questions about the use of symmetry as a baseline criterion for good posture.[30] Researchers should consider the variability of healthy posture when using straight plumb lines or lines of symmetry, and consider complementing the data with alternative forms of posture measurement and assessment. This is particularly true for Feldenkrais research, since FM does not actively seek to promote symmetry in positioning, but rather draws attention to asymmetry in positioning and function as a learning tool for promoting greater acuity in self-awareness.

Strategies for measuring head, shoulder and spine position

Since it is expected that the resting muscle tonus of postural control muscles will change as a result of FM lessons, researchers may be interested in examining key postural relationships for evidence of change in patterns of muscular activation. Researchers have devised different approaches to measure head, shoulder and spine positioning that could be useful in some FM research contexts. For example, forward head position is frequently measured as the angle formed between a line passing from the C7 vertebra through the ear tragus, and a horizontal line passing through C7 in the sagittal plane, while an individual is sitting or standing. Similarly, the angle formed between a horizontal line passing through the ear tragus, and the line connecting the ear tragus and the outer canthus of the eye have been used to assess the angle of the head at the atlas occipital joint.

Shoulder position is occasionally determined by measuring the horizontal and vertical displacement of a point on the shoulder in relation to the C7 joint to measure whether the shoulders are elevated or rest substantially forward from the body.[31] Other researchers have measured the angle between the line connecting a point on the shoulder and the C7 vertebra, and a horizontal line extending forward from the shoulder in the sagittal plane to represent the degree of forward shoulder posture.[32] Methods for measuring spine curvature vary widely, with different vertebrae chosen as landmarks from study to study.[33] Since measurement procedures for posture of the head, shoulders and spine have not been standardized, it is difficult to compare results across different studies examining similar postures. This means that researchers interested in measuring the impact of somatic training on pianists' posture must design their own measurement protocols according to their own needs and expertise.

Selecting posture variables for research on somatic training for pianists

Reports on changes to posture and movement as a result of somatic training are often descriptive, or non-specific, and understandably vary among individuals, making it difficult for researchers to choose specific parts of the body to measure when looking for meaningful changes in the context of piano playing. Since research has shown a connection between forward head posture and musculoskeletal pain in the neck in computer users, this position could be a good choice for measurement with pianists. However, researchers should be cautious about extending conclusions from research on computer users to pianists, since the two activities place different biomechanical demands on the upper body.

Although research associating elevated or forward shoulder positioning with musculoskeletal pain is not conclusive, piano teachers are often concerned about the elevation of shoulders during performance, since it might be an outward indication of excess tension or performance anxiety. Evidence does suggest that there is a correlation between having protracted shoulders and forward head position and incidence of musculoskeletal pain in musicians.[34] Therefore, researchers could consider measuring the vertical and forward displacement of the shoulders in respect to the spine and position of the head in relation to the torso as posture variables pertinent to piano playing.

Extreme angles of spine curvature held statically at length have also been implicated as problematic in the posture of musicians, warranting research on the impact of somatic training on the vertebral positioning and spine curvature of pianists.[35] Investigating these three regions of the body (the head, shoulders and spine) would give a comprehensive overview of the vertical postural alignment of performing pianists, allowing researchers to examine if FM lessons impact performance postures of the head and torso.

The challenge of assessing posture quality

Some studies suggest specific postural characteristics put musicians at greater risk for developing musculoskeletal pain.[36] It may therefore seem straightforward to simply measure whether FM helps pianists avoid body positions that are known to be problematic. However, research on risk factors for the development of PRMDs is heterogeneous, with many conflicting definitions of PRMD and methods of assessment, making it difficult to understand clear risk factors that may contribute to the development of pain syndromes in musicians.[37] Although some evidence points to relationships between postural factors and PRMDs in musicians, including dysfunction of the lumbopelvic stabilization muscles,[38] forward head posture and protracted shoulders,[39] so far posture has not been strongly implicated as one of the primary risk factors for developing PRMDs in prevalence studies. Available evidence instead points to factors like gender,[40] practice habits and anxiety as having a greater impact on a musicians' risk for developing a PRMD.[41] Most available research tends to diagnose perceived postural defects in musicians without empirically connecting the postures to PRMDs, illustrating instead that according to some clinical definitions of good posture, most, if not all, musicians could be considered to have defective posture.[42] The body of available research on postural interventions as a treatment for PRMDs is small, and so far the results have been inconclusive due to subjective forms of posture measurement.[43] Therefore, although retraining of posture is often recommended as an important part of a treatment plan for PRMDs,[44] there is not yet concrete evidence that interventions aimed at solving postural defects solve or reduce symptoms of PRMDs. More research is urgently needed to further address this issue.

As research proceeds, investigators should consider that establishing the true role of posture in the development of PRMDs will require objective forms of assessment. Conflicting results and theories about the influence of specific postures on musculoskeletal health hinder researchers' ability to interpret whether posture changes following interventions should be considered improvements. Since research has been unable to establish conclusively if certain posture characteristics are clinically problematic, and since posture variables have the potential to vary from day to day within an individual,[45] researchers must contend with the fact that it may be impractical, if not impossible, to apply universal criteria for assessing posture quality across all participants in a study.

Posture quality in piano performance

In the context of piano playing, definitions about what constitutes ideal posture are even more ambiguous. Posture and movement habits vary considerably among professional pianists, making it impossible to define good posture based on technical expertise or movement aesthetics. For instance, Arthur Rubinstein is noted for the erect yet supple nature of his posture, and his parsimonious movement of the torso.[46] His seemingly effortless interpretations, especially of the works of Chopin, are admired as masterful. However, Glenn Gould's peculiar manner of sitting, with a very low seat, hunched back, face nearly touching the keys and raised shoulders, did not seem to interfere with his ability to deliver virtuosic and original performances, even though he struggled with severe musculoskeletal pain during his lifetime.[47] Music educators who teach posture and movement usually draw on a variety of different experiences and movement education systems to formulate diverse opinions about what constitutes good posture, resulting in different preferences among expert educators. These examples demonstrate that there are no defined aesthetic criteria for judging the quality of pianists' posture and movement, making it difficult to judge if changes observed in post-intervention testing should be considered improvements or deteriorations from the perspectives of artistry or technical proficiency. Unless future research is able to specify criteria that can definitively label certain postural characteristics as problematic from the perspective of health or technical expertise, researchers will be unable to confidently interpret the results of intervention studies that objectively measure posture and movement. Until that problem is solved, researchers investigating the impact of somatic training on pianists' posture should look for evidence of change to posture and movement only, without applying criteria for whether the change should be considered better or worse. This will allow researchers to take a more objective first look at the possible influence of somatic training on posture in various areas of the body, instead of ascribing to preconceived expectations based on opinions about posture quality that may not be well-founded in research.

Conclusion: Considerations for measuring posture and movement in the context of the Feldenkrais Method

Choosing appropriate variables for measurement in the context of FM requires researchers to thoughtfully consider the true goals and techniques of the Method. First and foremost, it must be acknowledged that while habitual ways of positioning one's body might be expected to be influenced by the Method to a degree that could be measured with motion-tracking technologies or cameras, FM is not a postural intervention. The Method does not demonstrate specific principles of posture, nor does it require students to practise holding themselves in particular positions. Therefore, researchers studying the impact of FM on posture variables should take care to contextualize posture measurements as one of many possible indicators of change in motor behaviour, and not rely upon them as a means of gauging the success of the Method. Evidence from static positions should be assessed alongside other forms of data, and postural variables should always be interpreted within the context of their relationship to functional movement. It is preferable that studies attempt to include variables related to movement quality, such as range of motion, velocity, acceleration, or jerk, rather than only instantaneous measurements. In the case of research with pianists, variables within movement contexts are particularly important, since we are interested to learn how the motor functioning of pianists is impacted by FM lessons as they interact with their instrument. Instantaneous measurements of posture either before playing, or from selected moments during a performance, can offer only a single glimpse into the functioning of a complex moving system that is influenced not only by biomechanical factors, but also by the musical intentions of the performer.

Feldenkrais adhered to the tenet that posture should not be thought of as a static position but a dynamic process by which the brain solves problems of balance and movement as individuals move through their environment adaptively. He preferred not to use the word 'posture' at all due to its strongly encultured meanings related to ways of holding one's self imposed by societal expectations and physiological manifestations of anxiety.[48] When discussing postural alignment, he preferred to use the word 'acture' to highlight that, in his view, postural alignment is better understood as a dynamic process. 'Acture' describes musculoskeletal organization in the context of movement; the CNS (Central Nervous System) seeks to achieve a state of dynamic equilibrium, self-organizing to maintain balance and satisfy functions of daily life.[49]

He believed that through the exploratory process of learning to sense and feel one's self in movement, people could improve their functionality and ultimately enhance their quality of life[50]. In this view, any state of ideal skeletal alignment or functioning remains purely theoretical, with primacy always placed on individual expressions of movement behaviour, and not the attainment of functional ideals.[51] However, in the twelfth chapter, entitled 'Measuring' Posture (quotations added by himself), of his book *Body and Mature Behaviour* (1966), he writes the following in regard to the value of quantitative posture measurement:

> I am quite aware that in practice, these methods (of measuring posture) are not more than an indication. It is important, however, that it is possible to obtain some sort of measurement, even though indirect, of what is usually considered unfathomable. I have little doubt that with the accumulation of extensive data … very useful information would be obtained.[52]

Therefore, by opting for quantitative measurement of changes in body-positioning and movement as part of a research agenda for FM, we are able to fulfil one of Feldenkrais's own wishes. Motion-tracking tools offer the ability to do this, providing a precise means of measuring body-positioning and the possibility of examining movement dynamically through kinematic analyses. Finally, it should be emphasized that our discussion about the value of pursuing objective measures in Feldenkrais research with pianists is not intended to replace qualitative forms of evidence or discount the subjective experiences of practitioners and students. These forms of evidence will always remain of primal importance when evaluating the merits and potential of the Method to help people, including musicians. Quantitative measurements of movement and posture can never provide the entire story, but merely constitute an under-represented form of evidence in the current body of literature. Filling this gap could benefit musicians and practitioners of the Method alike by helping increase awareness of and confidence in FM in music education and performance.

Notes

1. Carl Czerny, *Complete Theoretical and Practical Piano Forte School: From the First Rudiments of Playing to the Highest and Most Refined State of Cultivation with the Requisite Numerous Examples Newly and Expressly Composed for the Occasion* (London: R. Cocks & Co, 1839), 1.

2. Samuel Nelson, 'Playing with the Entire Self: The Feldenkrais Method and Musicians', *Seminars in Neurology*, Vol. 9, No. 2 (1989), 97–104; Yochanan Rywerant, 'Chapter 12, Hanoch's Return to the Flute', in *The Feldenkrais Method: Teaching by Handling* (Laguna Beach, CA: Basic Health Publishers, 2003), 181–9; Yochanan Rywerant, 'Chapter 13, Improving the Ability to Perform', in *The Feldenkrais Method: Teaching by Handling* (Laguna Beach, CA: Basic Health Publishers, 2003), 191–8; Kristen Urbanski, 'Overcoming Performance Anxiety: A Systematic Review of the Benefits of Yoga, Alexander Technique, and the Feldenkrais Method', Bachelor of Arts, Ohio University, 2012. Available from: https://etd.ohiolink.edu/!etd.send_file?accession=ouhonors1343316242&disposition=attachment (accessed 14 May 2020).

3. Christine Zaza, 'Playing-Related Musculoskeletal Disorders in Musicians: A Systematic Review of Incidence and Prevalence', *Canadian Medical Association Journal*, Vol. 158, No. 8 (1998), 1019–25; Laura Kok et al., 'The Occurrence of Musculoskeletal Complaints Among Professional Musicians: A Systematic Review', *International Archives of Occupational and Environmental Health*, Vol. 89, No. 3 (2016), 373–96.

4. Danelle Cayea and Ralph Manchester, 'Instrument-Specific Rates of Upper-Extremity Injuries in Music Students', *Occupational Health and Industrial Medicine*, Vol. 6, No. 308 (1998), 308; Lisa Britsch, 'Investigating Performance-Related Problems of Young Musicians', *Medical Problems of Performing Artists*, Vol. 20, No. 1 (2005), 40–7; Alice G. Brandfonbrener, 'History of Playing-Related Pain in 330 University Freshman Music Students', *Medical Problems of Performing Artists*, Vol. 24, No. 1 (2009), 30–6.

5. Nicholas Quarrier, 'Survey of Music Teachers: Perceptions about Music Related Injury', *Medical Problems of the Performing Artist*, Vol. 10, No. 3 (1995), 106–10; Margaret Redmond and Anne Tierman, 'Knowledge and Practices of Piano Teachers in Preventing Playing-Related Injuries in High School Students', *Medical Problems of Performing Artists*, Vol. 16, No. 1 (2001), 32–8.

6. Kara Hagglund and Karen Jacobs, 'Physical and Mental Practices of Music Students as They Relate to the Occurrence of Music-Related Injuries', *Work*, Vol. 6, No. 1 (1996), 11–24.

7. Urbanski, 'Overcoming Performance Anxiety'.

8   *Scotty Barhnart Works with Feldenkrais Practitioner Alice Ferguson Boyd* [online video], 2015, https://www.youtube.com/watch?v=zOs_BuSU1_k (accessed 14 May 2020).

9   Samuel Nelson, 'Playing with the Entire Self', 97–104.

10 Sanjiv Jain, Kristy Janssen, and Sharon DeCelle, 'Alexander Technique and Feldenkrais Method: A Critical Overview', *Physical Medicine and Rehabilitation Clinics of North America*, Vol. 15, No. 4 (2004), 811–25.

11 E. Ernst and P.H. Canter, 'The Feldenkrais Method – A Systematic Review of Randomised Clinical Trials', *Physikalische Medizin, Rehabilitationsmedizin, Kurortmedizin*, Vol. 15, No. 3 (2005), 151–6.

12 Susan Hillier and Anthea Worley, 'The Effectiveness of the Feldenkrais Method: A Systematic Review of the Evidence', *Evidence-Based Complementary and Alternative Medicine*, Vol. 2015 (2015), 1–12.

13 Eva-Britt Malmgren-Olsson and Inga-Britt Bränholm, 'A Comparison between Three Physiotherapy Approaches with Regard to Health-Related Factors in Patients with Nonspecific Musculoskeletal Disorders', *Disability & Rehabilitation*, Vol. 24, No. 6 (2002), 308–17; Eva-Britt Malmgren-Olsson, Bengt-Ake Armelius, and Kerstin Armelius, 'A Comparative Outcome Study of Body Awareness Therapy, Feldenkrais, and Conventional Physiotherapy for Patients with Nonspecific Musculoskeletal Disorders: Changes in Psychological Symptoms, Pain, and Self-Image', *Physiotherapy Theory and Practice*, Vol. 17, No. 2 (2001), 77–95.

14 Eva-Britt Malmgren-Olsson and Bengt-Ake Armelius, 'Non-Specific Musculoskeletal Disorders in Patients in Primary Care: Subgroups with Different Outcome Patterns', *Physiotherapy Theory and Practice*, Vol. 19, No. 3 (2003), 161–73.

15 Patricia Buchanan and Beverly Ulrich, 'The Feldenkrais Method: A Dynamic Approach to Changing Motor Behavior', *Research Quarterly for Exercise and Sport*, Vol. 72, No. 4 (2001), 315–23.

16 Carl Ginsburg, 'Body-Image, Movement and Consciousness: Examples from a Somatic Practice in the Feldenkrais Method', *Journal of Consciousness Studies*, Vol. 6, No. 2–3 (1999), 79–91.

17 Ian Kutschke, 'The Effects of the Alexander Technique Training on Neck and Shoulder Biomechanics and Posture in Healthy People' (Master Thesis, McGill University, 2010). Available from: McGill University Library and Collections, http://www.fitavie.ca/documentation/alexander.pdf (accessed 14 May 2020).

18 Timothy Cacciatore, Fay Horak, and Sharon Henry, 'Improvement in Automatic Postural Coordination Following Alexander Lessons in a Person with Low Back Pain', *Physical Therapy*, Vol. 85, No. 6 (2005), 565–78; Timothy Cacciatore et al., 'Increased Dynamic Regulation of Postural Tone through Alexander Technique Training', *Human Movement Science*, Vol. 30, No. 1 (2011), 74–89.

19 Elizabeth Valentine and Aaron Williamon, 'Alexander Technique and Music Performance: Evidence for Improved "Use"', Thematic Session: Developing Musicians, *Proceedings of the Fifth Triennial ESCOM Conference* (Hanover, NH: Hanover University Press, 2003), 145–47.

20 Grace Wong, 'The Immediate Effects of Somatic Approach Workshops on the Body Usage and Musical Quality of Pianists' (Unpublished MA Thesis. University of Ottawa, Ottawa, Canada, 2015), 38–63, https://ruor.uottawa.ca/handle/10393/32166.

21 Christine Fedorak et al., 'Reliability of the Visual Assessment of Cervical and Lumbar Lordosis: How Good Are We?', *Spine*, Vol. 28, No. 16 (2003), 1857–59.

22 Andrew Aitken, 'Reliability of Visual Assessment of Forward Head Posture in Standing' (Master Thesis, Unitec Institute of Technology, New Zealand, 2008). Available from: Research Bank (accessed 5 March 2015).

23 Gail M. Sullivan, 'A Primer on the Validity of Assessment Instruments', *Journal of Graduate Medical Education*, Vol. 3, No. 2 (2011), 119–20.

24 Anabela Silva, T. David Punt, and Mark Johnson, 'Reliability and Validity of Head Posture Assessment by Observation and a Four-Category Scale', *Manual Therapy*, Vol. 15, No. 5 (2010), 490–5.

25 Sang-Hie Lee et al., 'Intervention Program in College Instrumental Musicians, with Kinematics Analysis of Cello and Flute Playing: A Combined Program of Yogic Breathing and Muscle Strengthening-Flexibility Exercises', *Medical Problems of Performing Artists*, Vol. 27, No. 2 (2012), 85–94.

26 F.M. Alexander, *The Use of the Self: Its Conscious Direction in Relation to Diagnosis, Functioning, and the Control of Reaction* (London: Methuen, 1932); Feldenkrais, *The Elusive Obvious* (Cupertino, CA: Meta Publications, 1981); Feldenkrais, *The Body and Mature Behaviour* (New York: International Universities Press Inc., 1966).

27 Jan Dommerholt, 'Performing Arts Medicine – Instrumentalist Musicians, Part II-Examination', *Journal of Bodywork and Movement Therapies*, Vol. 14, No. 1 (2010), 65–72; Rene Cailliet, 'Abnormalities of the Sitting Postures of Musicians', *Medical Problems of Performing Artists*, Vol. 5, No. 4 (1990), 131–5.

28 Donna Krasnow et al., 'Imagery and Conditioning Practices for Dancers', *Dance Research Journal*, Vol. 29, No. 1 (1997), 43–64; Florence Peterson Kendall et al., *Muscles Testing and Function with Posture and Pain*, 5th edn. (Baltimore, MD: Lippincott Williams & Wilkins, 2005).

29 Ann Woodhull, Kristine Maltrud, and Bruno Mello, 'Alignment of the Human Body in Standing', *European Journal of Applied Physiology and Occupational Physiology*, Vol. 54, No. 1 (1985), 109–15; Ann Woodhull-McNeal et al., 'How Linear Is Dancers' Posture', *Medical Problems of Performing Artists*, Vol. 5, No. 4 (1990), 151–4.

30 Elizabeth A.G. Ferreira et al., 'Postural Assessment Software (PAS/SAPO): Validation and Reliability', *Clinics*, Vol. 65, No. 7 (2010), 675–81.

31 Grace Szeto, Leon Straker, and Sally Raine, 'A Field Comparison of Neck and Shoulder Postures in Symptomatic and Asymptomatic Office Workers', *Applied Ergonomics*, Vol. 33, No. 1 (2002), 75–84.

32 Sally Raine and Lance Twomey, 'Head and Shoulder Posture Variations in 160 Asymptomatic Women and Men', *Archives of Physical Medicine and Rehabilitation*, Vol. 78, No. 11 (1997), 1215–23.

33 Miranda Bernhardt and Keith Bridwell, 'Segmental Analysis of the Sagittal Plane Alignment of the Normal Thoracic and Lumbar Spines and Thoracolumbar Junction', *Spine*, Vol. 14, No. 7 (1989), 717–21; Donald Harrison et al., 'Comparisons of Lordotic Cervical Spine Curvatures to a Theoretical Ideal Model of the Static Sagittal Cervical Spine', *Spine*, Vol. 21, No. 6 (1996), 667–75.

34 Emil Pascarelli and Yu Pin Hsu, 'Understanding Work-Related Upper Extremity Disorders: Clinical Findings in 485 Computer Users, Musicians, and Others', *Journal of Occupational Rehabilitation*, Vol. 11, No. 1 (2001), 1–21.

35 Patricia Blanco-Piñeiro, M. Pino Díaz-Pereira, and Aurora Martínez, 'Common Postural Defects among Music Students', *Journal of Bodywork and Movement Therapies*, Vol. 19, No. 3 (2015), 565–72.

36 Patricia Blanco-Piñeiro, M. Pino Díaz-Pereira, and Aurora Martínez, 'Musicians, Postural Quality and Musculoskeletal Health: A Literature Review', *Journal of Bodywork and Movement Therapies*, Vol. 21, No. 1 (2017), 157–72.

37 Peter Bragge, Andrea Bialocerkowski, and Joan McMeeken, 'A Systematic Review of Prevalence and Risk Factors Associated with Playing-Related Musculoskeletal Disorders in Pianists', *Occupational Medicine*, Vol. 56, No. 1 (2005), 28–38.

38 Anke Steinmetz, Wolfram Seidel, and Burkhard Muche, 'Impairment of Postural Stabilization Systems in Musicians with Playing-Related Musculoskeletal Disorders', *Journal of Manipulative and Physiological Therapeutics*, Vol. 33, No. 8 (2010), 603–11.

39 Pascarelli and Hsu, 'Understanding Work-Related Upper Extremity Disorders', 1–21.

40 Christine Zaza and Vernon Farewell, 'Musicians' Playing-Related Musculoskeletal Disorders: An Examination of Risk Factors', *American Journal of Industrial Medicine*, Vol. 32, No. 3 (1997), 292–300.

41 Shinichi Furuya et al., 'Prevalence and Causal Factors of Playing-Related Musculoskeletal Disorders of the Upper Extremity and Trunk among Japanese Pianists and Piano Students', *Medical Problems of Performing Artists*, Vol. 21, No. 3 (2006), 112–17.

42 Blanco-Piñeiro, Díaz-Pereira and Martínez, 'Common Postural Defects among Music Students', 565–72.

43 Blanco-Piñeiro, Díaz-Pereira and Martínez, 'Musicians, Postural Quality and Musculoskeletal Health', 157–72.

44 Richard J. Lederman, 'Neuromuscular and Musculoskeletal Problems in Instrumental Musicians', *Muscle & Nerve*, Vol. 27, No. 5 (2003), 549–61; Steinmetz, Seidel and Muche, 'Impairment of Postural Stabilization Systems in Musicians', 603–11.

45 Nadine Dunk et al., 'The Reliability of Quantifying Upright Standing Postures as a Baseline Diagnostic Clinical Tool', *Journal of Manipulative and Physiological Therapeutics*, Vol. 27, No. 2 (2004), 91–6; Philippa Pownall, Robert Moran, and Andrew Stewart, 'Consistency of Standing and Seated Posture of Asymptomatic Male Adults over a One-Week Interval: A Digital Camera Analysis of Multiple Landmarks', *International Journal of Osteopathic Medicine*, Vol. 11, No. 2 (2008), 43–51.

46 Bill Plake, *When Good Posture Becomes a Bad Idea* [website], 2011, http://billplakemusic.org/2011/07/21/when-good-posture-becomes-a-bad-idea-2/ (accessed 14 May 2020).

47 Kevin Bazzana, *Wondrous Strange: The Life and Art of Glenn Gould* (Toronto: McClelland & Stewart, 2004), 353–5.

48 Feldenkrais, *Awareness through Movement*, 66–7.

49 Feldenkrais, *The Potent Self* (Berkeley, CA: Frog Books, 1985), 119.

50 Feldenkrais, 'Mind and Body: Two Lectures Delivered at the Copenhagen Congress of Functional Movement and Relaxation', *The Journal for the Correlative Study of History, Philosophy and the Mind and Body*, Vol. 2, No. 1 (1964), 47–61.

51 Feldenkrais, *The Elusive Obvious*, 42–4.

52 Feldenkrais, *Body and Mature Behaviour*, 107.

CHAPTER 7
GAINING INSIGHT ON THE IMPACT OF FELDENKRAIS FUNCTIONAL INTEGRATION IN THE CONTEXT OF PIANO PLAYING: CONSIDERATIONS FOR MEASURING POSTURE AND MOVEMENT QUALITY

Jillian Beacon, Gilles Comeau and Donald Russell

PART I: THE FELDENKRAIS METHOD AND PIANISTS: A PILOT STUDY OF OBJECTIVE MEASUREMENT OF POSTURE AND MOVEMENT

Playing the piano is one of the most complex feats of motor control that human beings can accomplish.[1] Mastery involves over a decade of dedicated practice to refine and reinforce neurological connections distributed throughout the brain, which must coordinate seamlessly to allow a performer to play with control and expression.[2] The thousands of hours of practice also place formidable demands on the body. Recent research has revealed that playing-related pain is prevalent among professional and pre-professional musicians[3], including pianists.[4] Aspects of body use, such as postural misalignment,[5] excessive muscular tension[6] and biomechanically inefficient playing techniques, are often implicated as risk factors for playing-related pain.[7] Some musicians pursue somatic education as a means of retraining posture and movement to reduce or prevent playing-related pain.

Feldenkrais as holistic mind-body education for pianists

The Feldenkrais Method (FM) is one such form of somatic education. Musicians have used FM's holistic mind-body approach to enhance body awareness and explore new possibilities for coordinated movement. During lessons, students experience functional movement relationships between different parts of the body, helping them become aware of how their entire body coordinates in dexterous action. By exploring movements slowly and mindfully, students may become aware of habits of movement they did not notice before and learn new ways of moving more comfortably. For musicians, this may mean discovering more sustainable ways of playing to reduce or prevent playing-related pain.

Functional Integration in theory and practice

In FM, the style of one-on-one work in which a practitioner gently moves a student's body is known as Functional Integration (FI). While passively moving the student, the practitioner senses small details in (1) the quality of the student's movement, such as the degree of resistance and patterns of movement transfer between different segments of the body; (2) the body's position, such as asymmetries in orientation and positioning; and (3) the state of arousal in the nervous system, including evidence such as changes in the rate and depth of breathing, and changes in the resting tonus of muscles. Students are usually recumbent during these lessons to allow the postural support muscles (especially the extensors of the back) to relax without having to work against gravity to balance the body upright.[8]

In the short term, these lessons are intended to modulate neuromuscular control of posture globally, impacting the resting tonus of the muscles and students' proprioceptive representation of themselves.[9] Over time, they may lead to neuroplastic adaptations to motor control and an enhanced ability to perceive finer sensorimotor distinctions.[10] These changes may enhance the adaptability of motor behaviour, allowing individuals to move with greater spontaneity and variety. They may also confer other benefits, such as reduced pain or increased ease of movement.

Although each person's experience with FI is unique, it tends to elicit some common sensorial experiences that are reported by many students. People often report feeling taller, or more balanced over their feet in standing, or over their sitting bones in sitting immediately after FI.[11] Individuals may report feeling that some movements, such as walking or breathing, seem easier,[12] that they have increased range of motion at some joints, or that they have reduced musculoskeletal pain.[13] Some become aware of specific parts of themselves that they could not easily sense or perceive before the lesson.[14] People may also speak of sensory illusions, such as feeling that some parts of the body feel larger or longer than before.[15] These subjective experiences shared by many Feldenkrais students suggest that FM may lead to changes in the mental representation of the body-schema, or self-image, of the person in the central nervous system (CNS) via alterations of their proprioceptive experience. It may also lead to global changes in posture and coordination, stemming from changes in patterns of postural muscle activation that balance and redistribute patterns of resting muscle tonus across the musculoskeletal system. It is therefore reasonable to expect that some evidence of this learning process should be measurable through external measurements of body-positioning and coordination. However, researchers have not yet investigated whether changes in body-positioning or coordination patterns can be measured quantitatively.

Objective measurements of pianists before and after Feldenkrais training

As a first step towards addressing the need for objective measurement relating to posture and movement coordination in pianists participating in FM, the authors conducted a pilot project to track and measure pianists' body movements during performance from before and after a single FI lesson. This pilot study had two main objectives: (1) To determine if trends in the vertical alignment of postural points of balance were noted across a group of participants after a single FI lesson, and (2) if specific differences in posture and movement coordination were noted for individual participants. We hypothesized that no group trends in posture change would be observed after a single FI lesson (with Alan Fraser) due to the variability of posture between different individuals, and the natural variability of an individual's posture from day to day.[16] We also hypothesized that changes to specific posture variables might be noted for

The Feldenkrais Method in Creative Practice

some individuals, since somatic practitioners and their students often report differences in alignment or movement quality after short-term exposure to the Method.

Investigating Functional Integration with video-based motion-tracking of pianists

We used Dartfish video-based motion-tracking software to track anatomical points of interest on fifteen advanced pianists performing a contrary-motion C-major scale repeated three times, a sight-reading test, and the first section of Beethoven's *Für Elise WoO 59* immediately before and after receiving a thirty-minute FI lesson. We hypothesized that integration of sensorimotor experiences of the FI lesson may depend on the cognitive demands of the musical task, and therefore chose playing tests that placed different cognitive demands on the performer. We used Dartfish to track the movement of the pianists because it was simple to set up video cameras non-invasively next to acoustic pianos to permit comfortable and realistic performance conditions for participants. Although Dartfish measurements are limited to two dimensions, this method was appropriate for our study because we wished to measure the vertical alignment of specific anatomical points in the sagittal and coronal planes independently.

Figure 7.1 Placement of anatomical markers for Dartfish tracking (i) canthus (outer corner) of the right eye; (ii) ear tragus; (iii) anterior acromioclavicular joint (shoulder); (iv) C7 spinous process; (v, vi, vii, viii) – T4, T8, T12 and L5 spinous processes.

Gaining Insight on the Impact of Functional Integration

Posture variables: We fixed anatomical markers on the C7, T4, T8 and T12 vertebrae of participants, as well as the right eye canthus, right ear tragus, right acromion, right olecranon process and right lateral epicondyle of the humerus (Figure 7.1). We measured the postural variables described in Table 7.1 from videos recorded from the posterior and right sagittal views of the pianists as they performed the playing tests.

Table 7.1 Description of measurement of posture variables for Dartfish tracking

Variable	Description of measurement	Justification for measurement
Head region		
(i) forward head angle (°)	Angle formed between a horizontal line passing through the C7 spinous process and a line connecting the C7 process to the ear tragus	Found to be a good indicator of forward head position.[17] A smaller cervical angle has been associated with increased forward head position and neck pain in computer users.[18]
(ii) head height (cm)	Height of the ear-tragus marker above the origin of the Cartesian coordinate system	A simple way to determine if a person is sitting with more or less spine flexion overall between sessions.
Shoulder region		
(iii) shoulder protraction angle (°)	Angle formed between a line connecting a point on the shoulder and the C7 vertebra and a horizontal line extending forward from the shoulder in the sagittal plane	Gives information about the degree of protraction (forward rounding) in the shoulders.[19] Measured according to the procedure of van Niekerk et al.[20]
(iv) vertical and horizontal shoulder displacement (cm)	Difference between the y-axis value of C7 and the right shoulder	A measurement used by Szeto et al. (2002) to investigate shoulder elevation and shoulder protraction separately.
Spine region		
(v) origin-C7 angle (°)	Angle formed between the x-axis and a line joining C7 to the origin of the coordinate system at the back of the piano bench	Represents the angle of forward inclination of participants as they play.
(vi) T4 angle (°)	Angle formed between the C7, T4 and T8 vertebral markers	Gives an indication of curvature in the upper thoracic region of the spine.[21]
(vii) T8 angle (°)	Angle formed between the T4, T8 and T12 vertebral markers	Gives an indication of curvature in the lower thoracic region of the spine.[22]
(viii) T12 angle (°)	Angle formed between the T8, T12 and L5 vertebral markers	Gives an indication of the curvature in the lower thoracic/upper lumbar regions of the spine.[23]
(ix) height of vertebral markers (cm)	Height of spine markers (C7, T4, T8, T12, L5) above the origin of the Cartesian coordinate system	Used to measure changes in vertical positioning of specific vertebrae in the spine.

Table 7.2 Cross-participant average measurements of angular posture variables from before and after FI intervention in three playing conditions (°)

Variable	Playing condition	Pre-test	Post-test	Difference
Forward head angle (°)	Scale	31.3	31.7	0.4
	Für Elise	29.9	30.6	0.7
	Sight-reading	32.2	32.4	0.2
Shoulder protraction angle (°)	Scale	43.5	43.6	0.1
	Für Elise	49.6	49.4	−0.2
	Sight-reading	38.8	33.7	−5.1
T4 angle (°)	Scale	150.7	151.2	0.5
	Für Elise	150.8	151.2	0.4
	Sight-reading	150.8	150.9	0.1
T8 angle (°)	Scale	166.1	166.2	0.1
	Für Elise	166.0	166.4	0.4
	Sight-reading	166.0	166.2	0.2
T12 angle (°)	Scale	182.2	181.9	−0.3
	Für Elise	181.7	180.9	−0.8
	Sight-reading	182.7	180.7	−2.0

Notes. An increase in forward head angle means the head has moved backward into a more erect position. A decrease in shoulder protraction angle means the shoulders are moving forward, becoming more rounded.

Comparing group averages of posture variables: Results revealed that posture variables and movement patterns tended to remain consistent for most participants between the first and second sessions. No group trends in posture change were noted from pre- to post-test for any posture variables measured in the head, shoulders and spine regions. The group averages for spine angles were particularly stable between sessions and across playing conditions (see Table 7.2).

Changes to posture and movement characteristics of individual participants

We were also interested in finding out if significant changes in posture variables or movement patterns could be noted for individual participants. To answer this question, we examined time plots of posture variables of individual participants throughout the duration of their first and second sessions performing each playing test. The time plots from both the pre- and post-test recordings frequently displayed very similar movement patterns for a given participant, often containing even small details of torso movement at the exact same musical points in the phrases. The stability of the movement patterns can be clearly observed in Figure 7.2, which displays the pre- and post-test time plots of participant EF1's body flexion angle during their performance of *Für Elise*.

Gaining Insight on the Impact of Functional Integration

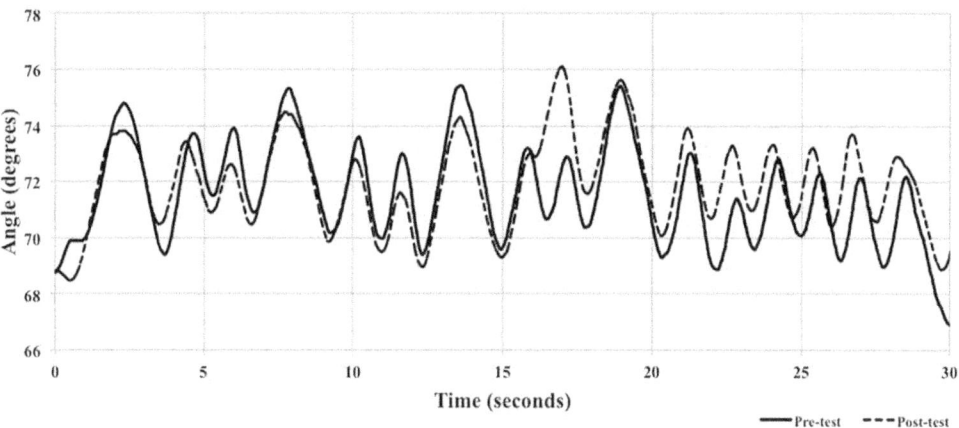

Figure 7.2 Pre- and post-test time plots of the angle between a line connecting the C7 marker and the point of origin on the bench, and the x-axis for participant EF1.

However, time-plot analysis also revealed that some individuals displayed strikingly different movement patterns in pre- and post-test recording sessions. For example, Figure 7.3 illustrates that in the pre-test, participant KP2 kept her head almost perfectly still. Her pre-test head movement appears jerky, with a limited range of only about 3 degrees. In the post-test, the participant's head appears to have moved in a smoother, wavelike pattern compared to the pre-test, and the range of motion increased to about 10 degrees. It is interesting to note that this difference in pre- and post-test head movement patterns was noticeable in both the scale and *Für Elise* performances, but not the sight-reading condition, suggesting the movements of the head may have been restricted when the participant was required to read unfamiliar music.

Figure 7.4 displays a second example of differences in movement quality, illustrating an increased range and apparent smoothness of movement of the head and torso of participant AL1 in the post-test compared to the pre-test performance of contrary-motion C-major scales. This example is interesting because it clearly depicts a consistent movement pattern in the torso throughout each of the three repetitions of the contrary-motion scale. The changes in movement quality appear to be integrated throughout the head and spine, since the differences appear for angles of head elevation (A), hip flexion (B) and lumbar curvature (C). The post-test movements had a greater range of motion and showed fewer instances of abrupt changes in positioning. However, it is noteworthy that these changes only appeared in the scale-playing condition for this participant, and not the other tests.

The Feldenkrais Method in Creative Practice

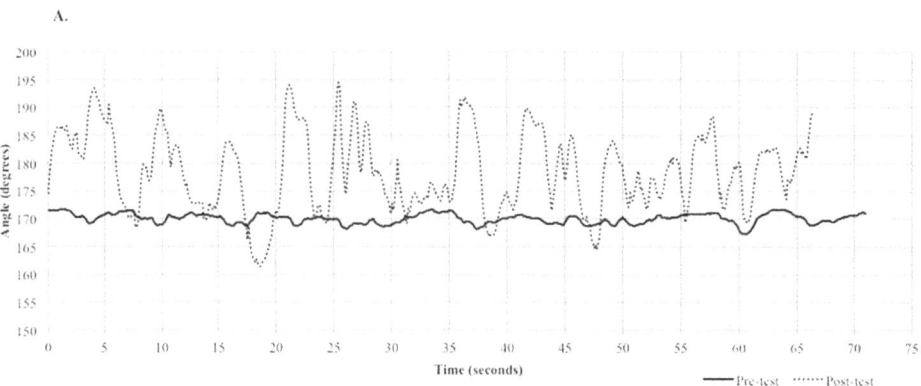

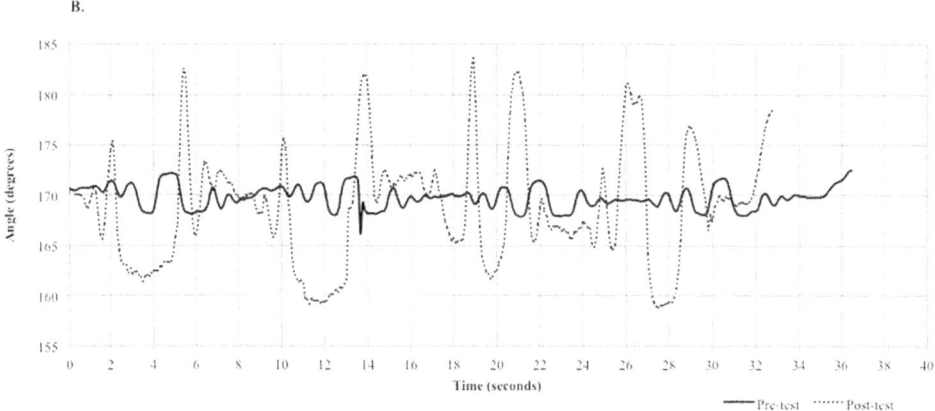

Figure 7.3 Pre- and post-test time plots of the angle formed between the horizontal plane and a line connecting the C7 vertebral marker and the eye-canthus marker for participant KP2 during (A) *Für Elise* and (B) scale performances.

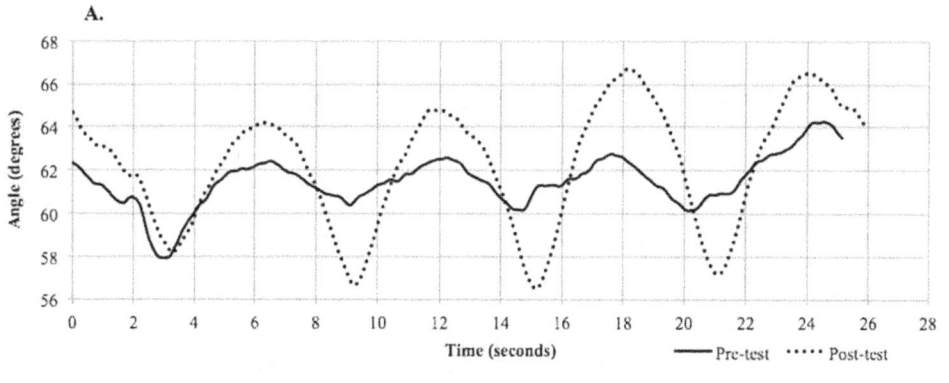
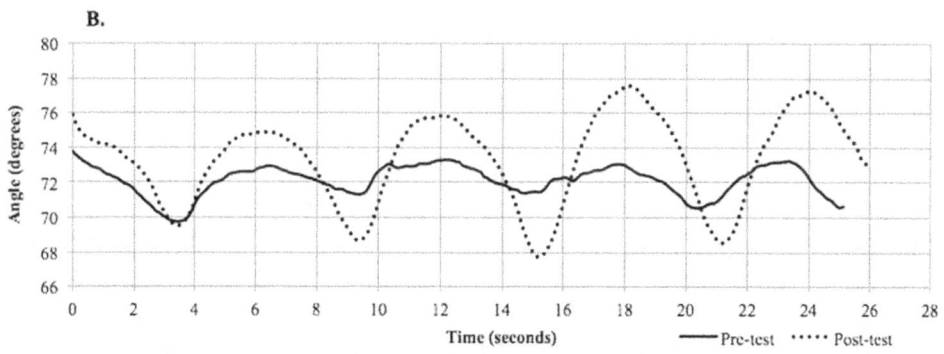
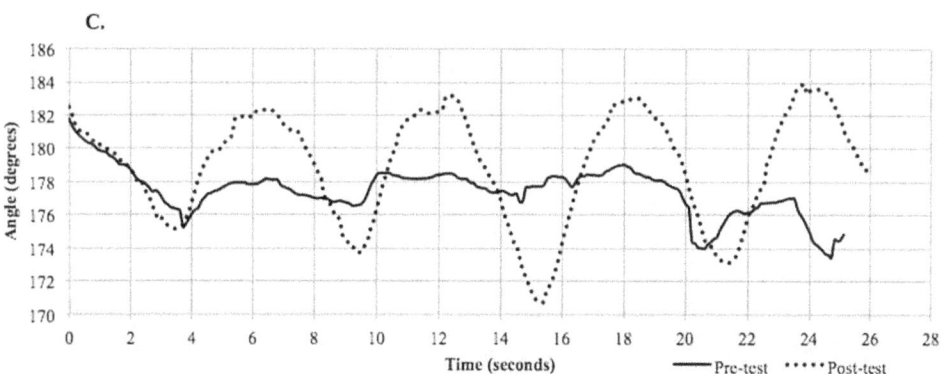

Figure 7.4 Pre- and post-test time plots of (A) eye-canthus, C7, horizontal angle, (B) C7 marker, horizontal angle, and (C) T12, L5, vertical angle for participant AL1's performance of scales.

PART II: DISCUSSION AND RECOMMENDATIONS FOR FUTURE RESEARCH

The results from this pilot study are intriguing and offer an opportunity to discuss many issues regarding the strengths and limitations of measuring posture as the dependent variable in repeated measures studies with FM. In the following sections we raise five important points stemming from our pilot investigation that future researchers may find helpful when constructing methodologies for quantitatively examining patterns of human movement in the context of music performance.

Recommendations for study design: Researching individuals instead of groups

The most interesting results from our pilot study came from examining data on an individual basis rather than looking for group trends. For instance, participant AP1's movement became more integrated throughout the torso during scale performances. We also observed larger, more graceful head movements in participant KP2's post-test recording compared with her pre-test recordings, which show that she held her head almost perfectly still before the FI. Although more than two measurement sessions would be required to determine if the changes observed reflect natural variability in movement or changes induced by FI, these examples are intriguing and warrant further investigation.

The fact that the two participants did not respond in the same way should not diminish the significance of the observations; it is expected that individuals will respond differently to FI since each participant has unique movement habits, and personal histories of training, pain and injuries. Researchers struggle to identify variables that could be meaningfully assessed across a large sample group in a large randomized controlled trial (RCT). Future research on FM may be best served by capitalizing on detailed, single-subject designs employing objective measurements of movement behaviour of individuals over longer periods of time. Although RCTs are still considered to be the gold standard of scientific evidence,[24] many human movement researchers are beginning to recognize that the dynamic, evolving and adapting nature of the human motor system requires detailed examination of unique individuals in single-subject methodological designs.[25] This style of investigation is certainly well suited to FM, achieving a necessary balance between the individualized attention afforded in case studies and the objectivity of the scientific method. This is especially true for pianists, who as a group vary in level of expertise, type of dysfunction or discomfort experienced, and playing history, making it difficult to achieve participant homogeneity in large-scale research projects.

Recommendations for variable selection: Measuring movement

Our pilot project raises questions about the limitations inherent in studying posture as a static position. Most studies that quantitatively measure posture use static standing or seated positions.[26] Up until recently, researchers have tended to prioritize methodologies which attempt to define ideal or average measurements for resting angles in spine curvature,[27] shoulder position,[28] or head and neck positions,[29] but without standardized measurement protocols it is difficult to compare results across different studies. Methodologies examining static posture variables could help assess some physiological outcomes of FI, but they are ultimately unable to address changes in movement quality, timing, orientation and coordination, which are central concerns of FM.[30] Moshe Feldenkrais believed in a principle of dynamic equilibrium, by which posture is thought of not as a position but rather as a process through which the CNS finds functional ways to move gracefully and find balance using sensory feedback.[31]

Researchers could address this perspective on posture by exploring analytical approaches that report on the quality of movement, such as smoothness and range of motion, rather than static joint positions. Researchers could also apply biomechanical strategies for studying coordination in intersegmental relationships to describe how changes in one area of the body impact or evolve with changes in another area dynamically during movement. One method to examine how changes in one joint angle relate to changes in another is to use parametric phase plots to describe the continuous relative phase between two moving oscillators.[32] Some motor control researchers have used this type of analysis to examine movement relationships between the head and thorax in walking,[33] and studies with pianists could conceivably use this method to examine how movements in joints of the arms are related to movements in the pelvis or thorax for repetitive playing tasks. However, this type of analysis is best suited to movements that repeat and can be described periodically. Since many pianistic movements are not typically periodic and may vary considerably depending on the technical and expressive demands of the music, this type of analysis may only be practical in a limited number of music performance contexts.

Principal component analysis (PCA) is another possible method for examining features of coordination in human motion-tracking data. PCA is a form of analysis used to reduce large kinematic data sets into components identifying specific movement relationships that account for portions of the variability in the entire moving system. PCA uses algorithms to identify mutually orthogonal directions of maximal variance in a data set to compile new data sets, or principal components (PCs), that are ordered according to the amount of variance they explain. Each PC is an independent linear transformation of the original data set, and in kinematic analysis these transformations are often interpreted to represent meaningful movement relationships within the entire system. The benefit of PCA is that it can reveal movement relationships between many different areas of the body at the same time, and researchers do not have to limit analysis to only one or two joints.[34]

This method has already been used in some applications with musicians. For example, researchers used PCA to extract movement features from the hands of four pianists with differing levels of expertise.[35] The researchers tracked twenty-six anatomical markers on the pianists' hands as they played six different piano pieces. Analysis revealed that often eight or more PCs were required to describe the movements of the more experienced pianists while fewer PCs were required for pianists with fewer years of experience. This suggests that the experts more flexibly exploit the degrees of freedom available in the hand and use a greater diversity of hand movements compared to amateurs. Although this study only examined four pianists, the ability of PCA to identify more degrees of freedom in the hand movements of expert compared to amateur pianists suggests future research is warranted. Researchers could investigate if PCA is suitable for comparing motor behaviour between musician populations expected to display differences in dexterity, such as injured and uninjured musicians, or musicians with and without somatic training experience.

Although PCA offers a powerful way to extract features from complex movement data, the method comes with limitations. The movement relationships uncovered using PCA may be difficult to interpret biomechanically since they do not necessarily represent real movements,[36] and there is a potential for loss of detail in explaining the variance if the variance threshold is set too low in the algorithm.[37] The results of the analysis can change drastically depending on the user-determined settings, such as the percentage of total variance the algorithm will explain in the data set or processes of data normalization. PCA is also more suitable for identifying differences between groups of movers already suspected of exhibiting differences in motor behaviour. It is not clear if PCA analysis is a suitable means for tracking subtle changes to coordination that may be brought about by somatic training across pre- and post-test trials. Although researchers have already used PCA to create movement profiles to describe individual pianists' movements,[38] researchers have not yet established if these profiles tend to remain consistent for repeated performances of the same piece. For these reasons, more testing will be required to determine its suitability as a measurement technique in repeated measures studies of FM with pianists.

Recommendations for baseline measurements: Assessing variability in baseline posture

Future studies on FM with musicians should incorporate comprehensive baseline testing to better understand the range of normal measurement values for each individual participant. Since our study did not conduct baseline testing over many days, we were unable to distinguish potential changes brought about by the intervention from natural fluctuations in motor behaviour. Human postural coordination varies day to day because it is mediated by complex and highly adaptable motor control strategies in the CNS that can easily be influenced by factors intrinsic to the participant or their environment and potentially lead to variability in baseline measurements.[39] Postural control can be impacted by cognitive loading[40] and attentional demands of competing tasks,[41] with the impact becoming more significant as age increases.[42]

Postural sway and the natural variability of head and spine positions present serious obstacles for researchers attempting to track changes to posture in repeated measures studies.[43] For instance, Dunk and colleagues found poor repeatability of posture measurement of thoracic, cervical and lumbar curves when measured across three sessions, with the first session conducted in the morning, and the second and third sessions taken a week later in the morning and afternoon.[44] Pownall and colleagues found that the posture variables of eleven healthy men remained stable during measurements taken over the course of one week, but posture variables in the sagittal plane, including spine variables, were more inconsistent compared to variables measured in the posterior or anterior view.[45] Whichever postural variables researchers choose to measure, it is important that researchers take the time to learn how their variables naturally fluctuate over a period of several days or weeks, and carefully control testing conditions to reduce the influence of environmental factors that may influence postural coordination.

Choosing musical tests: Task-dependent posture

Since research demonstrates that cognitive loading impacts neurological posture control strategies,[46] we hypothesized that the type of playing task performed by a pianist could significantly influence their postural characteristics during playing. The results of our pilot study lend preliminary support for this hypothesis. For instance, we noted that the relative size of forward head angle stayed consistent from pre- to post-test for a given participant performing a given playing task. This suggests that an individual adopts a different average position of the head depending on the task, and that these individual tendencies seem to remain consistent despite a single FI lesson. We also observed that each pianist displayed a greater average angle of elbow abduction on the right side compared to the left side from the anterior view in both the pre- and the post-tests (Figure 7.5). This is interesting because C-major contrary-motion scales involve identical biomechanical demands on the right and left side of the body; the movements are perfectly mirrored, the same fingers play at the same time in both hands, and the distance the individual's arm must travel on the keyboard is also the same. Since most individuals sat at the keyboard with middle-C very near to the centre of their bodies, one might expect biomechanical symmetry in the movements of the right and left arm to match the symmetry of the task demands. However, it appears that all participants have learned a right-side dominant strategy to perform the contrary-motion scale, regardless of handedness (there were three left-handed individuals in the study). This gives a clear example of how it is possible for the brain to use different movement strategies for the right and left side of the body even when they are completing the same task. In this case, this type of asymmetrical movement strategy seems to be common for the performance of this particular scale and this tendency did not seem to be impacted by the FI lesson.

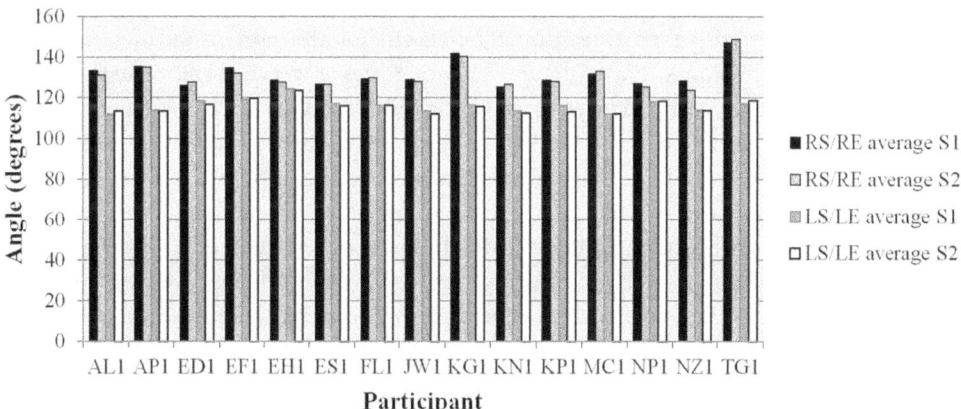

Figure 7.5 Average angle of abduction between a line connecting the elbow and shoulder, and a vertical line descending from the shoulder on the right and left sides in performances of contrary-motion scales before and after an FI intervention. RS/RE stands for 'angle of right shoulder to right elbow'. S1 is the pre-test and S2 is the post-test.

Our observations of task-dependent posture concur with other researchers' observations that musicians' movement characteristics differ between sight-reading and repertoire playing conditions.[47] Therefore, researchers investigating posture of pianists must consider that the varying cognitive demands of different types of performing tasks could significantly impact posture control strategies during performance, and should control for the type of activity the pianist is doing in repeated measures tests. Future research will be required to better understand task dependency on posture when constructing methodologies to investigate somatic training outcomes with pianists.

Drawing conclusions from posture research: What is an improvement?

Even if studies successfully measure posture variables, researchers have yet to reach a consensus about how to interpret the meaning of those measurements in terms of improvements to health or performance. Researchers struggle to define how extreme a postural measurement must be to count as pathological, and many cases have been unable to find clear correlations between certain posture characteristics and musculoskeletal pain. For instance, some evidence indicates that rounded shoulders are associated with higher incidences of musculoskeletal pain.[48] However, since the repeatability of shoulder measurement has been shown to be unreliable between different raters and across multiple measurements from the same rater for some measurement protocols, it is difficult to draw conclusions from available research.[49] Correlations of specific spine positions with musculoskeletal pain are particularly ambiguous.[50] Although research shows that variations in spinal curvature can alter how trunk muscles are activated to support the body,[51] the details about how certain characteristics of spinal curvature influence musculoskeletal health are not well understood, and diverging theories create confusion about the definition of healthy spine posture.[52] For instance, some researchers still disagree about whether a kyphosis or lordosis curvature in the lumbar spine is healthier for seated posture,[53] and how proper posture should be taught for the prevention of lower back pain.[54] Evidence also shows that structural abnormalities in cervical spine curvature are not correlated with higher incidences of neck pain, even though they are often considered to be the cause of pain in clinical settings.[55] The case against forward head position is much clearer, with more substantial evidence that smaller angles of forward head position (occurring when the head is held further away from the body anteriorly) correlate with higher incidences of musculoskeletal pain in the neck and shoulders.[56] However, some researchers have cautioned against drawing conclusions too quickly even in this case, since classifications of forward head position have varied across different studies.[57] These confusions illustrate that although superficially it may seem like a simple task to create criteria for judging posture quality and to choose posture variables for measurement in research, the many divergent opinions presented in the literature pose significant challenges to researchers. Although many modes of treatment for musculoskeletal disorders operate based on their own theoretical principles of correct postural alignment, currently there is no scientifically defensible criterion for judging whether posture could be said to have improved or deteriorated in repeated measures studies on somatic training.

Conclusion: New directions in research on the Feldenkrais Method with musicians

Our pilot study offers preliminary insight into the expected impact of FI lessons on body positioning and movement in pianists. This project yielded five main insights that could help guide researchers in future studies on FM with musicians: (1) Research on FM with musicians may benefit from single-subject designs that use rigorous empirical methods to study changes in motor behaviour in individuals; (2) Research on how FM influences movement quality and coordination may yield more poignant results compared to measuring static posture variables, or averaging positions from motion-tracking data; (3) Future studies should include comprehensive baseline measurements to better understand the natural variability of the dependent posture and movement variables; (4) The posture and movement exhibited by a musician may be significantly influenced by the type of playing task they perform; and (5) Researchers should acknowledge that it is difficult to interpret the meaning of posture measurements within the literature relating posture to health and function.

Since the current scope of research in this field is limited, researchers could consider applying some of these insights in investigations about longer-term impact of somatic training interventions, including FM. We have a paucity of data on the transition that a piano performer might experience as they learn new motor behaviour through FM, and the time scale over which these changes are observable. This should entice researchers to work to find ways to answer many important questions regarding the process and applications of somatic learning, including: (1) Which factors influence the development of biomechanical strategies such that some pianists are pain-free, while others encounter limits to their motor capacity or develop playing-related pain? (2) How do biomechanical strategies differ between injured and non-injured pianists and how can Feldenkrais lessons help? (3) How do biomechanical strategies evolve over somatic learning periods of different time scales? (4) Do biomechanical strategies keep evolving once somatic lessons are over? (5) Are specific biomechanical factors influenced differently by different somatic approaches?

A motivation behind the pursuit of such studies is the urgent need for new research that objectively examines somatic training outcomes, since most evidence suggesting that somatic training can lead to improvements in playing-related pain or musical expression comes from subjective sources. FM and other somatic approaches have helped many musicians feel more comfortable when performing, and increasing awareness about these methods may help to improve the quality of life of many performers, especially students who experience tremendous workloads and high degrees of physical and emotional stress during their study.[58] However, universities and conservatories will need credible evidence from research about the benefits of these methods to justify the cost of incorporating them into programming. Since somatic training lessons are not often covered by medical insurance plans, they are not always affordable for the musicians who may benefit from them. Improved research could pave the way for the eventual coverage of somatic training by insurance plans or may at least help students become informed about the potential benefits of somatic training, should they choose to invest their time and money into learning them. Finally, improving research methodologies could help FM practitioners better understand the specific mechanisms responsible for musicians' positive experiences with FM. This could lead to better adaptation of teaching strategies to the unique needs of performing musicians and improve the quality of somatic training in the context of music education.

Notes

1. Eckart Altenmüller and Wilfried Gruhn, 'Brain Mechanisms', in *The Science and Psychology of Music*, ed. R. Parncutt and G.E. McPherson (New York: Oxford University Press, 2006), 63–82.
2. Marc Bangert et al., 'Shared Networks for Auditory and Motor Processing in Professional Pianists: Evidence from fMRI Conjunction', *Neuroimage*, Vol. 30, No. 3 (2006), 917–26.
3. Alice G. Brandfonbrener, 'History of Playing-Related Pain in 330 University Freshman Music Students', *Medical Problems of Performing Artists*, Vol. 24, No. 1 (2009), 30–6; Christine Zaza, 'Playing-Related Musculoskeletal Disorders in Musicians: A Systematic Review of Incidence and Prevalence', *Canadian Medical Association Journal*, Vol. 158, No. 8 (1998), 1019–25.
4. Danelle Cayea and Ralph Manchester, 'Instrument-Specific Rates of Upper-Extremity Injuries in Music Students', *Occupational Health and Industrial Medicine*, Vol. 6, No. 308 (1998), 308; William J. Dawson, 'Upper-Extremity Problems Caused by Playing Specific Instruments', *Medical Problems of Performing Artists*, Vol. 17, No. 3 (2002), 135–40.
5. Rene Cailliet, 'Abnormalities of the Sitting Postures of Musicians', *Medical Problems of Performing Artists*, Vol. 5, No. 4 (1990), 131–5; Jan Dommerholt, 'Performing Arts Medicine – Instrumentalist Musicians, Part II-Examination', *Journal of Bodywork and Movement Therapies*, Vol. 14, No. 1 (2010), 65–72.
6. Alice G. Brandfonbrener, 'Pathogenesis and Prevention of Problems of Keyboardists', *Medical Problems of Performing Artists*, Vol. 12, No. 2 (1997), 57–9.
7. Lili Allsop and Tim Ackland, 'The Prevalence of Playing-Related Musculoskeletal Disorders in Relation to Piano Players' Playing Techniques and Practising Strategies', *Music Performance Research*, Vol. 3, No. 1 (2010), 61–78.
8. Feldenkrais, *The Elusive Obvious* (Berkeley, CA: Frog, 1985), 131.
9. Feldenkrais, 'Mind and Body', in *Embodied Wisdom*, ed. Elizabeth Beringer (Berkeley, CA: North Atlantic Books, 2010), 27–44.
10. Norman Doidge, 'Moshe Feldenkrais: Physicist, Black Belt, Healer – Healing Serious Brain Problems through Mental Awareness of Movement', in *The Brain That Changes Itself: Remarkable Discoveries and Recoveries from the Frontiers of Neuroplasticity* (New York: Viking, 2015), 160–96.
11. Carl Ginsburg, 'The Roots of Functional Integration: Part 1 – Biology and Feldenkrais', *Feldenkrais Journal*, Vol. 3 (1987), 13–23.
12. Carl Ginsburg, 'Body-Image, Movement, and Consciousness: Examples from a Somatic Practice in the Feldenkrais Method', *Journal of Consciousness Studies*, Vol. 6, No. 2–3 (1999), 79–91.
13. Lori Myers, 'Application of Neuroplasticity Theory through the Use of the Feldenkrais Method® with a Runner with Scoliosis and Hip and Lumbar Pain: A Case Report', *Journal of Bodywork and Movement Therapies*, Vol. 20, No. 2 (2016), 300–9.
14. Eva Scher, 'A Case Study from Three Perspectives: A Life Story', in *New York Feldenkrais Professional Training Program Readings & Handouts Volume 1*, ed. D. Zemach-Bersin (New York: Feldenkrais Institute of North America, 2008); Aliza Stewart, *Feldenkrais for Musicians Violin w/Aliza Stewart* [online video], 2010, https://www.youtube.com/watch?v=fKLjZRARwkU (accessed 15 May 2020).
15. Carl Ginsburg, 'Epistemology for the Feldenkrais Method', in *New York Feldenkrais Professional Training Program Readings & Handouts Volume 1*, ed. D. Zemach-Bersin (New York: Feldenkrais Institute of North America, 2008). http://iffresearchjournal.org/volume/4/ginsburg.
16. Nadine Dunk et al., 'The Reliability of Quantifying Upright Standing Postures as a Baseline Diagnostic Clinical Tool', *Journal of Manipulative and Physiological Therapeutics*, Vol. 27, No. 2 (2004), 91–6; Nadine Dunk, Jennifer Lalonde, and Jack Callaghan, 'Implications for the Use of Postural Analysis as a Clinical Diagnostic Tool: Reliability of Quantifying Upright Standing Spinal

Postures from Photographic Images', *Journal of Manipulative & Physiological Therapeutics*, Vol. 28, No. 6 (2005), 386–92; Karen Grimmer-Somers, Steve Milanese, and Quinette Louw, 'Measurement of Cervical Posture in the Sagittal Plane', *Journal of Manipulative and Physiological Therapeutics*, Vol. 31, No. 7 (2008), 509–17.

17 Philippa Pownall, Robert Moran, and Andrew Stewart, 'Consistency of Standing and Seated Posture of Asymptomatic Male Adults over a One-Week Interval: A Digital Camera Analysis of Multiple Landmarks', *International Journal of Osteopathic Medicine*, Vol. 11, No. 2 (2008), 43–51; Sally Raine and Lance Twomey, 'Head and Shoulder Posture Variations in 160 Asymptomatic Women and Men', *Archives of Physical Medicine and Rehabilitation*, Vol. 78, No. 11 (1997), 1215–23; Rodrigo Ruivo, Pedro Pezarat-Correia, and Ana Carita, 'Cervical and Shoulder Postural Assessment of Adolescents between 15 and 17 Years Old and Association with Upper Quadrant Pain', *Brazilian Journal of Physical Therapy*, Vol. 18, No. 4 (2014), 364–71.

18 Grace Szeto, Leon Straker, and Sally Raine, 'A Field Comparison of Neck and Shoulder Postures in Symptomatic and Asymptomatic Office Workers', *Applied Ergonomics*, Vol. 33, No. 1 (2002), 75–84.

19 Raine and Twomey, 'Head and Shoulder Posture Variations', 1215–23.

20 Sjan-Mari van Niekerk, Quinette Louw, Christopher Vaughan, Karen Grimmer-Somers, and Kristiaan Schreve, 'Photographic Measurement of Upper-body Sitting Posture of High School Students: A Reliability and Validity Study', *BMC Musculoskeletal Disorders*, Vol. 9, No. 1 (2008), 1–11.

21 Philippa Pownall et al., 'Consistency of Standing and Seated Posture', 43–51.

22 Pownall et al., 'Consistency of Standing and Seated Posture', 43–51.

23 Pownall et al., 'Consistency of Standing and Seated Posture', 43–51.

24 David Mullineaux, Roger Bartlett, and Simon Bennett, 'Research Design and Statistics in Biomechanics and Motor Control', *Journal of Sports Sciences*, Vol. 19, No. 10 (2001), 739–60.

25 Barry Bates, 'Single-Subject Methodology: An Alternative Approach', *Medicine and Science in Sports and Exercise*, Vol. 28, No. 5 (1996), 631–8; Steven Harrison and Nicholas Stergiou, 'Complex Adaptive Behavior and Dexterous Action', *Nonlinear Dynamics Psychology, and Life Sciences*, Vol. 19, No. 4 (2015), 345–94; Taisuke Kinugasa, Ester Cerin, and Sue Hooper, 'Single-Subject Research Designs and Data Analyses for Assessing Elite Athletes' Conditioning', *Sports Medicine*, Vol. 34, No. 15 (2004), 1035–50.

26 Nadine Dunk et al., 'Implications for the Use of Postural Analysis as a Clinical Diagnostic Tool', 386–92.

27 Philippa Pownall, Robert Moran, and Andrew Stewart, 'Consistency of Standing and Seated Posture of Asymptomatic Male Adults over a One-Week Interval: A Digital Camera Analysis of Multiple Landmarks', *International Journal of Osteopathic Medicine*, Vol. 11, No. 2 (2008), 43–51.

28 Debra Peterson et al., 'Investigation of the Validity and Reliability of Four Objective Techniques for Measuring Forward Shoulder Posture', *Journal of Orthopaedic & Sports Physical Therapy*, Vol. 25, No. 1 (1997), 34–42.

29 Herman Mun Chueng Lau, Thomas Tai Wing Chiu, and Tai-Hing Lam, 'Clinical Measurement of Craniovertebral Angle by Electronic Head Posture Instrument: A Test of Reliability and Validity', *Manual Therapy*, Vol. 14, No. 4 (2009), 363–8; Raine and Twomey, 'Head and Shoulder Posture Variations', 1215–23; Szeto et al., 'A Field Comparison of Neck and Shoulder Postures', 75–84.

30 Feldenkrais, *The Elusive Obvious*, 39–54.

31 Feldenkrais, *The Elusive Obvious*, 43–4; Feldenkrais, *The Potent Self*, (Berkeley, CA: Frog Books, 1985), 119. 53–5.

32 Joseph Hamill, Jeffrey Haddad, and William McDermott, 'Issues in Quantifying Variability from a Dynamical Systems Perspective', *Journal of Applied Biomechanics*, Vol. 16, No. 4 (2000), 407–18.

33 Richard van Emmerik and Robert Wagenaar, 'Effects of Walking Velocity on Relative Phase Dynamics in the Trunk in Human Walking', *Journal of Biomechanics*, Vol. 29, No. 9 (1996), 1175–84.

34 Peter Federolf et al., 'The Application of Principal Component Analysis to Quantify Technique in Sport', *Scandinavian Journal of Medicine and Science in Sports*, Vol. 24, No. 3 (2014), 491–9.

35 Mickaël Tits et al., 'Feature Extraction and Expertise Analysis of Pianists' Motion-Captured Finger Gestures', in *Proceedings of the International Computer Music Conference (ICMC15)* (Denton: University of North Texas, 2015), 102–5.

36 Peter Federolf, 'A Novel Approach to Study Human Posture Control: "Principal Movements" Obtained from a Principal Component Analysis of Kinematic Marker Data', *Journal of Biomechanics*, Vol. 49, No. 3 (2016), 364–70.

37 Kevin Deluzio and Janie Astephen, 'Biomechanical Features of Gait Waveform Data Associated with Knee Osteoarthritis: An Application of Principal Component Analysis', *Gait & Posture*, Vol. 25, No. 1 (2007), 86–93.

38 J. MacRitchie, B. Buck, and N.J. Bailey, 'Inferring Musical Structure through Bodily Gestures', *Musicae Scientiae*, Vol. 17, No. 1 (2013), 86–108.

39 Donna Krasnow, Rita Monasterio, and Steven Chatfield, 'Emerging Concepts of Posture and Alignment', *Medical Problems of Performing Artists*, Vol. 16, No. 1 (2001), 8–16.

40 Geraldine Pellecchia, 'Postural Sway Increases with Attentional Demands of Concurrent Cognitive Task', *Gait & Posture*, Vol. 18, No. 1 (2003), 29–34.

41 Anne Shumway-Cook and Marjorie Woollacott, 'Attentional Demands and Postural Control: The Effect of Sensory Context', *Journals of Gerontology-Biological Sciences and Medical Sciences*, Vol. 55, No. 1 (2000), 10–16.

42 Michel Lacour, Laurence Bernard-Demanze, and Michel Dumitrescu, 'Posture Control, Aging, and Attention Resources: Models and Posture-Analysis Methods', *Neurophysiologie Clinique/Clinical Neurophysiology*, Vol. 38, No. 6 (2008), 411–21.

43 Grimmer-Somers, Milanese and Louw, 'Measurement of Cervical Posture', 509–17.

44 Dunk et al., 'The Reliability of Quantifying Upright Standing Postures', 91–6; Dunk et al., 'Implications for the Use of Postural Analysis as a Clinical Diagnostic Tool', 386–92.

45 Pownall, Moran, and Stewart, 'Consistency of Standing and Seated Posture', 43–51.

46 Gerhard Andersson et al., 'Effect of Cognitive Load on Postural Control', *Brain Research Bulletin*, Vol. 58, No. 1 (2002), 135–39; Yves Lajoie et al., 'Attentional Demands for Static and Dynamic Equilibrium', *Experimental Brain Research*, Vol. 97, No. 1 (1993), 139–44.

47 Brenda Wristen, Sharon Evans, and Nicholas Stergiou, 'Sight-Reading versus Repertoire Performance on the Piano: A Case Study Using High-Speed Motion Analysis', *Medical Problems of Performing Artists*, Vol. 21, No. 2 (2006), 10–16.

48 Bruce Greenfield et al., 'Posture in Patients with Shoulder Overuse Injuries and Healthy Individuals', *Journal of Orthopaedic & Sports Physical Therapy*, Vol. 21, No. 5 (1995), 287–95; Emil Pascarelli, and Yu-Pin Hsu, 'Understanding Work-Related Upper Extremity Disorders: Clinical Findings in 485 Computer Users, Musicians, and Others', *Journal of Occupational Rehabilitation*, Vol. 11, No. 1 (2001), 1–21.

49 Peterson et al., 'Investigation of the Validity and Reliability of Four Objective Techniques', 34–42.

50 Andrew Claus et al., 'Is "Ideal" Sitting Posture Real?: Measurement of Spinal Curves in Four Sitting Postures', *Manual Therapy*, Vol. 14, No. 4 (2009), 404–8.

51 Kieran O'Sullivan et al., 'Neutral Lumbar Spine Sitting Posture in Pain-Free Subjects', *Manual Therapy*, Vol. 15, No. 6 (2010), 557–61; Andrew Claus et al., 'Is "Ideal" Sitting Posture Real?', 404–8.

52 Jenny Pynt, Joy Higgs, and Martin Mackey, 'Seeking the Optimal Posture of the Seated Lumbar Spine', *Physiotherapy Theory and Practice*, Vol. 17, No. 1 (2001), 5–21.

53 Joan Scannell and Stuart McGill, 'Lumbar Posture – Should It, and Can It, Be Modified? A Study of Passive Tissue Stiffness and Lumbar Position during Activities of Daily Living', *Physical Therapy*, Vol. 83, No. 10 (2003), 907–17.

54 Pynt et al., 'Seeking the Optimal Posture', 5–21; O'Sullivan et al., 'Neutral Lumbar Spine Sitting Posture', 557–61.

55 Dieter Grob, Hans Frauenfelder, and Anne Mannion, 'The Association between Cervical Spine Curvature and Neck Pain', *European Spine Journal*, Vol. 16, No. 5 (2007), 669–78.

56 Chris Ho Ting Yip, Thomas Tai Wing Chiu, and Anthony Tung Kuen Poon, 'The Relationship between Head Posture and Severity and Disability of Patients with Neck Pain', *Manual Therapy*, Vol. 13, No. 2 (2008), 148–54; Anabela Silva, Paul Sharples, and Mark Johnson, 'Studies Comparing Surrogate Measures for Head Posture in Individuals with and without Neck Pain', *Physical Therapy Reviews*, Vol. 15, No. 1 (2010), 12–22; Rodrigo Ruivo, Pedro Pezarat-Correia, and Ana Carita, 'Cervical and Shoulder Postural Assessment of Adolescents between 15 and 17 Years Old and Association with Upper Quadrant Pain', *Brazilian Journal of Physical Therapy*, Vol. 18, No. 4 (2014), 364–71.

57 Inae Gadotti, Edgar Vieira, and David J. Magee, 'Importance and Clarification of Measurement Properties in Rehabilitation', *Brazilian Journal of Physical Therapy*, Vol. 10, No. 2 (2006), 137–46.

58 Heather Kelly, 'Personality Types of Student Musicians: A Guide for Music Educators', *Canadian Music Educators* (June 2015), 13–17.

PART III
STUDIES IN CREATIVE PRACTICE

CHAPTER 8
MAPPING BODY AWARENESS ONTO PIANO PERFORMANCE FOR ARTISTIC REJUVENATION
Alan Fraser

This chapter applies the Feldenkrais Method to practical issues facing the musical performer, offering Feldenkrais-style exercises which enhance both the musical and the physical components of movement with one's instrument – exploring the link between physical gesture and artistic effect. A Feldenkrais lesson can enhance one's general sense of well-being, but bridging the gap to the improvement of goal-specific actions can be more problematic. Understanding the underlying movement functions unique to playing an instrument allows improved awareness of body structure and function to enhance musical interpretation.

Several anomalies common to present-day piano pedagogy are investigated: over-relaxation that inhibits the power inherent in skeletal structure; and arm weight technique, which when misapplied turns melodic lines into a series of plodding, one-note events. *Awareness Through Movement* strategies are introduced to offer the pianist's hand a 'pre-standing apprenticeship' like the year-long preparation a baby undergoes before standing and walking. The chapter's central thesis is 'everything you do, sounds'. Elements of physical organization that lead to an individual musicianship are presented, with physically precise movement strategies mapped onto specific musical structures instead of a generically expressive pianism.

The focus is on piano performance, but the principles can be extrapolated to other instrumentalists, singers, actors and dancers. Refinement of physical gesture is synonymous with refinement of musicianship and artistry. Savour the exercises in full while reading this chapter. They are most beneficial when experienced sensorially, with pauses in between to help digest and integrate the effects. Then extrapolate the exercise to passages in the repertoire where the particular physical organization evoked can improve the ease, elegance and expression of the artistic gesture.

A thorough grounding in these exercises demonstrates that applying a Feldenkrais mindset to musical performance is not just a 'feel-good' exercise, or a way of resolving injury, but a potent means of enhancing one's interpretive practice.

Physical gesture sculpts sound

For dancers and actors, the body is the instrument. A dancer's art lies in gestures; an actor's body language is as important as their speech. For them, the Feldenkrais Method refines the art by refining the gesture.

In piano playing, physical gestures create sounds. The shape of the *sound* constitutes the musical art: the sound alone acts on the emotions. Musical art is 'shaping the invisible'.[1] Here too the Method can refine the art by refining the gesture: improved physical organization has positive, precise effects on musical interpretation.

A hand walking on the keys

Feldenkrais deals with structural function. Improving skeletal mechanics improves how the central nervous system (CNS) manages movement, beginning with the basics such as sitting, standing, walking and running. There's a further benefit to pianists when the hand is understood as a mini-body. Seeing the fingers as legs, the hand as a pelvis, and the arm as a torso that breathes allows *Awareness through Movement* lessons (ATMs) originally applied to whole-body skeletal mechanics to be adapted to the hand, evoking a similar improvement in its lying, sitting, standing, walking, running, hopping and leaping on the keyboard.

Walking is not perceived as a series of falls

Treating the hand as a mini-body brings to light aspects of modern-day piano technique that are foreign to a Feldenkrais perspective – the most ubiquitous being that the weight of the arm is used to move the key. From the physicist's point of view, balance is lost each time the torso moves forward in human walking, and recovered as the leg swings forward to come under the pelvis. Feldenkrais said as much, but also noted that *we do not experience it so*. We do not feel the falling. At each step, the pelvis moves through a sophisticated three-dimensional figure-eight pattern to 'smooth out the bumps'. This pattern, absent when a child first stands and walks, develops fully only by the seventh year.[2] If children were told to notice how they lose and regain their balance at each step, or to 'use their torso weight' to get their foot onto the ground, their walking would quickly deteriorate.

Generations of pianists have been told to involve the weight of the arm in playing, to a similar detrimental effect:

(1) The hand, whose basic function should be to stand and walk on key, now needs to compensate for the falling arm by stiffening, or emptying out – robbing the arch structure of its potency.

(2) Arm 'relaxation' movements, addressing the tension caused by this lack of structural integrity, further destabilize the hand and lead to its bearing further stress.

The vicious circle of this skeletal dysfunction continues in a downward spiral, the pianist struggling more and more, the artistic result less and less convincing because the pianist is preoccupied with regaining a physical balance they never should have lost in the first place.[3]

Grasp to avoid falling

The hand's basic action is grasping. If you lie the hand palm down on key and grasp, keeping the fingers straight, the hand stands up, creating an arch structure of which the metacarpal-phalangeal (MCP) joint is the keystone – the hand's 'hip joint'. A functional 'hand hip joint' allows the fingers to walk on the keys, carrying the arm easily, just as the pelvis and legs easily carry the torso. The ease derives from *balance* – but sensing the weight of the arm disturbs this, impinging on the delicate yet potent functioning of the whole system. The weight is there, of course – but it is not experienced as *heavy*.

Straight vs. curled fingers

Granted, the fingers often curl to some extent in playing, just as the legs do in running, but if the potent work of the MCP joint is hampered by chronic curling, the hand becomes dysfunctional. Starting from a straight-fingered touch feeds the CNS initial healthy impressions of standing well on key.

Unstable equilibrium

The human body is designed to maintain a state of *unstable equilibrium* in standing, walking and running. The Feldenkrais Method aims to improve all human movement: one primary focus is to improve the delicate, functional balance of unstable equilibrium in basic functions such as sitting, standing and walking. It can do the same for the hand on key.

Shaping a phrase instead of weighting the phrase

An arm liberated from the sense of falling enters into 'pianistic unstable equilibrium' (certain adaptations must be made to the forearm's horizontality). It is now free to assume its natural role, shaping the phrase: moving with the fingers and hand as they walk and run on the keys just as the torso moves with the legs. Never does one leave the other behind: they remain in perfect synchrony, maintaining a balanced centre of gravity no matter how complex the dance step.

Move the key, but don't press it down

This happens best when piano playing is not perceived as pushing the keys down at all. Pushing the ground down would disturb the gait in walking, and, concomitantly, pushing the key down does the same at the piano. When the key is *manipulated*, free from any sense of dropping, the hand's centre of gravity is maintained with greater ease. When the vertical force is limited to the descent of the fingertip, the lateral movements of the arm gain transcendence and transform the quality of the phrase – it becomes a sinuous, expressive entity rather than the plodding, generic declamations produced by weight touch.

The piano key does indeed descend to sound a note, but when it is perceived as such, something within the player tends to descend with it – it's a quirk of human perception and reaction, a sort of embodied mimeticism – and a falling component is added to the motion of the key strike, separating this musical event from the next one.

The hand's arch structure and grasping

A healthy grasping function (the action that creates the hand's arch) works against the perceived fall, exerting a direct positive influence on piano tone. Again, lay the hand on a

The Feldenkrais Method in Creative Practice

surface; draw the tips of the flat fingers towards the heel – making the MCP joint rise to create an arch structure. At the piano, notice how this focuses the tone, just as a singer's dropping the chin reduces the amount of air escaping through the vocal cords. Play a note with a collapsed arch to imitate the singer's raised chin that engenders an airy, unfocused tone. Explore this both vocally and pianistically to experience the corollary with your senses.

The thumb's role in grasping

The function of the thumb is profoundly different from that of the fingers. It opposes itself to the fingers. Its fulcrum of movement, the metacarpal-carpal (MCC) joint, is at the wrist – far closer to the arm than the finger's fulcrum, the MCP joint.

When the thumb grasps, its metacarpal bone moves in an arc, bringing its distal phalange to lie against the fingers. All of the thumb participates. If only the proximal and distal phalanges flex, the thumb is emasculated: opposition becomes impossible.

How can the grasping/opposing action of the thumb apply to piano playing when the thumb moves upwards to meet the downward-moving fingers? Lay the hand flat on a surface or on a key with thumb and fifth finger wide apart. Oppose the thumb: it first moves *downwards* through an arc that eventually arrives at the finger pad. The surface, or keyboard, blocks the motion, and since for every action there is an equal and opposite reaction, the metacarpal-

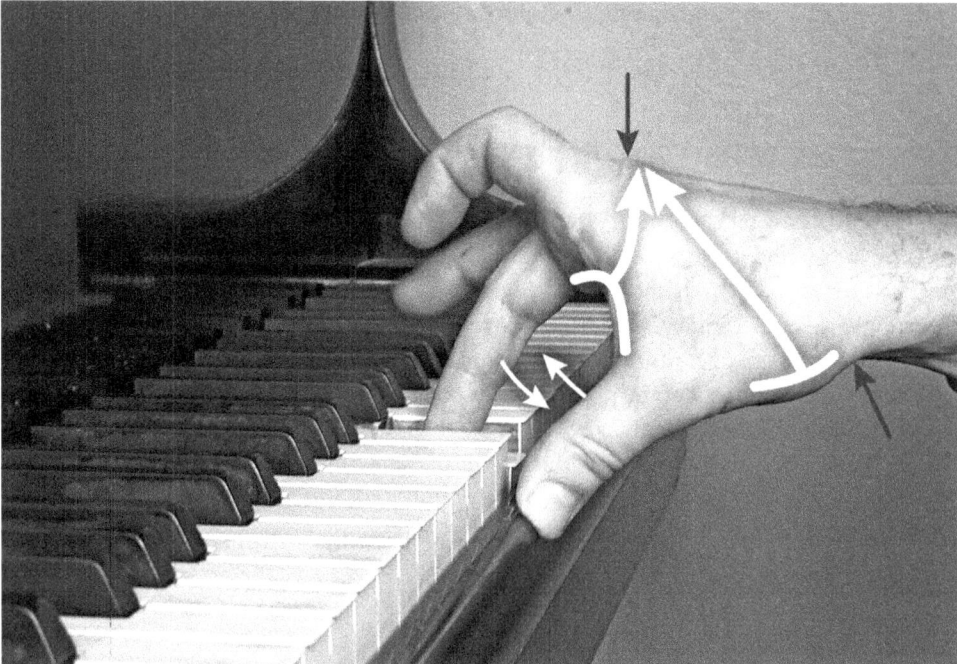

Figure 8.1 Action and reaction as the hand stands on key. Biomechanical integrity derives from the elastic loading of the hand's skeletal structure. Thumb and finger oppose to grow the hand arch; thumb metacarpal launches the MCP joint.

Mapping Body Awareness onto Piano Performance

phalangeal joints rise, confirming the hand's arch structure. Thus in arch creation, the thumb's role is even more crucial than that of whole-finger flexion. A finger grasping on a key raises its 'hip joint', but the thumb's 'hip joint' stays low as it grasps, getting under the MCP joints and launching them even higher.

Musical inflection and the standing function: Hand arch generation

Played with the standard arm weight technique, these chords from Debussy's *Prélude* from *Pour le piano* (Ex. 8.1) tend to sound plodding and possess limited dynamic range – the *forte* is strained. Ironically, the pianist's attempt to avoid harsh tone – by relaxing – is the very thing that causes it. Relaxation undermines the integrity of the hand's skeletal structure.

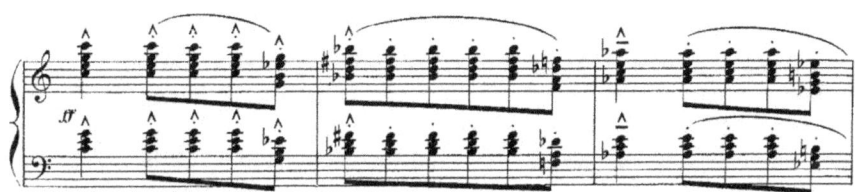

Ex. 8.1 Debussy – *Prélude* from *Pour le Piano*, b. 43–45.

Play the same chords with a quick, vigorous 'stand up' motion, beginning with the fingers on key. Make the fingers' primary goal launching the MCP joint sky high as they join to the key bed. The result: a gloriously rich, vibrant, singing, colourful orchestral tone. Physical freedom translates into free sonic vibration that radiates exuberant joy instead of cumbrous majesty. The arm doesn't fall; it follows the hand's 'hip joint' upward into balance. It need not compensate, nor relax: it simply floats on the vital, athletic motion of the hand. Debussy even indicates this 'up' motion in the notation – the 'dunce cap' or carrot top is the violinist's marking for an up bow. Thus are correlated notation, technique and musical result.

Musical inflection and the walking function: The fingers and arm

Removing falling from the equation allows arm and hand to collaborate in new ways in pianistic walking as well. Now each new phrase acquires a unique shape created through slight variations in time and horizontal trajectory – just as a dancer shapes his choreography anew at each performance. My teacher Phil Cohen called this 'expressively directed micro-timing'. The opening motive of the Chopin *Nocturne in F minor* Op. 55 No. 1 (Ex. 8.2) is repeated eleven times throughout the work. The danger of exact, stale repetitions is avoided by 'walking on key choreographically': subtle nuances of inflection arise spontaneously because of the free, natural moving relationship established between artist and instrument. Technique brings the interpretation to life.

Ex. 8.2 Chopin – *Nocturne in F minor*, Op. 55 No. 1, b. 1–4 with added tenuto bars to indicate plodding, weighted melodic notes.

The physical underpinnings of legato: Walking needs two potent hip joints

Crucial to 'artistic walking' along the melodic path is the functional transfer of weight from one 'hip joint' to another. This evolved legato is the very foundation of piano technique: the physical joining of two notes creates the arch structure that carries the arm from one note to the next, simultaneously empowering the piano's voice and rendering it sinuous and expressive. A single finger sounds a note by standing on key, and continues to stand while the neighbouring finger drops into its key. Any collapse in the initial finger's 'hip joint' would create a bump in the musical line. Only when the newly sounding finger completes *its* standing motion can the initial finger leave its key. In a functional melodic legato, there is always at least one and often two MCP joints that have risen fully into their potent standing state.

Compare the structure-functional integrity of this process to the laborious 'production of tone' on each successive melodic note when the arm's weight falls in behind each finger, as shown by the tenuto markings in Example 8.2.

With weight technique, each finger carries the arm in turn, but because the nervous system senses the arm's falling, the arch structure either gives way slightly as it 'catches' the arm, or stiffens in resistance, maintaining structural security at the expense of moveability. Imagine the torso 'falling' onto each leg at every step. There's no flow: who would dream of walking so?

Musical inflection and the walking function: Rotation

The complex gliding trajectory of the pelvis that smooths out human walking includes forward and back motion, lateral translation, and rotation. The hand also does all three, manifesting the third with a subtle rotation along the axis of the forearm. It shouldn't be overdone, but without it the hand's walking becomes stiff and mechanical.

Melodic shaping and the efficient division of labour between hand and arm

When the division of labour is clear – fingers producing tone; hand, wrist and forearm linking tones – the piano's sound blossoms with richness and clarity. The transformation almost defies explanation, but the underlying cause is clear: structure integrity and functionality are at work.

Making peace with gravity

The Feldenkrais Method has been defined as 'making peace with gravity'.[4] When we move well, we don't struggle against gravity – it doesn't overpower our efforts to stand; it informs them. The sophisticated mechanisms by which the skeleton maintains equilibrium allow this harmony. Parasitic contractions disturb it, but well-coordinated muscular efforts balance the down and up forces perfectly throughout the skeletal frame.[5] This applies equally to the body as a whole and to the hand – the 'pianistic body'.

Ex. 8.3 Chopin – *Nocturne in D flat major*, Op. 27 No. 2, b. 1–4.

Making peace with gravity at the piano may involve some unusual movement. Approach the first melodic note of Example 8.3 from below, sliding the fingertip horizontally onto the first note F, and continuing the slide as the tip drops into the key, standing the hand up on the finger. Playing this note with the third finger allows for richer tone (the third was Chopin's preferred finger for cantabile singing),[6] and a 3–5 finger substitution facilitates the sliding, undulating arm movement which lends the melody its sinuous quality. Buoy the forearm forward responsively, as an ice skater's body would, riding on a high MCP joint, then angle through subsequent notes creating an unbroken chain of melodic tones, just as the torso moves on the legs in an unbroken chain of balletic movement. Notice how different this feels from a habitual, weighted approach, and notice the difference in the sound and the expression.

Arm weight technique and the divorce with gravity

Playing the same melody with the standard, weighted touch, one feels how arm weight technique, aiming to utilize gravity's power to increase the beauty, achieves the opposite. Ironically, one is now divorced from gravity: in the fall, the arm is lost to gravity's thrall. The hand must resist, and has little energy left to move the key. Parasitic contractions ripple up through the body, breaking the kinematic chain in any number of places.[7] The body compensates the uncontrolled fall by stiffening, achieving stability but becoming dysfunctional.

The crucial functional moment: The transition from standing to walking

The finger stands to sound the note. The pianist moves on to the next note – the hand takes a step. The point of stability shifts. Here if the MCP joint loses potency, it is no longer the keystone of the arch. It drops. The arm follows it down, pushing the next finger into its key.

Who would walk down the street collapsing the hip joint at every step – but we pianists do it all the time: we were taught to relax. Example 8.3 offers an antidote: the forearm subtly manipulates its 'hip joint' towards the following note *while* the initial playing finger continues to 'stand', physically harmonizing with gravity *and* musically harmonizing with the melodic flow. In real walking, as the torso angles towards the new balance point, the leg swings forward, naturally moving the pelvis just enough to bring the new standing hip joint over its leg: so must the finger and hand interact with the forearm. When the new finger's MCP joint is directly over its key, the finger lever can drop into its note untrammelled by shear forces, creating a clean attack. Now the basis has been established for the new finger to take *its* step: the forearm now continues to move in the direction of the third melodic note, standing with more and more confidence on note two, allowing the initial finger to leave its key with no collapse: the standing function has been fully transferred to the finger on note two.

The complexity of this description reflects the complexity of the action – breaking it down in this way in practice allows the CNS to recalibrate and improve the movement, just as ATM lessons break down whole-body movements into their constituent parts to foster improvement. Remember that it takes a child a full seven years to master this complexity in whole-body walking. The Feldenkrais practitioner works with the neuro-mechanical nuts and bolts of movement rather than movement *per se* – reawakening the original learning process to evoke positive change in the motor cortex. Similarly the pianist can gain greater improvement by exploring every functional aspect of playing in analytical, sensorial and experiential detail.

The 'one-boned finger'

'Finger walking' is most easily learned in its primitive form, where the straight or even splayed finger functions as a one-boned structure through which kinetic forces transmit with relative ease. This helps the hand's 'hip joint', the MCP joint (too often neglected as the pianist diligently articulates by curling the fingers), finally to discover its innate power.

This primitive form of pianistic walking is used often in performance. Croatian pianist Kemal Gekić posits a simple axiom for enriching the tone: the greater the area of flesh-to-key contact, the richer the sonority. Curling the finger reduces the area of skin contact, but straightening or splaying it gets the juicy, thick part of the finger pad onto the key surface. I have seen Gekić hang his thumb off the keyboard completely, glue the heel of his hand to the key slip, and play a melody with the entire underside of all three phalanges in contact with each key, the palm brushing the white keys, gliding and sliding among them. The ringing sound this produces is extraordinary. It is skeletal mechanics used to artistic advantage.

Elastic loading and biotensegrity

Touching the entire underside of the finger to the key prior to standing it straight up evokes a natural elasticity throughout the hand, especially if the finger splays. This is biotensegrity in action – the state of elasticity in the human body that keeps movement potent, smooth and effective. The concept of biotensegrity, developed by Dr Steven Levin, recognizes that bones are held apart not only by synovial fluid in the joint, but by all the connective tissue: the fascia, ligaments, tendons and muscles, creating a wonderfully elastic and adaptable medium for movement.[8]

Biotensegrity is revolutionizing the way Feldenkrais practitioners approach their work. Lowered muscle tone does help the bones to better align, improving transmission of kinetic forces through the skeletal frame – but turning an FI client into a 'Feldenblob' and leaving the CNS to fend for itself in the reintegration process does not always foster the most effective learning.[9] A judicious elastic effort rendering an assemblage of bones more effective in their action can sometimes achieve greater improvement.

Exploit the stretch reflex

Feldenkrais scoffed at runners doing stretching exercises to warm up, because he knew his neurophysiology: the stretch reflex immediately shortens the very muscles that are being stretched. And he knew that if the person did succeed in lengthening the muscle by stretching it, she was actually stretching the tendon, making it less functional. I have seen Aikido masters with incredible 'flexibility', capable of amazing feats in martial arts, who could not walk normally – whose gait was somehow deformed by their overly stretched hamstrings.

Why work to overcome the stretch reflex when it plays such a crucial role in maintaining effective, lithe movement? The stretch reflex is the lynchpin of biotensegrity. Feldenkrais did access the stretch reflex to improve movement,[10] and splaying the finger as it presses juicily into the key does the same at the piano, triggering the stretch reflex in the lumbrical muscle, elasticizing the finger and empowering its relationship to the key.

Elastic loading in keyboard leaps

The sense of lithe elasticity empowers leaping on the keyboard as well. Imagine yourself leaping from stepping stone to stepping stone across a creek. Which would you prefer?

1. A big derrick lifts you up by a hook attached to a body harness, angling you over to the next stone and lowering you until your feet touch.
2. You bend your knees slightly and with the springing action of a diver leap adroitly to the next stone. Your leg is so elastically primed that you hardly notice the distance. Elastically loading the muscles gives you accuracy as well as energy.

Leap on key comparing these techniques. Sense the cumbersome quality of the arm weight, 'derrick lifting' technique. Sense the hand's innate elastic power fostering a nimbler and more accurate movement in the leaping technique.

Elastic loading in running

Running on the spot can give you a sense of how elastic loading empowers. First run at a moderate gait. The feeling is somewhat sluggish; it seems to take a lot of energy to move the

The Feldenkrais Method in Creative Practice

bulky legs. Increasing the gait threefold should require three times as much effort, but the step actually becomes lighter and easier.

At the slower rate, muscular contraction is the only animating force. At the faster speed, elastic loading kicks in. As the heel reaches the ground, the calf muscle, which is already contracted, is stretched and loaded elastically. When the knee thrusts forward, the elastic energy is released, launching the runner forward.[11] This is biotensegrity powering a basic human movement.

Elastic loading in trills and fast passagework

Lifting the fingers in scales and trills initiates a similar process. Play a slow trill, between second and third fingers, and as one finger plays, lift the other high, keeping its tip pointed downward. Extend the proximal phalange while flexing the medial and distal phalanges (see Figure 8.2).

This loads the lumbrical elastically and uses elastic energy to help power the next downward stroke. Lifting the fingers helps agonist and antagonist cooperate more efficiently, as if the trill is played more with 'up' than 'down' movements. Don't lift in isolation: 'breathe' the forearm upward as each finger lifts. As the trill speed increases, the forearm can no longer move up and down with each finger – but keep it free and floating. This is not the Inquisitional isolation of the old finger action school, but a biomechanically sound organization. Effective elastic loading can be seen in the hand of Wanda Landowska (Figure 8.3), the pre-eminent twentieth-century pianist and harpsichordist noted for her articulate variety and 'illuminated' sound.

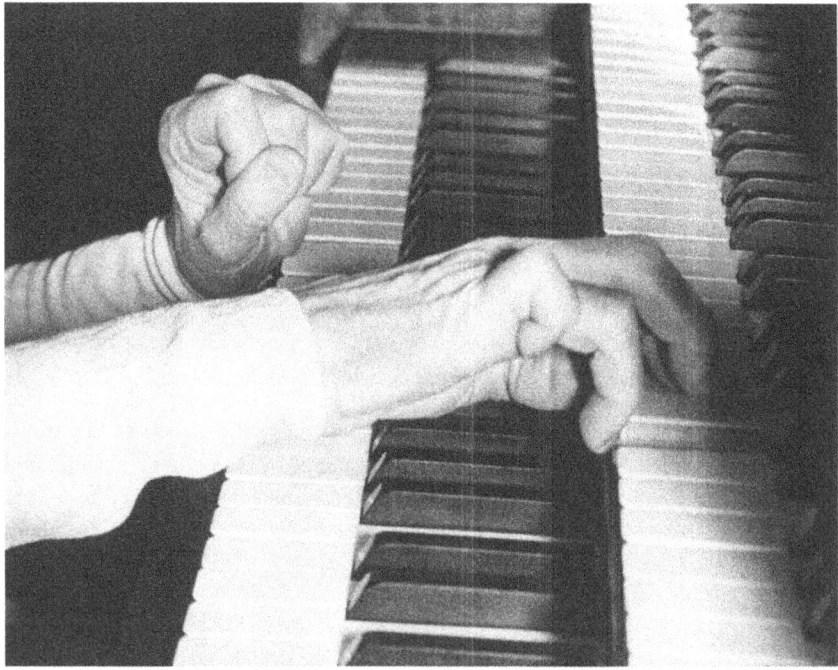

Figure 8.2 Extend the proximal phalange while flexing the medial and distal. The MCP joint appears collapsed, but in fact is buoyed by elastic loading of both the extensors and the flexors.

Mapping Body Awareness onto Piano Performance

Figure 8.3 Wanda Landowska loads the lumbricals elastically to 'prime' the fingers for clear, varied articulation.

Her hands appear tense – but this 'tension' is functional: elastic loading brought to bear on her scintillating articulative practice. Though it may not seem so, these elastic loading movements do reflect the spirit of Feldenkrais Method, which cultivates *functionality* – guiding the learning towards empowering solutions specific to the technique involved.

Musical inflection and the lying down function

We've compared the hand on key to the whole body in standing, walking, leaping and running, but perhaps the most transformative corollary is the most radical: lying down. This last seems to have little to do with playing – how can you play a note by lying down in it – but it is one of the most effective ways of bringing Feldenkrais-style 'skeletal illumination' to piano technique.

Transferring a 'whole body' ATM to the pianistic body on key

In one ATM lesson,[12] the student lies on the side, let's say the left, with legs drawn up and arms stretched out on the floor at shoulder level, the right palm and fingers lying snugly on the left palm and fingers.[13] Do this now, and move the right arm in a big arc towards the ceiling then continuing behind you, ascertaining how far it can go comfortably. Explore this reference movement (Figure 8.4) several times.

Figure 8.4 The reference movement.

Returning the right hand to lie on the left, begin to slide it little by little out on to the floor in front of you, then back onto the left hand, then farther up the left forearm. Keep the elbow straight the whole time to evoke new, unusual sensations in the shoulder area. The brain reduces tonus in certain muscles to allow the bones of the arm, shoulder and torso to discover a new interrelationship: movement becomes more ergonomically efficient, smoother and more pleasant – force vectors are transmitted more cleanly through the bones, reducing the need for muscular work. Greater power is achieved with less effort. When you return to the reference move, the arm can move farther behind with no strain.

Add a pianistic dimension to this lesson with finger individuation movements. With the hand on the floor, 'pulse' one finger at a time into the floor: use a gentle whole-finger flexion to put the entire underside of the finger in more intense contact with the floor. Can you sense an 'echo' of this movement further up the arm: contractions in the shoulder area … around the shoulder blade … the collarbone … and even the rib cage? When you change the pressing finger, does the location of this echo change? Here the sense of elastic skeletal connection is palpable. One *experiences* how effective movement ripples all the way through the kinematic chain.

Brought to Scriabin's iconic *C sharp minor Étude*, Op. 2 No. 1 (Ex. 8.4), this 'lying down' technique transforms the physical experience, the sonority *and* the emotional impact of the music.

Mapping Body Awareness onto Piano Performance

Ex. 8.4 Scriabin – *Étude in C sharp minor*, Op. 2 No. 1, b. 1–4.

Don't 'play the piano' at all; simply lie down flat-fingered in the keys. Give the entire underside of each playing finger intimate contact with the key surface; 'drown' it in the key bed. To finish the note, lighten the finger imperceptibly; allowing the key to float the finger back up to the resting position. There is no sense of depressing the key, only lying down and then floating.

Done well, this frees the pianist from parasitic contractions not only in the hand and arm but throughout the body. The effort to stand, even when done well, tends to evoke excessive muscular effort somewhere in the system. Here the standing effort is replaced with a delicious let-go in the hand, wrist and forearm all the way up through the elbow, upper arm, shoulder area, clavicle, shoulder blade, ribs and spine and even to the pelvis. A new sense of 'skeletal neutral' develops, along with the astonishing discovery that it is possible to manipulate the keys while remaining true to this neutral. Both the physical experience of playing and the musical result are transformed.

A skeletal touch begets musical transformation

The physical transformation would mean nothing without the musical benefit. Miraculously, the absence of parasitic contractions in the body is felt by the soundboard. The piano vibrates with more colour, power and sheen than was thought possible. This sound leads not only to new possibilities in orchestration – bold solo voices, accompanying voices that whisper yet still possess harmonic colour, basses that are resonant, distant and supportive – but also to a completely new phrasing aesthetic. The sound itself is so beautiful, the penetrating colour of the solo voice's every note so ongoing in time that the need to manipulate the melody for expressive purposes fades away. It is already expressive in and of itself. It is the essence of expression. The pianist is so much *with* the moving melody at every physical and auditory level that she is freed from the need to *try* to be expressive, to impose expressivity on the melody's natural contour. Now she can spontaneously insert subtle nuances which lend the melody humanity, individuality, that lend it personality one way one day, another way the next – but always allowing it to remain true to its essential nature.[14]

Lying down and a pianistic pre-standing apprenticeship

A baby lies down for a long time before crawling. Its first locomotion is 'commando crawling', or creeping, on the belly. Later it gets its belly off the floor by rising to the hands and knees. Later still it sits, and still much later, stands. It takes its first steps only after a year-long apprenticeship. Nobody learned to walk by walking.

The pianist's hand by contrast is made to stand up and walk the first day. Is it any wonder that there are so many problems, so much stiffness, so many injuries? A series of ATMs for the hand – dissolving it into the keys, laying it down to sink its 'belly' into sensorially rich contact with its environment – can make up for missed experience, offering the pianist's hand a 'sensory bath' equivalent to the year-long sensory enrichment of infancy.

From lying to standing: A crucial developmental stage in movement

When a baby lifts it head, its extensors work for the first time. These muscles will eventually raise the body to a balanced verticality – lifting the head offers them a first rudimentary training. The hand can embark on an equivalent training by lying flat and doing a whole-finger flexion so slight that at first there is no visible movement, only a subtle inner effort. Done long enough, this subtle inner work can dissolve parasitic contractions that have existed in the hand and arm sometimes for decades, and set the stage for a new, skeletally aware hand to take the stage.

This sensorial re-education can continue by allowing that same, gentle whole-finger flexion to manifest in slight movement, the MCP joint beginning to rise at first only a millimetre … then two … then three … and so on. The greater the sensorial detail brought to this exercise, the more the sensory image of the hand is renewed from within. The changes in the hand's comportment are neurological in nature, because they stem from changes in the sensory-motor feedback loop. If I tell a young student that his hand is an awakening monster in a swamp, and make a game of this exercise, the student's playing can transform in minutes from a weighted loping from note to note to a healthy walking that makes the melody sing, without my ever having said a word about the hand's arch. Directed sensory experience evokes the learning. This particular strategy is functionally derived: improve the function of pianistic walking by returning to the 'nuts and bolts' of that action. The first gentle flexion of the whole finger equals the first extensions of the neck and back in head lifting.

We have stated that perhaps the greatest illusion in piano playing is that the key goes down. Although it does indeed descend, when we perceive it as such, something in us inevitably goes down with it, and the balance of the down and up forces is lost. We are caught in a vicious circle, the loss and regaining of balance. Lying on and crawling around the keyboard kills two birds with one stone: it improves the hand's physical organization by applying ATM techniques directly to the piano, and improves the musical result by avoiding the pitfalls of 'making the key go down'.

Perceiving the key as a lever to be manipulated frees one from all the problems of verticality. A lever can be moved equally well sideways, forward and back, or up and down. The latter is no different from the first two; it is only by chance that the vertical movement of the key goes with or against the gravitational pull.

This new, extra-vertical relation to the key can be cultivated through altered perception: one can experience playing as simply joining finger to key lever, or as 'tunnelling' the finger through one key to another. Many ATM-like movements on key cultivate this perception in the CNS. For instance, lay a finger in the depths of a white key and slide its tip up the side of the neighbouring black key until the key descends 'by accident', simply because the finger 'crawled' into the space it occupied. The sensorial richness of this practice has profound neuromotor implications: the massage-like contact of skin and key surface evokes a richer sensorial awareness of the finger skeleton within, evoking positive changes in the brain's motor organization.

Silent 'pancake' glissandi

This intimate developmental relationship to the keyboard can be brought to the whole hand by doing a silent palm *glissando* along the key bed. Lay the entire palm and all the undersides of the fingers on the keys, depressing them, and drag the hand in the direction of its heel so slowly that the only sound is of the action quietly going *thunk, thunk, thunk* as one key after another is released and rises to the surface.

Mashing the hand is a developmental step

The mashed hand is seldom used in actual playing, but transferring the *feel* of the mashed hand to playing alters its internal neurology, just as ATM informs our entire neuro-motor functioning to improve sitting, standing and walking.

Rhythm

Many so-called technical problems stem from not any physical limitation but a musical one: the failure to generate healthy rhythm. The hand's skeleton comes into its own when it serves rhythmic pulse – music's skeleton. The relationship is symbiotic: just as attention to the body's skeletal relationships improves rhythm, attention to rhythm can improve the body's skeletal organization.

Preparing a new piece: A transformational approach

'Injecting' rhythmic pulse fully into the skeleton may require an extreme approach, such as combining skeletal precision with high energy in this next exercise to create a rhythmic élan where the pulse is derived not from weight but from bones.

The Feldenkrais Method in Creative Practice

Ex. 8.5 Chopin – *Étude in F major*, Op. 10 No. 8, b. 1–2.

Step 1: Play the passage in Example 8.5 ultra-slowly, standing a fully elasticized, 'one-boned' finger on each and every note at an angle of about 70 degrees to produce the richest, loudest, most ringing tone possible. *Do not use weight*. Stand *up* to confirm and enrich the sense of skeletal connection in the hand. This high-energy exercise does not seem very 'Feldenkrais-like', but has profound implications for skeleto-functional integration.

Step 2: In each four-note group, still exclusively standing *up*, play the first note *forte-fortissimo*, the next three *piano-pianissimo*, making the dynamic differences as great as physically possible. This is the deeper meaning of the accents. Any sort of weighted touch is intolerable. Do the accents, *really*, but absolutely avoid pounding the piano, attacking it or abusing it. Let circumstance force you to become skeletally wise. Understand the vigorous standing action sensorially, experientially, because the musical circumstances dictate that you *must*.

There is no 'down' in standing

Step 3: Get out of a chair. What went down? Nothing! The feet meet the ground but they do not go down: the skeleton unfolds to rise up. This is still true if you get up suddenly.

Now throw the finger at the key with a seeming complete absence of muscular effort, moving the wrist lightly up and forward allowing the bones to stand themselves up similarly. Feel a shock through the entire bone structure that stands the finger up suddenly, totally and weightlessly. For the three lighter notes, dangle the fingers so their tips barely reach the bottom of the key – let them swim through the key instead of walking on the key bed. Keep full potency in the standing finger's keystone, the MCP joint, through the entire light three-note group.

An extreme, non-weighted rhythmic pulse gives a sense of elation, especially in passages that are *played* with this extreme dynamic treatment. Gekić, for instance, not only practises the last chromatic run in the Chopin *B minor scherzo* (Ex. 8.6) with every sixth note *fortissimo*, the other five *pianissimo*, he plays it that way in performance to brilliant, electrifying effect.[15]

Mapping Body Awareness onto Piano Performance

Ex. 8.6 Chopin – *Scherzo No. 1 in B minor*, Op. 20, b. 606–617.

Rhythmic practice to resolve a dystonia

A skeletal approach to rhythmic accentuation is one effective strategy in dystonia resolution. Many dystonias result from a chronic, insidious collapse of the arch that, over time, results in the CNS 'fighting back' with a dystonic movement. A chronically extending finger is trying to pull the MCP joint up into a functional position. A chronically flexing finger is trying to grow the hand's arch. Unfortunately, the pianist's training is so firmly rooted in relaxation and the resulting, unsuspected emasculation of hand structure that these strategies fail – the dystonia remains.

The CNS may learn the dystonic reaction so well that it continues even when functionality *is* restored to the hand. A radically different sensory experience is needed to cut through the 'neurological static' of the dystonic pattern. The vigorous, skeletal 'stand up' motion of extreme rhythmical pulse offers just that. The sense of the skeleton doing 99 per cent of the work effectively creates a completely new neurological image of playing, written on a *tabula rasa*. All the usual muscular contractions have been 'decoupled', and the action takes place free from dystonic overtones. The restoration of a rhythmically and physically skeletal sense of self frees one from the dystonia.[16]

Making music with the whole self – skeletally

The movements of a musician's fingers, hands and arms constitute one of the most complex activities known to humanity. The CNS tends to stabilize the body to offer these complex movements a clear point of departure. Arnold Schultz even advises stiffening the hip joints to offer the arms a stable fulcrum in *forte* playing.[17] However, we now know that the body is a tensegrity, where each bone is one element in a kinematic chain that stretches from one end of the body to the other – no fixed fulcrums needed.

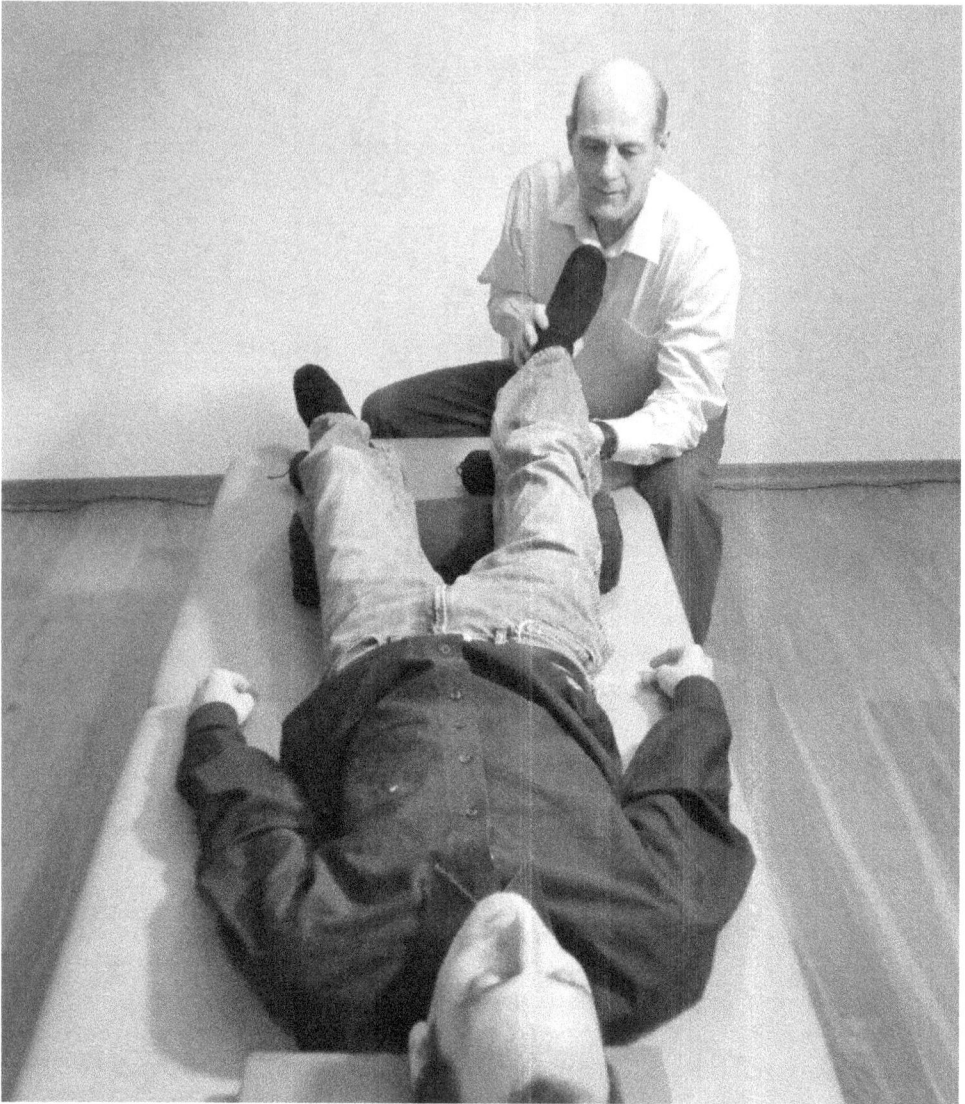

Figure 8.5 Pushing through the foot, leg and pelvis into the spine and all the way to the head in FI.

In my work with pianists, singers and instrumentalists, I almost always encounter a slightly hyper-extended spine, the lower back thrust just a little too far forward and stuck there in the body's attempt, with no little amount of effort, to *support* the movements of the hands on the instrument or the breath on the vocal cords. The ensuing stiffness blocks the kinematic chain. The amazing wisdom of skeletal design is to have movement transmit all the way through the skeletal frame. We cultivate it in FI when we push on a client's foot and evaluate how far up the skeleton the movement reaches (see Fig. 8.5). The force transmits through when the joints remain moveable. Much of our work in FI involves facilitating this by dissolving parasitic contractions.

If the client resumes the parasitic contractions when she sits up, our work has been for naught. When she learns to cultivate and enhance the supple movement of all the vertebrae in sitting, for instance by practising the three cardinal directions of movement *while playing*, the full power of her skeleton becomes available to her artistry.[18]

Skeletally, the two arms attach to the body at the origins of the clavicle which are only about an inch and a half apart on the sternum, making the sternum the crucial point of connection between arm and torso. When the sternum moves freely in breathing, all the ribs are moveable and all the vertebrae as well, and the movements of the pelvis can ripple up through the entire system and out through the arms. The sound of any instrumentalist – pianist, string player, wind player, percussionist – is profoundly enhanced when functionality is restored to the body's kinematic chain, connecting the whole self to the instrument. Feldenkrais said that life is movement – life without movement is unthinkable. In musical performance the spine, in supporting the sternum moveably, becomes the tree of melodic, rhythmic and harmonic life.

The spine – the tree of musical life

Singers benefit especially from a functional spine. Muscular contractions that keep vertebrae immoveable interfere with the free movement of the diaphragm and ribs. When the vertebrae are balanced and moveable, the diaphragm is free from cross-motivation: no longer obliged simultaneously to fill the lungs and support the skeleton. This enhancement of the singer's spinal functionality produces a ringing, intense vocal sonority full of overtones with far less than the singer's habitual effort. It is the *reduction* of effort that makes this amazing sound possible. I have often given a singer an FI, then watched as they vocalized with a look of stupefaction, not believing the sound being produced or the way it is being produced. It's so simple (yet tricky) to achieve – simply get the torso over the hip joints by means of a balancing act instead of muscular effort.

Coaching pianists, singers or other instrumentalists in this work on the spine, I may sit behind them with my hands on certain vertebrae, mostly just sensing but also subtly guiding, bringing the body closer to the point of balance where magic happens. Of course there are organic fluctuations – the body moves a little to the left of the point of absolute balance, or to the right, or a little in front or behind – but it always moves through the neutral point, never contradicting the laws of skeletal mechanics. When I work like this, after some time the uncanny impression arises that I can tell what the performer is going to do musically before he or she does it. I sense the phrase – the music's contour, its intensity, its expression – gestating in the back an instant or two before I hear it in the sound. This is indeed making music with the whole self.

Everything you do *sounds*

Why is the palpable sense of skeletal connection to oneself and one's instrument so important? Avoiding injury is a prime concern, but far more compelling is the resulting artistic transformation. When the body naturally follows the phrase contour inherent in the musical structure, phrase inflection becomes the manifestation of music's inner nature rather than an imposed aesthetic. Starkly bold orchestrations on the piano become possible when muscular interference is absent and the bones can align effectively to transmit kinetic forces efficiently. When movement ripples unhindered through the skeleton's entire kinematic chain, the whole self takes part in the artistic process, with the accompanying, astonishing blossoming of emotionally expressive content. Music speaks from deep within the self.

The key perceived as a three-dimensional entity to be entered, one element of an implied tensegrity, becomes an effective instrument for colour creation at the piano, a tool for rich orchestrations with huge dynamic differences which increase as control of the key becomes more precise. Greater precision arises through Feldenkrais-style physical differentiations in the hand's 'mini-body' as well as in the body as a whole. The shape of every gesture affects not only the sound, but also one's basic inner state, the level of background tonus throughout the entire body that allows more sophisticated skeletal differentiation, that *experiences* the musical conception physically, not just intellectually – that touches the soundboard with true artistic profundity.

In the past, piano technique has been seen as scales and arpeggios, Czerny and Hanon exercises, the diligent cultivation of mechanical dexterity through the slavish repetition of exercises without that much attention paid to the 'how'. Even the young Liszt read the newspaper while he did his hour or two of finger exercises each day. Extending a Feldenkrais mindset into the realm of piano technique changes all that. Becoming aware of *how* one plays enhances the physical and mechanical result. Physical blockages melt away, making one feel not only more potent but also artistically more free. It is crucial that this 'how' be *felt* at the sensory level, not just understood intellectually – hence the Feldenkrais-style exercises.

We hope the reader will be inspired to develop this exploration further, through further reading, by taking Feldenkrais lessons especially oriented towards music performance (of which there are an ever-increasing number), and by extrapolating this mindset to the solution of specific musical and technical challenges presented in the repertoire.

The refining influence of the Feldenkrais Method for pianists and other musicians is not just about feeling good, not just about relaxing, nor even just about improving movement – it is about connecting the deepest parts of the artist to the instrument to create performances full of drama and sensitivity, power and subtlety, to engender a voice that speaks with artistic command.

Notes

1   Phil Cohen, private conversation.

2   Yvon Brenière and Blandine Bril, 'Development of Postural Control of Gravity Forces in Children During the First 5 Years of Walking', in *Exploratory Brain Research* (Heidelberg: Springer Verlag, 1998), 1–2.

3   Weight technique as originally conceived by Rudolph Breithaupt in Germany and Tobias Matthay in England may not have had this effect, but the widespread misapplication of the technique certainly does.

4   Myriam Pfeffer, Feldenkrais trainer, private conversation.
5   Parasitic contractions are contractions that have no use, that interfere with movement.
6   Jean-Jacques Eigeldinger, *Chopin: Pianist and Teacher* (Cambridge: Cambridge University Press, 1986), 57.
7   The kinematic chain: kinetic forces are transmitted through a chain of bones when the 'links' are neither too tightly connected nor so loose that there's no connection.
8   A tensegrity structure is an arrangement of wires and struts where none of the struts touch. Its structural integrity derives from tensile relationships. Levin coined the term 'biotensegrity' to describe the same dynamic at work in the human body. The classical concept of the spine as a 'stack of bricks' fails to reflect the elegance, mechanical sophistication and adaptability of our structure.
9   FI: Functional Integration, a one-on-one private Feldenkrais lesson.
10 Feldenkrais discusses the stretch reflex at length in chapter 15 of *Body and Mature Behavior*, and in chapters 12 and 13 of *The Potent Self*. Trainer Paul Rubin tells of Feldenkrais bending a scoliosis *more*, to eventually reduce the curve by evoking the stretch reflex in the spine's antagonist muscles (private email).
11 Dr Mark Cuccazella, *Principles of Natural Running* (Shepherdstown, WV: The Natural Running Center, 2012), available at https://www.youtube.com/watch?v=zSIDRHUWlVo
12 Awareness through Movement (ATM): a group Feldenkrais lesson.
13 Moshe Feldenkrais, *San Francisco Evening Class, Volume 1* audio recording (San Francisco: Feldenkrais Resources, 1980), Lesson 3.
14 Cf. Feldenkrais trainer Ruthy Alon's seminal series of ATM lessons, 'The Grammar of Spontaneity'.
15 Private conversation with Kemal Gekić, November 2017.
16 Dystonia is a complex and sometimes unresolvable neurological condition. This approach can work, when combined with others, in some relatively mild cases.
17 Arnold Schultz, *The Riddle of the Pianist's Finger* (New York: Carl Fischer, 1936), 70.
18 *The Three Cardinal Directions of Movement in Sitting*: a classic ATM that explores flexion/extension, side bending and rotation of the spine.

CHAPTER 9
BUILDING A MODEL FOR INJURY PREVENTION IN MUSIC PEDAGOGY ROOTED IN FELDENKRAIS'S PHILOSOPHY AND METHODOLOGY FOR LEARNING

Lisa M. Burrell

Introduction

Several years ago a colleague and I were lamenting the growing prevalence of career-ending neurological disorders in musicians, recounting personal struggles and those of students and other professionals. My colleague told me the story of a classmate from his conservatory days, a student, like many, who hoped eventually to win a job in a top-tier professional orchestra. This young trombonist practised for many hours daily to refine and streamline his technique in pursuit of flawless performance, following the well-known tenet 'Don't just practise until you get it right; practise until you cannot get it wrong'.

As with many pre-professional brass players, his practice began to centre on his primary difficulty, his embouchure. Conquering his technical weakness progressed from an area of focus to an obsessive fixation. He kept a camera in his practice room, and each time he produced a tone in a particular register that satisfied him, he would freeze his face in the current embouchure and take a photo. Within months, his walls were covered with photos of his mouth and face in various positions. His practice gradually narrowed towards the singular goal of reproducing the perfect embouchure on each note, at each dynamic and in each register.

In a matter of years the sustained and unvaried use of highly specific neural pathways for several hours each day began to produce a dysfunction in him. By the age of thirty, he was forced to stop playing due to a condition known as musicians' dystonia, a neurological dysfunction that often involves permanent loss of control of the muscles – in this case, those of his embouchure. As with many musicians facing neurological injury, he had little success with rehabilitation and eventually abandoned his career in music.

This story may seem an extreme example of compulsive overuse leading to injury, but it is a widespread and growing issue in instrumental musicians. Recent studies in Great Britain, Australia and Denmark have revealed that an average of 86 per cent of full-time musicians in major symphony orchestras were injured while continuing to fulfil their regular professional commitments.[1] Studies of pre-professionals, including college and conservatory students, from the 1990s through the early 2000s show varied results, but also showed an injury average of 84 per cent among the students studied.[2] Although these studies do not correlate directly with each other, they point to a pattern of musicians developing traits of long-term serious injury during their professional training.

With children who are beginning to study music it is standard pedagogy to add games, experimentation and variation to practice, but as students begin to advance towards professionalism the games and creativity disappear. A new seriousness overtakes their study with a focus on refinement of skill. Often this transition promotes a new self-consciousness that brings about performance anxiety and creates a perfectionist mentality. Perfectionism becomes synonymous with narrowing of focus and resistance to new ideas and change.

Furthermore, as young musicians make the transition from students into professionals, their learning patterns are often shaped by allegiances to 'schools of technique'. Students begin to model their playing on that of their teachers who inherited traditions of technique and artistry from a lineage of historical master teachers. While many of these methods offer valuable tools for learning, they can lead to further narrowing of approach when students blindly adhere to them in the name of tradition rather than using them as a basis for more varied and autonomous exploration.

Recent studies into the neurology of musicians' injuries suggest a correlation between long-term dysfunction and the way in which we approach refinement and specificity of skill. These studies have begun to look at injuries among musicians as neurological in nature and as direct products of our process of learning and honing skill from pre-professional through professional levels. The results challenge earlier assumptions that these injuries are local or purely orthopaedic in nature. They also suggest that musicians' injuries are less a product of the specifics of individual technique and more a product of how we learn to limit our options for adaption and change.

Musicians who become injured often find it difficult to change their approach once injury begins to surface. This is because each musician has constructed a complex network of connections in the brain and nervous system over many years, which supports the very specific demands of musical performance. For teachers seeking to address the issue of long-term health in playing, this research offers insights into processes of learning that are rooted in the culture of our pedagogy and practice.

My struggles as a violinist with musician's dystonia and as an educator seeking to address musicians' injury led me to the work of Moshe Feldenkrais.[3] Feldenkrais's goal was to create a method of learning that would both acknowledge and facilitate change by establishing internal authority in his students. He was interested in creating conditions for learning rather than telling students what needed to be learned. From my own observations in implementing these ideas in my teaching of instrumentalists, Feldenkrais offers a useful model for reframing how we approach learning and practice in musicians.

In what follows, my purpose is threefold. Firstly, I will summarize current research that backs this new understanding of musicians' injury as hyper-development alongside studies that demonstrate how this occurs on a neurological level through traditional music pedagogy and practice. Secondly, I will introduce some of the unique components of the Feldenkrais Method, including how Feldenkrais differentiated along the spectrum of function in the development of his own ATM lessons, which have become a model for my practice and pedagogy. Finally, I will demonstrate how my teaching has evolved based on this model, including case studies, alongside suggestions for reshaping approaches to teaching and playing to reduce the growing tendency towards serious neurological injury.

The Feldenkrais Method in Creative Practice

Evolutions in research: Musicians' injuries as hyper-learning disorders

Musicians' overuse injuries have been noted in studies going back at least 250 years, with references as early as those of the physician Bernardo Ramazini in 1713.[4] These injuries, however, have long been categorized with typical repetitive-strain injuries experienced equally by non-musicians who perform repetitive tasks in their daily work. An example is the often-referenced dystonia research of Michael Merzenich in the 1990s,[5] in which primates were subjected to repeated grasping tasks over hundreds of hours combined with targeted sensory stimulation.[6] In orthopaedic studies, correlations were drawn between athletes and musicians, labelling musicians 'small-muscle athletes'.[7] Even research that targeted musicians' injuries, specifically, drew a clear distinction between serious neurological injuries like musicians' dystonia and physiological injuries of repetitive strain, which were thought to be purely orthopaedic and mechanical.

Only in last fifteen years or so, however, have researchers begun to study musicians' injuries for their unique neurological characteristics. These recent studies acknowledge changes in the brain and nervous system that occur over thousands of hours towards the development of highly specific and complex habits, requiring networking of multiple parts of the brain. Thanks to research initiatives that are specific to musicians' injuries, we have access to knowledge about issues of hyper-development in the brain, tendencies towards over-learning, or hyper-plasticity, and the resulting dysfunction in homeostatic mechanisms, or self-regulation, in the nervous system. This work has resulted in new classifications of musicians' injuries based on their neurological components.

In 2014 Eckart Altenmüller and his team of researchers from the Hochschule fur Musik, Hannover, and the Deutche Sporthochschule in Köln, proposed a system for musicians' injuries outlining a spectrum of neurological dysfunction.[8] Unlike previous classifications, which categorize musicians' injuries as either musculoskeletal or neurological, this new system identifies *all* musicians' injuries as neurological due to the significant changes in the brain and nervous system that accompany each condition. Where disorders like focal dystonia were once thought to be uniquely governed by cortical blurring and overdeveloped plasticity, this new system of classification suggests that musicians' injuries are ranked on a continuum of increasing severity of neurological dysfunction. These categories also correlate with the ease of reversibility/rehabilitation based on the degree of overdevelopment involved in each category. The five categories from least severe and most reversible to extreme plastic overdevelopment are

1. **motor fatigue**, which includes short-term loss of control, tension, and nerve and/or muscle fatigue due to an isolated period of repetition such as playing trills or a fast tremolo with the bow of a stringed instrument, and often employing small, fast peripheral movements;

2. **overuse injury**, which differs from motor fatigue in that it might involve the spread of agonist/antagonist muscular contractions in compensation for overused peripheral muscles due to repetition of similar movements over an isolated lengthy period of practice or performance, including the preparation for and performance of a fast or technically demanding work over a period of days or weeks;

3. **choking under pressure**, which represents a recurring performance failure that becomes repetitively associated with specific circumstances in performance, such as a violinist who experiences shaking while passing through one area of the bow, or a trumpet player who literally chokes, cutting off the breath by contracting the diaphragm, tongue and muscles of the throat, at the initiation of a phrase, often after a long period of rest, or at the beginning of a performance;
4. **dynamic stereotype in musicians**, which includes more complex loss of control that has become networked into automatic response at multiple levels of the brain and nervous system and involves loss of precision, increased agonist/antagonist contraction and rapid motor fatigue sustained over a period of weeks and months despite attempts at rest and rehabilitation;
5. **focal dystonia**, which likely involves some genetic and/or proprioceptive dysfunction, which, when combined with overdevelopment issues in the previous categories, gives rise to networking and sensory integration issues, including loss of function in the negative feedback mechanisms which normally keep control of excess plastic growth; these changes cause dysfunctional sensory-motor problems to spread rapidly in response to added repetitive sensory-motor stimulus resulting in cramping, oscillating tremor, loss of precision, and abnormal postures and movements.[9]

In Altenmüller's research, musicians' brains are shown to exhibit structural changes in other ways that, on the one hand, allow them to learn and perform increasingly complex sequences with greater efficiency over time, but, on the other hand, begin to prioritize certain kinds of learning. Prioritization of highly specific tasks begins to elicit systemic compensations that increase the neurological complexity in situations of overuse and overdevelopment in any one area. This makes the idea of 'simple' overuse injury anything but simple, in comparison to these injuries in non-musicians.[10]

One important functional and structural factor in cognition for musicians is the powerful network of feedback between the auditory and the kinaesthetic. For professional musicians the feedback loops represented in these networks are the primary pathways for detecting and correcting error. In musicians the auditory-kinaesthetic connection is stronger and more integrated into each function than sensations of pain or discomfort that normally serve in a self-regulating capacity. Responses in sensation and movement become highly networked to their auditory output. This auditory-kinaesthetic networking accounts for some of the most significant structural/plastic changes throughout the brain.[11]

Researchers are also beginning to link excessive plastic growth in musicians to the positive emotional experiences of playing and of practising. In the brain these emotional connections are mediated by the limbic system. The limbic system is also networked to areas of the brain responsible for action selection, like the basal ganglia, and, therefore, plays a major role in the development of new networks and the strengthening of synapses. The limbic system plays an important part of self-regulation by producing negative feedback in response to error. In musicians, however, neurotransmitters like dopamine actually provide positive feedback in response to exact kinds of over-learning that lead to loss of control – musicians develop a kind of addiction to and a craving for these feelings of hyper-plastic change. In a way, the positive stimulus of music and feelings of pleasure might become associated with synaptic strengthening and, thus, override the negative signals normally required to maintain a kind of homeostasis that helps control how much synapses are allowed to grow and strengthen in balance with the whole nervous system.[12]

Research from the early 2000s to the present has begun to explore this concept known as homeostatic synaptic plasticity and, likewise, its dysfunction.[13] Homeostatic plasticity controls the strength of a synapse and measures it against the demands of the system. Homeostatic plastic regulation helps prevent excess excitation that would overwhelm the nervous system particularly in the case of complex tasks involving frequent repetition. Research is beginning to show how this kind of regulation works at a global level, regulating synapses in coordination with each other in the whole nervous system.

When viewing musicians' injuries from a neurological perspective, this research suggests that this critical synaptic regulation can become compromised due to training and practice. This model supports the idea of faulty inhibition at play after the onset of dystonia, and during dystonic cycles; it also suggests that the lack of fully functioning negative feedback mechanisms that normally underlie homeostatic plasticity may eventually be recognized as precursors to the development of dystonia.[14]

Feldenkrais, functional integration and the asymptotic ideal

The prominence of injuries among musicians at both professional and pre-professional levels alongside new characterizations of musicians' injuries on a continuum of increasing severity of neurological dysfunction suggests a need for re-evaluation of pedagogical tools in training young musicians. We also need a better understanding of neurological pitfalls in working with those who have become injured. If we acknowledge what the latest research tells us about the way in which musicians' injuries are linked to the ways we traditionally learn, practise and teach music, it also follows that we should be looking towards pedagogical philosophies that offer more diversification, choice and adaptability.

Among the pedagogical elements that first appealed to me about the work of Moshe Feldenkrais was his non-linear approach to learning which acknowledged the complexity of variables within the human nervous system and which he derived, in part, from his background in the mathematics of complex function. Feldenkrais's early study and work in mathematics are evident in the terminology and philosophy of his method of learning.[15] Feldenkrais's language is the language of mathematics using words like 'differentiation', 'function', 'integration' and 'asymptotic' relationships. This is the language of discovery within complex systems without a primary concern for reaching a goal, but instead questioning and exploring in a way that creates new possibilities, new pathways, new networks that refine and clarify who we are.

In mathematics, a *function* is a relationship between variables where the values of some depend on the values of others. The relationship between Fahrenheit and Centigrade is an example of a simple function, where the temperature value in one system depends on the value of the other. Simple functions are relatable to some of the early models of understanding of musicians' injury.

Feldenkrais was interested in the tools involved in exploring complex function, or those which involved non-linear relationships. Studying complex function in mathematics involves disciplines such as calculus. Calculus is used, for example, in examining the distance travelled by a car over time where the speed varies during the journey. A complex relationship like this might be represented by a curve, rather than a straight line, between vertical (distance) and horizontal (time) axes. In order to study this kind of non-linear function, due to varying speeds or infinite changes in the slope of the curve, a mathematician goes through a process of breaking down and examining changes in the curve over smaller and smaller segments of time. This process, well known in Feldenkrais's terminology, is called *differentiation*. The process of examining accumulated changes over a number of segments, in the case of the car example, to approximate the distance travelled over time, is called *integration*. Because complex function involves constant change, the process of differentiating and integrating is one that is designed to refine and clarify infinitely, rather than offering singular solutions.

Feldenkrais used terms that have very explicit technical meanings in mathematics and several other areas of significance to him, in order to communicate some essential premises of his work with precision. Examining Feldenkrais's use of this terminology in the context of his pedagogy has provided useful insight into how to work with musicians in and around the learning-based components of musicians' injury and dysfunction.

Functions in the Feldenkrais Method are the infinite and complex relationships that make up action. These include both relationships within ourselves and between ourselves and our environment. Feldenkrais was intrigued by processes that could improve action by breaking it down and examining its functional components. Even a seemingly simple action comprises a complex function. For example, if we pick up a glass of water, we must be aware of factors in ourselves like coordination and proprioception alongside external factors, such as gravity, temperature and texture.

For a musician the functional relationship is within each individual, between that individual and the demands for performance on his or her instrument, and in that person's connection to the world through an instrument – the latter being as enigmatic as trying to connect to an audience through expression, or as practical as dealing with temperature or acoustics in a concert hall.

Differentiation in Feldenkrais's work is the process of breaking down actions and functions of those actions into new and varied functional components. We might differentiate function in playing an instrument by exploring how a pianist brings a finger to a key on the piano, or a violinist plays a staccato articulation with the bow. We might further differentiate by exploring the differences in louder or softer dynamics or staccato articulations in Mozart versus Stravinsky. Differentiation is not about defining a particular moment, but, rather, about exploring the relationship between two limits or constraints, parsing a function into smaller connections within that function to attend to it in detail.

Feldenkrais's concept of integration is the regrouping of the differentiated elements into a new approximation of an ideal of some part of that function or an intended action. Each time we differentiate, or parse some unexplored detail of the overall function, we gain new insights into the whole – a single change in articulation or timing in a Bach Sarabande may affect how we choose to shape the entire phrase, convey an emotion or set the tone of an entire work.

The process of differentiation and successive integration comes closer and closer to an ideal as the differentiated elements are explored through finer constraints, or self-imposed limits, and integrated over that spectrum of functional possibility. Feldenkrais referred to this process as approaching an 'asymptotic ideal', another term derived from mathematics. This process for musicians can be applied to the art of practising an instrument as an alternative to repetition and narrowing of focus.

In his book *Awareness through Movement*, Feldenkrais describes the relationship that a person might discover between the spine and the floor in one of his lessons:

> As you proceed with this lesson you will discover that your judgment is different in the two cases, but that the subjective evaluation converges on the objective evaluation asymptotically. In other words, the subjective sensation has a wider field of operation than objective evaluation, which limits our capacity for knowledge to the simple material reality around us.[16]

He speaks of the asymptotic relationship between a person and his/her subjective perceptions, often formed by habituation, and contrasts it with a kind of internal process of refinement through differentiation and integration by exploring the elements of function as they pertain to individual experience.

For me, this kind of thinking is important to our learning as musicians in order to prevent long-term neurological injury. When we are working at refining function that is highly specific, highly intentional, and potentially repetitive over many hours and has increasingly rapid execution, we need to be exploring the full 'curve' of that function through differentiation within limits that we are able to *objectively* define for ourselves. Function among musicians, because of its specificity, has to approach the ideal of each individual's relationship to playing and expression asymptotically in order to avoid the dangers of learning in traditional ways. A cellist with small hands, for example, may have as much functional potential as another cellist with long fingers, but the way in which each person must explore function safely will vary significantly.[17]

Feldenkrais's Awareness through Movement lessons as a model for teaching musicians how to practise

Feldenkrais's use of differentiation and integration as pedagogy can be traced through his probing of functional themes in his many hundreds of Awareness through Movement (ATM) lessons. Feldenkrais taught ATM lessons in varied settings, from his lessons to long-time clients on Alexander Yanai Street in Tel Aviv, to those given spontaneously in public workshops and trainings, to the examples he included in his book for the general public, *Awareness through Movement*. For me, this array of resources has become valuable for understanding just how extensively he varies his exploration of relatively simple functional ideas to illuminate complex relationships in the body and nervous system. The sometimes thought-out, but often spontaneous pedagogical process in these lessons is something I have worked to integrate into my own teaching in my violin studio, classroom teaching and individual practice with musicians.

If we choose any functional theme to trace among the many hundreds of ATM lessons Feldenkrais taught in his career, we will see certain pedagogical objectives emerge – creating conditions for learning, establishing individual autonomy, and exploring a broad and detailed range of relationships in functional connections. Feldenkrais crafted these lessons with the intent to bring his students into personal relationships with human function in a way that would prevent them from imposing limits on their learning. He set up puzzles and sequences to examine micro-segments of differentiation and their subsequent integration to widespread functional relationships over the course of multiple lessons. No two lessons are the same in scope or depth. He alternated between increasingly targeted differentiation, using constraints, and the introduction of auxiliary movements in areas more peripheral to the primary relationship he was exploring. He worked with varied positions from sitting, reclining, standing, to supine, prone, and side lying to create new constraints to open up underexplored movements and connections. He included common habitual and developmental relationships as well as many 'out of phase' movements to challenge students to feel themselves in new ways. He made sure that by continuously exploring new relationships they were exploring infinite potential within themselves rather than principles or ideals dictated by him.

In my combined role as a Feldenkrais practitioner and violinist, I continue to study these lessons to gain insights into how to vary the work I do with students to help prevent long-term injury in my own, often spontaneous process. I believe we can tailor the pedagogical elements of Feldenkrais's work to the process of teaching musicians how to learn and improve upon the functions of playing. Specifically, we can make the string studio, classroom and even Feldenkrais lessons themselves laboratories for discovering how to move the art of practising in the direction of exploring variation/change, personal awareness and potential by encouraging experimentation and expansion even when teaching the specifics of technique and musicianship.

In my private teaching studio, I bring my specific knowledge of how the violin works and my years of study and performance to each lesson, but in integrating ideas from Feldenkrais, I have come to use my knowledge of playing as just a part of the equation of what teaching each individual student entails. Studying Feldenkrais's lessons has made me more attuned to the unique aspects of human function that each student brings to the table. This allows me to create conditions for learning that are tailored to specific techniques, but also specific to the needs of the student. When exploring a difficulty that does not fit my own experience, I can enter into a dialogue by giving a student a series of experiments to conduct, looking at a technique or a musical idea in relation to an aspect of listening, or sensing, or physical relationships or movements. I may have a hypothesis in mind, but I try to let both my sense of the scope for the infinite connections to function, provided by the many examples in Feldenkrais's ATM lessons, and the student's actual experience lead us through the lesson.

For example, if a student is struggling with a difficult bowing, I might ask her to pay attention to how she might be distributing her weight over her feet if I notice that she tends to favour one side over the other. If that student then tells me that she senses more weight in her heels, I could ask her to play the passage shifting weight between right and left heels, then front to back, then between right and left toes and observe the differences both in sound and in sensation. We might integrate this into another technique, looking at how shifting of the weight coordinates differently between moving right to left on a down bow versus left to right how do direction and balance relate to momentum and friction in playing, and how do they change the quality of sound, texture or volume?

In another lesson, I might look at how this relationship to standing creates changes in stability/flexibility in the shoulder joint, or how eye gaze might be connected to the weight of the bow on the string or the way in which the sternum and jaw support the instrument. In this sense, the student is gaining experience with a technique along with a sense of the whole body's involvement in the function of playing and that no single relationship can define a function in every circumstance of playing.

In the music classroom, my objective, very much like that in Feldenkrais's public ATM lessons given to large and widely varied groups, is to account for and encourage personal exploration while covering the necessary array of technical and musical functions we all must include in our musical and technical development. I present lessons as sensory experiments for students to initially explore internal awareness, but then bring some of the distinctions to light in the group, encouraging students to share their personal observations and to discuss some of the similarities and differences they find. This process can be valuable in ensemble training, as well, because students can explore how they might each differently engage in practice towards a unified performance goal.

When I teach rhythm, for example, I often begin a lesson by exploring developmental connections to the vestibular, like balancing, turning or crossing the midline. I might ask students to explore various rhythms, tempi, on-beats and off-beats, while walking in circles, marching in contralateral and ipsilateral motion, twisting, passing balls with one hand etc. Sometimes I draw directly from Feldenkrais's ATM lessons, but, most often, I create variations inspired by these lessons that suit the group of students at hand. I then integrate these variations with techniques on the instrument like playing a rhythm near the frog of the bow, requiring students to cross the midline of the body, or circling the bow around the head during a rest.

If I want to emphasize a left-hand technique, I might have students practise sliding between left-hand positions on the instrument (shifting positions) while moving from sitting to standing. Exposing students to an array of variations in each lesson begins to engage them in thinking about ways they might creatively explore problem-solving and substitute for repetition in individual practice.

The Feldenkrais practitioner's studio can become a venue for teaching musicians to expand and vary their own practice to include relationships outside of the already highly differentiated areas that they tend to overdevelop, whether or not they are musicians themselves. This is one area, though, where I want to insert a note of caution. When working with professional musicians, I think it is important to remember that there are likely areas of individual development that have already become extremely differentiated to a point where 'normal' homeostatic mechanisms may have become compromised. This was the extreme case with me in my own Feldenkrais training, where I entered feeling confident in my physical and neurological capacity to handle this kind of learning only to experience what can only be described as an 'explosion' of my own musicians' dystonia within the first ten days of lessons.

Early in my work with clients, in spite of my own experience, I had to learn the dangers of adding increased differentiation to overdeveloped areas of their playing, contributing to plastic development in unwanted ways. In many ways these areas drew my attention because of how quickly my clients seemed to learn in a lesson when I worked with a hand or a shoulder developing small, detailed connections they had not felt before, but very often these lessons left my clients confused or with an intensification of the problems they had already struggled with in the days after a lesson, almost as if the brain and nervous system had added complexity to the problem, rather than helping balance or stabilize.

As I grew in experience and understanding of musicians' injury, I learned how much more powerfully helpful, and safe, I could be by helping musicians build functional relationships with parts of themselves that are the least known to them in ways that help to balance the overdevelopment in the areas they consider primary to playing. Teaching injured string players to derive support from their legs, pelvis and spine, or finding how the arm, hand and shoulder can stabilize individual fingers can help them transform their own practice to include more rather than less of themselves. Likewise, instead of focusing on breathing or embouchure in a brass or wind player, I might direct attention to the legs or the pelvic floor, doing a lesson focused in a way related to breath and support, but adding a stabilizing element. Most professional musicians thrive when they can learn to regain some equality in the nervous system between over- and under-used areas of their own functional curves.

Three examples of Feldenkrais pedagogy with musicians

My pedagogy draws from my own experience as a musician struggling with neurological injury and my inquiry into both the challenges and the advantages of adapting this work for targeted use with musicians. While I feel comfortable outlining a general protocol for how this work can be used as a model for working in private studios, classrooms and in Feldenkrais practices, I also stress that this pedagogy really took shape as a more spontaneous outgrowth of my personal, real-time experiences with many students and clients, as I worked to understand this method for myself. My sense is that this is something similar to the process Feldenkrais went through in creating his own lessons, and through those lessons what we now call the Feldenkrais Method. Feldenkrais was a strong believer that the intuited sense of an idea and the many experiences with exploring that idea in multiple contexts necessarily came long before its verbalization. Therefore, I offer the following specific samples from my experience using Feldenkrais in my teaching and work with musician clients to demonstrate a range of applications from teaching fundamentals of playing, to working with a student with particular physical constraints, to working with a client with a playing-related injury.

Kathryn – integrating Feldenkrais concepts into violin teaching

Near the end of the first week of my Feldenkrais training, while teaching a lesson to a high school student, I felt a new kind of intuition begin to pervade my teaching. After several days of lying on the floor doing ATM lessons and exploring multiple differentiations of function in my own brain and body, I started to feel my toolbox filling with more alternatives to traditional teaching, modelling my own playing, and repetition-based practice to which I had often succumbed due to lack of alternatives. After most of my training days, I would try to squeeze in a few hours of private teaching. It was, foremost, a professional necessity, but it gradually also became a valuable laboratory for assimilating the learning I was doing in the training.

On this particular day, I was working with my student, Kathryn, on playing chords – an advanced skill on the violin involving multiple strings at the same time and requiring access to very targeted and efficient use of force/power. Kathryn was struggling to make a beautiful sound in her chords, which came out as either weak or overly harsh. I remember going down a sizeable list of successful strategies for teaching chords that had worked with other students. Each attempt showed mild improvement, but nothing really struck me as connecting with her from a place that she could continue to build upon in her practice. I tried to determine which element was really missing for Kathryn. She continued to approximate the way I was demonstrating them, using *my* strategies for power and accuracy, developed through *my* own internal connection to what was a relative comfortable technique for *me*.

Then, as I sat back and watched and listened to Kathryn review the exercises we had tried over the last weeks, something fascinating happened. As she played, I stopped thinking about how I played the chords and began to attend to how Kathryn approached this challenge. For the first time, I had sense of who Kathryn was in that instant: her personal relationship with the violin and with the world, how she carried herself, how she reacted to mistakes, how she moved, from whence was she willing this elusive force and precision. From there I began to notice the missing areas in her sensation and awareness. I did not understand what I was seeing, but I knew I was seeing Kathryn, not me, and not any other student, playing these chords in a way I had never noticed before. Something absolutely new in my own awareness of my relationship to her as her teacher surfaced.

I got up and stood behind Kathryn with my hands on her shoulder blades, and I asked her to lean back into my support ever so slightly. I told her to try playing the chords again only when she felt fully supported. When Kathryn lifted her bow this time, there was a lightness, freedom and ease in her right arm, followed by a tremendous connection to power from her back. She absolutely nailed it. She turned to me with a smile. When she returned to playing on her own, she felt the connection clearly. Her work in the next weeks built on her success, as she integrated the technique into her personal music-making.

In pedagogy of all kinds, novel ideas that once created successful individual learning find their way into universalized practices in the name of streamlined and efficient teaching. These ideas often become normalized in a practice or pedagogy quite simply because a teacher or practitioner discovers a strategy that works well with one student or in her own playing, and that strategy gradually becomes adopted as a broader truth in that teacher's pedagogy. This is a classic example of how a process-based exploration of function becomes a prescriptive exercise we adopt to 'fix' a problem. My Feldenkrais training's educational director, Paul Rubin, introduced the word 'reification' in the first week of our study to explain this common tendency in human behaviour to begin to confuse a process with a fixed reality while alerting us to beware of this tendency over the course of our studies and practice.

My first experiments with Feldenkrais's ideas in my violin studio began to show me that a new approach to musicians' pedagogy might be hidden in the strategies for individualized experiential learning of this Method, particularly when these strategies were used for developing new avenues of discovery rather than as ways to 'fix' problems. Studying the many variations of Feldenkrais's ATM lessons also reinforced the idea that this work was really about reimagining function from continually changing perspectives in order to elicit personalized learning. This strategy accounts for infinitely varied approaches to similar functional ideas and allows for unique pathways of change in each student.

Alexa – working around constraints

From a developmental perspective, particularly those theories espoused in recently accepted models, we know that the learning of function takes many paths to the same basic ends.[18] Steering away from the traditional process of passing down pedagogical systems from one generation to the next encourages educators to observe and support differences between individuals. Sometimes it is even the case that an individual's physical or other constraints can unleash an unforeseen potential that might not be valued in traditional training.

My college student, Alexa, has grown up with a brachio-plexus injury to her right shoulder, caused by the stretching and severing of nerves during her birth. Alexa has an extremely limited range of movement in her right arm, and very little stabilization in her shoulder joint as a result of the permanent shortening of muscles from prolonged spasticity. Nevertheless, Alexa is not only well on her way to becoming a professional violinist, she has also become one of the highest-functioning brachio-plexus injury patients in the world, according to her doctors at the Mayo Clinic.

When Alexa and I first began working together four years ago, she was largely self-taught. She found it difficult to employ many aspects of traditional technique and follow the kind of regimen used to teach these techniques due to her specific movement limitations. She cannot lift her right arm more than a couple of inches, so any kind of isolated or suspended use of her bow arm was impossible. Furthermore, the rigour of repeated practice of mainstream technique involved significant compensation from surrounding muscle groups and served to increase the pain and physical tension in her playing.

Fortunately, Alexa was very cognizant of her capabilities, and moved into her own way of learning with truly remarkable results, already evident when we first met. Her capacity to feel, sense and articulate how things worked in her body with each new experiment made the adventure of our work together immediately productive. With Alexa's guidance we began to explore the untouched areas around her 'disability' in order to plumb for valuable links to what she *could* do.

Initially I believed Alexa would likely find limitations when it came to the demands of higher-level technique and performance on the violin. My idea was to understand her limits and work towards an ideal within the potential I could envision. We talked early about gradually trying to define what was achievable within the confines of what she could reasonably handle. I provided challenges within a particular range that would push the limits a little bit, but not enough to discourage. We experimented with new movements and new sensations, including unused but functional parts of Alexa's body and nervous system, and then tried to examine where we fell short or reached an obstacle we could not overcome.

After working this way for several months some completely unexpected phenomena began to occur in Alexa's learning. Each time I anticipated a limitation, we found a new way around it. She began to progress through upper-level repertoire, playing solo Bach, Wieniawski, Saint-Saëns and Bruch concerti, alongside pyrotechnical études and studies. She began to look for the next potential obstacle in order to discover how far she could push the boundaries.

What I realized, finally, with Alexa is that although she had a number of physical constraints that altered her approach to the violin, she had a brain that could learn multiple routes around each problem. She could map every functioning part of herself in relation to these challenges, and by bringing online all available resources, she had a functional potential that was no different from anyone else.

Alexa's potential function was, also like everyone else, defined not by her orthopaedic constraints, but by the places we had not yet explored. For her, like everyone else, the possibilities were infinite, as long as we kept looking for what was missing and not focusing narrowly on the problems. In a way, Alexa's injury forced both of us to look farther along the curve than either of our experiences suggested so far, and I think this is in many ways at the heart of her enormous success.

Jeb – working with playing-related dysfunction

As I have discussed, musicians who demonstrate patterns of overdevelopment in very specific ways can benefit from varying their areas of focus from peripheral to central in order to begin to identify places that are underexplored. One of the ways that Feldenkrais successfully bypasses pathways of overdevelopment in many of his ATM lessons is to work on the initiation of a movement. In working with the thoughts, feelings, changes in breath, changes in balance etc., before a movement begins, we find places where we can often choose a non-habitual next step in the movement. This kind of work is especially valuable when a musician is strongly engaged in a pattern of action that has become dysfunctional and finds that the dysfunction has already become networked into many deeply unconscious mechanisms of playing.

A few years ago, I worked briefly with a horn player, Jeb, who feared the onset of some early dystonia symptoms. He found growing tension in his embouchure and jaw, and he felt that in times of more strain and stress the tension was spreading into his neck and shoulders.

When Jeb spoke about his difficulty I noticed significant unconscious starts and stops in his breath. I was concerned about initially addressing such a familiar mechanism to horn playing as breath, but it seemed like such an obvious place to begin that I thought it was worth a try, especially if we could approach his breathing from someplace totally new.

I recalled Feldenkrais's lesson, 'Stopping the Breath',[19] and thought that it might allow Jeb to feel what he was doing in the moments before he started to play. I worked with Jeb first in lying, supporting his low back, his shoulders and eventually his head with my hands, providing just enough extra feedback so that he could sense in different places the parts of himself that engaged when he went through the experiments of stopping his breath – after inhaling, exhaling and mid-way through each part of a breath cycle. Gradually Jeb began to notice how certain familiar ways of stopping his breath were triggering parts of the tension patterns he was experiencing. He also began to notice a particular 'stop' at a specific point in deep inhalation that he closely associated with playing. We worked further on stopping the breath in ways unrelated to the tension patterns by controlling starts and stops with changes in the musculature of his abdomen in order to control his airflow, while easily moving his head and shoulders so that his whole system did not need to be wired into this control.

Jeb's face and jaw began to soften as we worked. In a relatively short time he was able to discriminate between ways of initiating movement outside of even strongly unconscious patterns of tension in his breathing, his most developed and ingrained mechanism of playing.

Conclusions and thoughts for future development

In an age where standards of playing are pushing the limits of human potential, injuries among musicians will continue to increase in prevalence as long as we remain complacent in examining the roles of our practice and pedagogy in their construction. We know that professional musicians spend thousands of hours practising an art reinforced by strong emotional connections to the work they do. We now understand that musicians' brains are transformed by this process in a way that creates a systemic dependency prioritizing their functional relationship with their instrument and communication through music.

We can observe outcomes of recent research into the distinct qualities of musicians' injuries that demonstrate how elements of our practice and pedagogy are contributing to a long-term process that is potentially harming us. These injuries, which were once treated as purely physiological, have become recognized for their neurological complexity, involving changes in networking, changes in self-regulation, and changes in perception and feedback.

On the positive side, these latest findings point directly to ways in which we, as educators, might change our approach pedagogically to decrease the likelihood of both short- and long-term problems. These include increasing individual autonomy, adding variation to replace repetitive practice habits, fostering ongoing adaptability, and exploring the function of playing in a way that engages some of the peripheral parts of ourselves directly related to playing to a more global sense of self-image.

Moshe Feldenkrais's work offers a model for learning that can be successfully integrated into arts teaching, not only in the broad sense of teaching these lessons in their original form, but directly into safer functional exploration with instruments in lessons and classroom settings. Since incorporating this methodology and philosophy into my studio and classroom pedagogy, I have begun to see generation of self-sufficient, creative and thoughtful young musicians emerge. For practitioners, educators and creative thinkers it is important to consider the nature of these injuries and the ways that our traditions reinforce our practice and teaching. Developing intentional pedagogy that creates conditions for learning and avoids systematized protocols and quick fixes may provide the key to creating a new generation of musicians more resilient and adaptable in their playing careers.

Notes

1. Bronwen J. Ackermann, Dianna T. Kenny, Ian O'Brien, and Tim R. Driscoll, 'Sound Practice: Improving Occupational Health and Safety for Professional Orchestral Musicians in Australia', *Frontiers in Psychology*, Vol. 5 (2014), 973–90. Richard Leaver, E. Clare Harris, and Keith T. Palmer, 'Musculoskeletal Pain in Elite Professional Musicians from British Symphony Orchestras', *Occupational Medicine*, Vol. 8 (2012), 549–55, and Helene M. Paarup, Jesper Baelum, Jonas W. Holm, Claus Manniche, and Niels Wedderkopp, 'Prevalence and Consequences of Musculoskeletal Symptoms in Symphony Orchestra Musicians Vary by Gender: A Cross-Sectional Study', *BMC Musculoskeletal Disorders*, Vol. 12 (2011), 223–38.
2. Joseph Bejiani, Glenn M. Kaye, and Melody Benham, 'Musculo-skeletal and Neuromuscular Conditions of Instrumental Musicians', *Archives of Physical and Medical Rehabilitation*, Vol. 77 (1996), 406–13.
3. Lisa Burrell, 'My Journey with Dystonia and the Feldenkrais Method: Beginning a Discussion on Contraindications for Aspects of Our Practice', *The Feldenkrais Journal*, Vol. 28 (2015), 7–19.
4. Beijiani, 'Musculo-skeletal and Neuromuscular Conditions of Instrumental Musicians', 406.
5. Norman Doidge, *The Brain's Way of Healing* (New York: Viking, 2015), 173.
6. Peter Stein, Eliot Saltzman, Kenneth Holt, and Dagmar Sternad, 'Is Failed Predictive Control a Risk Factor in Focal Dystonia?', *Movement Disorders*, Vol. 31, No. 6 (2016), 1772–6.

7   Eckart Altenmüller, with Christos Ioannou, Markus Raab, and Babett Lobinger, 'Apollo's Curse: Neurological Causes of Motor Impairments in Musicians', *Progress in Brain Research*, Vol. 217 (2015), 91.

8   Altenmüller et al., 'Apollo's Curse', 89–96.

9   Altenmüller et al., 'Apollo's Curse', 89–96.

10 Altenmüller and Shinichi Furuya, 'Apollo's Gift and Curse', *Neuroforum*, Vol. 23, No. 2 (2017), A57.

11 From Altenmüller and Furuya, 'Apollo's Gift and Curse', *Neuroforum*, Vol. 23, No. 2 (2017), 59.

12 Altenmüller and Furuya, 'Apollo's Gift and Curse', 61.

13 Siegrid Löwel, 'Selection of Intrinsic Horizontal Connections in the Visual Cortex by Correlated Neuronal Activity', *Science*, Vol. 255, No. 5041 (1992), 209–12.

14 From Tamura et al., 'Disordered Plasticity in the Primary Somatosensory Cortex in Focal Hand Dystonia', *Brain*, Vol. 123, No. 3 (2009), 750.

15 Mark Reese, *Moshe Feldenkrais: A Life in Movement*, Vol. I (San Rafael, CA: ReeseKress Somatics Press, 2015), 66–8.

16 Moshe Feldenkrais, *Awareness through Movement* (New York: HarperCollins, 1977), 120.

17 Esther Thelen and Linda B. Smith, 'Dynamic Systems Theories', in *Handbook of Child Psychology*, Vol. 1 (Hoboken, NJ: John Wiley and Sons, 2006), 258–312.

18 Thelen and Smith, 'Dynamic Systems Theories', 255–312.

19 Ellen Soloway Feldenkrais (ed.), 'Stopping the Breath', in *Alexander Yanai Lessons*, No. 172 (Paris: International Feldenkrais Federation, 1995).

CHAPTER 10
A SENSE OF SAFETY: POLYVAGAL THEORY, THE FELDENKRAIS METHOD AND THE ACTING PROCESS

Victoria Worsley

Safety is a powerful metaphor ... if we feel safe, we have access to the neural regulation of the facial muscles, we have access to a myelinated vagal circuit that is capable of down regulating more traditional fight/flight and stress responses, and we have an opportunity to play ... Play requires an ability to mobilize with the sympathetic nervous system and then to down-regulate the sympathetic excitation with face-to-face social interaction and the social engagement system.[1]

It's very hard to play when you are anxious, but the opposite is also true: It's very hard to be anxious when you are truly playing.[2]

Introduction

It is not immediately obvious how the acting process is enabled by a somatic method of re-education such as the Feldenkrais Method, or why the Polyvagal Theory, more usually valued for its contribution in the field of trauma therapy, illuminates that relationship. However, exploring these connections helps answer some of the most fundamental questions asked in any rehearsal room or acting class: what makes a performance 'live' or 'die'? What sustains the interest of the audience in a performance or causes it to fail?

Stephen Porges's Polyvagal Theory examines the nature of the vagal nerve complex and its role in modulating our responses to danger in order to keep us safe. In any 'Awareness through Movement' (ATM) lesson from the Feldenkrais Method, students are invited to explore their habitual responses and patterns of movement and what facilitates or limits the choices they are able to spontaneously make. In that process, many students encounter shifts, not only in their physicality, but in their behaviour, emotional well-being and ability to respond to the world; to their sense of ease, comfort and – crucially for this chapter – safety.

In the quotation above, Porges locates the ability to connect socially and to play within the person's sense of safety. An actor's process involves the need to connect with audience and with other actors and to play. It is this connection and ability to play that keeps a performance alive. Looking into the Polyvagal Theory in more detail could improve our understanding of the conditions acting students and working actors may need in order to learn, create and flourish, and to enable individual actors to resource themselves better when in the challenging arena of performance. It could also help explain why lessons from the Feldenkrais Method can be so enabling in this context.

The ideas and connections made in this article are drawn from years of experience as an actor, as a teacher of performers and as a Feldenkrais Method practitioner. They are not the result of evidence-based research. However, thinking based on direct experience in the field is necessary to illuminate significant areas for further investigation and that is where the value of this article lies. The following real-life examples provide an opportunity to clarify and discuss the importance of the connection between actors and actors and audience, its relationship to a sense of safety and how the performance 'dies' when that connection fails.

Example 1

August 1986 at the Edinburgh Festival: one sweaty, beery night, a young southern lad tries out as a stand-up comic. The slightly (or very) drunk audience watches briefly and then rapidly ignores him. The lad falters. His jokes become louder and harsher as he tries to push his way into conversations and grab the audience's attention back. The audience ignores him. He begins to strut about the stage shouting and swearing as if he can conquer it with sheer aggression. Nothing. He adds a few barbed insults to the jokes he hurls out like grenades. At last he gets his response: a roar begins to build from a row at the back and erupts with a cheery chorus of heavy Scottish voices,

Show us your bum!

The would-be stand-up stands stock-still. Arrested in mid-flight, he deflates like a burst balloon. His face pale and damp, he slips away and no one registers he has gone. On comes the compère, Arthur Smith, with his easy saunter. He is also a little rough with the audience, but in a knowing 'one of the lads' kind of way. His resonant voice and weathered banter soon takes hold of the space. The audience shuts up. Laughter bursts out obligingly across the room in all the right moments.

Example 2

An audition room, many years later: an actor starts her speech. She is energized and animated, on the balls of her feet. The panel sits back and watches, carefully giving little response. The actor leans a little more forward. Her eyes widen; her expressions and gestures become a little more intense. The panel leans further back. The actor eyeballs each member of the panel, enthusiastically radiating warmth and charm as hard as she can. The panel's eyes glaze a little, some look slightly away. The actor's chest lifts and swells. She puts her all into the end of the speech, breaking down in real tears. The speech ends in silence. The actor looks up eagerly with her shiny, shiny smile. A member of the panel politely ushers her out. They will 'let her know'.

Example 3

The Barbican Theatre in London *c.* 1994: A classy Shakespeare comedy with a handful of well-known British actors and a rising star in the lead. Even the unknown actors do a good job. The verse is well-spoken and coherent, the overall direction and design serve them well. And I am mostly bored. I find I am only engaged when the rising star is on. He listens to the other actors, gives things time, responds to what they do. His verse is playful and easy. I am not alone: the audience clearly hangs on his every word. We find ourselves with him in a way that we are not with anyone else, even though the delivery of every part is good. This division between how we are with him and with the other actors pulls the production apart, but at least there is someone we are keen to watch.

Connection: Complicité

Philippe Gaulier and another well-known European teacher, Jacques Lecoq, coined the term 'complicité' to mean the mutual connection between the actor(s) and audience.[3] These three examples illustrate different ways a performance dies when complicité is disrupted. In the first two examples, the would-be stand-up and auditioning actress fall out of complicité with the audience very quickly, and their attempts to reconnect are through aggression or begging. These do not work because they are trying to force the audience to respond, unlike the MC in the first example, Arthur Smith, who simply meets the audience where it is and builds a connection from there.

The third example shows the difference between an actor who is in complicité and the actors who are not. The connection with the audience, even when indirect, provides a sense of timing and impulse for performance as does the connection with the other actor(s). Where there is a shared connection there is life, playfulness, spontaneity, a true dynamic and a context that an actor's emotional or comedic response can emerge from, as with the lead actor in this show. Where there is not enough complicité there is nothing for the actor to work off and it becomes a run-through of the moves and words along with – perhaps – a disconnected display of emotional or technical fireworks with no real foundation within the show. Even if the performance is technically 'skilled', there is nothing much going on for an audience to be engaged with, which is what was happening with most of the cast.

Understanding the need for a connection between actors and audience is not new. Most schools have their 'Lecoq' teacher preaching complicité via clown and mask modules. It appears in popular American methods like the Meisner Technique, where the interdependence of actors is key:

What you do doesn't depend on you, it depends on the other fellow.[4]

Going further back, Konstantin Stanislavski, the grandfather of many modern methods, stresses it. Here he describes disconnection (lack of complicité) beautifully:

What torture to play opposite an actor who looks at you and yet sees someone else, who constantly adjusts himself to that person and not to you. Such actors are separated from the very persons with whom they should be in closer relationship. They cannot take in your words, your intonations or anything else. Their eyes are veiled as they look at you.

And here he describes play and the triangle of 'complicité' between actor, actor and audience:

> We are in relation with our partner and simultaneously with the spectator … The remarkable thing is that with both our relation is mutual …. To play to a large and sympathetic audience is like singing in a room with perfect acoustics. The audience constitute the spiritual acoustics for us. They give back what they receive from us as living, human emotions.[5]

However this element of Stanislavski's method is often utterly lost. Actors frequently use his method carefully to work out what their character is attempting to do to another character at every moment and then play those decisions with great dedication and very little reference to how the other actors respond – let alone the audience. Indeed the acting process can still end up being thought of as something an actor does essentially by themselves: researching their part as necessary, making decisions about the intention and motivation for the character at any time and taking it on themselves to find an appropriate emotional state: the crucial importance of what happens in the space between actors disappears. Sometimes, when filming, connection with the other performer is considered so unimportant that an actor finds themselves acting with a cross on a stick, or with a fellow actor 'saving themselves' for their own close-up.

A sense of safety

The link between complicité and the actor's sense of safety is, in my experience, even less acknowledged. Teachers' and directors' methods can range from excitingly challenging to verging on cruel. I am not about to reference that statement, however I can mention Lecoq, Gaulier and some of their followers, who have been known for their well-intentioned espousal of a version of the 'via negativa'.[6] This approach was named by Grotowski and is meant to encourage students to strip away an actor's conscious intentions and enable a performance to emerge instead. The theory is laudable, however, in practice, saying 'No, that's not it. NEXT!' to actors whenever they are not succeeding in an exercise or improvisation can, over time, produce a level of insecurity that makes it even harder to connect and play freely[7]. Even without harsh methods of teaching or rehearsing, actors may have their own reasons for struggling to find a place from which they feel safe to play and connect easily. It is an area that needs more consideration. The Feldenkrais Method can offer a way of enabling an actor to resource themselves here.

The effect of a Feldenkrais lesson

The Feldenkrais Method can help provide a sense of ease and comfort that seems to enable actors to connect better. For many years I have used a 'presentation' exercise modified from versions I learnt from director Annie Griffin and performance artist Rose English. In this exercise the class sits at one end of the room being 'audience', while one member of the class enters, stands and just looks at the 'audience'. The instruction is to do nothing but keep eye contact with the 'audience' for a minute or so. Each member of the class has a turn. In every group I have done this exercise with, the students have reported that they could recognize their fellow student's level of discomfort on stage (their tension, the ways they fidget, hold their breath and so on) as well as how hard it was to do it themselves. I also know from experience that if the class does an ATM lesson from the Feldenkrais Method after this exercise and then repeats it, most students will find the exercise much easier the second time: they will be more comfortable and better able to stay connected to the audience. As audience members, they will also say that most participants seemed more relaxed and open and that they found themselves more engaged with them too.

The recognition that comes with this exercise is very significant: the ability to connect with the audience is what keeps the performance alive and a sense of ease has something to do with enabling that connection. However a greater understanding of what is going on could enable actors, directors, teachers and Feldenkrais Teachers more. This is where the Polyvagal Theory can help.

The Polyvagal Theory

Why the Polyvagal Theory? Acting as social engagement

The Polyvagal Theory is just one contribution to the much wider fields of neuroscience, psychology, sociology, philosophy and evolution and has caught attention mostly in the study and treatment of trauma.[8] However, this theory connects our sense of safety to our ability to socially engage in ways that are particularly illuminating and clarifying.

Acting (or any kind of performing), as I have described it above in terms of complicité and play, is a social activity, even when mediated by a screen. If we consider other social activities, the aggressive response of the young stand-up in the first example, and the fawning response of the actress in the second become clearer. For example, when we walk into a room full of friends most of us are usually at ease. We can talk, joke or just be quietly present among those we know and love. However, when we walk into a room full of strangers it can be a very different experience. Some people rise to the occasion and feel at ease quickly; some are daunted at the prospect but soon relax when someone makes a friendly overture; some become overly animated, awkwardly silent or just leave as soon as possible.[9] An actor's situation walking into an audition, rehearsal, on stage or in front of a camera is arguably very like walking into a room of strangers.

In his Polyvagal Theory, Porges points out that our decisions about what is safe for us do not always involve a cognitive decision (or may not match it if we have one), but that our nervous system has evolved to scan for signs of safety or danger in the environment and can initiate a response without conscious control to protect us. He has coined the term 'neuroception' for this.[10] Walking into a room full of strangers is not usually physically dangerous, but it can still resonate as such (via 'neuroception') and our ability to be comfortable depends on our ability to come to feel safe in the way we do among friends. The same could be said of walking onto stage or camera: we say a performer 'dies' on stage when it goes badly after all. Philippe Gaulier encourages his students to see and treat the audience as 'a bunch of mates',[11] which is what Arthur Smith did very successfully in the first example, while the young stand-up did not.

To take a closer look at Polyvagal Theory, we need to delve into anatomy and physiology. I am attempting a brief and rather simplified summary of a very large, dense body of research and I will not be able to capture all of it. I am focusing on what I believe to be most relevant for the theme, but it may well be that there are yet more riches to unearth for actors from this source. The Polyvagal Theory modifies the traditional view of the autonomic system in some crucial ways, so that is where we will start.

The autonomic system and Polyvagal Theory

The autonomic system is the part of the nervous system which regulates internal processes such as digestion, breathing and heart rate so that we do not consciously have to instigate or take charge of these ourselves even though we can affect some of these functions to a degree (such as breathing). It also regulates levels of arousal (known as the sympathetic state) so that we can meet day-to-day challenges and come back to a state of calm (parasympathetic state) as appropriate. Traditionally the job of autonomic regulation has been considered to be one of balancing states of arousal and calm (or sympathetic and parasympathetic) to meet the circumstances.

The autonomic system also has the job of keeping us safe. The sympathetic system mobilizes us to meet life-threatening situations or those that trigger feelings of intense threat. This is known as the 'fight or flight' setting which involves a hormonal release that affects breath, heart rate, muscular tonus, digestion, immune system and more to optimize efficiency for the defensive tasks ahead. (Our poor young comedian clearly went into a fight/flight mode when he met the challenge of an uninterested audience.) Being stuck in this state of arousal or having a system that goes there at the least provocation is problematic on many counts and, according to Porges, until recently this has been the main model that therapeutic circles have been working with in treating Post Traumatic Stress Disorder.

In the Polyvagal Theory, Porges brings more pieces of the autonomic system into the picture which changes the model in ways that have been very helpful for trauma therapy, but also, I believe, sheds some useful light on what is going on for actors. Porges did this by noticing some aspects of anatomy and physiology that had not been taken into account. He starts with the anatomy of the vagus nerve.

The vagus nerve

The vagus nerve is the part of the autonomic system that organizes the parasympathetic (calming) response. Named after the Latin word 'to wander', this long nerve travels from the brain stem to the face, heart, lungs, other organs and down to the guts. What Porges brings attention to, however, is that the vagus is not really just one nerve but a 'complex' of nerves. The vagus has many branches that run to different organs; it has a right brain and left brain pathway which have slightly different jobs; it has fibres that run in both directions to and from the brain stem and, most importantly for this chapter and for the theory overall, its fibres emanate from two different parts of the brain stem – hence the term 'Poly(many)vagal'. One set of fibres run from the Dorsal Motor Nucleus, which influences the heart but runs all the way down below the diaphragm into the stomach and guts; the other set runs from the Nucleus Ambiguous which also (separately) influences the heart as well as lungs and (along with other connected cranial nerves V, VII, IX and XI) the muscles of the face, eyes, middle ear, throat and neck. These two main parts of the vagus nerve have been named dorsal (back) vagus and ventral (front) vagus, respectively.

The character of these two vagal pathways led Porges to reconsider how the autonomic system works. Instead of describing its job as one of maintaining a simple balance between arousal and calm, Porges suggests a hierarchy of three defensive systems from old to new in evolutionary terms, and he posits that these systems are recruited in order, the newest and most sophisticated first, resorting to older ones in the event of those newer systems proving insufficient or failing.[12]

The dorsal vagus that reaches down into the guts is the oldest pathway which we find in reptiles. It is unmyelinated,[13] which means it is a little slower but also less efficient and precise.[14] The dorsal vagus regulates basic vegetative states of the organs and the guts, but it can also produce its own defensive response that is not to do with the fight/flight response. It is a slowing of the heart rate (bradycardia) so it is essentially a parasympathetic or calming response, but in extreme danger it produces a slowing to the point of immobilization and even shut down, as when a deer falls down as if dead in the face of a lion, or when a person freezes to the spot, fails to defend themselves, defecates or faints under serious threat. Anecdotally, we all know it happens for example 'she froze in fear' or 'he fainted from shock', but Porges along with others in the field (for example Peter Levine) have explored and described its significance.[15] As the oldest system (and dangerous to humans because of the reduction of oxygen to our large oxygen-hungry brains), it is usually a last resort when other newer options fail. It is likely to be what is behind some forms of stage fright when an actor freezes or completely blanks, but actually that is not the most interesting aspect of the theory with reference to acting.

The better-known mammalian sympathetic 'fight or flight' response enables us to mobilize in the face of threat instead of immobilize, and involves a cascade of physiological events as described earlier. However, even though it is not as life threatening as the freeze response, it is also a major event and takes some time to return from. We have therefore, as humans, developed a third, much more sophisticated system that involves the other vagal pathway – the ventral vagus. This branch of the vagus works as a brake on sympathetic arousal (again by affecting the heart), inhibiting the fight/flight response, but can also still enable a level of mobilization at the same time, unlike the freeze response. Lifting the brake does not mean that the person has gone into fight or flight mode, it simply allows for that possibility if the situation develops that requirement. Porges describes a typical event in a conversation between colleagues if one disengages. He notes that it is possible to see the change in the one who is talking at the time – their facial expression, level of muscle tension and so on: this is the moment the vagal brake comes off.[16] It would also be true, however, that if the conversation turned a corner soon after – the colleague re-engaged, restoring harmony – the vagal brake would go back on and all those effects could be reversed easily, making it a very adaptable system rather than a simple 'all or nothing' event. This is where it becomes most interesting for actors.

The Social Engagement System

Porges describes the ventral vagus as being central to the newest defence system in evolutionary terms and the one of first resort. He calls it 'The Social Engagement System'.[17] It is a defence system not in the sense of a call to action or a freeze, but because it seeks to establish safety by way of sophisticated human communication skills – modulation of vocal tone and facial gesture – which signal that we are not a threat to another person and which help us elicit a reassuring response from them. The Social Engagement System can allow mobilization while keeping a dampener on any full-blown sympathetic state which, as the quote at the start of this piece explains, is also what enables human beings to play. It is the explanation for why connection with the audience and other actors is so vital for an actor – the neural explanation for complicité.

The ventral vagus, along with four other connected cranial nerves (V, VII, IX, XI), links the heart to the muscles of facial expression, the middle ear, throat and neck. Porges suggests that a human's first resort when scanning for safety is both to offer and to look for reassurance that an attack or a rejection is not in the offing: that the situation is a safe one and does not require increased mobilization. This is what goes on when the actor looks for and successfully establishes a connection with the other actors (and audience), or indeed when anyone engages in play. Equally important for actors, he also points out that when a connection cannot be satisfactorily made, indicates hostility or is suddenly withdrawn, the Social Engagement System will begin to fail. Here is Porges's list of effects 'which occurs spontaneously in response to a neuroception of danger or a life threat … :

- The eyelids droop;
- The voice loses inflection;
- Positive facial expressions dwindle;
- Awareness of the sound of the human voice becomes less acute; and
- Sensitivity to others' social engagement behaviours decreases'[18]

This is a disastrous list for an actor. Eventually, if the fight/flight response comes online, the Social Engagement System is overwhelmed and the system switches into full-blown sympathetic state, or, if there is no chance of fighting or fleeing, the dorsal vagus takes over and begins to shut the person down.

This would suggest that if an actor cannot make a good enough connection with other actors and the audience to feel 'safe' (or, cannot feel safe enough to make that connection in the first place), they will be less able to engage the audience via expression, gesture, vocal tone, in fact all of the communication skills essential for acting because they will be on the way to, or stuck in, either a hyper- (fight/flight) or hypo- (freeze) setting that will affect the volume, pitch and modulation of their voice, rate of breathing and either flatten or accentuate aspects of their facial gestures. If the brake stays off, the sympathetic arousal or dorsal vagus shutdown can affect the functioning of many of their organs and the level of muscular tonus (resting tension) throughout their whole body, which will create serious difficulty in performance.

We see this clearly in the first example of the stand-up comedian who goes into fight mode when he fails to make a connection: his voice becomes harsh, his muscles tense, his energy focused into aggression. Then at the heckle he begins to freeze: his muscles slackening, his facial expression flattening and his voice simply disappearing. In the second example, the actor is working overtime to establish a connection, but it is not working. Her desperation and rising fear have triggered an adrenalized response with wide, over-focused eyes, raised eyebrows, a tense, forward-pressing delivery, rapid breathing and a raised vocal pitch which is in turn reading as a danger signal to the audition panel's nervous systems. Neither of these actors is able to establish a connection and neither of these actors finds a safe enough place to play.

The third example is more complex. In the absence of the safety of social connection, an actor may well (subconsciously) search for a different strategy to help return them to some sense of calm. This might prevent them from being engulfed by a debilitating state of arousal and give them a chance of bringing the Social Engagement System back online. Our system detects dangers not just in the environment but from within ourselves (e.g. when we are sick or our structure is failing).[19] My observation is that an actor may seek to restore some sense of safety from within themselves through, for example, self-calming motion of some kind such as walking around the space, gesturing repeatedly. They may adjust their posture, looking for more support (maybe shifting from leg to leg or pulling themselves up 'straight'), or reassure themselves by focusing on their vocal technique. They may even try to behave 'as if' the connection with the audience is there, a little in the way that we smile to feel better sometimes.

In the very bald presentation game I described earlier, these strategies do not usually succeed, although they may prevent the actor from tipping as far into fight/flight or freeze as our wretched stand-up did. The actor's presence still 'dies' to the degree that they fail to restore social engagement. With a strong script or scenario however, the actors have some structure to support them, and through rehearsal they are provided with some kind of safe container at least, and so, with a measure of technical skill, they can deliver a performance which works at a certain level. However it is likely that with a lack of social engagement, the cost will still be a 'disconnect': the timing, spontaneity, ease, ability to listen and appropriateness of response may all be slightly off. They are not really playing, just very busy with pretending to play. I remember Philippe Gaulier rebuking his students for not being in complicité with the words: 'Vous êtes dans votre couloir' ('you are in your own corridor'), that is, you are so far away from connecting with anyone that you might as well be somewhere off-stage.

That is evident in my example 3: one actor was clearly in complicité, while the others were all doing their own technically competent but very individual versions of 'as if' outside of complicité. He was inside the safe container of the Social Engagement System and they, whatever they did, were not. It was problematic because his complicité ended up being mostly with us, the audience, as the other actors could not meet his level of responsiveness and that pulled the play apart.

Play, creativity and safety

Porges's Polyvagal Theory, in summary, concerns the way human systems seek safety and it articulates three defence mechanisms that are recruited in order, from newest and most sophisticated to oldest and least precise. Firstly the Social Engagement System centring on the ventral vagus complex, secondly the sympathetic arousal system's fight/flight response, and thirdly the immobilization or 'freeze' response produced by the dorsal vagus.

I have suggested that the Social Engagement System, when considered in terms of acting, amounts to a neural description of complicité, and that when actors are not sufficiently in complicité, their system is more likely to detect danger, eliciting sympathetic or even dorsal vagus responses to some degree with all the pursuant effects that will impair their performance, even if they can find other strategies to give them some sense of safety and keep themselves from tipping too far into sympathetic arousal or dorsal vagus freeze.

But, it could be argued, humans do not always seek safety. They like variety and get bored without change. And furthermore, you might say, acting is not about being safe, it is about walking the high wire and taking creative risks. Leaving aside the issue of dysregulated systems that are addicted to an adrenalized state, Porges does address creative risk in what he says about the Social Engagement System and play, as in the quote at the start of this chapter and elsewhere.[20] As I have been pointing out, his idea of play maps pretty much exactly onto what actors do when they are performing in complicité. Play is a mobilized state which is allowed by our nervous system without tipping into a full sympathetic state because it recruits and requires the Social Engagement System which dampens arousal. We can mobilize even in aggressive ways when we play, because we are able to signify to others and pick up cues that no harm is intended: it is a game we are in together, not an attack. Within this safe container we can try out all kinds of activities without triggering a full sympathetic response.

How then can we help facilitate the Social Engagement System so that an actor can easily access the safety offered by that connection with the audience and the other actors in order to be spontaneous, access all their communication skills and feel able to take creative risks?

How does Feldenkrais help?

Firstly, I should acknowledge that many of the ways of thinking about or working with the vagal nerve and with the autonomic system are either new and still developing, or come from very old traditions which have not yet been recognized by Western research methods. That includes many applications of the Feldenkrais Method itself, although an evidence base for it is growing.[21] While much of what I am suggesting for the Feldenkrais Method is hypothesis at this stage, I am presenting it as a potentially useful direction to consider in relation to acting.

Secondly, there are Feldenkrais practitioners developing a variety of interesting ways of working to affect the tone of the vagus nerve and encourage a better balance between the parasympathetic and sympathetic states which I will only briefly mention here. Most ways of working take advantage of the fact that the vagus is bi-directional (i.e. it has nerve fibres carrying information from the organs to the brain stem as well as from the brain stem to the organs), so affecting a function or organ in some way can bring about a vagal response. Practitioners with an understanding of gut health (like US Feldenkrais practitioner Elinor Silverstein) are able to include that understanding in their practice to influence the information flow from gut to brain to improve the tone of the vagus nerve and facilitate balance in autonomic regulation. Silverstein also teaches how to use the 'listening touch' which Feldenkrais practitioners develop for hands-on sessions ('Functional Integration' – FI) to listen to and facilitate the movement of viscera, to influence the vagal nerve. Porges goes into some depth discussing the impact of sound and music on the vagus nerve through the ventral vagus connections to the middle ear:[22] this is beginning to inform the work of some of the Feldenkrais teachers who specialize in voice and music.[23] Then there are some Feldenkrais practitioners[24] also trained in modalities addressing trauma which encompass this idea of the vagal complex, such as Peter Levine's Somatic Experiencing.[25] I cannot discuss all of these modalities here. Instead I am focusing on a discussion of the possible effects of a classic ATM or FI lesson.

The Feldenkrais Method

A Feldenkrais lesson (class or hands-on) seeks to enable the student to learn something about the way they respond to a stimulus, through an invitation (via touch or words) to move, breathe, pay attention to themselves or use their imagination. In noticing how they respond, the student begins to uncover their particular matrix of unconscious patterns and to open up new possibilities. These lessons can affect breath, facial muscles, eyes, jaw, throat, carriage of the head, posture and the ways we organize and support ourselves in a myriad of movements, many of which are likely to affect vagal tone and enable access to a more balanced autonomic state. I will consider here just a few of these.

Breath

One of the ways of directly affecting the vagus that Porges includes is breathing. The bi-directional nature of the vagus means that while the vagus can affect the rhythm of the breath (for example), the rhythm of the breath can also affect vagal tone. Porges mentions yogic pranayama (and playing the clarinet!) in this context,[26] noting the significance of long out-breaths, while paying attention and the involvement of the muscles of the face. The ability of such breathing to shift the system towards the parasympathetic state has been studied elsewhere too.[27] There are a number of lessons in the Feldenkrais Method that also explore breath. Several explore equalizing the length of in-breath,[28] out-breath and pauses to bring attention to whatever habit we have and to develop each of the four parts of the breath. Some equalize between the nostrils reminiscent of yogic practice.[29] Others systematically bring attention to, and further enable, the many parts of ourselves involved in breathing, including the movement of the ribs and each part of the abdomen and a more complete descent and return of the diaphragm, to enable more variety in the ways we can breathe and develop greater adaptability to circumstances.[30] These lessons do not seek to define what kind of breathing we should use at any one time, but to make more available for our system to recruit from appropriately.

However almost every Feldenkrais lesson will affect what parts of ourselves we have available for breath even when breath is not the prime focus of the lesson. Any of the array of lessons that involve twisting, side-bending or flexing and extending the ribs and thoracic spine is likely to enable the ribs to respond better to the breath. Lessons that enable length in the lower back or release in the abdomen – either as a direct result of the lesson or as a by-product of finding fluidity in the movement of the pelvis and hip joints (for example) – may accommodate the downward motion of the diaphragm. It might be possible to keep expanding this list of lessons that affect the breath to those centring on the jaw or eyes, carriage of the head and shoulders, how we maintain ourselves upright, until we have pretty much covered the entire cannon.

Ventral vagus

Lessons we could choose to directly affect the ventral vagus might be specific lessons that involve the muscles of the face in lessons that explore, for example, cavities of the mouth with the tongue and discover the movement of the jaw[31] or those that focus on the eyes.[32]

But once again, the freedom of the jaw and eyes can be part of many lessons, and once we are considering the throat we have to include a great many lessons that enable the carriage of the head in different movements and relationships to space. It starts to seem like every Feldenkrais lesson is likely to have an effect on the vagus nerve and our autonomic balance in some way. However, I would also like to consider some other ways of thinking about how the Method might be impacting.

The safety of skeletal support

Porges talks and writes more about the implications of hearing, vocalizing, breathing and using the muscles of the face for vagal tone, but my first assumption when I noticed that students were better able to be more comfortable and make better contact with the audience after a Feldenkrais lesson was that they were better able to take support from the ground. Jeff Haller asserts that a well-functioning organism will never simply let itself fall down, and it will switch on muscular effort as required to prevent itself from falling when support from the structure designed for the purpose is lacking and collapse is threatened.[33] Finding a better architecture of – and so support from – the skeleton means the extra work can be switched off. This may already have an effect on the autonomic balance since higher tonicity is associated with arousal, but it may be that simply the sense of clear support enables the person to feel safer and less anxious. I have also frequently seen how severe an anxiety is produced by the loss of balance for any reason and that re-finding the safety of being better able to balance again is a great relief. Finding balance is a part of what is learnt in discovering the support of the skeleton in many different activities and relations to gravity, and it is one of the areas where the Feldenkrais Method is gathering a recognized evidence base (especially where older people are concerned).[34]

Listening to edges and reversing

There are many other filters through which one could consider how sympathetic and parasympathetic systems are affected and so how the Social Engagement System is facilitated or inhibited. However, I would like to mention just a few fundamentals of any Feldenkrais lesson relevant here:

In every ATM lesson, the student is invited to listen to what feels easy and comfortable and to notice when they tip over into making a greater effort or when a movement starts to become uncomfortable, a strain or even painful. Learning to listen to signals of ease, comfort and safety in movement enables the student to recognize signals of the opposite – or even better, the moment before those signals are likely to appear. Developing this kind of awareness can have a broader impact: it can alert an actor to recognizing the signs that they are moving out of a place of ease and safety in performance and are in danger of moving towards a state of arousal or freeze that will compromise their ability to engage. If they can notice this then they may be able to resource themselves before it has gone too far.

What can they do? They may have learnt to change their breath, notice support from the ground, but within the Feldenkrais Method there is also the notion of reversibility. Feldenkrais asserts that every good movement is reversible and discusses reversibility in general as a sign of health and maturity. He talks, for example, about the importance of emotion and indeed of sexual arousal as being reversible.[35] Practise with being able to reverse movements easily opens the door to these other kinds of reversibility and this may well be a resource for actors on the edge of sympathetic arousal taking over. Once they can recognize their own pathway that leads to a sympathetic state of arousal, they may be able to learn to reverse it and bring themselves back into balance – and even finally to make a choice that doesn't lead them to that edge.

Play

Finally, I began with Porges's quote about play which is partly what drew me to this topic, and I would like to finish with where play is directly involved in the Feldenkrais Method. The Feldenkrais Method is not a set of routines designed to achieve specific ends. It is a learning method in which the participant is invited to feel, try out and explore in order to find something out about themselves and their habitual ways of behaving and being. The lessons are shaped in different kinds of ways. As in a game there may be something specific that is being tried out (how to roll up to sit) but as in less structured play, the participant may not know that could be the end result: it may simply emerge out of the progression of the lesson. Indeed the lesson may run more along lines of questioning such as 'what happens when you … ', 'how do you … ', 'what is the difference when you … ' which could all be the beginning of any game – or any inquiry in a rehearsal room indeed.

A Feldenkrais lesson doesn't often call on our need to mobilize by working on the edge of threat as playing can do, but it does include the ability to go into the unknown and to allow new possibilities to unfold rather than insisting on a pre-ordained sequence of events. Playing, rehearsing, performing, doing a Feldenkrais lesson: all are adventures into the unknown, improvisations on a theme.

While a one-to-one hands-on (FI) lesson involves the close interaction of teacher and student, most ATM lessons don't require interaction with other people. However they do invite a relation to the floor and often to the space which may also include awareness of those in it, especially in a dynamic lesson. Most importantly though, the careful listening to self and environment and the invitation to explore a variety of responses and let go of rigid choices can enable a participant to be better able to do the same in their relationships with others too.[36]

Conclusion

This chapter started with the fundamental questions: what makes a performance 'live' or 'die'? What sustains the interest of the audience in a performance or causes it to fail? The Polyvagal Theory provides a useful answer from the realm of neurophysiology: it explains how tipping into a more 'adrenalized' state switches off the ability to engage with others (audience or fellow actors in this case), as shown in different ways by both the young stand-up and the auditioning actress in the first two examples I gave. The Polyvagal Theory points to the importance of enabling or resourcing actors to have enough of a sense of safety to be able to engage and play without being taken over by the arousal performance can evoke. I illustrated the difference in the third example of the actor in the Shakespeare play who was able to connect far more than the rest of the cast. In the light of this we can begin to see how an ATM lesson is likely to affect vagal tone directly or indirectly, enabling an actor to engage better even under the challenging conditions of performance, and so why the Feldenkrais Method appears to be such a useful learning tool for actors in this respect.

There is further to go in exploring and understanding the many ways a Feldenkrais lesson could affect vagal tone and promote a sense of safety which may help teachers think about what lessons to choose and how to contextualize them. The ideas here need building on to improve rehearsal, filming, auditioning and teaching processes. They offer a basis for more exploration of strategies to help actors understand the importance of complicité, recognize when and why their performance is failing and develop strategies to resource themselves better under the pressure of performance.

Addendum: A practical application

This article is all about the interaction between actors, not about what they can create on their own, so to apply this mini-Feldenkrais lesson in any meaningful way you need a minimum group of three people but preferably at least five or more. It may work even better with people who don't know each other too well. Go slowly and mindfully in the Feldenkrais lesson. It is an exploration, not an exercise. Take a break in between the numbered sections, letting your legs down and feeling any differences. Don't do anything that hurts or strains, and if the unusual movement of the eyes is difficult for you, go very lightly, slowly, keep it small and do not do it for long.

1) Begin by walking around the room, shaking hands and greeting each other as you meet. Notice the quality of this interaction. What does their handshake feel like? How easy is your interaction? How does it make you feel? How present are you both able to be? How long does this simple interaction naturally last and when do you feel the need to move on? Don't discuss it, just notice for yourself. You may not know what you have noticed anyway, but it is likely to be clearer when you compare by doing this again at the end.

2) Lie on your back on the floor with long legs if your back is comfortable with that (plant your feet if not) with some space to your right and left. You may need a mat or blanket to be comfortable with what is coming, but nothing too spongy or soggy that will limit your movement and ability to feel your contact with the ground too much. Spend a little time noticing how you are supported by the floor: what parts of you really give their weight to the ground, which places touch but lie less heavily and which places do not touch at all.

3) Bend your knees and plant your feet. Notice how your contact with the ground changes. Bring your right hand to your left collar bone and begin to slide it along the collar bone from your breast bone outwards towards your left shoulder. Gently, slowly. Let your right hand be as soft, easy and caressing as possible.

4) Continue with this movement, but direct your right hand more clearly to the left, so towards the outside of your left shoulder/top of your left arm (rather than the top of your shoulder/side of your neck). Notice whether your fingers are able to slide around the outside of your shoulder and find the floor without changing the quality and level

of work in your movement. Does your head move at all? Do you feel your weight shifting to the other side of your chest or even pelvis? Don't create it; just notice.

5) Swap sides, and slide the left hand to the right as in steps 3 and 4. Take your time. Is it different with this arm and this side? In what ways?

6) Bring your left hand across you under your right armpit (keep your thumb with your fingers so your arm can slide under and around the ribs as far as it will go comfortably. For some it might even find the inner edge of the shoulder blade, but do not force it. Just go wherever your arm reaches very easily). Bring your right arm over the top and around the left shoulder: hugging yourself, not crossing your arms. Notice the width now between your shoulder blades in your back.

7) Begin to alternate lifting the right shoulder with your left hand, and then the left shoulder with the right hand in a smooth, even manner, so that you begin to rock your whole rib cage a little to the left and right. Feel your back rolling easy and gently on the floor. Let your pelvis stay more or less quiet for now and your knees stay upright, towards the ceiling, without swaying left or right even if that is a smaller movement. Keep making the movement smoother and easier – making it smaller if you need to. Notice your breathing. Can you make this movement without holding or even altering your breathing? Allow the quality, speed and size of the movement to adjust until you can.

8) Come back to the same organization of your arms and the same movement. What does your head do? Does it stay still? Does it roll? If so, which way?

   Keep the movement of rolling the chest going and deliberately let your head roll with it too. So everything rolls right and left together (not pelvis and legs). Feel your eyes resting in the back of their sockets and being carried along with the movement of the head. Notice if your teeth touch, your jaw is clenched, your lips press together or your tongue is pressing strongly against any place in your mouth. Can those places let go of that unnecessary work?

   Now change the direction of the head rolling so it goes opposite to the movement of your arms and chest. You may need to make the movement smaller to keep the quality of ease.

9) Explore both steps with your arms the other way around, right under and left on top.

10) Go back to the first 'hugging' organization of your arms and once again roll your chest left and right with your arms. What does your head do now? Let your head roll with the movement again. Once you have an easy size and quality for the movement, without changing your breath or making any extra effort, begin to take your eyes in the opposite direction to your head (and chest). Spend a little time slowing down and finding how to do that without changing your breath, tightening your jaw or fixing your tongue. Then return to letting the eyes be carried by the head. Is it in any way different in quality or range?

11) Come back to the rocking movement with your arms the other way around. Now let your head roll opposite to the movement. Once you have an easy gentle range and quality, take your eyes in the opposite direction to your head (so with your chest and arms this time). Take your time to work it out. Go slower, smaller, easier. Once you

have found it come back to everything rolling the same way together with the eyes carried in the sockets. Notice any difference.

12) Go back to the very first movement of sliding the right hand along the left collar bone and over the outer (not upper) edge of the shoulder towards the floor and maybe even along the floor if that is available to you. Let your head roll to the left and see if that helps your weight shift more to the left to enable your right shoulder to lift and your arm to travel. At what point would it help to use your right foot on the floor to encourage the pelvis to roll to help. Can you find how to keep the right foot planted and the knee upright so you can use that connection to the ground to help the pelvis turn? (You could even lengthen the left leg to get it out of the way and help the pelvis roll.)

13) Try the same thing to the left. Be alive to any differences. Each time look for more ease, less effort, even if that means a smaller movement for a while. Let your eyes be carried by your head rolling, notice if your jaw is soft and your lips and tongue are not pressing.

14) Come back to lying on your back with long legs and notice any differences in how you give your weight to the ground.

15) Come back to standing and once again go around the room shaking hands and greeting each other. How does their handshake (or yours!) feel now? What is the quality of, and time given to, your interactions now? How present are you with each other now?

Notes

1 Stephen W. Porges, *The Polyvagal Theory for Treating Trauma* (Nicabm teleseminar interview with Ruth Buczynski), 18, retrieved from https://static1.squarespace.com/static/5c1d025fb27e390a78569537/t/5cce03089b747a3598c57947/1557005065155/porges_nicabm_treating_trauma.pdf (accessed 10 May 2020).
2 Victoria Worsley, *Feldenkrais for Actors* (London: Nick Hern Books, 2016), 244.
3 On complicité, see Jacques Lecoq, *The Moving Body* (London: Bloomsbury Methuen, 2014), 34 and 156.
4 Sanford Meisner, *On Acting* (New York and Toronto: Vintage Original, Random House 1987), 8.
5 Konstantin Stanislavski, *An Actor Prepares* (London: Methuen, 1980), 202–4 (1st publ. UK: Geoffrey Bles Ltd., 1937).
6 Alison Hodge, *Actor Training* (London: Routledge, 2010), 207.
7 Philippe Gaulier's 'Non. Suivant!' was engraved on my heart for many years.
8 There is a good brief description of the fundamental way a somatic approach differs and is given by Porges from 2.04 mins in this podcast: https://www.youtube.com/watch?v=8tz146HQotY (accessed 29 April 2020).
9 Based on what Porges says in an interview with Ravi Dykema, 'How Your Nervous System Sabotages Your Ability to Relate', published by NexusPub but retrieved from https://acusticusneurinom.dk/wp-content/uploads/2015/10/polyvagal_interview_porges.pdf (accessed 10 May 2020).

10 Stephen Porges, *The Polyvagal Theory* (New York: Norton, 2011), 11–19.
11 As a student of Philippe Gaulier I know this first-hand.
12 Porges, *The Polyvagal Theory*, 16, 17, and 54.
13 Myelin is a fatty white substance (or more specifically an extended and modified plasma membrane) that is wrapped around the axon of some nerve cells in a spiral fashion, forming an electrically insulating layer.
14 Porges's description of an unmyelinated nerve cf. myelinated. https://www.youtube.com/watch?v=8tz146HQotY 8 mins 10–25 (accessed 5 May 2020).
15 Peter A. Levine, *In An Unspoken Voice* (New York: Norton, 2010), 97–109.
16 https://www.youtube.com/watch?v=8tz146HQotY from 10 mins 44 secs (accessed 10 May 2020).
17 Porges, *The Polyvagal Theory*, 125–6.
18 Porges, *The Polyvagal Theory*, 15.
19 Porges, *The Polyvagal Theory*, 15.
20 Porges, *The Polyvagal Theory*, 275–8.
21 See the research page at www.feldenkrais-method.org.
22 Porges, *The Polyvagal Theory*, 246–54.
23 IUK Feldenkrais Practitioner and singer Maggy Burrowes first introduced me to the Polyvagal Theory. https://maggyburrowes.com/ (accessed 10 May 2020).
24 For example, Irene Lyon.
25 Peter A. Levine, *Waking the Tiger* (Berkeley, CA: North Atlantic Books, 2017) and, *In An Unspoken Voice* (Berkeley, CA: North Atlantic Books, 2010).
26 https://www.youtube.com/watch?v=8tz146HQotY from 22 mins 30 secs (accessed 10 May 2020).
27 Jerath et al., 'Physiology of Long Pranayamic Breathing: Neural Respiratory Elements May Provide a Mechanism That Explains How Slow Deep Breathing Shifts the Autonomic Nervous System', *Med Hypotheses*, Vol. 67, No. 3 (2006), 566–71. Epub 2006, 18 April.
28 Feldenkrais, 'Breathing Rhythmically', series #1-6: Lessons 180, 185–9, Alexander Yanai, Vol. 4 part B; Copyright January 1997. All rights reserved by the International Feldenkrais Federation, Paris, France in co-operation with The Feldenkrais Institute, Tel Aviv, Israel.
29 Feldenkrais, 'Equalizing the Nostrils', Alexander Yanai lesson 5, Vol. 1 Part 1; Copyright May 1994. All rights reserved by the International Feldenkrais Federation, Paris, France in co-operation with The Feldenkrais Institute, Tel Aviv, Israel.
30 For example, Feldenkrais, 'Gluing in the Lungs', series parts 1–4: lessons 201–204, Alexander Yanai, Vol. 5 Part A; Copyright December 1997. All rights reserved by the International Feldenkrais Federation, Paris, France in co-operation with The Feldenkrais Institute, Tel Aviv, Israel; 'Differentiation of Parts and Functions in Breathing', in *Awareness through Movement*, ed. Moshe Feldenkrais (London: Penguin, 1990), 100–8.
31 Feldenkrais, 'Palate, Mouth and Teeth', lesson 23, Alexander Yana, Vol. 1 Part 1; Copyright May 1994. All rights reserved by the International Feldenkrais Federation, Paris, France in co-operation with The Feldenkrais Institute, Tel Aviv, Israel, 'The Mouth and Head Cavity', lesson 126 Alexander Yanai, Vol. 3b, and the jaw lessons in week 7 of the Amherst training.
32 Feldenkrais, 'Eyes 1', lesson 15, Alexander Yanai, Vol. 1 Part 1; Copyright May 1994. All rights reserved by the International Feldenkrais Federation, Paris, France in co-operation with The Feldenkrais Institute, Tel Aviv, Israel, 'The Eyeball Lesson', lesson 165, Alexander Yanai, Vol. 4a, and 'Lines', Lesson 453, Alexander Yanai, Vol. 10a.
33 In Jeff Haller's Advanced Training: Finding the Internal Roots of Strength. The specific quote is transcribed in Worsley, *Feldenkrais for Actors*, 104.

34 See https://www.ncbi.nlm.nih.gov/pubmed/25949266 (accessed 10 May 2020).
35 Feldenkrais, *The Potent Self* (Berkeley, CA: Frog Publications, 2003), 113–14.
36 At the Actors Centre in London recently, the group reported that the Feldenkrais lesson had established enough of a calm place for the chatter in their heads to stop so that they were freer to simply listen to and engage with the audience afterwards.

CHAPTER 11
CURING THE ACTING HABIT: THE FELDENKRAIS METHOD, ACTORS, COMPULSION AND THE PERFORMING ARTS INDUSTRY
Mark Lacey

> The actor should be able to stop, start again, or do something else. Only then can he play ten nights, one after the other, and do the same thing.[1]

Introduction

The scholarship concerning the Feldenkrais Method and actor development has to date tended to focus on the direct improvement of the embodied functioning of the physical, vocal or sensory apparatus in a training context. This has included such themes as stage presence, expressive range, aesthetics, applied stage-craft and physical rehabilitation among other conceptual and practical research applications.[2] These are of great value; however, it is notable that mention of one of Moshe Feldenkrais's core themes is often absent from these studies: the capacity to develop awareness that helps a learner to make independent, effective and integrated decisions that are non-neurotic, so leading to greater autonomy and therefore sense of maturity.[3] Feldenkrais does not use the term 'autonomy' in its socio-economic context, referring to capital or status that provides security, but autonomy in its innate sense, as being the individual's capacity to self-govern, or adapt effectively amid adversity with minimum damage to their core sense of self. There is a paucity of information available that applies to this specific area in relation to actors and their development – whether referring to their personal resilience, to their craft or to their relationship with the industry in which they endeavour to function.

This is surprising since the behaviours of actors seem to point towards an activity that might possibly be fuelled by some kind of compulsion. After all, public appearances are often cited as a great, if not the greatest, human fear.[4] As such, risking self-security against all reasoning for a shot at something that is rarely clearly defined points to a potentially neurotic and compulsive dynamic within the actor. In her book *Feldenkrais for Actors*, Victoria Worsley touches upon the subject of performance anxiety, but mostly refers to the phenomenon of 'Stage Fright' which is in itself a generic term for any anxiety-inducing event triggered by any public appearance rather than an identifiable phenomenon peculiar to actors.[5]

The Feldenkrais practitioner and writer Campbell Edinborough, in his thesis *Exploring Integral Transformative Education for Actors*, partly addresses this issue by demonstrating how the top-down approach to actor training might potentially exploit the neuroses of actors by tapping into their compulsion to please.[6] This is similar to what Feldenkrais himself touched upon in his interview with Richard and Helen Schechner for *The Tulane Review*:

> If I start to tell you that the movement is wrong, I will convince you by rules, aspects, definitions that everybody will try … But with Stanislavski and others, if he said something was right or wrong, it was only his own impression. He was right very often because he was a great man.[7]

This study builds upon Edinborough's ideas and puts forward the hypothesis that the potential impact of the Feldenkrais Method upon identified compulsions within actors is relevant not only to actor training but to the entire experience of being a professional actor within a performing arts industry. This study first looks at defining compulsion as it might apply to actors, then compares the approach of the Feldenkrais Method to other psycho-physiological models of this subject. It then goes on to address how compulsion might affect the actor within their working context and how compulsions have been recognized and addressed by practitioners and the performing arts industry in general, before finally looking at how the Feldenkrais Method might usefully be applied, the changes one might expect to occur, and the potential scope of these changes in a broader context.

Acting as disease

In an interview, the British actress Sheila Hancock was asked why she acted. She replied (with zero irony): 'It's a Disease!'[8] Many actors, however, may ascribe this same urge to a 'passion' or 'calling'. Amid a successful career I experienced 'stage fright' and visited a psychoanalyst specializing in this area. Simultaneously I embarked on a four-year training to become a Feldenkrais practitioner. During this intense period of self-reorganization, instead of reinstating some sense of security in the capacity to go on stage, I began to entertain the unsettling idea that perhaps Sheila Hancock had been right all along. Perhaps I wasn't driven to act by some unseen calling, but perhaps I was actually 'ill'; perhaps the motivating force within me was not some romantic passion, but an unhealthy compulsive behaviour. Nature/nurture may have provided me with a particular aptitude or interest in the dramatic arts, but the integrity of the motivations that led me to become a professional actor was dramatically put into question.

As a result of these experiences, as well as through empirical observation of others (including my many acting students), there emerged a troubling awareness of a deep paradox. It appeared that the less actors needed to act the better they became. If one takes on board Feldenkrais's idea that behaviours resulting from compulsion, by their very definition, always contain within them some aspect of inauthenticity, then perhaps this comes as no surprise, since authenticity is a key aspect of the actor's art.[9] However this idea creates a problem since it turns on its head the traditional advice that one shouldn't enter the industry unless one absolutely has to, since it can be a savage environment in which to work. This gives rise to a second paradox:

a) By losing their compulsion to act, an actor can become more authentic. This makes them both more accomplished in their work and more autonomous as an artist.

However:

b) Without the compulsion to act there is no reason to risk going on stage within a potentially ruthless industry context. Particularly when the industry can often be seen to not necessarily differentiate compulsive actors from authentic actors when casting.

Even though:

c) A capacity for authenticity could be seen as the primary tool for good acting.

If we take this thinking through to its logical end we come to a rather peculiar conclusion that the best actors might be those who don't actually pursue it, and that those with a drive to pursue success within the industry may not actually be the best people for the job. As such it raises certain questions about the efficacy of the current, normative actor/industry infrastructure (as it is) and its implications on quality of output.

I would argue that there is an unhealthy tradition of co-dependency between actors and the industry that is held in place by the individual compulsions of many who call themselves actors, and the collective compulsions of the institution of acting itself, and that addressing these aspects would have positive implications for both quality of work and personal satisfaction for all involved. In this study I also contend that the application of the Feldenkrais Method is a potent way of beginning to address this issue.

In order to address this we need to identify what Feldenkrais understood as compulsion in relation to other models and identify how this might apply to actors.

Actors, compulsions and habits: Feldenkrais and compulsion

The term 'compulsion' as used in this chapter does not refer to the specific diagnosis psychologists apply to aspects of personality disorders (such as OCD) which is at an extreme end of compulsive behaviour and is usually measured by the clustering, uniqueness or severity of the compulsions.[10] Rather, it refers to the general state of repeated action without satisfaction. It is something that may be better understood by the term 'habit'; however, this also has its own connotations. In his canon of work Feldenkrais often uses the terms 'habit', 'compulsion' and 'neurosis' interchangeably. However, when necessary, he would take care to differentiate the dynamic patterns behind the terms, particularly focusing upon the relationship between their causality and outcome.[11] Although there is a recognition that reflexes, habits and compulsions share similar – in some cases identical – neurological structures, he puts forward the idea that they can be separated based upon the conditions under which they are formed, the environmental context in which they occur, and the way they are experienced by the student.[12] In some ways this can be seen as a semantic argument; however, it is worth looking at this differentiation in order to clarify what is meant by compulsiveness for actors, as well as to clarify Feldenkrais's approach as compared to other physiological and psychological models.

With no agreement on a positivist model of sanity, it can be seen that the famous relativist, behaviourist description of insanity as 'repeating an action without satisfying an intention, and each time expecting a different result' might be regarded as identical to compulsion.[13] Similarly this continued dissatisfaction, for Feldenkrais, was one of the essential ways of differentiating a compulsion from an innocuous habit.[14]

Throughout his early book *Body and Mature Behaviour*, Feldenkrais goes into detail about how habits and compulsions become instated into the nervous system.[15] He impresses on the reader, however, that this process cannot be mapped linearly, nor piecemeal, and that the perceived tensions between the physiologist's empirical approach and the psychologists conceptual ones are not useful.[16] Instead he puts forward a model whereby the nervous system, the mind and the environment are inextricably linked to survival and could be said to define each other.[17] Similarly, he considers the way that any experienced moment contains within itself a sensory, an emotional, a motor and a thinking aspect, and that these cannot be separated, nor, in terms of study, does one realm have dominance over any of the others when defining the personality.[18]

As such the Feldenkrais Method is a monist, empirical system that views habits as a structure of neuro-physiological patterns that, when triggered by a familiar or unfamiliar environment, reinstate or challenge a total situation that is experienced phenomenologically by the individual, and is responded to appropriately or inappropriately.[19] It is the inappropriate response that might be said to differentiate a compulsion from a mere habit. Feldenkrais calls the neurological mechanism that creates the compulsive response 'cross motivation' and uses the example of the itch that cannot be relieved by eating a bun, and the hunger that cannot be relieved by scratching oneself.[20] This 'cross motivation' is always instated during a period of dependence when the feeling of security is threatened, and when autonomous learning and behaviour are deferred to another's will.[21] As a result it contains within its neurological patterning some kind of inappropriate physio-psychological response that is reinstated whenever any aspect of the total situation is triggered.[22]

According to Feldenkrais a compulsion can be recognized by the following:

- Repetition of an action with continued dissatisfaction.[23]
- An inner sense of resistance to an action.[24]
- Inappropriate emotional charge triggered by perceived loss of security.[25]
- Conscious muscular effort replacing necessary effort.[26]

The actor then, who is driven to act and yet is not satisfied by either the process of acting or its relationship with the industry, would probably be considered compulsive by Feldenkrais's definition. Equally an industry that continually looks to traditional models of casting, for example, and never examines why this is not a fail-safe method to minimize the risk of failure might also be considered organizationally compulsive.

To compare Feldenkrais's model of compulsion to the overwhelming number of alternative ones is way beyond the scope of this chapter, however we can get a broad idea by visiting some of the more widely accepted theories.

Neuro-anthropology

From the traditional neuro-anthropological perspective it has been argued that the purpose of habits is to give the human race an evolutionary advantage. That by deeply wiring these repeated actions into the nervous system they can be relegated to the subconscious leaving the conscious mind free to think, imagine and reason.[27] Apart from the obvious argument over whether or not conscious rationality alone puts the human race at an evolutionary advantage, there is also little explanation as to why one action becomes hardwired while another does not. Neither is there any rationale given to why we experience some habits as useful and relatively innocuous, while others have inherent resistance and can be painful. As has been seen, actors put themselves at high risk whenever they perform and often feel compelled to do so regardless of their level of perceived satisfaction, which, in survivalist terms, is incongruent. It is evident, therefore, that habits alone, if viewed from a survival perspective, do not account for the motivation of actors. Interestingly, however, contemporary neuro-anthropology has adopted, and is one of the primary espousers of, 'neuro-plasticity'; a relatively recent term given to a phenomenon that scientifically supports much of the Feldenkrais Method.[28]

Conditioning

Although built upon many of its concepts, the Feldenkrais Method ultimately differs from classic conditioning methods, such as Pavlov's 'respondent' and Skinner's 'operant' models, in that it inherently contains within it a necessity for dependency rather than merely reinforcement of action.[29] If compulsive behaviours were simply a case of reward responses to external stimuli (Pavlov) or repeated actions (Skinner), then there would not need to be any traumatic, emotional content associated with action. One might say that some compulsions *may* have emerged in Pavlov's dogs or Skinner's rats, but this would have been more to do with the relationship between the researcher and the animals than on the intensity of the bells that were rung or the complexity of the mazes that were constructed. It would be a strange idea indeed to meet actors who are simply *conditioned* to act, and even if they did exist it would be relatively easy to extinguish their behaviour by simply removing the stimuli.

Of course, the idea that there needs to be some kind of trauma present to create a compulsion is not unique to Feldenkrais. Even Skinner's extreme behaviourist theory recognized that this was necessary for deeply conditioned behaviour.[30] In fact, one would be hard pushed to find a personality theory that doesn't use it as a base assumption. What tends to differ between these theories is not so much ideas about the origins of compulsions, rather the perceived mechanism of how it is instated, where it is instated, the role the environment plays and the therapeutic focus of how it is to be addressed.

Psychoanalysis

The psychoanalytic view of how compulsion occurs in actors is mostly based on Freud's theory of repression, where abstract psychic material is pushed below the level of consciousness and struggles to find expression without re-experiencing original guilt or pain.[31] In general terms, we can see echoes of this all the way through analytic and behaviourist theories to contemporary humanistic approaches.[32] However, in spite of the wealth of papers on the subject there is still little clear agreement – without cyclically referring to Freud himself – on the mechanism that governs what is being repressed or pinpointing where it (whatever 'it' is) is being repressed to.

In the March 1960 issue of *The Tulane Drama Review*, Otto Fenichel and Edmund Bergler independently use the Freudian model to demonstrate that the drive to act is 'compulsive exhibitionism'.³³ This drive to act derives from either a sexually repressed desire to expose the genitals in public in order to obtain magical power (Fenichel) or suppressed guilt about being a voyeur which is then projected on to the world (Bergler). Aside from anything else, such elaborate ideas can be read as specious to say the least: there is no causation between infant relationships with the genitals, being an actor or having a desire for voyeurism. The idea, also, that all actors are exhibitionists, or that all exhibitionists become actors, as a kind of explanation of a self-selecting vocation choice is dubious and could be seen as convenient *a posteriori* reasoning. It is also one example of the use of romantic assumptions made by non-actors about actors which can often be problematic. Fenichel, for example, puts forward the idea that actor's motivations come from repressed impulses surrounding their heritage as nomads and gypsies.³⁴ Aside from being historically inaccurate, these views demonstrate how extreme a theory might be 'off beam' without empirical understanding of the actor's lived experience.

Feldenkrais himself was well read in psychological theory and would often refer to Freud in his writings (for more on this see Chapter 2 in this volume). He held the view that psychoanalytical terminology was not always useful to the analysand, and that it ran the risk of embedding in the latter's self-image a chronically distorted concept of themselves.³⁵ By introducing them, instead, to a corporeal experience of their embodied functioning, he provided a more direct route to the potential kinks (cross motivations) in their nervous system that bypassed the potentially overwhelming verbal symbolism required to engage in psychoanalysis.³⁶ From this embodied, phenomenological perspective, compulsion is viewed not merely as a single dynamic entity residing in the Cartesian psyche, but as a holistic expression of the entire being responding to its environment and situation. Psychoanalysis, he believed, could never fully extinguish a habit as the pattern would always be reinstated once exposed to any aspect of the original stimuli.³⁷ Once again, as with Fenichel, we find a subtle warning of the dangers of transplanting holistic vitality with conceptual intellectualism when addressing human functioning.³⁸

Cognitive psychology

The cognitive psychological view takes a more teleological approach to habits and defines them in terms of learned behaviour and the level of success in achieving a predicted goal. Habitual functions are defined by their intended outcomes and compulsions might be regarded as unwanted habits.³⁹ How these unwanted habits are experienced as inessential or dissatisfying, and the functional reasons for their repetition are not considered, since the focus is more on the conceptual mechanisms of the mind and its capacity to achieve a goal than on an empirical embodied experience of what it might be like to achieve that goal. This is contrary to Feldenkrais's Method, which measures the successful completion of an outcome by the efficiency, satisfaction, ease, organization and pleasure experienced by the individual while engaging in the action, as much as the objectively perceived completion of the action itself.⁴⁰ Many actors are extraordinarily well adept at reaching towards a perceived reward somewhere outside of themselves – acclaim, approval, money or excitement – but if we accept the cognitive model absolutely while ignoring the effect of corporeal experience, then there is the temptation for them to contort themselves artificially to achieve these aims, and this will have an effect on the authenticity they can bring to their lives and their work. Feldenkrais himself recognized this:

Today you can find an actor portraying a hunchback and talking like a gigolo, because he doesn't feel any connection. He wants a nice voice, no matter what the role he speaks the same way.[41]

Similarly, Feldenkrais practitioner Ruthy Alon describes the profound effect of stereotyped movement on the Method in her book *Mindful Spontaneity*:

> When Bodily Movements appear to us straight and one-dimensional, so does our thinking become superficial ... we ... dry up the inventive powers of the imagination, preventing them from playing with the manifold possibilities of ourselves in space.[42]

The result, she explains, is 'superficiality' which is the absolute anathema to an actor and their art. We see then that any actor training, rehearsal or career direction that is compulsively orientated towards an external outcome or goal could be seen to be vulnerable to resultant stereotypical action and possible dissatisfaction.

Compulsion, environment and acting approaches

An examination of these different approaches to the concept of compulsion has revealed a core difference in their viewpoint of the dynamic relationship between the compulsive person and the environment. In each case there is considered a dominant causal aspect – either the mind or the environment. Feldenkrais, however, uses the idea of symbiosis to describe the continued development of the nervous system around the environment, and it is around this understanding that his method is built.[43]

Interestingly we may find a similar differentiation of environment/mind dominance in acting approaches, such as in the outside-in and inside-out methods of, say, Meisner and Strasberg, respectively.[44] In both these methods there is an assumption made that the skill of the actor lies in their capacity to be able to respond primarily to either the external world, in the case of Meisner, or to their imagination, in the case of Strasberg. Like the physio-psychologists there is a binary differentiation of primary cause against which the resultant behaviour/performance is measured. The problem with this is that the compulsive actor, as we have seen, may learn very quickly to hoodwink the practitioner by faking behaviour that provides the most immediate reward, thereby pushing them further away from authenticity as opposed to bringing them closer.

Feldenkrais differs from other schools of thinking about compulsion, in that he embraces both physiological and psychological approaches and creates a holistic, embodied model that focuses upon the quality of both process and outcome, rather than just the perceived achievement of outcome. There is also a sensitivity in his work to the idea of aesthetic inherent in non-neurotic activity which, unlike many of the conceptual systems, has been used to directly address questions concerning the actor's craft.[45] This link between absence of compulsion, free movement, self-expression and aesthetic is crucial.

In practice this might provide for the actor a holistic idea of their own efficacy. That is that there is a symbiotic, embodied awareness of their internal experience, how this is being presented, and how this is being received by the audience both in that moment and with a global overview. As such it reinstates autonomy for the actor, as opposed to a compulsive action that, when triggered, emotionally defers to an outsider with the power to aid or exploit their instability.

Compulsivity amid actors and industries

If we are to accept the idea that the drive to act may be compulsive in Feldenkraisian terms, then there must be some 'cross motivation' present: the need to act, and enter the industry, might actually be a need to satisfy some other drive. Whatever this may be, it points to an unhealthy co-dependence on something, or someone, environmental, whether real or imagined, that is wrongly perceived as being able to provide satisfaction for an original trauma. It also points to the inability for the actor to satisfy this drive autonomously, and as such free themselves from the behaviours and frustrations it creates. Whether or not this compulsion is fed or challenged depends very much on the behaviour of the object being depended upon, since the power balance places them in a position of potential exploitation.

Of course, this dynamic is often regarded as evident and normal in the relationship between professional actors and the industry where an actor's need for, say, recognition can easily make them vulnerable to the idea of overriding their own personal integrity on the promise of a few minutes of fame by an impresario with their own personal agenda. What is interesting, however, is that the erosion of authenticity within the actor, which as we have seen might be the natural by-product of such a contract, could, in such a case, diminish the quality of the product. It would, by analogy, be like a choreographer kicking their dancers in the shins before asking them to dance. As he often does, Feldenkrais turns this same idea on its head when he states that 'a talented pianist must have an audience that can understand that talented pianist'.[46] In other words, an effective performing arts industry can only reach its highest potential if it has the capacity itself to recognize authenticity within its artists and itself.

If an actor's authenticity is to be nurtured, therefore, then either the actor has to address the trauma, or the employer/practitioner has to have the maturity not to exploit the actor by having some idea of the actor experience from the point of view of the actor. This is very difficult in the current postmodern context since anybody can call themselves an actor; value is frequently based on recognizable aspects of existing successful actors; and reward can be achieved by constructing a false self that fits this bill. When directing a play, for example, I often find myself auditioning actors doing impressions of other performances. Since such actors exhibit neurotic tensions in their movement and muscularity, as a result of cross motivation, their veneer is empirically recognizable – but mostly only to the specialist (or intuitive) eye.[47] When working on audition panels it is not uncommon that I become surprised by the extent that some panel members are persuaded by the presented veneer of an auditionee, only to discover that they are ill-equipped for the actual job.

Actor's phenomenology

Any professional actor will tell you that to satisfy their drive to act is not merely a case of fulfilling lofty, philosophical notions about expressive storytelling or the audience/actor/stage relationship (for example) but equally about negotiating a world of agents, casting directors, trends, schmoozing, nepotism, disappointment, prejudice, backbiting, manipulation, bullying and ruthlessness. From the actor perspective, these are not objective by-products of an unfortunate career choice that can be separated from rarefied, academic idealism, but are integral to their experience of themselves in terms of status and self-image. So, when studying performer neuroses (as in any study involving actors), it is vital that a full, holistic picture of the phenomenological experience of the actor, while acting, is understood. This means how they experience themselves:

a) as individuals
b) in the creative process
c) before an audience
d) in the industry

When researching actor neuroses it is notable that any phenomenological perspective of the actor – either in terms of their personality or in their experience of themselves while acting – is rarely considered nor referred to by the practitioner or theorist. It is often as if there is a pre-supposition that actors possess 'actor–ness', in the same way that a rat possesses 'rat-ness'.

A fundamental, elusively obvious aspect of the actor's experience of themselves that is often ignored by practitioners without performance experience is that the actor cannot see themselves while acting. As such they are reliant upon their environment for feedback on their efficacy. This leaves them open to vulnerability by those who are unable or unwilling to work *with* the actor but merely want the actor to recreate something visually *for* them. For the actor who wishes to please the director this means they may have the compulsion to manipulate themselves in order to fit in with their ideals rather than bring the whole of their spontaneous, responsive selves to each moment. This may also be true of the actor who contorts to get the maximum immediate response from an audience, regardless of the long-term effect it may have on their performance or its impact on the integrity of the piece as a whole.

Campbell Edinborough has recognized that the result is that many practitioners are given carte blanche to build their own systems by inducting ideas and systems into their students that compound their own vision or theory.[48] Sanford Meisner, for example, famously refers to the infantile nature of actors.[49] However, he seems to leave it as a critical observation, rather than seeing the benefit to his work in helping them mature.[50] This is not to make a judgement on his method, only that it is noticeable in many 'how to' acting books that there is little comment made of the relationship between the potential quality of output and the actor's experience of themselves.

Uta Hagen takes a more mature approach and recognizes the need for a sense of self-possession and well-being in her actors:

> Nor should sensitivity be confused with neuroses or their personal display. Theoretically, the actor ought to be sounder in mind and body than other people, since he learns to understand the psychological problems of human beings when putting his own passions, his loves.[51]

However, she does not put forward an idea of how this is to be achieved, only a demand that it should be so. This might only serve to compound the actor's neuroses by placing more guilt and anxiety into their already impotent state in a need to please the practitioner.[52]

Grotowski, Boal and Brecht, for all their socialist ideals, never once refer in their writings explicitly to any kind of inclusivity in the way an actor is integrated into the creative process, and the ideal conditions in which they might work, only what is expected of them technically or poetically.[53] Thus, it can be seen that the demands upon actors in training, rehearsals and performance have mostly been summative rather than formative, and this has become the normal environment within which actors are expected to create their work. In fact, Stanislavski, an actor himself, is one of the few practitioners whose system truly recognizes that an actor's awareness of the way they experience themselves is integral to the quality of performance.[54]

Among academic theorists, too, we can see even more examples of the marginalization of the actor's status, this time resulting from educated guesswork based on romantic myths about how the actors experience themselves. Compare, for example, the following statements, which are a random selection of theories about the actor's personality. As psychologists specializing in performing arts application, Susan E. Marchant-Haycox and Glenn D. Wilson state:

> The Eysenck Personality Profiler and a stress symptom checklist were given to 162 performing artists ... and scores were compared against test norms and a control group. Actors emerged as extraverted and expressive.[55]

With Thalia R. Goldstein, a psychologist specializing in aesthetics and creativity, stating: 'Children who went on to become actors were lonely, shy and introverted'.[56]

Aside from being wildly contradictory, it appears that basic research assumptions have been made about the nature of actors that are naive. These might be summarized in the following ways:

a) That all people who call themselves professional actors are good actors
b) That all professional actors tell the truth about themselves
c) That professional actors are self-aware
d) That professional actors cannot fake empathy
e) That good actors cannot be introverted, closed and disagreeable

In none of the above examples, neither where their actors have been sourced from nor whether the definition of 'actor' is referring to a label, a vocation, an action, a craft, a level of skill or an experiential state is mentioned. To the non-actor or researcher these may all be the same thing, but to the actor these are important, inherent differentiations that have to be considered for any theory considering their alleged phenomenological state to have relevance.

We see then a 'disconnect' between the phenomenological experience of the actor and the perceived beliefs of the theorist and practitioner in both industrial and academic contexts.

When looking at context then, it is not enough simply to address actor's compulsions as a separate entity but to understand the scope and depth of the environment that keeps the compulsion in place. It might even be argued that it is compulsion that embeds within the culture the idea that actors work *for* the industry on the industry's terms, not *with* it on its own terms.

Application of the Method for actors

What value, then, might the Feldenkrais Method have as a further addition to the already potentially overwhelming number of skills and theories the actor is already exposed to? Firstly, it needs to be understood that the Method is not a system with a repeatable cause-and-effect paradigm. It consists of a series of suggestions that helps the student to directly experience their own functioning, become aware of its level of efficacy, and then entertain more efficient methods, probably by bringing more of their sense of self into the picture.[57] With relevance to the themes of this study, Ruthy Alon describes this process as reinstating 'functional honesty'.[58] How this is experienced, the level to which the student wishes to go and to what skills this is applied are private and subjective to each student. Never are they asked to defer or place trust in the specialist, nor pursue the goals of a fixed model or cosmology.[59] Instead it places all the power in the hands of the student and regards them as an individual rather than a stereotype.

As such rather than introducing an ideal, prescribed goal that the actor has to meet in order to feel 'professional', it reintroduces to the actor a way of evaluating their own functional efficacy, for themselves. It is a Method, then, that can be applied not only to improve skill sets, but to personalize them and thus reintroduce to the actor their own authentic capacity.

When exploring their own functioning through either group or individual lessons, the actor is not just trying to develop physical or vocal range but is exposed to many different aspects of themselves simultaneously, all of which help to reinstate their inherent experience of true autonomy. There are three here that are of particular relevance to the actor.

1. *Sensory-motor aspect.* How the student responds to the functional questions that are brought up in each lesson, which the actor might apply to stage movement, vocal range or character development. Rather like Hamlet to the players, Feldenkrais simply says to actors: 'Good movement is that which suits the part.'[60]
2. *Attention aspect.* How the student learns to use their attention. In actor training this is similar to focus exercises or Stanislavski's Circles of attention, in which the capacity to develop choice over what and how much is perceived.[61]
3. *Awareness aspect.* This is the media without which there is no conscious moment of perception. It is the way this experience of awareness is accessed and experienced by the student that reinstates true autonomy. It has the capacity to extricate the student from their compulsion, since it is a precursor to the delusion that embedded it. Neuro-anthropologically it is an aspect that is hardwired in each of us to recognize, enjoy and repeat an action that is useful and pleasant to us and without which we would never have learned to roll, crawl, sit or walk. It is this part that is contorted or lost when we deferred an action to a well-meaning or despotic other. It is my belief that reintroduction of the student to this aspect of themselves is the most profound and important aspect of the actors work currently missing from most trainings. Once this been reintroduced, the student can learn to apply it to everything with the confidence that they now have the capacity to measure their own sense of success or failure in terms of their own satisfaction rather than through a contorted projection of their environment.

The Feldenkrais Method in Creative Practice

As we have seen this reinstated true autonomy is, in effect, an antidote to compulsion. It allows the actor to remove its stereotyped response from the neurotic context upon which it has relied, and develop more mature insight, freedom and responsibility to themselves, their work and the conditions within which they work. In addition, autonomy reintroduces the actor to an embodied recognition of what it is like to feel authentic, which as we have seen is often the most eroded state experienced by those who have compulsively manipulated themselves to fit in with the desires of those viewed as gatekeepers to their primary goal. This authenticity, by contrast to compulsion, is not a static state but a capacity to easily adapt and function within a given environment or situation, however complex, in a way that is satisfying to the actor and appropriate to the creative or political context in which they are working (given circumstances). Of course, not only does it expand their own authenticity, but it also expands their capacity to develop more authentic characters, rather than mechanical ones limited by the actors' own stereotypical nuances.

Potential scope

If we allow a final Utopian flourish for a moment and imagine that Feldenkrais has cured all actors (or those who call themselves actors) of their compulsions to act or enter the industry, and that what they have found is a more authentic, as opposed to neurotic, response to their own relationship with acting, and the acting profession. What might happen?

Firstly, the large percentage that have no interest in acting but are attracted to the romance of it may disperse. As would those that may genuinely enjoy the idea of acting but realize their 'drive' to act in fact points to a displaced need to have an alternative drive satisfied and so seek satisfaction elsewhere. Those who remain would be those who have a genuine, healthy passion to act, but may no longer *have* to get on stage in the compulsive sense. They would therefore have more autonomy over themselves, their career and their art and therefore may be more selective and specific in their job choices, for whom they work and how they work best. This would mean the acting industry will no longer be a buyer's market. Practitioners will no longer be able to rely on the compulsive servitude of actors to compound their own ideals and the industry would need to address its own collective neuroses and re-examine the traditional patriarchal structure and methodologies on which it has relied for its own status and outcomes. The definition of actor and celebrity would be usefully separated in terms of their motivation, degree of authenticity and what they are prepared to do. There will be a clearer appreciation of the authentic, as opposed to the mechanical, as useful currency. Directors and casting directors would have to become specialists in spotting authenticity. A new method will need to be created which reinstates the status of the actor and appreciates the phenomenological response to their art in themselves, in the creative process, before an audience and in the industry. Essentially it would reinstate dignity to the actor. The result might be more authentic work that is more efficiently created and is more satisfying for all involved: actors, industry executives and audience.

Conclusion

This study has investigated the potential presence and effect of compulsive behaviours within actors, the world of acting and it has shown that it is reasonable to suggest compulsions may make up some of the motivational aspects in some actors. Whether or not this is so is only truly known by the actors themselves, but there are some behaviours that point towards recognized compulsive patterns of behaviour in actors, and these can be empirically observed by the trained eye.

This has ramifications in terms of the actor's experience of themselves, their work and the context in which they work. Some of this is due to a complex, potentially toxic co-dependent relationship between professional actors and the industry within which they endeavour to function and survive. This creates a dysfunctional loop which is held, I contend, by collective compulsion, and which ultimately negatively affects the quality of the work and the authentic well-being of all involved.

Since it is a developmental issue, compulsion can be reversed by careful application of awareness and embodied curiosity. This is the core aim of the Feldenkrais Method, and in doing so the authenticity of the actor may be reinstated. This perspective has huge potential for redefining actors' own experience of themselves, their creativity, and the context in which they live and work and is an area that is ripe for continued investigation.

Addendum

If you would like to try applying the Feldenkrais Method in such a way that you can begin to familiarize yourself with your own neuro-somatic habits, then you may like to try the following:

Choose a recorded ATM lesson from one of the many online. If you are a performer a good place to start may be Falk Feddersen's 'paradoxical breathing in many position' found at openatm.org and which was recorded on 17 May 2010.

Do the lesson once through as recorded.
Sometime after, when you feel like it, revisit the lesson.

One of the interesting things about any ATM lesson is that if you change your focal intention it makes it a different lesson. Repeat then, the lesson, and become interested in your attitude to the given movements, as well as their dynamic components.

Things you may be curious about are: Do you have a tendency to assume the way you are performing some movements are better or worse based on their quality or outcome? Is higher better than lower for you? Is faster better than slower? Even if you feel you know cognitively that this may or may not be correct, notice whether particular movements seem to have habits of their own that are difficult to control using just your will. Are there parts of the movement that you want to move through quickly? Do you find that you push through some movements using a lot of effort if you cannot achieve what you perceive to be the intended outcome, or are you able to stay within your own limits and be curious? Do you sense this as a failure? Or do you have a sense that you are doing it so well that you want somebody to see it?

When you find a particularly pleasant quality to a movement you may want to ask yourself: 'How do I know that this feels right?' What is your personal, organic measure? It is likely that you will start to develop an increasingly refined sense of ease which is different from being 'relaxed', 'effortless', 'comfortable' or 'familiar', and has more to do with the level of efficiency with which you consciously or unconsciously perform a function. Indications that you may be on the right track are you may find you want to repeat a move for no other reason than it feels pleasant; or finding a new-found curiosity in how the movement affects you.

Once you have a more refined experience of yourself you might want to put yourself into the recruiter role and watch others and imagine how they are experiencing themselves by recreating the quality and dynamic of a particular aspect of their physicality. You may get a further insight into the potential inner state of somebody or a state that is novel to you (Resist the temptation to diagnose somebody's personality based on this, since we can never know the associations that someone places on their self-image). You may sense that, for example, how the A list type with the puffed out chest and six pack may have inhibited functioning, while the one with the prosthetic limb has learned to use herself intelligently. The latter would be able to act a role responsively, while the former would be more likely to present a character than be able to inhabit it. This is of course a massive generalization for the purposes of putting forward an example, but with practice and close observation of one's own, as well as other's *quality* of movement and self-organization, rather than how they present themselves, one can develop a deeper, and potentially more reliable, way of matching the suitability of a candidate to the ideal job description, as well as oneself to a given role.

Notes

1 Moshe Feldenkrais, 'Image, Movement, and Actor: Restoration of Potentiality', trans. Kelly Morris *Tulane Drama Review*, Vol. 10, No. 3 (1966), 112–26.

2 See for example: Michael Purcell, 'Feldenkrais for Actors & Acters', *The Feldenkrais Journal*, No. 5 (1990), 41–7; Mara Della Pergolla, 'Working with Actors', *The Feldenkrais Journal*, No. 16 (2003), 33–42; Kristin Linklater, *Freeing the Natural Voice* (New York: Drama Book Publishers, 1976); Scott D. Harrison and Jessica O'Bryan (eds), *Teaching Singing in the 21st Century* (Netherlands: Springer, 2014), 175–85; Thomas Kampe, 'Eros and Enquiry: The Feldenkrais Method as Complex Resource', *Theatre, Dance and Performance Training*, Vol. 6, No. 2 (2015), 200–18; Martin. H. Weiner, 'Beyond Technique', *The Feldenkrais Journal*, No. 2 (1992), 4–6; Richard Allen Cave, 'Feldenkrais and Actors: Working with the Royal Shakespeare Company', *Theatre, Dance and Performance Training*, Vol. 6, No. 2 (1015), 174–86; and Michael Johnson-Chase, 'Expanding into Vocal Expression', *Feldenkrais Journal*, No. 5 (1990), 24–30.

3 See Feldenkrais, *The Potent Self* (Berkeley, CA: Frog Ltd., 1985), 6–13.

4 Glenn Croston, 'The Thing We Fear More Than Death', *Psychologytoday.Com* (2012), https://www.psychologytoday.com/us/blog/thereal-story-of-risk/201211/the-thing-we-fear-more-than-death (accessed 28 August 2018).

5 Victoria Worsley, *Feldenkrais for Actors* (London: Nick Hern, 2016), 240–50.

6 Campbell Edinborough, *Exploring Integral Transformative Education for Actors*, PhD thesis, Royal Holloway University of London (2009), 10–20.

7 Feldenkrais, 'Image, Movement, and Actor: Restoration of Potentiality', 112–26.

8   Sheila Hancock, 'Acting Is like Childbirth … You Forget How Painful It Is', https://lady.co.uk/acting-chidbirthyou-forget-how-painful-it-0 (accessed 28 August 2018).
9   Feldenkrais, *The Potent Self*, 6.
10 OCD: *Differential Diagnosis and Screening Questions*; see https://www.swlstg.nhs.uk/resources/ocd-bdd/ocd-a-guide-for-professionals/ocd.
11 Feldenkrais, *Body and Mature Behaviour* (Berkeley, CA: North Atlantic Books, 2005), 100.
12 Feldenkrais, *The Potent Self*, 6–29 and Feldenkrais, *Body and Mature Behaviour*, 100.
13 Adam Phillips, *Going Sane* (London: Penguin, 2005), 55.
14 Feldenkrais, *Body and Mature Behaviour*, 50.
15 Feldenkrais, *Body and Mature Behaviour*, 50.
16 Feldenkrais, *Body and Mature Behaviour*, 32.
17 Feldenkrais, *Body and Mature Behaviour*, 38–48.
18 Feldenkrais, *Awareness through Movement* (London: Penguin Books, 1990), 11.
19 Feldenkrais, *Body and Mature Behaviour*, 50–3.
20 Feldenkrais, *The Potent Self*, 26.
21 Feldenkrais, *The Potent Self*, 100.
22 Feldenkrais, *The Potent Self*, 11.
23 Feldenkrais, *The Potent Self*, 11.
24 Feldenkrais, *The Potent Self*, 24.
25 Feldenkrais, *The Potent Self*, 100.
26 Feldenkrais, *Body and Mature Behaviour*, 97.
27 E. Domany, J.L. Van Hemmen, and K. Schulte (eds), *Models of Neural Networks II* (Berlin: Springer, 1991), 1–93.
28 Leandro M. Gaitan and Javier S. Castresana, 'On Habit and the Mind-Body Problem. The View of Felix Ravaisson', *Frontiers in Human Neuroscience*, Vol. 8, No. 684 (2014), see PMC free article: https://www.ncbi.nlm.nih.gov/pmc/articles/PMC4158773/ (accessed 31 September 2018).
29 Feldenkrais, *Body and Mature Behaviour*, 52.
30 W.F. Meyer, C. Moore, and H.G. Viljoen, *Personality Theories – From Freud to Frankl* (Johannesburg: Lexicon Publishers, 1989), 18.
31 Meyer, Moore, and Viljoen, *Personality Theories – From Freud to Frankl*, 43–59.
32 Meyer, Moore, and Viljoen, *Personality Theories – From Freud to Frankl*, 43–59.
33 Otto Fenichel, 'On Acting', *The Tulane Drama Review*, Vol. 4, No. 3 (1960), 148–59; Edmund Bergler, 'On Acting and Stage Fright', *The Tulane Drama Review*, Vol. 4, No. 3 (1960), 159–65.
34 Fenichel, 'On Acting', 158.
35 Feldenkrais, *Body and Mature Behaviour*, 152.
36 Feldenkrais, *Body and Mature Behaviour*, 152.
37 Feldenkrais, *Body and Mature Behaviour*, 89.
38 Feldenkrais, *Body and Mature Behaviour*, 94.
39 Wendy Wood and Dennis Runger, 'The Psychology of Habit', *Annual Review of Psychology*, Vol. 67, No. 11 (2016), 1–26.
40 Feldenkrais, *Awareness through Movement*, 57–62.
41 Feldenkrais, 'Image, Movement and Actor: Restoration of Potentiality', 112–26.
42 Ruthy Alon, *Mindful Spontaneity* (Dorset: Prism Press, 1990), 8.

43 Feldenkrais, *Amherst Training Transcripts*, year 2, 8 June, 1981 (Paris, IFF), 1.
44 Sanford Meisner, *On Acting* (New York: Random House, 1987); Lee Strasberg, *A Dream of Passion* (London: Bloomsbury Publishing Ltd., 1987).
45 Feldenkrais, *The Potent Self*, 100.
46 Feldenkrais, 'Image, Movement and Actor: Restoration of Potentiality', 112–26.
47 Feldenkrais, *Body and Mature Behaviour*, 57.
48 Edinborough, *Exploring Integral Transformative Education for Actors*, 10–20.
49 Jean Shiffman, 'The Unbearable Neurosis of Acting', *Backstage.com*, https: //www.backstage.com/news/the-cradft-the-unbearbale-neurosis-of-acting-are-actors-destined-to-fulfil-their-self-absorbed-stereotypes, posted 21 February 2001 (accessed 28 August 2018).
50 Meisner, *On Acting* (New York: Random House, 1987).
51 Uta Hagen, *A Challenge for the Actor* (London: Simon & Schuster, 1991), xiii.
52 Hagen, *A Challenge for the Actor*, xiii.
53 Jerzy Grotowski, *Towards a Poor Theatre* (London: Eyre Methuen, 1986). Augusto Boal, *Theatre of the Oppressed* (London: Pluto, 1998). Bertolt Brecht, *Brecht on Theatre* (London: Methuen, 1978).
54 Konstantin Stanislavski, *An Actor Prepares* (London: Eyre Methuen, 1980).
55 Susan E. Marchant-Haycox and Glenn D. Wilson, 'Personality and Stress in Performing Artists', *ISSID*, Vol. 13, No. 10 (1992), 1061–6.
56 Thalia R. Goldstein, 'Psychological Perspectives On Acting', *Psychology of Aesthetics, Creativity, and the Arts*, Vol. 3, No. 1 (2009), 6–9.
57 Alon, *Mindful Spontaneity*, 7.
58 Alon, *Mindful Spontaneity*, 1.
59 Alon, *Mindful Spontaneity*, 1–21.
60 Feldenkrais, 'Image, Movement and Actor: Restoration of Potentiality', 112–26.
61 Stanislavski, *An Actor Prepares* (London: Eyre Methuen, 1980), 72–94.

CHAPTER 12
TUNING THE BODY: ACTING, DANCING AND SINGING FROM REHEARSAL TO PERFORMANCE
Marcia Carr

Feldenkrais practitioner and theatre theorist Richard Cave once posed a question to his students that caused a moment of confusion.[1] All the students were asked to adopt a semi-supine position.[2] Slowly we lifted each vertebrae from the pelvis (peeling each one from the floor), to the bottom of the nape of the neck, resting the weight of the body on both the shoulders and the feet. He then asked us to create a sound: 'Can you feel the sound in the pelvis?' In formal singing training, when approaching resonance, we consider the primary and secondary resonators but rarely consider the pelvis as a place for sound or for feeling sound.

This 'confusion' became a dawning moment when I was later given a Functional Integration (FI) lesson by Feldenkrais trainer Mara della Pergola.[3] Mara instantly began working on an unconsciously held tension in my neck and shoulders. The FI overall focused on the head. The top of the head was in contact with the table and there was a tracing of an imaginary clock face below the head, moving slowly and with slight weight on each of the numbers of the clock. After, when asked to stand, the feel of the pelvis and the connection of this part of my body through the spine opened a resonance that was completely new to me. In this moment the deconstruction of 'anchoring', as a taught singing technique, began to occur.[4] The interest went from the suggestion of an external image to help achieve a note to what was needed internally, so that physical effort was reduced. The sense of being required to hold a 'functional' position with effort now seemed an unnecessary 'sticking plaster' to the very nature of realizing a release that is at the heart of creating sound. This is amplified in musical theatre training where many students use consistent effort rather than an internal focus on finding less effort in the process of acquiring technique.

Part of my work at the London College of Music – LCM (University of West London) – was in the creation of an environment, encouraging work alongside vocal specialists, musical directors and directors to engage and foster a burgeoning understanding in finding connections between developmental habits and training habits. This understanding was fostered through an exploration of skeletal structure and function in the production and enhancement of sound. Through training as a Feldenkrais practitioner, this renewed clarity led to finding a working practice in which the performer was given more choices that allowed them to reduce the effort they thought they needed to move. This work had a concomitant effect on the sung voice, on technique, and on the ways in which technical training was 'sitting' within the body. By working together with voice specialists at LCM, we came to an understanding of where posture and habit were inhibiting sound and therefore potentially technical advancement.

As Feldenkrais practitioners, we are asked to find a sense of listening or hearing through touch; finding a state of being calm allows us to negotiate the conversation, the 'dance' with another's nervous system that is perhaps resisting change as a result of habitual doing. Through the application of Feldenkrais's thought to the voice, there could be a 'tuning of the body', finding the best frame in which to house the voice. 'Tuning the body' is the way I understand a form of actualization of technical training; it involves a translation of taught technique through an integration of practitioner and performer in the moment of making sound.

This chapter therefore presents some case studies, or snapshots, from working with singer-actors taken from work at St Louis College of Music, a specialist music college in the heart of Rome, Italy, of how the Feldenkrais Method could be incorporated into technical training. In particular, the chapter focuses on the complex negotiation for the performer of how they prepare to move from the rehearsal room to the performance environment. This work highlighted the ways in which, as Feldenkrais practitioners, we can engage with vocal specialists to translate and bring technique directly into the function of a vocal user. The St Louis workshops also opened up ways of working with singers, and it has ramifications for how musicians connect to their instruments, where bodily effort can hamper technical fluency and the quality of sound created.

In a reflection on this workshop, one student stated:

> The workshop was a revelation. In two days, I discovered that I have all the ability to change what I wanted changed. It was possible for me to dance and move freely …..
> Above all I … moved with what Feldenkrais called awareness.[5]

There were only two working days at St Louis and within these two days students and tutors became aware not only of how they moved but of the importance of introducing this to the course. There was also a stronger focus on understanding and cementing a practice, and a way of working that demonstrates the importance of the adaptation of the Feldenkrais Method within conservatoire training.

Students on the workshop studied Jazz, and the course had, up until the point of this Erasmus exchange, no movement provision.[6] There was little thought or consideration given in this institution to the ways in which the body was part of the instrument being played, or to the importance of the relationship between the body and breath, and especially for singers, there was little understanding of how singers could access a greater quality of sound along with effortless playing. Narciso Yepes, a celebrated Spanish flamenco guitarist renowned for not using any amplification in concerts, claimed that Feldenkrais was 'personally responsible for the regeneration of his career'.[7] I would suggest that Feldenkrais's work helped physically re-organize Yepes's response to the environment and enabled his nervous system to create a type of sound which did not require amplification. Feldenkrais's Method, in a quasi-psychoanalytical vein, suggests that in order to understand our response we need to work on what stimulus evokes the symptom.[8] My students were beginning to understand the re-organization experienced by Yepes, and to examine the stimuli with which their technique engaged.

There is a vulnerability in the training of performers that allows a Feldenkrais practitioner to delve deeply into the habit-forming structures active in everyday life. This training facilitates an examination of how these can be moulded into a trained technique and a codified individual system that could respond to the demands of performance. Every performer has a physical biography, and it is this biography that informs choices in supporting the training of technique and the decisions made in the creation of specific responses to texts or other stimuli in performance. As a practitioner working with the training of performers, it is important to note whether you are working to break down the habit of 'taught technique' or that of a developmental response that informs everyday habit. If this distinction is not made at the start of working with a performer, then the actuality of how a performer is working will not allow the difference between the pressures of the rehearsal room and the performance stage to be overcome.

My concern in the present chapter is with the way the Feldenkrais Method can be used to help breach this gap. Being 'aware'[9] of how we move is the intrinsic nature of the work we deliver as practitioners using Feldenkrais's Method. Feldenkrais's teaching helps us to understand the concept of function and how to engage with a performer's curiosity, to help move action from habit, to delve into a questioning of the nature of the nervous system and its response to the nervous tension created by performance culture and the environment.

There is a further complexity in the training of performers, a duality in self-image; there is self-image in the everyday environment, and self-image as a performer within the rehearsal and performance environment. It needs to be clarified that performers try to remove everyday self-image from the performer self-image, and it is this duality that leads to a complication in their response to the Method and to training. The everyday self-image (understood psychoanalytically as the way in which the person looks, presents themself to, and sees themselves, in the world) can create a battleground with developmental learning (which requires a repurposing of these formants). In turn, the performers self-image creates a battle with taught technique that in some cases began as early as six years of age (or earlier) and with a negotiation of different teachers' and role-models' thought, sometimes in multiple disciplines.

It would be easy to suggest that this duality does not exist but, as a performer, there is, unless discussed in the preparatory grounds of training, little sense of connecting developmental habit and trained habit. There are many instances in teaching where a young performer will suggest that there is a difference between posture in terms of everyday action and activity, and the 'turning on' of posture for audition and performance. It is into this arena then that self-punishment comes, and the question for the student of how much 'performer posture' can hurt or be tolerated. There have been many instances, in my experience, where a performer has indicated the presence of pain after an audition, stating that 'performer posture' is complex and difficult to sustain. As practitioners, we can negotiate a connection and discussion with the nervous system, but the question remains of how we begin to work with the mental ordering of a system that is sometimes clearly questioning itself. To 'dance' with another's nervous system through FI is easy as long as there is only one partner; with a performer they bring along a whole biography to the dance.

The language and vocabulary we use are important formants of this discussion. Feldenkrais states in *The Potent Self* that reaction to environment is a necessity, and without this we have no means of influence over the choices we make. When negotiating technique, we are in an environment that is clear, but this can lack a sense of connection with a goal once a room within a conservatoire is left for the day. Performers often speak of what is real and what is imagined. This paradigm in fact can allow habits to become even more fixed; such talk gives an artificial stability to an environment, which may work counter to one of the aims of training: to become aware of habits, and to break them down so they can be rebuilt.

A form of safety and security comes from having fixed structures that we can hold onto, and these enable a performer to survive in a world with an ever-changing environment and with ever-changing demands. Feldenkrais suggests that 'to alter the course of an existence, the whole attitude and manner must be changed'.[10] Of course, there is a sense of suggesting that this new rehearsal, training or performance environment is just part of a single existence and self-image, but this does not assist us in trying to locate a semblance of a cohesive nature within the self-image or in bringing a closer connection of the sense of everyday action and self-image to that of technique, and what I would like to call the 'performer-image'.

The 'proof' comes when asking performers where they feel most at home. Many say the stage; this is the place where action has been analysed, structured and is responsive to environment and realizes a greater sense of appreciation and acceptance than they ever had for choices made in society and within the everyday environment. The heart of what Feldenkrais determines as the developmental process is so important in allowing us to be responsive to, and to condition these responses to the environment. This helps bring a form of calm and balance to the nervous system we are reliant on in order to live.

Once a performer decides to move towards conservatoire training, then the concepts discussed here are brought into focus by the heightened physical demands required. Within the close conservatoire environment, we have a greater potential ability to understand the constraints each body is placing upon itself and to realize freedom in choices with accessing training techniques to achieve professional performance standards.

The Feldenkrais Method offers and encourages the possibility of a greater self-questioning of the ways in which we access our own (and others') physical histories that we arrive with in terms of technique and belief. It allows us to consider our physical biography beyond character biography, and to access the resources of the self as a centre for creative choices. This move is consistent with the demands for a 'higher thinking', and it inspires and requires a search for a vocabulary that enables discussion and further self-understanding of the processes being actioned and enabled. It is the quality of questions that allows a performer to really find the ability to repeat consciously, something that is the mark of a strong performer when requested to realize similar but subtly divergent choices within multiple performances. The process of conscious repetition of action also allows a greater level of functional recognition, and a questioning of how to make this with less effort, thereby avoiding injury.

In his book *Higher Judo*, Feldenkrais discusses the uniqueness of action, suggesting that 'the simplest movement we can produce is of immense complexity if we consider all that is happening in the body to make it occur'.[11] The complexities of working at St Louis came from not having any equipment, no rollers, no tables, no blocks, no rooms large enough, to explore the obvious curiosity in working with movement or to work with so many participants who were curious about how they move. The experience resulted in going back to basics, back to the fundamental meaning of function in the purest form, examining its simplicity and complexity. This required a certain form of thinking and resourcefulness to ensure that the potency of the Feldenkrais Method was sustained through both Awareness through Movement (ATM) and FI.

The aim here was to create a learning environment that realized curiosity: curiosity in wanting to feel difference beyond the simplest of movements, and to open pathways to feel and therefore hear our actions. As a practitioner, there is a simple realization that students need to feel a sense of differentiation, but this can be complex when the normal vocabulary of movement is absent and when what is being asked of them seems to be differentiated from the study of technique in itself. Norman Doidge, in *The Brain's Way of Healing*, defines differentiation as 'making the smallest possible sensory distinctions between movements', and he discusses building brain maps but also makes us aware differentiation is easily felt when the stimulus is the smallest:

> Feldenkrais wrote, 'If I raise an iron bar I shall not feel the difference if a fly either lights on it or leaves it. If, on the other hand I am holding a feather, I shall feel a distinct difference if the fly were to settle on it. The same applies to all senses: hearing, sight, smell, taste, heat and cold.' If a sensory stimulus is very great (say, very loud music), we can notice a change in the level of that stimulus only if the change is quite significant. If the stimulus is small to begin with, then we detect very small changes.[12]

This refers to the Weber-Fechner law, discussed in the Introduction to this volume, and illustrated through the image of the autumn leaf on the front cover. In a large-group session it was easy to use the equipment within the world of the musicians to enhance a realization of how sitting differently on a piano stool enabled effortless use of the entire keyboard and a lightness of touch. This came from both a consideration of the pelvis, and how a small lesson based on the arms moving above the head could have a profound impact on the technical requirements and movement of a drummer who suddenly realized new differences in the dynamic qualities of his playing. These small realizations showed how simplified thought and how becoming aware of the smallest stimulus allowed the realization of greater potential in a performer.

As a practitioner, the process of realizing these things was progressive, and it took a sustained analysis of my own work and on that of others during my training and after to examine the issues behind activity. Feldenkrais trainer Garet Newell suggested two ideas in training.[13] Firstly, focus away from the issue, and looking towards the distal rather than proximal aspects of what we are doing. This turning of focus away from activity becomes a complex idea when teaching technique as we focus on the issue and find the technique that will solve and assist a performer. Secondly, it is important to consider emphasizing an issue (meaning focus on a particular area to emphasize the issue further) in order to really find a way of placing questions to and into the nervous system.

In a similar vein, Feldenkrais practitioner Roger Russell, on the Sussex VIII training (see Chapter 5 of this book), held a discussion of how to move focus from our 'habit forming centre' to the questioning 'pre-frontal cortex'.[14] It is this concept that the first day of the St Louis seminars brought into practical focus, and for students here. The demands on the mind and body as a performer and the nature of anxiety and the response of this via the nervous system began a journey into working on understanding developmental stages of growth (the everyday role and function of action), physical biography (the understanding of the everyday and performer training), and technique (training that places emphasis on performance that requires amplification of action to achieve a required response to text, director or environment).

As suggested at the start, it took two days to begin to realize and understand the nature of differentiation: habit and change. Day two at St Louis College was organized differently, moving from group sessions to one-to-one singing sessions. The organization of the course provided exactly the same technique at each level. Every tutor was teaching 'their' chosen technique and nothing else beyond this (lead staff chose what technique would be taught at each level to students, and any visiting tutor needed to teach only this). The key was to find ways to engage the demands of the individual singer and voice. The sessions had a singing tutor (voice specialist), translator and practitioner. The practitioner in the room was supposed to view and perhaps discuss ideas based on their training and comparisons between conservatoires. However, it was in the moment of watching others that clarified the start of a discovery. At times in training, there is a sense of compartmentalizing the nature of influence and at times of using methods and systems in a way that is potent due to the pureness rendered in each teaching technique. Every institution demands a role or function for a practitioner; you teach movement, acting or singing/voice and you certainly never hear of a choreographer as a musical director. As a practitioner, your worth is weighted through this singular attention to self-development, and there is a tendency not to cross into other disciplines, as you need to be defined as a 'master' rather than competent at all and many disciplines. As a practitioner, such focus had always realized a sense of looking at organization, even before Feldenkrais training occurred and this was a factor heavily influenced by training with Richard Cave.

The ways of realizing difference and being open to a heightened sense of self-image and environment had left many questions that could not be answered, and a realization that movement needed to be organized for greater efficiency. The moment of watching the first young performer training at first-year undergraduate degree level seemingly brought together every element from over fifteen years of teaching dance and movement, of understanding the voice, sung voice and acting together with musicianship. There was a view of a body that was at a structural, skeletal level so analysis was purely through function. The process went from observation to a form of listening. Observation moved from watching the body and hearing the voice (always seen as two separate things to solve), to hearing the resonance of the voice within the skeletal structure and realizing where a habit or the posture choices made were hampering connectivity and therefore the quality of the sound. In that moment, the struggle of three months' training was solved. Observation and listening through the hands then led to altering the feet and the eyes and recognizing developmental habit. The process reminded me of sitting and watching the tuning of a piano; in that moment you are listening in so many differing ways and working through the hands to tune each string, so when played there is greater sense of integration and beauty. In a translation of FI work to the rehearsal studio, I was able to help a translation of vocal technique into the skeletal system. Therefore, as practitioner and performer we danced as one.

On day one at St Louis, during at an initial one-to-one session, the voice tutor had suggested that they had been on the same journey for over three months trying to find success through repetition of technique and the student just seemed very lost trying to access what was required. It was clear that the question being asked of the student about the quality of sound and the connection of this to breath was confusing. The student was clearly frustrated at not being able to implement what was being requested, despite 'working hard'. As a Feldenkrais practitioner, it was easy to see and hear the issues limiting technical fluency, to hear the quality of resonance and to suggest where connections are not being made, where intention and function are not integrated. There was a realization that two very different images of the student were in the room; one self-image (what I have called the performer self-image) was rising to the new challenge of this environment led by technique, and the other was holding onto a developmental self-image that was safe. But this developmental self-image was full of habits built through childhood to deal with the environment beyond the present room and as such was fighting to hold control and so going against the performer self-image. It might seem odd not to discuss a single self-image, but the technique required by a performer is not required to enhance everyday action in response to an everyday environment that does not include a stage or performance hall. The developmental self-image supports the performer and generally technique is formed around this. Sometimes technique enhances our everyday self-image (seen as personality performers), and then there are those performers where it is left at the rehearsal room door (chameleon performers who use technique to separate developmental self-image and performer self-image). In this moment, for this student, there needed to be a consideration of working in a way realized in Feldenkrais's FI – to find a sense of understanding of how their singing technique was informed by tensions and superfluous effort informed by habit, habit that was 'holding' a sense of safety. In FI lessons, ordinarily a practitioner will try to find comfort for a student by using a table and rollers etc., but in the rehearsal studio at St Louis other methods needed to be employed. The 'hands-on' technique of FI is a form of communication through touch. As a practitioner we do nothing, but as Feldenkrais discusses in *The Master Moves* this 'nothing' is not passive; you feel what is required for the student to learn, and it is through a double feedback loop that the student experiences a new pattern of possibility. Feldenkrais calls this 'dancing together'.[15]

As a practitioner, it was easy to see why the student could not access the technique required, and although the singing teacher was working physically and vocally with the student, the element that was missing was the very thing that Feldenkrais worked for in FI. It was necessary to realize what the student was holding habitually, tensing or locking a part of the body, and in understanding this, to oppose this, taking over the activity directly for the student. The student seemed to be holding significant jaw tension that stopped the quality of sound the teacher wished to produce, and this was not allowing clarity of sound or diction. There was also a lack of connection to the breath to support the work. It became clear that posture was an issue, the feet incorrectly placed, encouraged by the knees in hyper-extension created tension in the pelvis which tilted too far forward. This tendency then did not allow full access to the diaphragm for breathing. As part of the pattern of physical compensation, the eyeline was focused downwards and as such this hampered head position. This also had an impact in the amount of tension in the jaw.

By altering postural alignment, and doing work with the eyes, the student's head was able to 'float' with ease above the feet and the pelvis, the jaw released, and this created a sense of reduced effort in the body. Suddenly the sound that was intended and required began to emerge. More work was necessary, but as a foundation, this triggered an interest in the students' physical autobiography, and the teacher was able to help realize an improvement of technique through engagement with the body. The student was asked to sing. With my hands in contact with the neck and spine, the student began to sense though this the feedback of my touch where technical change could occur: a tuning of the body. This tuning facilitated a 'dance' between habit and technique to find and experience new potentials in the development of their sound.

Training in the Feldenkrais Method enables a kind of 'listening', a metaphor frequently used by Feldenkrais.[16] In creative practice, this in turn enables a specific quality of understanding sung technique, the training process, and an understanding of how the nature of tension for performers had led to 'hearing' blockages in their own understanding and awareness. I found that it was possible to work on these aspects simultaneously, when student and practitioner 'danced', in a way that refined the quality of the student's technique. More importantly there was a sense that the student had found a moment of maturity through the curiosity aroused by this process. Feldenkrais frames this process in a more devastating way:

> Just like the person who adopts a crippling use of her body when confronted with a task for which her previous experience has not equipped her, so does humanity as a whole adopt crippling methods for achieving security.[17]

For Feldenkrais, human nature is inherited, and as such cannot be altered, but if through awareness we can start understanding how we do something, other ways of performing and other choices, in his eyes commensurate with human freedom, come into focus. Tuning the body through creative practice is an outcome of these aims. My role as a practitioner working with others was like that of a translator, one small and subtle step at a time. In going to the 'distal point', focusing away from the issue as Newell had suggested, each small step built towards the nature of what the singing teacher required, until we could work slowly and in harmony and in our differing languages (English and Italian) towards the heart of technique.

The second one-to-one student in the workshop at St Louis College was a Level 6 student (final year student in the UK). The training in this year had a sense of final preparation. Even more so, the nature of the work concretized a realization that as a practitioner there was a need to translate technique into functional vocabulary – placing technique into the body by locating the areas that seemed to be lacking resonance and that could not negotiate the physiological changes required as part of technique. This session focused even more on sound as a fulcrum for the negotiation of physical responses to material and technique. It was clear that there were some habits that were held for security. The student had a tendency to move their right hand upwards and downwards in response to a vocal scale or a movement of the voice to a register that caused tension and difficulty. To accommodate this and to make this parasitic movement easier, the student responded by moving the right foot forward in relation to the left.[18] The nature of this movement shifted weight onto the right foot, lengthened the ribs on the right and shortened the ribs on the left.

It was clear that this was not allowing the full breath to support the vocal work. By amplifying the movement of the hand and the weight on the right foot there was a new awareness of this habit. To alter this without consideration of the breath and the immense questioning of habit in the time we had would have been irresponsible. Again, I placed my hands as I would for FI, and slowly we began to 'dance' our way from habit to a moment of freedom creating a sound that the teacher wanted and the student had always wished for.

I found that if I worked with the breath, feeling the space between the ribs on the left-hand side, the student responded by placing weight on the left foot. The diaphragm also responded, and the sound became fully supported. Work through the left shoulder enabled the student to begin to understand the involvement of the left arm. The shoulders started to align, which reversed a natural right rotation through the spine, into pelvis. This allowed weight to be rested on the right foot when singing scales and as such this stopped the raising of the right shoulder, realized through the habitual movement of the right arm. The student, rather than 'reaching' for the top of a scale of a difficult note with the hand, began to reach with the breath and anchor sound through weight that was balanced.

A change in the focus of the sound was noticeable to all; a very small habit therefore impacted a really exciting exploration and release of sound. The moment of excitement, as a practitioner, came from using the resonant connection between two skeletal structures, my own and the student and to work out where sound was not passing with ease. It was easy to note where sound was inhibited to realize where movement was required. New choices were introduced and a developmental vocabulary was re-awakened. The habit was responsive to environment and nerves and also as reflection of an external image of what a physical representation of a jazz singer could or should be; however, these habits were hampering sound. The conclusion for the student was a realization that this habit, although it was only in the hand, actually hid postural and other faults within it, and therefore an access to full breath. In this student, it was easy to bring about curiosity, moving from the hand (the distal point) inwards. In doing so, they realized that their weight balance was not even and therefore breath was hampered on one side. Once the hand stopped and the body found an alignment that responded to the intervention from the practitioner, the quality of sound improved. At this point the student realized that they had held these habits through their whole technical journey and as such this limitation prevented the potential afforded by greater choice in their actions. For this student tension was actually linked to a sense of security in performance. Feldenkrais underlined how our personal biography has developed and sustained such misunderstandings, when he stated that 'in a society, social existence is as important as physical existence. The habits we acquire from earliest childhood, knowingly or unwittingly, prepare us'.[19] 'Society' here signals that if, for example, a jazz singer in a conservatoire is preparing to enter a world where there is a hope to be consistently employable, habit, sustained by willpower, only seems to help us up to a point, but 'our object is to discover what … you really want. It is not an easy task'.[20]

Posture is a natural discussion point in relation to habit, as it is a universal language across many forms of technique and across disciplines. We are constantly dealing with 'faulty posture' and the minute we begin to consider emotional stress, there is a sense of being able to journey with a performer in recognizing learned habit that is entrenched. Performers tend to return to the entrenched habit when pressure and tension is heightened by the environment. They either move towards the developmental self-image or bravely go with what has a shorter history, that of the performer self-image. The practitioner's role is to work in finding ways of working with tutors in technique. Voice specialists especially need to translate technique into function. Voice and movement 'specialists' most often do not have the opportunity of coming together and working, but the importance of this integration is immensely important. Feldenkrais practitioners understand the integrative power of the nervous system that allows control over the influences of environment. In this moment, there is the ability to bring developmental self-image and the performer self-image together – to bring acceptance that they inform each other. It is at the moment of integration that the mind can map a new integrated image.[21] As such there is an alteration of the dependency of old behaviours, and, even under stress, something new begins to happen. This new difference is the integration of technique as a new habit, or a new choice.

It is clear from these cases studies above the importance that movement can have in the development of any performer. Technique is more potent when integrated with the aid of a practitioner who can enhance the sense of understanding old and even bad habits and the transition to new habits that enable a response to any environment to be prepared. One of the considerations that it was easy to leave with all students who came to experience movement was the nature of looking at their own personal physical biography. Noting and more importantly engaging with developmental stages and also noting *when* technique was learnt help a performer to start the process of recognizing habit and how this impacts upon achievement. By recognizing jaw tension, for example, a performer, through the aid of a practitioner, can start to look at the uses of the eyes in everyday action. Through this learning process, they can start to create choices that encourage ease in achieving a technique that will be sustainable beyond the rehearsal environment.

By noting the changes especially in puberty of how the developmental self-image was formed, the student can realize new ways of standing and walking, and bring a greater understanding of exactly where a habit came from and started. As such, the ease with which a practitioner can then access function is heightened. The study of our physical biographies, as illustrated with the St Louis students, can start the process of curiosity and asking questions. Technique is complex as it has use for a single function, in this case playing or singing. This has little place outside of this environment unless some of the function can be seen as enhancing the social environment and making a greater ease in response to society. It is sometimes about playing with the order of events in terms of habit, and as such we start to really harness imagination. This in turn provides a spontaneous response to any environment by recognizing useful habits and those that create greater effort and require consideration.

What needs to be remembered is the power of bringing two disciplines that form a whole communicative structure together, that of movement and voice. It is clear that just as a violin has a body shaped to make the most of the strings, our bodies house an instrument able of creating sound and meaning. But if the body does not operate with ease and without effort, then the voice will not have freedom and as such will never fulfil its true potential.

When a child is born, the first instinct is to breathe and then make sound. The ease and lack of effort in creating sound makes children able to find a voice that cuts through the world and realizes response (see Roger Russell's chapter in this book for more on this thinking). The challenge is to find this sense of effortless exploration of sound, and to locate the moments where habits formed create a structure within the body that hampers our ability to communicate with ease. Victoria Worsley in her book *Feldenkrais for Actors* discusses Feldenkrais and his work with Peter Brook and how Frank Wildman suggested that although Feldenkrais worked with many people the world over and from all walks of life, Feldenkrais himself believed that his work could be the most fully embodied in an 'actor' because 'they need to address the use of themselves'.[22] I believe that this is not just actors but singers too, whether singing in jazz, musical theatre or classical idioms.

In *The Master Moves* Feldenkrais states: 'I hear and forget. I see and remember. I do and understand.'[23] The Chinese have a different version of this that is revealing:

> Not hearing is not as good as hearing, hearing is not as good as seeing, seeing is not as good as knowing, knowing is not as good as acting; true learning continues until it is put into action.[24]

Both quotations advocate the value of learning by doing. It is by doing at St Louis that there started to be a development of the ways in which it became possible to understand function, habit and effort in a way that helps a practitioner to tune a body. By listening to sound with both ears and hands, we can help work to translate experience for students and find effortless integration of function and technique.

Addendum: A lesson inspired by St Louis and an FI with Mara della Pergola[25]

Fundamental awareness of the base

Take a moment to play or sing, and listen carefully as you do this. Focus on your effort, how hard it is to play or to reach notes. Is there a feeling of tension when moving between phrases? What happens with your breath, and are you breathing with ease or are you holding your breath?[26]

Take a moment to consider how you stand or sit just before connecting with the instrument or voice. Close your eyes slowly; bring attention from the feet through every part of the body to the head. Take a moment to ask questions while scanning the body – 'how does this part feel today?' for example.

If standing: imagine a clock face under the feet: 12 o'clock at the front of the feet, 3 o'clock at the right side of the right foot, 6 o'clock in the heels of the feet, 9 o'clock at the left side of the left foot.
If sitting: imagine a clock face under the pelvis. 12 o'clock at the front of the pelvis, 3 o'clock on the right side of the pelvis, 6 o'clock at the back of the pelvis, 9 o'clock on the left side of the pelvis.

At any point if the feet need to be moved, or the pelvis needs to be moved, do so and note the difference with relation to the clock face. Let this thinking inform your choices. Ensure the arms are at the side of the body.

Always consider where the quality in the movement changes, and become curious about the quality and how you can find a similar quality as you move.

Cardinal explorations

- Explore the starting position to each cardinal direction of the clock.
- Explore 12 o'clock to 6 o'clock and then 3 o'clock to 9 o'clock

Working the circle of the clock

Consider the clock face again. Throughout exploring the numbers on the clock face, always return to 12 o'clock.

- Consider the quality of movement from 12 o'clock to 1 o'clock and then move round the right side of the clock face to 6 o'clock noting the quality.
- Move on to the left-hand side of the clock, from 6 o'clock, exploring each number towards 12 o'clock.
- Explore the whole clock face – clockwise and anticlockwise and note the quality of the movement.

An extension of this lesson

- Consider the clock face beneath the feet or pelvis. This time close your eyes and allow the shoulders to explore the clock face in the same way. Throughout this, keep upright, so think about allowing the top of the head to project the clock from the pelvis onto the ceiling.

Always take a moment to find any differences. Always consider breath and remember to check the difference in the quality of playing before and after.

Arousing curiosity

Once the lesson is complete, engage your curiosity in your stance before preparing to create sound. Where is there less effort in playing or singing through considering how we sit or stand in preparation to perform. Move between what you know and have rehearsed for many years and what has been discovered that brings a sense of difference. Listen to the quality of the sound and any differences that occur when shifting between differing positions as you prepare to create sound. At conservatoire level, 'stance' becomes fixed through technique over many years, and in looking at the base from which we play we can start to become curious about how this can impact the quality of our sound.

Notes

1. This Module was studied as part of the BA Drama and Theatre Arts Degree Course, 1992–5. Richard Cave taught Movement for Actors on the BA Theatre and Drama degree at Royal Holloway, University of London, and is also a graduate from Garet Newell's Sussex trainings.
2. Semi-supine – laying flat on the back, knees bent, feet on the floor.
3. The FI lesson occurred on Sussex VIII training, FITC.
4. 'Anchoring' – placing the body into different positions to achieve a particularly difficult note.
5. Moshe Feldenkrais, 'Introduction', in *The Master Moves* (Capitola, CA: Meta Publications, 1984), 3.
6. This chapter is based on work conducted with students at the St Louis College of Music in Rome between 21 and 24 February 2017. St Louis and London College of Music had a strong Erasmus scheme and until this date the choice of tutors had been from Music Technology. This was the first time a Lecturer from Performing Arts had been invited and this seemed to cause confusion. No one was really sure what could be shared with an institution that had no movement provision.
7. 'Appendix II', of Alan Fraser's *The Craft of Piano Playing: A New Approach to Piano Technique*, 2nd edn. (Lanham, MD; and Plymouth: Scarecrow Press, 2011), 402. See Donald Thompson, and Francis Schwartz, *Concert Life in Puerto Rico, 1957–1992: Views and Reviews* (San Juan: Universidad De Puerto Rico, 1998), 623–4.
8. See Feldenkrais, *The Potent Self: A Study of Spontaneity and Compulsion* (Palm Springs, CA: Frog Publications, 1985) [orig. c. 1949], 36.
9. Feldenkrais, *Awareness through Movement* (London: Penguin, 1980), 36–7.
10. Feldenkrais, *The Potent Self*, 33.
11. Feldenkrais, *Higher Judo* (London: Frederick Warne, 1962) [orig. 1952], 42.
12. Norman Doidge, *The Brain's Way of Healing* (London: Allen Lane, 2015), 171.

13 Garet Newell came to the UK in the early 1980s and has facilitated Professional Practitioner Training since 1987.
14 *Sussex VIII* Training with Garet Newell. Visiting Practitioner Roger Russell 2016–17. FITC, Lewes. Roger Russell attended training and is a Feldenkrais practitioner who introduced the co-ordination cascade, or roll-map (Figure 5.2) discussed in Chapter 5 of this book.
15 Feldenkrais, *The Master Moves*, 7.
16 On listening, see Robert Sholl, 'Feldenkrais's Touch, Ephram's Laughter, Gould's Sensorium: Listening and Musical Practice between Thinking and Doing', *Journal of the Royal Musical Association*, Vol. 144, No. 2, 397–428.
17 Feldenkrais, *The Potent Self*, 61.
18 A parasitic movement is an unconscious movement that is felt to be necessary, but that is in fact unnecessary to the movement function.
19 Feldenkrais, *The Potent Self*, 30.
20 Feldenkrais, *The Potent Self*, 215.
21 Feldenkrais, *The Potent Self*, 37.
22 Victoria Worsley, *Feldenkrais for Actors* (London: Nick Hern Books, 2016), 4.
23 Feldenkrais, *The Master Moves*, 9.
24 *Xunxi: A Translation and Study of the Complete Works*, trans. John Knoblock, Vol. 2, Books 7 to 16, Section: Notes, Footnotes 99, 289 (Palo Alto, CA: Stanford University Press, 1990).
25 This lesson can be read in conjunction with Lisa Burrell's work in Chapter 9 of this book.
26 Such questions are an important part of the sensory-motor feedback loop that gives us information about ourselves.

CHAPTER 13
FOOD FOR NO-THOUGHT ... MEANDERING BETWEEN A PERSONAL SOMATIC PRACTICE AND FELDENKRAIS TEACHING

Sylvie Fortin

Prologue

Each morning over the last few years, I have immersed myself in what I call, by default, a 'nameless morning practice', which borrows from a variety of Somatic practices, including the Feldenkrais Method, as well as non-somatic techniques to which I apply somatic principles[1]. In my daily one-hour session, I might play with movements influenced by the Feldenkrais Method, Continuum, Body-Mind Centering, typical stretching and strengthening exercises and yoga asanas.[2] Or I could play singularly in a Feldenkrais manner with head, pelvis and feet for an hour finding the connectedness. But, as Sondra Fraleigh has remarked, I think that movement is not *the thing* we are pursuing in such a personal practice, but rather a medium that allows us to explore and develop our perception of the tremendous potentialities of human beings in a perspective of non-duality.[3]

In this solitary creative practice, I like to experience coherence and incoherence in my multiple encounters with the world. By this, I mean that I acknowledge the blurriness of my transient self, along with what I feel steadier in me. Through sensing, moving, stretching, strengthening somatically, I like to feel my weaknesses, my playfulness, my seriousness and my contemplativeness: the witch as well as the fairy. My intimate practice has a loose form that falls somewhere between ritualistic act and structured improvisation. Progressively, my nameless morning practice has come to feed all the dimensions of my being, therefore irradiating into my Feldenkrais work as a professor and researcher in a university dance department, and as a Feldenkrais teacher for children with special needs in a private healthcare setting.

In this chapter, I humbly present a few narratives describing dimensions of my intimate practice, while intercalating short reflections on arising issues migrating in my Feldenkrais work, in both Awareness through Movement (ATM) and Functional Integration (FI). Of course, many people have a personal practice that is more or less similar to my own. In describing a fraction of my practice through a few narratives, my point is not to render explicit what is implicit in my morning experiences. On the contrary, I feel quite satisfied with its phenomenological nature. I accepted the invitation to contribute to this book because it afforded me a way to further understand the ramifications of my intimate practice, within both my work and my life in general, and to contribute to the limited body of critical literature on the Feldenkrais Method. This chapter is a reflection on my nameless morning practice, which is a practice of embodiment: a moment devoted to my multifaceted experiences of being in the world.

Morning in colour

This morning, I feel a faithful and integrated connection towards things and beings in the world: a state of simultaneous emptiness and fullness, a sensation of borders dissolving, a place without words. I do so like these pristine morning moments of deep embodiment that, puzzlingly, sometimes feel like complete disembodiment: a belonging to everything and participating in the 'hereness' of the moment. In these moments, ordinary semantic meanings lose their grasp on daily experience. Without having completely disappeared, words no longer hold meaning over daily things. Ordinary things become more and more clear. In fact, the ordinary reveals a layer of the extraordinary: it is like glimpsing a faint black and white image that gradually evolves, acquiring more and more colour. Of course, I still have an inner dialogue, but I become more and more drawn to letting parasitic thoughts vanish, thus entering a world without words.

Different points of view on wordless experiences

Accepting the invitation to join this book is also a pretext to expand the experiential to the conceptual. In my practice, I sometimes feel a dissolution of duality, maybe close to *mushin*, a word used in Zen philosophy meaning 'no thought'.[4] This makes me comb through my bookshelves to recover Maxine Sheets-Johnstone's famous article 'Thinking in movement'. In this article, she wrote: 'I am wondering the world directly in movement, I am actively exploring its possibilities and what I perceive in the course of that wondering or exploration in enfolded in the very process of moving'.[5] To complement Sheets-Johnson's writing, Glenna Batson expanded this idea of thinking in movement with the concept of meta-kinaesthesia, which she describes as 'a way of knowing the material body as well as the route through the physical, the meta-physical and spiritual'.[6] And if considered through the field of psychology, my morning experiences could be similar to what Russell Hurlburt called 'unsymbolized thinking'.[7] However, there is a counterpoint to the idea that we don't need symbols to mediate between experience and understanding, which suggests that experiencing the world is necessarily embedded in language. All these notions point towards a transcending of duality[8], a controversial topic that appeals to artists, psychologists, philosophers, neuroscientists, to name just a few.

Of course, I could endlessly attempt to link my nameless morning practice to any number of different theories. However, I admit that analysing notions such as 'thinking in movement', 'meta-kinaesthesia', 'unsymbolized thinking' or 'mushin' at an ontological level has never appealed to me. In these 'altered states of consciousness' or 'different kinds of body consciousness' as many label them, we are understood as non-dualist, neither subject nor object, with no separation between mover and movement. Yet the act of analysing this non-dual experience inevitably re-imposes the duality of subject and object, mover and movement. Cowardly perhaps, I will leave to others the task of capturing, without destroying, these very notions that non-duality intends to capture. With this chapter, I am more interested in developing pedagogical language skills that may lead students to experience the many dimensions or qualities of their somatic being.

Using words to go beyond words

In my teaching, I do not specifically focus on the non-dual experiences I have just discussed, yet I do not exclude them either. I simply invite students to be open to themselves and to the physical, cognitive, emotional, social and spiritual resonances that an ATM class might reveal within them. While my nameless personal practice sometimes seems wordless, carefully choosing words is of prime importance in my ATM classes. This is a paradox that Moshe Feldenkrais recognized. 'In self-knowledge', he wrote, 'one cannot get at fundamentals without undoing the link between thought and speech.'[9] To undo this link, David Kaetz explains that we have to carefully refine our language: 'As we seek more precise and accurate inner image of movement, one that corresponds to the way the body/mind is put together, it is imperative that we use language with precision and accuracy. By so doing, we can side-step habitual responses to habitual language, "change the pattern" and enter the realm of learning.'[10]

To David Kaetz, using words to go beyond language is a matter of poetry, asserting that the Feldenkrais Method in fact has a lot in common with poetry.[11] In line with the Jewish tradition in which stories are used as pedagogical tools to transmit ancient wisdom, Feldenkrais teachers often interject stories or jokes during their teaching. Personally, I am more comfortable with inserting sentences from poems here and there within my ATM classes. For example, in a recent class, after inviting students to rock their upper torsos from side to side, I borrowed the following passage from the mime Étienne Decroux: 'Beauty contains sadness like a hammock holds a body. That which it can't forget or dissolve, it cradles.'[12] By inserting such quotes in my teaching, I challenge our linguistically habitual modes of relating to the world and offer an unconventional way to open up new horizons. But because I recognize that the manner in which I speak to the students partially conditions the possibilities for their individual experiences, I often invite those who wish to share a single word, metaphor, colour, onomatopoeia or gesture that captures any experience they might have had at the end of an ATM lesson. The representation of one's embodiment is complex; as such, I value both discursive and non-discursive knowledge and invite the students to share their experience in different manners.

The delicate distance from one's own embodiment while teaching

Although the goal of my nameless morning practice is not to improve my Feldenkrais teaching, how I talk while I teach is inevitably influenced by my various life experiences, including this nameless morning practice. The language I choose echoes my own journey, but at the same time, it must go beyond my personal experience and invite students to explore the diversity and depth of their own experiences. Here lies another paradox: my personal practice is a reliable source of knowledge, but at the same time, I must detach myself from it in order to create a 'distanced experience of embodiment' to help foster each student's own singular learning process. Because all individuals are different, 'it always takes imagination to go beyond one's own experience' when trying to approximate the embodied experience of another.[13]

On one hand, as a white, heterosexual, female, financially privileged baby-boomer Canadian, I cannot presume that my own embodiment of a given moment will match the embodiment of someone with a wholly different background. On the other hand, I should neither assume that it might not. My teaching of dance and the Feldenkrais Method in North and South American, European, African and Asian countries drives me to assert that there is simultaneously sameness and difference between my own experiences and the experiences of others. Whereas in dance, these experiences are primarily mediated through visual communication, the mediation in the group modality of the Feldenkrais Method occurs through verbal communication. Explicit attention to the relationship between my own embodiment and the language I use in my teaching helps me to take into account the possible diversity of others. And being attentive to this diversity draws attention to social, cultural and political dimensions that are often absent in published and non-published accounts of the Feldenkrais Method. Indeed, according to Margherita De Giorgi, the field of Somatics is often presented with few considerations of how cultural context or local influences might impact people's lived experiences.[14]

Morning tick tock tick tock

This morning, I am frustrated as I begin my practice. I do the Feldenkrais' pelvic clock lesson studiously. Tick tock tick tock.[15] Yesterday, my old back injury came back after swimming with new fins, and my embodied response is in my lungs, viscera, spine ... basically everywhere. In the face of this adversity, I come back to one of the Feldenkrais Method's core principles: Differentiation. Feldenkrais mastered his knee problem by monitoring the details of his experience with the slowest movement and smallest possible sensory input, based on his understanding of the neuro-scientific knowledge available at the time and inspired by his practice of the meditative aspects of Eastern martial arts. Tick tock tick tock .... I progressively become totally absorbed in the lesson by pushing different parts of my feet into the floor and observing how the movement translates into my pelvis. I feel when a movement I initiate from my head is taken over by gravity. Almost unnoticeably ... Tick tock tick tock .... I drift from the choreographed pelvic clock lesson to the wonder of improvisation. I function as an antenna-like receptor, allowing what emerges to lead the way ... Wu-wei, we-wei ... The Chinese word for non-doing, for letting the activity perform itself. Surreptitiously, I initiate the same head movement and let it go again. My chest is warm. I hear the sound of my quietly beating heart. I am a boat between-ocean-and sky. Wonders disappear. I am grateful for this time, since I know that not everybody has this luxury of such nameless mornings.

Embodiment in marginalized social communities

Isabelle Ginot deplores that Moshe Feldenkrais wrote a lot about the general social aspects of the construction of self-image, yet kept an individualistic outlook in his practice.[16] To Ginot, Feldenkrais underestimated how adverse social contexts might prevent the exercising of individual agency because he assumed that by developing a better self-image, individuals would evolve towards more autonomy, self-reliance and freedom. She points out that when working in social institutions, 'the possibility of a change for a person, the nature of the change to be obtained, and the role of the person him/herself are not carried individually but collectively'.[17] Like Isabelle Ginot, I contend that the Feldenkrais Method is often presented as abstracted from a situated milieu. Much like Ginot's Feldenkrais work in France with either migrant communities, people living with chronic health conditions such as HIV and individuals in situations of social exclusion,[18] my own action research projects in Canada with women suffering from fibromyalgia,[19] women living in housing shelters because of major depressive disorders,[20] and women with eating disorders[21] provide insight about working with the Feldenkrais Method in marginalized environments. For example, in one of my action-research projects involving women living in a shelter, after a few weeks the participants reported being able to feel their ribs and abdomen moving, allowing deep and calm breathing patterns. But one must ask: would returning to a family setting with a violent partner, or returning to work environment with hostile colleagues prevent these women from integrating their new way of breathing into their daily life? In other words, will their environment allow them to integrate a new breathing pattern into their sense of self, which could in turn contribute to lessening their anxiety, since a fluid diaphragm is commonly associated with a calmer sense of self?

Considering the wider context of different people's lives has led a growing number of somatic educators to engage in what is called 'somaction' at an individual and collective level.[22] The task then is not only to guide the sensing experiences of the students, but also to understand it in what Mark Peterson calls 'sensuous dispositions', which he defines as 'the sophisticated construction of the sensorium, its reproduction over time and its alteration through contexts and technologies'.[23] The most physical of sensations are always filtered through one's upbringing and socio-cultural context, which partially frame the experiences, dreams and opportunities available to the person who is sensing. Even though the Feldenkrais Method focuses on individual processes, it should not encourage a decollectivization of the work that needs to be done to improve the lives of people living in marginal situations. Indeed, Feldenkrais teachers and researchers must consider how situated first person experience may run the risk of ignoring or depoliticizing some of the forces that create and maintain inequity, whether it be domestic violence, racial disparities, ecological imbalances or health deterioration. These kinds of questions appear vital to me, since the micro- and macro-politics of the body are always inherently intermingled. Clearly, involvement in social somatics or politicized somatics stems from activism, a desire for common good, and a desire to frame verbal and non-verbal compassion in teaching the Feldenkrais Method as an integrative process, rather than simply as spontaneous feelings.[24]

From embodiment to compassion

In other articles, I have written about how the Feldenkrais Method can be understood as an act of deep compassion, an act of mutual acceptance and connectedness.[25] This stance resonates in my Feldenkrais private practice where I work with children with special needs. For example, I have recently been seeing an extremely bright and cheerful eight-year-old girl from the Orthodox Hassidic Jewish community on a weekly basis. I have used every tool imaginable to try to help her overcome certain physical limitations that she has. Because she is fed with a tube through the navel, I often sing to her and ask her to sing with me in order to stimulate her diaphragm and the digestive organs that cause some of her problems. Recently, her mother laughed when the little girl started singing a song that was a kind of invocation for me to become pregnant because having children is highly valued in her culture and she probably wanted to do something for me. These kinds of moments are fuelled by palpable empathy and compassion. Of course, nobody advertises the Feldenkrais Method in terms of compassion and mutual acceptance. It could be a little tricky in today's society, as it was in Feldenkrais's time, since it could be interpreted as being esoteric. Instead, the Method is advertised as promoting ease of movement, reduction of pain and feeling of calmness. Many of the deeper values of the Feldenkrais Method are more implicit than explicit. Compassion, which is textual in the sharing of words, and material in the sharing of touch, is therefore not identified as a main benefit of the Feldenkrais method. Because compassion is a behavioural communicative process, I cultivate it as a state of becoming, both when I accompany children with special needs and when I teach groups of women having what the feminist sociologist Susan Bordo calls 'a complex crystallization of culture in the body'.[26]

Morning after singing

This morning, I wish I could keep moving gently all day long. Yesterday, I finished late singing traditional sacred Corsican polyphony. I felt blessed to have this weekly opportunity to create audible beauty with my five friends, supporting each other's voices. To me, the placement of each note appears to be the result of centuries of refinement by monks in monasteries. Maybe this is why this morning I perceive myself as the result of years of wonderful evolution. Inspired by Body-Mind Centering and Continuum, I dive deeply into the life of my body, the life of my tissues, the life of my cells, the vibratory organism that I am. I am extremely busy in my organs, escaping the obsessive attraction I have to this little curved-felt spot where my microbiome often loses the rhythm of its optimal digestive functioning. Isn't everything in my body shared ... as it is in the world? My nameless practice enhances my livingness. Thanks to my morning practice, this kind of space-time process enfolded in my daily activities: it recalibrates everything I encounter. Nothing is too small to be wondered about. My practice, this morning, is a moving, sensing, feeling prayer or contemplation of the magnificence of the ever-evolving living body.

Spirituality in and around a practice

Bonnie Bainbridge Cohen, Emilie Conrad and Moshe Feldenkrais all share the same evolutionary perspective that human beings share ancestral processes with all other living organisms.[27] One's rapport to evolution can be scientific or experiential, religious or secular. From a scientific perspective, Isabelle Ginot provides a sharp criticism of Feldenkrais's use of scientific theory, mainly in regard to his anthropocentric view of human beings, whom he placed at the top of the evolutionary ladder, even going so far as entailing a eugenic discourse at times.[28] While advocating for the need of an updated conceptual framework for the Feldenkrais Method in light of contemporary theories of evolution and neuroscience, Isabelle Ginot also acknowledges Moshe Feldenkrais's forward thinking in developing an experientially based method that rejected binary concepts of mind and body. According to Mark Reese, 'Moshe's evolutionary orientation was not religious, but neither was it reducible to science.'[29]

He describes his work as secular, but many recognize the leverage for actualizing an embodied spirituality in his Method. Ruthy Alon and Russell Dellman's work are two prominent examples of this embodied spirituality.[30]

In my nameless morning practice, my relationship to evolution is also experientially based. Spirituality is present as a dimension of the larger ecosystem we live in. Spiritual components may pop up when, for example, connecting with my breath or my internal rhythms. Ancestral wisdom connects me to others and to universal patterns. In my early training in dance and Somatics, I often felt that spirituality was a taboo, although it was often elusively embedded in class material or ingrained in the way teachers presented their content. Deep sensory unification with oneself, with others and with the environment is an undisclosed spiritual dimension of Somatics that I do not directly address in my teaching, but that I carry with me in my being. For Sharon Janis, anything can be a spiritual practice, depending on your attitude, since spirituality is simply the experience of one's own personal relationship with the divine.[31] In the previous section, I emphasized how the individual body is socially constructed, yet the body itself is so much more than a social construction. I deeply relate to Diane Butler's view that the manner in which we go through life can be the 'living out of prayer itself ... a way to bring to life an attitude of bowing, offering, and praying in a context of humans, nature, and God/the Source of Life'.[32] For Glenna Batson, spirituality is defined 'as the deepening of relationships in life that enable a person to transcend the ego/self-focused existence towards more meaningful, blended bonding with humanity and other powers of expanding consciousness'.[33]

A practice that exceeds the time of the practice

It is not surprising to postulate that my practice exceeds the time of my morning practice per se. I came to understand my practice as a specific time to settle ritualistically into some forms of movement explorations that informs everything I do. This idea came to me from a conversation between one of my doctoral students, who is an expert in calligraphy, and her sensei. As she told him about her practice of calligraphy, the sensei asked her, 'Do you really have a practice?' Faced with her astonishment, he continued: 'Do you cross the street as you practice calligraphy? Do you eat your meals as you practice calligraphy?' For the sensei, indulging in calligraphic activity was not enough to have a practice: rather, it was necessary that the values embedded in the practice of calligraphy interfere in each moment of the life.

What I could call my 'extended practice' is the ways that my morning practice provides me with occasion to deploy a quality of presence in my daily personal and professional life. One of my main incentives for engaging in my somatically informed morning practice is to deepen my experience of connectedness. As noted earlier, I sometimes get an incredible feeling of unity. By this I mean that there is a kind of boundary line that separates 'self' from everything that is 'not-self'. Of course, according to Ken Wilber, this is an artificial boundary line that can frequently shift, and even, as I have experienced, sometimes disappear. Similarly, for Bonnie Bainbridge Cohen and Emilie Conrad, being present with ourselves, connecting with our cellular breathing, our internal rhythms and our ancestral wisdom, is an important step towards connecting to others and to universal patterns.

Morning distracted

This morning, I attend to myself through my ribcage, which made me think of two of my former students.[34] *The first was injured on the right side of her rib cage, and any question I posed to her about her experience in class would be answered in terms of whether it increased or decreased her pain. Her pattern was to relate any verbal discussion or movement exploration to a four inch-square area of herself. This morning I have to keep telling myself: 'Sylvie, stop thinking about that ... your head is spinning, come back to your morning practice ... feel the floor ... yield ... ' The second student was a mesomorph type of dancer, strong, direct, and not inclined towards the process of sensing, feeling or perceiving. Her way of paying attention to anything was laser like. All events took on an equal weight. She simply did not know how to take anything lightly. To me, the first student seemed to be indulging herself too much, and the second was not listening to herself enough. 'Sylvie, yield ... roll the head from side to side ... pay attention to your breathing ... ' What these two students had in common was a fixation of attention. 'Sylvie, let's try working with the big inflated ball, maybe it will help stop your head from spinning ... push and roll, pull and roll ... '. I give up. My mind keeps swirling. Like my two students, I am stuck in a certain field of perception that restricts me and prevents me from tapping into my creativity today. My nameless morning practice is not always an embodied practice. This morning I am far from the 'aha' moments. But I must take this as an occasion to not be judgmental toward myself. Tomorrow will be another morning.*

Active perception

As illustrated in the narrative above, my nameless morning practice is at times bumpy and has room for improvement. But as Dan Harris and Jeff Warren wrote, 'falling off the wagon' is not just excusable, it is the whole point, since it's the exact moment when the skill of paying attention is developed. 'Every time you catch yourself wandering and escort your attention back to the breath, it is like a biceps curl for the brain.'[35] Studies of perception often suggest that perception is passive in nature, but several branches of neurophysiology agree on the fact that active and passive functions are both present in sensory receptors.[36]

Exercising one's own perception is essential for artists: an artist's task is to expand their own perceptual capacities in order to absorb an infinitesimal portion of the world, and through movement, sound, metaphor, colour or image offer something back to an audience, who in turn may possibly alter their own perception of the world. Through my nameless morning practice, I have come to identify some of the reasons why it can be important for artists to engage in Somatics and hopefully develop a personal practice of their own. First, by enlarging their perception, they might become more creative, since freeing habitual ways of 'attentioning' allows us to experience life differently. Second, by paying attention to themselves, they might feel and identify potential risks in their training or working environment that could jeopardize their physical and psychological health. Third, by enriching their perception, they might acquire a more critical stance towards both dominant and alternative discourses in the larger contexts within which they function and become aware of how such discourses may partially contribute to shape and restrict them. And finally, because of the three points outlined above, they might respectfully give voice to their choices in the public arena, based on the security of their embodied knowledge.

From perception to empowerment

These empowering facets of engaging in Somatics were evident in an action-research project I conducted with a group of pre-professional dancers who were enrolled in a Feldenkrais ATM class twice a week.[37] This group was working with a guest choreographer at the time of the research action, who had asked them to show more commitment towards their final performance by losing weight and adding rehearsal time during their lunch hour and weekends. Seeing this request as excessive, they collectively put limits on the choreographer's demands: the students presented a united front by drawing-up together a schedule of extra rehearsal time that they could all manage without any loss of income coming from their weekend jobs. 'He's afraid that the piece won't be any good', a dancer said in interview. 'He's scared that we don't have enough time. His reputation in Montreal is not our problem. But we're working together on this and we will do what we can to make the piece good', the dancer added. In this situation, the experience of the Feldenkrais Method had allowed these students to develop an internal sense of authority. For dancers and laypeople alike, involvement in a somatic class may lead to developing a fuller sense of autonomy, since it offers the opportunity to suspend the relationship with the numerous others – teachers, choreographers, family members, friends – who, even with the best of intentions, sometimes offer advice which is based on their own experiences and not those of the person receiving it.

Perceiving the connections between our lived experiences and the socio-political agendas integral to any context may certainly be emancipatory. Another example of this comes from the action-research project I conducted with women suffering from eating disorders. After participating in a series of ATM classes, one of the women openly became a volunteer activist in the prevention of eating disorders.[38] Through her experiences in these classes, she became aware of how she had embodied the patriarchal society in which she lived and how this society had negatively affected her self-image. 'It is not my female body that is the problem, it's the hatred towards women', she said in an interview. 'To do activities such as Feldenkrais helps me to get rid of my hatred that I have unwillingly adopted. We all live in a man's world. Even if I don't live with a partner that beats me, that threatens me, I feel threatened. How many ways do I try to elude myself. How many times do I hush, swallow, repress eat, vomit, or seclude myself in my home and not allow myself to go out for fear of offending.'

A much-needed critical stance

Both the Feldenkrais Method and my nameless morning practice are tools, and as with any tool, they can be used in different ways. Despite the two examples of empowerment shared in the previous section, the first one at a collective level and the second one at an individual level, the Feldenkrais Method should not, as mentioned earlier, be seen as unproblematic, since all tools can potentially be emancipatory and oppressive. Indeed, it is not the tools themselves that should be celebrated, but rather the multiple possibilities of empowerment a tool can provide.

In the two examples cited earlier, these tools aided people in expanding their perception and in connecting the dots between their personal bodily experience and larger socio-political issues.

While acknowledging the efficiency of all sorts of corporeal techniques and the pleasure one might get from them, I argue that the tools provided by the Feldenkrais Method can contribute to the lives of various groups of people, such as women with eating disorders, women suffering from depression, women having fibromyalgia and pre-professional dancers. This is an important point, specifically in the case of dance where the aesthetics of professional demands can prioritize the form of a movement over the sensing, often with negative consequences in the dancer's life. Of course, overemphasis of sensing also comes with its own set of problems, but I maintain that Somatics is a great tool for both dancers and laypersons. This tool does not encourage a selfish escape into private narcissism but rather, on the contrary, might create pathways towards social and spiritual consciousness when a somatic practice is accompanied with critical stance. Our heightened awareness has the potential to change the way we perceive ourselves and the world around us and to render us more capable of intentional action.

A creative morning practice

> *This morning I play with what is called in the Feldenkrais community the bell hand, the jellyfish hand or the octopus hand: and exercise which consists of opening and closing the hand while differentiating the centre of the palm from the extremity of the fingers. This is a rhythmical movement that recalls the concentric and eccentric movement of our ancestral mode of locomotion as bilaminar sea creatures. Gradually, I move away from the initial template of the Feldenkrais lesson as if I was being pulled by the currents of a deep open sea. Movement ideas swirling on wave swell; my entire body-self is in my hands. Around me, there is the illusion of infinite space, while within me, the illusion of a water creature. I am sitting on a chair because tonight I will lead a public workshop in a museum and would like to offer the hand gesture as a departure point for each person to develop connectedness with self, others and the world around us. Actually, my workshop accompanies a large-scale video installation[39] showing the life affirming quality of the Sabbath candle-lighting ceremony. The installation evokes an impressionistic mosaic of shared spiritual experience that draws and builds on hand gestures. My participation consists of using the Feldenkrais method to invite people to resonate with the video by playing creatively at the interface of sensing and moving.*

Creativity: A common thread

As a dancer, I began learning the Feldenkrais Method of somatic education out of curiosity, but quickly realized how it much fed my creative processes. The museum workshop outlined above is an example of this, where I allow myself to depart from the typical format of the Feldenkrais Method. To some extent, all somatic practitioners deal with the tension between their own experiences and how to follow the typical format or procedures of a method, or, in other words, how they remain 'authentic' with the method. Indeed, in the last few years, many somatic practitioners have developed their own practices informed by the work of the original pioneers. For example, Anat Baniel and Ruthy Alon have developed their own somatic method, transgressing the formatted way of practising the Feldenkrais Method. Creativity, or the capacity to perceive, think and act in innovative ways, springs from different sources and finds a fertile ground in my dance, somatic and nameless morning practice.

Getting out of a certain prescribed way of doing things is often thought as a given for the artists, but I don't think this is always the case. For example, artists might choose to follow a specific choreographic style, devoting deliberate periods of time to acquire a specific dance idiom through daily technical dance, just as they might choose to engage in a more personal journey. In a similar manner, in a spiritual quest one might decide to follow a given structured tradition by cultivating one's relationship with the sacred through devotional activities such as specific prayer or inspirational reading. In the book *Creative Spirituality: The Way of the Artist*, Robert Wuthnow contends that 'to be creative about one's spiritual life means recognizing that the teachings one learns in Sunday school and the insights observed from friends and family have to be *personalized* to be meaningful'.[40] Similarly, in Somatics, one can decide to practise a method in a dogmatic manner or to engage in a personalized manner.

Far from the maddening panacea

The following anecdote from one action-research project I conducted with a group of women living with fibromyalgia illustrates how participants can be engaged in a personalized manner. The aim of the project was, in one participant's own words, 'to put more Feldenkrais in their daily lives'. Over the course of the study, the participants had noticed during the weekly classes a decrease of their fibromyalgia symptoms and an increase in their feelings of well-being. At the end of this project, they reported doing their chores more slowly, reducing their efforts in various activities and taking pauses between tasks. For some of these women, the pedagogical approach presented in the Feldenkrais classes became a kind of philosophy of life or art of living. At first glance, this outcome could seem desirable, but it is important to remember that to consider the Feldenkrais pedagogical approach as representing a 'good' lifestyle versus a 'bad' lifestyle would be inconsistent with the goals of the Feldenkrais Method. Both teachers and students must avoid the pitfalls of glorifying a method: Somatics is not a panacea in and of itself.

Epilogue

My nameless morning practice is a continually evolving mysterious pathway. As a teacher, it keeps me in a delicious persistent questioning: How to go from the unutterable to the speakable? What kind of verbal and corporeal presence alludes to multiple dimensions of embodiment? How to acknowledge different values attributed to similar experiences? How can language encourage meaningfulness and a diversity of learning experiences for the students? What is the relationship between my own embodiment and the embodiment of others? What are the conditions required to create individual and collective agency? Finally, how to trust, on the spur of a pedagogic moment, the embodied liminal synthesis within me, wherein lies the convergence of, to borrow Howard Gardner's term, my 'multiple intelligences'. In conclusion,

I would rather not respond with words, but instead trust my nameless morning practice and allow it to have the last embodied expression … tomorrow morning.

Notes

1. My sincere thanks to Linda Rabin, Odile Rouquet and Warwick Long for assisting me in the preparation of this manuscript. Thank you also to Yvan Joly, my Feldenkrais teacher for many years.
2. For information about the Feldenkrais Method: https://feldenkraismethod.org/fr/archive/feldenkrais-method/. For information about Continuum developed by Emilie Conrad: http://continuummovement.com/. For information about Body-Mind Centering developed by Bonnie Bainbridge Cohen: https://www.bodymindcentering.com/
3. Sondra Fraleigh, 'Teaching through Movement: A Detective Story', *Feldenkrais Research Journal*, Vol. 5 (2016), 10. Available at: http://iffresearchjournal.org/volume/5/fraleig
4. Daisetz Suzuki, *Zen and Japanese Culture* (Princeton, NJ: Princeton University Press, 1993), 26.
5. Maxine Sheets-Johnstone, 'Thinking in Movement', *Journal of Aesthetics and Art Criticism*, Vol. 39, No. 4 (1981), 403.
6. Glenna Batson, 'Intimate to Ultimate: The Meta-Kinesthetic Flow of Embodied Engagement', in *Dance, Somatics and Spiritualities: Contemporary Sacred Narratives*, ed. A. Williamson, G. Batson, and R. Weber (Chicago: The University of Chicago Press, 2014), 226.
7. Russell Hurlburt and Sarah Akhter, 'Unsymbolized thinking', *Consciousness and Cognition*, Vol. 17 (2008), 1364.
8. Shunryu Suzuki, *Zen Mind, Beginner's Mind* (New York: Weatherhill, 1970), 7.
9. Moshe Feldenkrais, *The Elusive Obvious* (Cupertino, CA: Meta Publications, 1981), 146.
10. David Kaetz, *Making Connections* (Needham, MA: River Center, 2007), 112.
11. Kaetz, *La réparation du monde* (Needham, MA: River Center, 2014), 133. Personal translation.
12. Etienne Decroux, *Paroles sur le mime* (Paris: Gallimard, 1994), 84. My translation.
13. Gorel Rasmark, Bengt Richt, and Carl Rudebeck, 'Touch and Relate: Body Experience among Staff in Habilitation Services', *International Journal of Qualitative Studies on Health and Well-being*, Vol. 9 (2014), 10.
14. Margherita De Giorgi, 'Shaping the Living Body: Paradigms of Soma and Authority in Thomas Hanna's Writing', *Brazilian Journal on Presence Studies*, Vol. 5, No. 1 (2015), 56.
15. See the lesson titled 'The Differentiation of Pelvic Movements by Means of an Imaginary Clock', in Moshe Feldenkrais's *Awareness through Movement* (London: Harper and Row, 1977), 115–22.
16. Isabelle Ginot, 'Body Schema and Body Image. At the Crossroad of Somatics and Social Work', *Journal of Dance and Somatic Practices*, Vol. 3, No. 1+2 (2011), 160.
17. Ginot, 'Body Schema and Body Image', 160.
18. Ginot, *Penser les Somatiques avec Feldenkrais* (Montpellier: Éditions l'Entre-Temps, Lignes de corps, 2014).
19. Sylvie Fortin and Élise Hardy, 'Fibromyalgia and the Feldenkrais Method: Action Research Examining the Teacher-student Dynamic in Transfer of Learning', *Journal of Dance and Somatic Practices*, Vol. 10, No. 2 (2018), 261–74.
20. Fortin and Danièle Chouinard, 'Gymnastique Holistique par des femmes souffrant de dépression et de troubles du comportement alimentaire', *Scientific Journal of the Faculty of Arts of Paraná/*

FAP-UNESPAR, Vol. 13 (2015), 32–53. Available at: http://www.fap.pr.gov.br/modules/conteudo/conteudo.php?conteudo=333

21 Fortin and Chantal Vanasse, 'The Feldenkrais Method and Women with Eating Disorders', *Journal of Dance and Somatic Practices*, Vol. 3, No. 1+2 (2011), 127–41.

22 Martha Eddy, *Mindful Movement: The Evolution of the Somatic Arts and Conscious Action* (Chicago: The University of Chicago Press, 2016), 235.

23 Mark Paterson, 'Haptic Geographies: Ethnography, Haptic Knowledges and Sensuous Dispositions', *Progress in Human Geography*, Vol. 33, No. 6 (2009), 779.

24 Fortin, 'Looking for Blind Spots in Somatics: Evolving Pathways', *Journal of Dance and Somatic Practices*, Vol. 9, No. 2 (2017), 145–57.

25 Fortin, 'Looking for Blind Spots', 145–57.

26 Susan Bordo, *Unbearable Weight: Feminism, Western Culture, and the Body* (Berkeley: University of California Press, 1993), 52.

27 Fortin, 'Living in Movement: A Transcultural Perspective', *Journal of Dance Education*, Vol. 2, No. 4 (2002), 128–36.

28 Ginot, 'Body Schema and Body Image', 155.

29 Mark Reese, *Moshe Feldenkrais: A Life in Movement* (San Rafael, CA: ReeseKress Somatics Press, 2015), 441.

30 For information about Ruthy Alon's work: http://www.bonesforlife.com/ For information about Russell Delman's work: https://www.russelldelman.com/

31 Sharon Janis, *Spirituality for Dummies* (Hoboken, NJ: John Wiley, 2008), 12.

32 Diane Butler, 'Awakening Art and Dharma Nature Time', in *Embodied Lives: Reflections on the Influence of Suprapto Suryodarmo and Amerta Movement*, ed. K. Bloom, M. Galanter, and S. Reeve (Charmouth: Triarchy Press, 2014), 290.

33 Batson, 'Intimate to Ultimate: The Meta-Kinesthetic Flow of Embodied Engagement', in *Dance, Somatics and Spiritualities: Contemporary Sacred Narratives*, ed. A. Williamson, G. Batson, and R. Weber (Chicago: The University of Chicago Press, 2014), 226.

34 Fortin, 'Keynote Dancing on the Möbius Band', in *New Connectivity: Somatics and Creative Practices in Dance Education*, ed. M. Hargreaves, Papers from Laban Research Conference (London: Laban Center, 2003), 3–10.

35 Dan Harris and Jeff Warren, *Meditation for Fidgety Skeptics* (New York: Spiegel & Grau, 2017), 201.

36 Alain Berthoz, *Perspectives in Cognitive Neuroscience. The Brain's Sense of Movement* (Cambridge: Harvard University Press, 2000).

37 Fortin, Adriane Vieria, and Martyne Tremblay, 'The Experience of Discourses in Dance and Somatics', *Journal of Dance and Somatic Practices*, Vol. 1, No. 1 (2009), 47–64.

38 Fortin and Vanasse, 'The Feldenkrais Method and Women with Eating Disorders', 127–41.

39 http://mouvementperpetuel.net/fr/filmography/1001-lights-a-multi-channel-installation-in-production/

40 Robert Wuthnow, *Creative Spirituality: The Way of the Artist* (Berkeley: University of California Press, 2001), 269.

BIBLIOGRAPHY

Writings of Moshe Feldenkrais

Higher Judo (London: Frederick Warne, 1962) [orig. 1952].
'Mind and Body: Two Lectures Delivered at the Copenhagen Congress of Functional Movement and Relaxation', *Systematics: The Journal for the Correlative Study of History, Philosophy and the Mind and Body*, Vol. 2, No. 1 (1964), 47–61.
'Image, Movement, and Actor: Restoration of Potentiality', *The Tulane Drama Review*, Vol. 10, No. 3 (1966), trans. and ed. Kelly Morris, 112–26.
Body and Mature Behaviour: A Study of Anxiety, Sex, Gravitation and Learning (New York: International Universities Press Inc., 1966).
Awareness through Movement (New York: HarperCollins, 1977; London: Penguin, 1990).
The Case of Nora (Berkeley, CA: Somatic Resources and Frog Ltd, 1977).
San Francisco Evening Classes (San Diego: Feldenkrais Resources, 1980).
The Elusive Obvious (Cupertino: Meta Publications, 1981).
New York Quest Workshop, 1981 (San Diego: Feldenkrais Resources, n.d.).
The Master Moves (Capitola, CA: Meta Publications, 1984).
The Potent Self: A Study of Spontaneity and Compulsion (California: Frog Publications, 1985). [orig. c. 1949].
'Functional Integration with Cerebral Palsy, Session I', *The Work of Dr Mosche Feldenkrais*, 2 DVDs (San Diego, CA: Feldenkrais Resources, 2007); also available at https://www.facebook.com/watch/?v=136092850277964 (accessed 25 March 2019).
Embodied Wisdom, ed. Elizabeth Beringer (Berkeley, CA: Somatic Resources and North Atlantic Books, 2010).
Thinking and Doing (Longmont, CO: Genesis II, 2013).

Selected bibliography

Advanced Training: A Dynamic Systems Approach to Development with Esther Thelen, Ph.D, Feldenkrais Resources [DVD set].
Allsop, L. and T. Ackland, 'The Prevalence of Playing-Related Musculoskeletal Disorders in Relation to Piano Players – Playing Techniques and Practising Strategies', *Music Performance Research*, Vol. 3, No. 1 (2010), 61–78.
Alon, Ruthy, *Mindful Spontaneity* (Dorset: Prism Press, 1990).
Altenmüller, Eckart and Shinichi Furuya, 'Brain Plasticity and the Concept of Metaplasticity in Skilled Musicians', in J. Laczko and M. Latash (eds), *Progress in Motor Control. Advances in Experimental Medicine and Biology*, Vol. 957 (New York: Springer, 2016).
Altenmüller, Eckart, Christos Ioannou, Markus Raab and Babett Lobinger, 'Apollo's Curse: Neurological Causes of Motor Impairments in Musicians', *Progress in Brain Research*, Vol. 217 (2015), 89–116.
Andersson, G. et al., 'Effect of Cognitive Load on Postural Control', *Brain Research Bulletin*, Vol. 58, No. 1 (2002), 135–9.
Batson, Glenna. 'Intimate to Ultimate: The Meta-Kinesthetic Flow of Embodied Engagement', in A. Williamson, G. Batson and R. Weber (eds), *Dance, Somatics and Spiritualities: Contemporary Sacred Narratives* (Chicago: The University of Chicago Press, 2014), 221–38.

Bibliography

Batson, Glenna and J.E. Deutsch, 'Effects of Feldenkrais Awareness through Movement on Balance in Adults with Chronic Neurological Deficits Following Stroke: A Preliminary Study', *Complementary Health Practice Review*, Vol. 10, No. 3 (2005), 203–10.

Beacon, Jillian et al., 'Assessing Kinect Suitability for Measuring the Impact of a Weeklong Feldenkrais Method Workshop on Pianists' Posture and Movement', *Journal of Music, Education, and Technology*, Vol. 10, No. 1 (2017), 51–72.

Bella, Simone Dalla, 'Music and Brian Plasticity', in Susan Hallam, Ian Cross and Michael Thaut (ed.), *The Oxford Handbook of Music Psychology* (New York: Oxford University Press, 2016), 325–42.

Bernstein, Nikolai, *The Co-ordination and Regulation of Movements* (Oxford: Pergamon Press, 1967); *Dexterity and Its Development*, ed. Mark Latash, Michael Turvey (New York: Psychology Press, 1996).

Berthoz, Alain, *The Brain's Sense of Movement* (Cambridge, MA: Harvard University Press, 2000).

Blanco-Piñeiro, Patricia, M.P. Díaz-Pereira and A. Martínez, 'Common Postural Defects among Music Students', *Journal of Bodywork and Movement Therapies*, Vol. 19, No. 3 (2015), 565–72.

Blanco-Piñeiro, Patricia, M.P. Díaz-Pereira and A. Martínez, 'Musicians, Postural Quality and Musculoskeletal Health: A Literature Review', *Journal of Bodywork and Movement Therapies*, Vol. 21, No. 1 (2017), 157–72.

Brook, Peter, 'Eight Lessons in Awareness through Movement', taught in 1978 at the Théâtre des Bouffes du Nord, Paris, and ed. François Combeau and Sabine Pfeffer. available at https://b.org/book/5494611/9168d8 (accessed 31 October 2020).

Burckard, C., *Moshe Feldenkrais – Der Mensch hinter der Methode* (Berlin: Piper published CDs, 2015).

Buchanan, Patricia and B.D. Ulrich, 'The Feldenkrais Method: A Dynamic Approach to Changing Motor Behavior', *Research Quarterly for Exercise and Sport*, Vol. 72, No. 4 (2001), 315–23.

Burrell, Lisa, 'My Journey with Dystonia and the Feldenkrais Method: Beginning a Discussion on Contraindications for Aspects of Our Practice', *The Feldenkrais Journal*, Vol. 28 (2015), 7–19.

Cacciatore, Timothy, F.B. Horak and S.M. Henry, 'Improvement in Automatic Postural Coordination Following Alexander Lessons in a Person with Low Back Pain', *Physical Therapy*, Vol. 85, No. 6 (2005), 565–78.

Cave, Richard Allen, 'Feldenkrais and Actors: Working with the Royal Shakespeare Company', *Theatre, Dance and Performance Training*, Vol. 6, No. 2 (2015), 174–86.

Connors, K.A., C. Pile and M.E. Nichols, 'Does the Feldenkrais Method Make a Difference? An Investigation into the Use of Outcome Measurement Tools for Evaluating Changes in Clients', *Journal of Bodywork and Movement Therapies*, Vol. 15, No. 4 (2011), 446–52.

Della Pergolla, Mara, 'Working with Actors', *The Feldenkrais Journal*, No. 16 (2003), 33–42.

Demos, A.P. and R. Chaffin, 'Removing Obstacles to the Analysis of Movement in Musical Performance: Recurrence, Mixed Models, and Surrogates', in M. Lesaffre, P. Maes and M. Leman (eds), *The Routledge Companion to Embodied Music Interaction* (New York: Routledge, 2017), 341–9.

Demos, Alexander, R. Chaffin and T. Logan, 'Musicians Body Sway Embodies Musical Structure and Expression: A Recurrence-Based Approach', *Musicae Scientiae*, Vol. 22, No. 2 (2018), 244–63.

Depraz, Natalie, Francesco Varela and Pierre Vermersch, *On Becoming Aware* (Amsterdam: John Benjamins Publishing, 2003).

Doidge, Norman, *The Brain's Way of Healing* (London: Allen Lane, 2015).

Doidge, Norman, *The Brain That Changes Itself: Remarkable Discoveries and Recoveries from the Frontiers of Neuroplasticity* (New York: Viking, 2015).

Eddy, Martha, *Mindful Movement, The Evolution of the Somatic Arts and Conscious Action* (Bristol: Intellect, 2015).

Eddy, Martha, 'A Brief History of Somatic Practices and Dance: Historical Development of the Field of Somatic Education and Its Relationship to Dance', *Journal of Dance and Somatic Practices*, Vol. 1, No.1 (2009), 5–27.

Edinborough, Campbell, 'The Resilient Body: Developing Resilience and Presence Using the Feldenkrais Method', in Sandra Reeve (ed.), *Ways of Being a Body: Body and Performance* (Axminster: Triarchy Press, 2013), 111–22.

Bibliography

Ernst, E. and P.H. Canter, 'The Feldenkrais Method – A Systematic Review of Randomised Clinical Trials', *Physikalische Medizin, Rehabilitationsmedizin, Kurortmedizin*, Vol. 15, No. 3 (2005), 151–6.

Fogel, Alan, *Body Sense: The Science and Practice of Embodied Self Awareness* (New York: Norton, 2013).

Fortin, Sylvie, 'Looking for Blind Spots in Somatics' Evolving Pathways', *Journal of Dance and Somatic Practices*, Vol. 9, No. 2 (2017), 145–57.

Fortin, Sylvie and Elise Hardy, 'Fibromyalgia and the Feldenkrais Method: Action Research Examining the Teacher-Student Dynamic in Transfer of Learning', *Journal of Dance and Somatic Practices*, Vol. 10, No. 2 (2018), 261–84.

Fortin, Adriane Vieria and Martyne Tremblay, 'The Experience of Discourses in Dance and Somatics', *Journal of Dance and Somatic Practices*, Vol. 1, No. 1 (2009), 47–64.

Fraser, Alan, *Play the Piano with Your Whole Self* (Novi Sad: Piano Somatics Press, projected 2021).

Fraser, Alan, 'Feldenkrais Method and Piano Somatics: From the General towards the Specific in Piano Technique', *Feldenkrais Research Journal*, Vol. 6 (2018–19): *Practices of Freedom: The Feldenkrais Method and Creativity*.

Fraser, Alan, *All Thumbs: Well-Coordinated Piano Technique* (Novi Sad: Maple Grove Music, 2012).

Fraser, Alan, *The Craft of Piano Playing: A New Approach to Piano Technique* (Lanham, MD: Scarecrow Press, 2003, 2nd edn, 2011).

Fraser, *Honing the Pianistic Self-Image: Skeletal-Based Piano Technique* (Novi Sad: Maple Grove Music, 2010).

Furuya, Shinichi and E. Altenmüller, 'Flexibility of Movement Organization in Piano Performance', *Frontiers in Human Neuroscience*, Vol. 7, No. 173 (2013), 1–10.

Gallagher, Shaun, *Action and Interaction* (New York: Oxford University Press, 2020).

Gallagher, Shaun, *Enactivist Interventions: Rethinking the Mind* (New York: Oxford University Press, 2017).

Gallagher, Shaun, *How the Body Shapes the Mind* (Oxford: Oxford University Press, 2005).

Ginot, Isabelle, 'Body Schema and Body Image. At the Crossroad of Somatics and Social Work', *Journal of Dance and Somatic Practices*, Vol. 3, No. 1+2 (2011), 151–65.

Ginsburg, Carl, *The Intelligence of Moving Bodies: A Somatic View of Life and Its Consequences* (Santa Fe, NM: AWAREing Press, 2010).

Ginsburg, Carl, Foreword to *Body and Mature Behaviour* (Berkeley, CA: Frog Books, 2005), vii–xxv.

Ginsburg, Carl, 'Body-Image, Movement, and Consciousness: Examples from a Somatic Practice in the Feldenkrais Method', *Journal of Consciousness Studies*, Vol. 6, No. 2–3 (1999), 79–91.

Ginsburg, Carl, 'Epistemology for the Feldenkrais Method', in D. Zemach-Bersin (ed.), *New York Feldenkrais Professional Training Program, Readings & Handouts Volume 1* (New York: Feldenkrais Institute of North America, n.d.).

Ginsburg, Carl, 'Bernstein and Feldenkrais: The Fathers of Movement Science', *The Feldenkrais Journal*, No. 12 (1998).

Ginsburg, Carl, 'The Roots of Functional Integration: Part 1 – Biology and Feldenkrais', *Feldenkrais Journal*, Vol. 3 (1987), 13–23.

Gould, Glenn, *The Glenn Gould Reader*, ed. Tim Page (London: Faber 1984).

Hancock, Dianne, 'Teaching the FM in UK Higher Education Performer Training', *Theatre, Dance and Performance Training*, Vol. 6, No. 2 (2015), ed. Worth and McCaw, 159–73.

Hecker, Tim, 'Glenn Gould, the Vanishing Performer and the Ambivalence of the Studio', *Leonardo Music Journal*, Vol. 18, *Why Live? Performance in the Age of Digital Reproduction* (2008), 77–83.

Hillier, Susan and A. Worley, 'The Effectiveness of the Feldenkrais Method: A Systematic Review of the Evidence', *Evidence-Based Complementary and Alternative Medicine*, Vol. 2015 (2015), 1–12.

Johnson, Don Hanlon, ed., *Bone, Breath and Gesture: Practices of Embodiment* (Berkeley, CA: North Atlantic Books, 1995).

Johnson, Mark, *Embodied Mind, Meaning and Reason* (Chicago: The University of Chicago Press, 2017).

Kampe, Thomas, 'The Art of Making Choices: the Feldenkrais Method as Soma-critique', in Sarah Whatley, Natalie Garrett-Brown and Kirsty Alexander (ed.), *Attending to Movement: Somatic Perspectives on Living in This World* (Axminster: Triarchy Press, 2015), 77–89.

Kampe, Thomas and Clifford Smyth (eds), *The Feldenkrais Journal*, Vol. VI (May 2019).

Latash, Mark, 'Motor Control: On a Way to Physics of Living Systems', in M. Levin (ed.), *Advances in Experimental Medicine and Biology*, Vol. 826 (New York: Springer, 2014), 1–16.

Bibliography

Linklater, Kristin, *Freeing the Natural Voice* (New York: Drama Book Publishers, 1976).
Malony, S. Timothy, 'Glenn Gould, Autistic Savant', in Neil Lerner and Joseph N. Straus (ed.), *Sounding Off: Theorizing Disability in Music* (New York: Routledge, 2006), 121–35.
McCaw, Dick, *Training the Actor's Body: A Guide* (London: Bloomsbury Methuen, 2018).
McCaw, Dick, *Rethinking the Actor's Body: Dialogues with Neuroscience* (London: Methuen, 2020).
Nelson, Samuel, 'Playing with the Entire Self: The Feldenkrais Method and Musicians', *Seminars in Neurology*, Vol. 9, No. 2 (1989), 97–104.
Nelson, Samuel and Elizabeth Blades, *Singing with Your Whole Self: A Singer's Guide to the Feldenkrais Method*, 2nd edn. (Lanham, MD: Rowman & Littlefield, 2018).
Newell, Karl M., 'Change in Movement and Skill: Learning, Retention, and Transfer', in Mark L. Latash and Michael T. Turvey (eds), *Dexterity and Its development* (Mahwah, NJ: Lawrence Erlbaum, 1996), 393–429.
Newell, Karl M. and D.M. Corcos, *Variability and Motor Control* (Champaign, IL: Human Kinetics Publishers, 1993).
Newell, Karl M. and P. Vernon, 'The Evolving Perceptual-Motor Workspace in Infancy', in Geert. J.P. Savelsbergh (ed.), *Advances in Psychology*, Vol. 97. *The Development of Coordination in Infancy* (North-Holland: Elsevier Science Publishers, 1993), 175–99.
Newell, Karl M., Yeou-Teh Liu and Gottfried Mayer-Kress, 'A Dynamical Systems Interpretation of Epigenetic Landscapes for Infant Motor Development', *Infant Behavior & Development*, Vol. 26 (2003), 449–72.
Nogueira, Pedro, 'Motion Capture Fundamentals: A Critical and Comparative Analysis on Real-World Applications', Faculdade de Engenharia da Universidade do Porto, 2011, https://paginas.fe.up.pt/~prodei/dsie12/papers/paper_7.pdf (accessed 20 February 2018).
Nonaka, T. and B. Bril, 'Fractal Dynamics in Dexterous Tool Use: The Case of Hammering Behavior of Bead Craftsmen', *Journal of Experimental Psychology: Human Perception and Performance*, Vol. 40, No. 1 (2014), 218–31.
Ockelford, Adam and Graham F. Welch, 'Mapping Musical Development in Learners with the Most Complex Needs: The Sounds of Intent Project', in Gary E. McPherson and Graham F. Welch (ed.), *The Oxford Handbook of Music Education*, 2 vols. (Oxford: Oxford University Press, 2012), Vol. II, 11–30.
Oram, Daron, 'Research and Practice in Voice Studies: Searching for a Methodology', *Voice and Speech Review*, Vol. 9, No. 1 (2015), 15–27.
Porges, Stephen, *The Polyvagal Theory* (New York: Norton, 2011).
Potter, Nicole, Barbara Adrian and Mary Fleisher (eds), *Movement for Actors*, 2nd edn. (New York: Allworth Press, 2017).
Pozo, Karine and Yukiko Goda, 'Unraveling Mechanisms of Homeostatic Plasticity', *Neuron*, Vol. 66, No. 3 (2010), 337–51.
Prucell, Michael, 'Feldenkrais for Actors & Acters', *The Feldenkrais Journal*, No. 5 (1990), 41–7.
Pugh, J.D. and A.M. Williams, 'Feldenkrais Method Empowers Adults with Chronic Back Pain', *Holistic Nursing Practice*, Vol. 28, No. 3 (2014), 171–83.
Reese, Mark, 'The Feldenkrais Method and Dynamic System Principles', A personal communication to Esther Thelen, unpublished document available from https://pdfs.semanticscholar.org/c09b/c049c73246ddc96d9257074807af39cec365.pdf (accessed 15 May 2020).
Reese, *Moshe Feldenkrais: A Life in Movement*, Vol. I (San Rafael, CA: ReeseKress Somatics Press, 2015).
Rochat, Philippe, 'What Is It Like to Be a Newborn', in Shaun Gallagher (ed.), *The Oxford Handbook of The Self* (Oxford: Oxford University Press, 2013), 57–79.
Rochat, Philippe, *The Infant's World* (Cambridge, MA: Harvard University Press, 2004).
Roche, Jennifer, 'Shifting Embodied Perspectives in Dance Teaching', *Journal for Dance and Somatic Practices*, Vol. 8, No. 2 (2016), 143–56.
Rose, Debra and R.W. Christina, *A Multilevel Approach to the Study of Motor Control and Learning*, 2nd edn. (San Francisco, CA: Pearson Education Inc., 2006).
Rosenfeld, Albert, 'Teaching the Body How to Program the Brain Is Mosche's Miracle', *Smithsonian Magazine*, Vol. 11, No. 10 (January 1981), 1–6.

Russell, Roger, 'The Weber-Fechner-Henneman Movement Optimization Cycle', *The Feldenkrais Journal*, #30, Feldenkrais Guild of North America (2017), 28–40, https://issuu.com/thefeldenkraisjournal/docs/2017_feldenkrais_final

Russell, Roger, *Dem Schmerz den Rücken kehren* (Paderborn: Junfermann Verlag, 2002).

Russell, Roger and Ulla Schläfke, 'The Growing World of the Child', *The Feldenkrais Journal, No. 12*, Feldenkrais Guild of North America (1997), 16–31.

Rywerant, Yochanan, *The Feldenkrais Method: Teaching by Handling* (Laguna Beach, CA: Basic Health Publishers, 2003).

Sacks, Oliver, 'Neurology and the Soul', *New York Review* (22 November 1990), 44–50.

Sheets-Johnstone, Maxine, 'Body and Movement: Basic Dynamic Principles', in Shaun Gallagher and Daniel Schmicking (eds), *Handbook of Phenomenology and Cognitive Science* (Dordrecht: Springer, 2010), 217–34.

Sheets-Johnstone, Maxine, *The Primacy of Movement*, 2nd edn. (Amsterdam: John Benjamins, 2011).

Sholl, Robert, 'Feldenkrais's Touch, Ephram's Laughter, Gould's Sensorium: Listening and Musical Practice between Thinking and Doing', *Journal of the Royal Musical Association*, Vol. 144, No. 2 (2019), 397–428.

Spire, Mary, *How to Understand and Work Effectively with Musicians* (San Diego, CA: Feldenkrais Resources, n.d.).

Stern, Daniel N., *The Interpersonal World of the Infant*, 2nd edn. (New York: Basic Books, 2000).

Suzuki, Daisetz, *Zen and Japanese Culture* (Princeton: Princeton University Press, 1993).

Suzuki, Shunryu, *Zen Mind, Beginner's Mind* (New York: Weatherhill, 1970).

Thelen, Esther, 'The Central Role of Action in Typical and Atypical Development', in Ida J. Stockman (ed.), *Movement and Action in Learning and Development: Clinical Implications of Pervasive Developmental Disorders* (San Diego, CA: Academic Press, 2004), 49–73.

Thelen, Esther and Linda B. Smith, 'Dynamic Systems Theories', in *Handbook of Child Psychology*, ed. Richard M. Lerner, Vol. 1, Ch. 6 (Hoboken, NJ: John Wiley and Sons, 2006), 258–312.

Thelen, Esther and Linda B. Smith, *A Dynamic Systems Approach to the Development of Cognition and Action* (Cambridge, MA: MIT Press, 1994).

Todd, Mable, *Early Writings*, Reprint with a Foreword by Fritz E. Popken (New York: Dance Horizons, 1977).

Urbanski, Kristen, 'Overcoming Performance Anxiety: A Systematic Review of the Benefits of Yoga, Alexander Technique, and the Feldenkrais Method', Bachelor of Arts, Ohio University, 2012. Available from: https://etd.ohiolink.edu/!etd.send_file?accession=ouhonors1343316242&disposition=attachment (accessed 14 May 2020).

Valentine, Elizabeth and A. Williamon, 'Alexander Technique and Music Performance: Evidence for Improved "Use"', in *Thematic Session: Developing Musicians, Proceedings of the Fifth Triennial ESCOM Conference* ed. R. Kopiez, A.C. Lehmann, I. Wolther and C. Wolf (Hanover: Hanover University Press, 2003), 145–7.

Weiner, Martin H. 'Beyond Technique', *The Feldenkrais Journal*, No. 2 (1992), 4–6.

Worsley, Victoria, *Feldenkrais for Actors* (London: Nick Hern Books, 2016).

Worth, Libby and Dick McCaw (eds), Special Edition of *Theatre, Dance and Performance Training*, Vol. 6 No. 2 (2015).

INDEX

Arrau, Claudio 5–6

Barkai, Yael 27
Barker, Clive 55–6, 65–7
Bateson, Gregory 86
Batson, Glenna 221
Bernstein, Nicolai
    and Dexterity 56–7
    and Feldenkrais 60–2
    and sensation 59–60
Bodenweiser, Gertrud 17, 19, 20
Brook, Peter 55–6, 59, 67
Brown, Caro 18–19

Cortot, Alfred 4–5

Damasio, Antonio 86

Eshkol, Noa 27

Feldenkrais, Moshe
    and babies 86–90, 137, 150, 216
    and biotensegrity 144–5
    and brass players 158, 170
    and comfort 43, 104, 176
    and compulsion and spontaneity 39, 44–5, 192–4, 196–8, 201–3
    and disability 2
    and education 3, 86
    and 'the elusive obvious' 50–1, 199
    and emancipation xv, 1, 21–6, 31–2, 227
    and embodiment 222–5
    on feeling and awareness 78–9, 201
    and gravity 143–4
    and habits 46, 63–4, 78, 94–6, 105–6, 211
    and injury 4, 169
    and learning 3–5, 39, 49–51, 62–3, 77, 85–6, 89–94, 165–7, 211–16
    and lessons 90–2, 164–7, 167–70, 182–8, 203–4, 217–18, 222
    and martial arts 30–1, 145, 210
    and mathematics 162–4
    and maturity 44
    and neurological disorders (including focal dystonia) 153, 158–62, 167
    and organists 50
    and the parasitic 39, 194
    and patriarchy 30–2
    and pianists 109–10, 117–23, 137–56

    and posture 107–10, 117–23, 128, 209, 215
    and practice 60, 84–6
    and 'proximal-distal' relationships 211
    and qualitative research 105–8
    and quantitative research 107–8, 117–28
    and self-image 2, 64–5, 80, 86, 209, 215–16
    and singers 50, 155, 207, 211–15, 225
    and the skeleton 143, 153–5, 164, 184, 207, 214
    and string players 50, 165, 167–70
    and spirituality 225–6, 230
    and teaching 75–80, 87–92
    and the Weber-Fechner law 6, 211
Freud, Sigmund 195–6
    and aggression 41–2
    and civilisation 39–41, 45
    and jokes 38
    and the 'Neighbour' 40–1
    and resistance 39

Gaulier, Philippe 175
Gindler, Elsa 17, 27, 29–31
Ginsburg, Carl 56
Gould, Glenn
    and Beethoven 49
    and recording 39
    and uniqueness 9, 42, 46–9

Jaques-Dalcroze, Émile 17
Johnson, Mark 83–4, 97

Kristeller, Lotte 27, 29

Laban, Rudolf 17, 27
Lacan, Jacques
    and *Das Ding* 38–9, 42–3, 50
    and *jouissance* 39, 42–3
    and *objet petit a* 39
    and the *Sinthome* 43–4
Landowska, Wanda 146–7
Lecoq, Jacques 175–6
Linklater, Kristin 68–9
listening 50–1, 184–5, 207, 212–13

Meisner, Sanford 175, 199
Mensendieck, Bess 17, 19, 23–6
Menuhin, Yehudi xv, 1

Ornstein, Margalit 17, 20–3

Playing-relatedPain (PRP) 103, 109–10
Porges, Stephen
    and the Feldenkrais Method 182–6
    and the Polyvagal Theory 173, 177–81
    and safety 173, 176, 181–2

Reese, Mark 1, 56, 225
Rössler, Tile 26, 28

Stanislavski, Konstantin 18, 175–6, 201
Stern, Daniel 87, 97

Thelen, Esther and Linda B. Smith 1, 4, 45, 89–90

Yepes, Narciso 2, 208

www.ingramcontent.com/pod-product-compliance
Lightning Source LLC
Chambersburg PA
CBHW080537300426
44111CB00017B/2765